# SHAKESPEARE AND THE CULTURE OF ROMANTICISM

# Shakespeare and the Culture of Romanticism

Edited by
JOSEPH M. ORTIZ
*University of Texas at El Paso, USA*

LONDON AND NEW YORK

First published 2013 by Ashgate Publishing

Published 2016 by Routledge
2 Park Square, Milton Park, Abingdon, Oxon OX14 4RN
711 Third Avenue, New York, NY 10017, USA

*Routledge is an imprint of the Taylor & Francis Group, an informa business*

Copyright © Joseph M. Ortiz and the contributors 2013

Joseph M. Ortiz has asserted his right under the Copyright, Designs and Patents Act, 1988, to be identified as the editor of this work.

All rights reserved. No part of this book may be reprinted or reproduced or utilised in any form or by any electronic, mechanical, or other means, now known or hereafter invented, including photocopying and recording, or in any information storage or retrieval system, without permission in writing from the publishers.

Notice:
Product or corporate names may be trademarks or registered trademarks, and are used only for identification and explanation without intent to infringe.

**British Library Cataloguing in Publication Data**
Shakespeare and the culture of Romanticism.
   1. Shakespeare, William, 1564–1616 – Appreciation – Great Britain – History – 19th century. 2. Shakespeare, William, 1564–1616 – Influence. 3. Influence (Literary, artistic, etc.) – History – 19th century. 4. Imitation in literature. 5. Politics and literature – Great Britain – History – 19th century. 6. Romanticism – Great Britain.
   I. Ortiz, Joseph M.
   822.3'3-dc23

**The Library of Congress has cataloged the printed edition as follows:**
Shakespeare and the culture of romanticism / [edited by] Joseph M. Ortiz.
    pages cm
  Includes bibliographical references and index.
  ISBN 978-1-4094-5581-3 (hardcover: alk. paper)
  1. Shakespeare, William, 1564–1616—Criticism and interpretation. 2. Shakespeare, William, 1564-1616—Influence. 3. Popular culture—Great Britain—History—18th century. 4. Popular culture—Great Britain—History—19th century. 5. Influence (Literary, artistic, etc.) I. Ortiz, Joseph M., 1972–
  PR2976.S33715 2013
  822.3'3—dc23

2012047028

ISBN 9781409455813(hbk)

# Contents

*List of Figures* vii
*List of Tables* viii
*Notes on Contributors* ix
*Acknowledgments* xi

Introduction 1
Joseph M. Ortiz

**Part I   Rethinking the Romantic Critic**

1  "Small reverence for station": Walter Savage Landor's Subversive Shakespeare 13
   David Chandler

2  Peer Reviewed: Elizabeth Inchbald's Shakespeare Criticism 31
   Karen Bloom Gevirtz

3  "My God! Madam, there must be only *one* black figure in this play": *Hamlet*, Ophelia, and the Romantic Hero 51
   Karen Britland

**Part II   Shakespeare and the Making of the Romantic Poet**

4  The State of Unfeigned Nature: Poetic Imagination from Shakespeare to Wordsworth 77
   Thomas Festa

5  "Mature Poets Steal": Charlotte Smith's Appropriations of Shakespeare 99
   Joy Currie

6  The Sublimity of *Hamlet* in Emily Dickinson's Poem, "He Fumbles at Your Soul" 121
   Marianne Noble

**Part III   The Romantic Stage**

7  "The Translucence of Eternity in Time": Shakespeare and Coleridge's *Zapolya* 139
   Paola Degli Esposti

8  Contextual Hauntings: Shakespearean Ghosts on the Gothic Stage 161
   Francesca Saggini

9   Shakespeare Reception in France: The Case of Ambroise Thomas's
    *Hamlet*                                                              183
    *Suddhaseel Sen*

**Part IV   Harnessing the Renaissance: Markets, Religion, Politics**

10  Reconstructing the Boydell Shakspeare Gallery                         207
    *Ann R. Hawkins*

11  *Pericles* and the Spiritual Wisdom of Joanna Baillie's Sacred Dramas
    *The Martyr* and *The Bride*                                          231
    *Marjean D. Purinton and Marliss C. Desens*

12  A Written Warning: Lady Caroline Lamb, Noblesse Oblige, and the
    Works of John Ford                                                    245
    *Leigh Wetherall-Dickson*

*Bibliography*                                                            *267*
*Index*                                                                   *287*

# List of Figures

1.1 Ford Madox Brown, *William Shakespeare*, 1849. © Manchester Art Gallery. Reproduced by permission.     26

8.1 Robert Thew after Henri Fuseli. The Platform Before the Palace of Elsinore—Hamlet, Horatio, Marcellus, and the Ghost (Hamlet I.iv). John & Josiah Boydell (London) 1796. The Metropolitan Museum of Art (New York) © Foto Scala Firenze.     177

# List of Tables

| | | |
|---|---|---|
| 10.1 | Paintings added each year to the Boydell Gallery by genre. | 214 |
| 10.2 | Cumulative growth of the Boydell Gallery by genre. | 214 |

# Notes on Contributors

**Karen Britland** is Associate Professor of English at the University of Wisconsin, Madison. She is the author *Drama at the Courts of Queen Henrietta Maria* (Cambridge University Press, 2006) and is currently preparing an edition of James Shirley's *The Imposture* for Oxford's *Complete Works of James Shirley*.

**David Chandler** is Associate Professor of English at Doshisha University, Kyoto. He has published over 50 essays, including essays in the *Charles Lamb Bulletin, Eighteenth-Century Studies, Journal of Popular Culture, The Dickensian,* and *Ecumenica.*

**Joy Currie** was a lecturer in the Department of English at the University of Nebraska, Lincoln. She received her PhD in English literature at Nebraska, where her research focused on British Renaissance literature and Romantic poetry.

**Marliss C. Desens** is Associate Professor of English at Texas Tech University. She is the author of *The Bed-Trick in English Renaissance Drama: Explorations in Gender, Sexuality, and Power* (University of Delaware Press, 1994).

**Paola Degli Esposti** is a lecturer of History of Drama at the Università di Padova. She has published extensively on Romantic drama. Her book, *La Scena Tentatrice* (Padova, 2008) examines the stage works of Coleridge, Byron, and Baillie.

**Thomas Festa** is Associate Professor of English at the State University of New York, New Paltz. He is the author of *The End of Learning: Milton and Education* (Routledge, 2006) and co-editor of *Early Modern Women on the Fall: An Anthology* (MRTS, forthcoming).

**Karen Bloom Gevirtz** is Associate Professor of Eighteenth-Century British Literature at Seton Hall University. She is the author of *Life after Death: Widows and the English Novel, Defoe to Austen* (University of Delaware Press, 2005).

**Ann R. Hawkins** is Professor of Bibliography and Book History in the Department of English at Texas Tech University. She is editor of the multivolume set *Romantic Women Writers Reviewed, 1789–1819* (Pickering & Chatto, 2012), as well as co-editor of *Women Writers and the Artifacts of Celebrity* (Ashgate, 2011).

**Marianne Noble** is Associate Professor of Literature at American University. She is the author of *The Masochistic Pleasures of Sentimental Literature* (Princeton University Press, 2000), which won a Choice Outstanding Book Award.

**Joseph M. Ortiz** is Associate Professor of English at the University of Texas at El Paso. He is the author of *Broken Harmony: Shakespeare and the Politics of Music* (Cornell University Press, 2011). He is currently working on a book-length study of the relationship between form and translation in Renaissance literature.

**Marjean D. Purinton** is Professor of English and Associate Dean of the University Honors College at Texas Tech University. She is the author of *Romantic Ideology Unmasked: The Mentally Constructed Tyrannies in Dramas of William Wordsworth, Lord Byron, Percy Shelley, and Joanna Baillie* (Associate University Presses, 1994).

**Francesca Saggini** is Associate Professor of English Literature at the University of Tuscia, Viterbo (Italy). She is the author of *La messinscena dell'identità. Teatro e teatralità nel romanzo inglese moderna* (Viterbo, 2004), which won the 2005 Best Work in Historical and Philological Criticism prize from the Italian Academy of Science.

**Suddhaseel Sen** is a postdoctoral teaching fellow at the University of British Columbia. He has published a chapter on Richard Wagner and T. S. Eliot, and articles on Satyajit Ray, Vishal Bhardwaj, and cinematic adaptations of Shakespeare.

**Leigh Wetherall-Dickson** is a lecturer in eighteenth- and nineteenth-century literature at Northumbria University. She has published on the life of Lady Caroline Lamb and co-edited Pickering & Chatto's edition of *The Works of Lady Caroline Lamb*.

# Acknowledgments

Only those people who have been closely involved with the making of this book will know how much generosity, good will, and patience made possible its publication. I wish especially to thank Ann Hawkins and David Chandler for their confidence in me as an editor and for their sage advice at crucial moments in the process. Kristen Lacefield contributed much to the planning and organization of this book, and I am very grateful for her unwavering support of the project throughout its many stages. Ann Donahue has been an ideal editor at Ashgate, shepherding the project with copious amounts of enthusiasm and efficiency. I also wish to thank Stephen Buhler, Beatrice Beaup, Whitney Feininger, Seth F. Hibbert, and the anonymous reader at Ashgate for their valuable contributions to the project.

It would be impossible to assess adequately the contribution that Douglas A. Brooks made to this project. Without him, this book would never have existed. Although he was not able to see the project to its completion, his intellectual acumen and his generosity as a colleague have exerted a profound influence on each of the essays in this volume. The contributors and I dedicate this book to his memory.

# Introduction

## Joseph M. Ortiz

After attending his production of Shakespeare's *The Winter's Tale* at Drury Lane in 1802, the actor and theater manager John Philip Kemble is said to have commented on the stunning presence of the actress playing Hermione in the play's final scene:

> I have already remarked the studies of Mrs. Siddons after the antique; in Paulina's chapel, she now stood one of the noblest statues, that even Grecian taste ever invented. ... Upon the magical words pronounced by Paulina, "Music awake her: strike!" the sudden action of the head absolutely *startled*, as though such a miracle had really vivified the marble; and the descent from the pedestal was equally graceful and affecting.[1]

As a demonstration of Shakespearean sublimity, Kemble's production is, in his own estimation, wildly successful. The performance of the play's final scene "absolutely startles" the audience at Drury Lane, and the transformation of Hermione is felt to be nothing short of "miraculous." However, while he gives the nod to the idea of a sublime, awe-inspiring Shakespeare, Kemble shows an even greater preoccupation with the visual aspects of the scene, especially as they showcase his ability to reproduce a classical aesthetic as impressive as anything "Grecian taste ever invented." Romantic productions of *The Winter's Tale* had often emphasized its pagan elements, but Kemble took particular pains to capitalize on the current vogue for Hellenism, using his production as an opportunity to stage an elaborate display of classical architecture and sculpture. His efforts were not wasted. Contemporary reviews of Kemble's production lauded its classical authenticity, most notably the "Grecian" appearance of Sarah Siddons's Hermione in the play's final scene. Thomas Campbell, for example, remarked that Hermione "looked the statue, even to literal allusion; and, whilst the drapery hid her lower limbs, it shewed a beauty of head, neck, shoulders, and arms, that Praxiteles might have studied."[2]

The classicizing impulse in Kemble's production may be understood as an effort to construct a paradigmatically "Romantic" Shakespeare. In other words, the elision of classical art and Shakespearean drama in Kemble's theater—made easier by the fact that Shakespeare anachronistically includes many pagan

---

[1] James Boaden, *Memoirs of the Life of John Philip Kemble*, 1825, 2 vols. (New York: Benjamin Blom, 1969), 2:314.

[2] Quoted in Dennis Bartholomeusz, *"The Winter's Tale" in Performance in England and America 1611–1976* (Cambridge: Cambridge University Press, 1982), 59.

elements in *The Winter's Tale*—can be seen as an embodiment of the popular idea that Shakespeare's intuitive grasp of nature was rivaled only by the ancients. At the same time, when compared with other nineteenth-century productions of *The Winter's Tale*, Kemble's staging is remarkable for the way in which it draws attention to the production's visual artistry, rather than for its ability to evoke a sense of nature unveiled. For one thing, Kemble's production was purposely designed to evoke the sense of a picture frame, and the Grecian architecture that served as the opening set opened to reveal a Gothic interior; this "framing" of Gothic tragedy by Grecian classicism caused more than one contemporary critic to fault Kemble for historical inaccuracy.[3] Moreover, in contrast to other Romantic productions, the presence of music in the final scene was all but occluded in Kemble's production. In the playtext, the statue's transformation is represented as the effect of a musical spell ("Music, awake her. Strike!"), and many Romantic productions, such as those at Drury Lane and Covent Garden, used musical effects to create the appearance of an otherworldly presence.[4] Kemble, by contrast, accomplished the transformation through a carefully orchestrated set of physical gestures, effectively focusing the audience's attention on the statue's poise and movement. In this way, the production did not pretend to deliver a timeless nature, so much as it sought to showcase the impressiveness of its own artifice—a goal that it apparently achieved, in light of the reviewer's comparison to Praxiteles.

The essays in *Shakespeare and the Culture of Romanticism* document the myriad ways in which theater directors, actors, poets, political philosophers, gallery owners, and other professionals in the nineteenth century often turned to Shakespeare to advance their own political, artistic, or commercial interests. Sometimes, as in Kemble's staging of *The Winter's Tale*, Shakespeare provided a platform—literally, for Kemble—on which to demonstrate publicly the desirability of a particular set of tastes or point of view. This is the case, for instance, when Samuel Johnson uses the example of Shakespeare to articulate his own views on the moral imperative of literature, famously chastising Shakespeare for his apparent lack of didactic fervor: "He sacrifices virtue to convenience, and is so much more careful to please than to instruct that he seems to write without any moral purpose. … This fault the barbarity of his age cannot extenuate; for it is always a writer's duty to make the world better, and justice is a virtue independent on time or place."[5] At other times, the use of Shakespeare is less overtly appropriative. Many Romantic writers find in Shakespeare's works a set of rhetorical and theatrical tools through which to form and develop their own public *personae*, whether poetic or political. In each of these cases, the Romantic writer harnesses the Shakespearean

---

[3] Ibid., 48.

[4] For example, the productions of the play at Drury Lane and Covent Garden by William Macready, which held the stage from 1823 to 1843, coordinated the statue's movement with "solemn" music. See ibid., 68.

[5] Samuel Johnson, "The Plays of William Shakespeare," 1765, in *Samuel Johnson*, ed. Donald Greene (New York: Oxford University Press, 1984), 427.

phrase but is also shaped by it, thus exemplifying the "dialogic" relationship that Peter Sabor and Paul Yachnin see as central to much Shakespearean reception in the eighteenth century.[6] In the nineteenth century, what emerges into view in both the appropriative and dialogic responses to Shakespeare is a body of poetic and theatrical material that is remarkably labile and tractable. Romantic writers of all persuasions—Whig and Tory, male and female, intellectual and commercial—continually use Shakespeare as a powerful medium through which to claim authority for their particular interests.

The idea that there are many Shakespeares in the nineteenth century productively complicates the popular notion of a distinctly "Romantic" Shakespeare. In his landmark study of the presence of Shakespeare in English Romantic poetry, Jonathan Bate adduces an attitude toward Shakespeare that views "creative imagination," as opposed to a disciplined adherence to aesthetic principles, as the *sine qua non* of great poetry:

> If we had to pick out a single premiss at the core of English Romanticism, it would probably be the ascription of a central place to the power of the creative imagination, a belief that imagination, genius, and poetry are closely associated with each other. Like the movement in which it plays so large a part, the Romantic approach to Shakespeare has its roots deep in the eighteenth century. Those critics and aestheticians of the second half of the eighteenth century who laid the groundwork for the Romantics by exploring the creative power of imagination turned again and again to Shakespeare for examples of that power. The rise of Romanticism and the growth of Shakespeare idolatry are parallel phenomena.[7]

This book does not aim to diminish Bate's claim that the idolization of Shakespearean imagination profoundly informs Romantic representations of poetry. It does, however, seek to demonstrate that the picture looks significantly different when one moves away from the six poets that Bate discusses—or even when one moves away from a particular set of works by these poets. For example, in her essay that appears in this volume, Paola Degli Esposti argues that Coleridge's *Zapolya*, a play deeply indebted to Shakespeare's later works, represents an attempt to reform the Romantic theater and make it a suitable vehicle for moral and political education. Here, the imaginative genius that Coleridge elsewhere identifies with Shakespeare is pursued not as an end in itself, but as a quality that can be harnessed in the service of practical, political ends. For Bate, however, *Zapolya* is simply "unreadable," a crude pastiche of plot and structural elements taken from *Cymbeline* and *The Winter's Tale*. Seen from this perspective, *Zapolya* is only marginally better than the other dramas that held the stage in the nineteenth century, which Bate characterizes as the work of "hacks"

---

[6] Peter Sabor and Paul Yachnin, eds., *Shakespeare and the Eighteenth Century* (Aldershot, UK: Ashgate, 2008), 4.

[7] Jonathan Bate, *Shakespeare and the English Romantic Imagination* (Oxford: Clarendon, 1986), 6.

and "derivative dramatists." Producing a witty imitation of his own, Bate adapts Coleridge's description of Beaumont and Fletcher as a patchwork piece of fruit to suggest the mechanical style of imitation in Coleridge's own dramas: "In his plays Coleridge frequently took a quarter of a Hamlet, a quarter of a Lear, and the like of a Macbeth and of an Othello, and tried to make it look like one round diverse Shakespearean fruit."[8]

By suggesting that much Romantic drama is hackneyed and opportunistic, especially when compared to Romantic poetry, Bate rehearses a strand of polemic that was often expressed by Romantic critics themselves. Several poets and critics in the nineteenth century frequently made the point that Shakespearean genius is best appreciated by reading his plays as poetry, not by seeing them performed. In his *Characters of Shakespeare's Plays* (1817), the critic William Hazlitt went so far as to argue that Shakespeare's plays are distorted in the very act of performance:

> We do not like to see our author's plays acted, and least of all, HAMLET. There is no play that suffers so much in being transferred to the stage. Hamlet himself seems hardly capable of being acted. ... He is, as it were, wrapped up in his reflections, and only *thinks aloud*. There should therefore be no attempt to impress what he says upon others by a studied exaggeration of emphasis or manner; no *talking at* his hearers. There should be as much of the gentleman and scholar as possible infused into the part, and as little of the actor. A pensive air of sadness should sit reluctantly upon his brow, but no appearance of fixed and sullen gloom. He is full of weakness and melancholy, but there is no harshness in his nature.[9]

I have argued elsewhere that the attempt to frame Shakespeare's works as poetry rather than drama in the Romantic period often represents a desire to cordon off aspects of the plays that trouble the notion of Shakespearean sublimity.[10] For instance, Hazlitt's assertion that there should be "as little of the actor" in Hamlet leads naturally to his reading of Ophelia as "a character almost too exquisitely touching to be dwelt upon." In this case, the elevation of poetry over drama justifies Hazlitt's decision to use Gertrude's purple speech at the end of Act Four as the basis for his reading of Ophelia, effectively ignoring the theatrical effects of the loud, singing Ophelia who appears a few scenes earlier. Others, however, did not downplay the theatrical aspects of Shakespeare's plays. As Karen Britland, Francesca Saggini, and Suddhaseel Sen demonstrate in their respective essays in this volume, visual and theatrical depictions of Shakespeare play an important role not only in the development of nineteenth-century theatrical conventions, but also in the critical debates over drama and art. Moreover, when this emphasis on

---

[8] Ibid., 50–51.

[9] William Hazlitt, *Characters of Shakespeare's Plays* (1916; repr., London: Oxford University Press, 1966), 87–8.

[10] Joseph M. Ortiz, *Broken Harmony: Shakespeare and the Politics of Music* (Ithaca, NY: Cornell University Press, 2011), 53–9.

Shakespearean theatricality is evident—either on the page or on the stage—it often points to a "minority" strand of aesthetic criticism that powerfully problematizes the monolithic theories of art propagated by critics like Hazlitt.

It would be a mistake to suggest that theatrically minded critics in the nineteenth century produce a version of Shakespeare that is somehow more accurate, or more "whole," than the portrait of imaginative genius constructed by Romantic poets. Just as some Romantic critics and poets surreptitiously cut or ignored certain aspects of the plays so that they could better portray Shakespeare as the model of sublimity, writers and directors interested in the theatrical dimensions of Shakespeare were also selective in their handling of the works. For example, when the director William Macready launched his production of *The Winter's Tale* at Drury Lane in 1823, he moved the setting of the pastoral scene in Act Four from the English countryside to a Grecian valley, in the name of maintaining "archaeological correctness."[11] (Macready was apparently not bothered by the other anachronisms that were actually amplified by his changes, such as the scene's references to Puritans and morris dancers.) In this way, Macready's production exemplifies the tendency to carve up and rearrange Shakespeare's plays to make them appear more unified and coherent *to a particular, targeted consumer*. This principle of dramatic fragmentation and reconstruction in the service of particular commercial tastes is perhaps nowhere more evident than in the history of the Boydell Shakespeare Gallery, the collection of paintings of Shakespearean scenes that was displayed in the 1790s by John Boydell as an intended accompaniment to an elaborate illustrated edition of the works. As Ann Hawkins shows in her essay in this volume, despite critical attempts to treat the Boydell Gallery's presentation of sculpture and paintings as a "completed artifact," the historical accounts of the Gallery show a collection that is remarkably in flux: paintings are frequently added and removed, arranged and rearranged, altered and retouched—almost always in response to perceived changes in aesthetic and literary tastes. Thus, if there *is* a principle underlying the Romantic appropriation of Shakespeare, it may be better exemplified by the volatile, fragmentary nature of the Boydell project than by the vision of a transcendent Shakespeare who converts "multitude into unity."[12] In this respect, Bate's colorful description of the mangling of the Shakespearean corpus—"a quarter of a Hamlet, a quarter of a Lear, and the like of a Macbeth and of an Othello"—aptly characterizes not only the work of hackneyed Romantic dramatists, but also the wider appropriation of Shakespeare's works by Romantic poets, critics, stage directors, politicians, and entrepreneurs.

The essays in this collection highlight the fragmenting effect of Romantic culture on Shakespeare; in doing so, they make a timely intervention in recent

---

[11] Bartholomeusz, *Winter's Tale*, 64.

[12] Coleridge, *Biographia Literaria*, quoted in Bate, *Shakespeare*, 20. See also Jonathan Bate, *Shakespearean Constitutions: Politics, Theatre, Criticism 1730–1830* (Oxford: Oxford University Press, 1989), which gives more attention to the appropriation of Shakespeare by political actors in the eighteenth and nineteenth centuries.

critical conversations about the cultural and political dimensions of Shakespeare scholarship itself. In the last twenty years, a number of scholars have turned their attention to the history of the idea of Shakespeare, and collectively they have done much to destabilize the perceived naturalness of any particular meaning of "Shakespeare"—whether as imaginative genius, as national poet, as a cohesive body of literary works, or even as single author. Jeffrey Knapp, citing this body of work, describes its propensity to view the idea of Shakespeare's authorialness as "a form of denial that blinds us to the inescapably social nature of drama."[13] Knapp counters this view with the suggestion that, while the collaborative nature of Renaissance drama often problematizes modern notions of an author, a model of single authorship is self-consciously inscribed by Shakespeare in the plays and poems themselves. In this case, Knapp is responding to scholars who argue that conventional representations of Shakespeare are the products of specific historic periods rather than inevitable outcomes of the extant playtexts. For example, in *Shakespeare Verbatim*, Margreta de Grazia argues that the very notion of an "authentic" Shakespeare whose true intentions are the only legitimate goal of literary study is itself historically contingent, made conceivable only after a dramatic change in textual editing practices in the late eighteenth century.[14] Other studies by Michael Dobson, Richard Helgerson, Leah Marcus, Jeffrey Masten, Stephen Orgel, David Scott Kastan, and Lukas Erne also historicize the idea of an "essential" Shakespeare, though with differing explanations about when and how this idea decisively took hold.[15]

Yet, as the current debate over the true source of Shakespearean exceptionalism plays out, what is remarkable in all of these studies is the extent to which the Romantics are assumed to have bought wholesale the notion of Shakespearean autonomy. In other words, the idea of Shakespearean genius that is said to be foreign to the publishers of the 1623 Folio is portrayed as Romantic gospel, ready to be deconstructed once "we awaken from the sleep of Romanticism ... and return to a Renaissance sense of the embeddedness of texts in the specific

---

[13] Jeffrey Knapp, *Shakespeare Only* (Chicago: University of Chicago Press, 2009), 2.

[14] Margreta de Grazia, *Shakespeare Verbatim: The Reproduction of Authenticity and the 1790 Apparatus* (Oxford: Clarendon, 1991), 13.

[15] Michael Dobson, *The Making of the National Poet: Shakespeare, Adaptation and Authorship, 1660–1792* (Oxford: Clarendon, 1992); Richard Helgerson, *Forms of Nationhood: The Elizabethan Writing of England* (Chicago: University of Chicago Press, 1992); Leah Marcus, *Unediting the Renaissance: Shakespeare, Marlowe, Milton* (New York: Routledge, 1996); Jeffrey Masten, *Textual Intercourse: Collaboration, Authorship, and Sexualities in Renaissance Drama* (Cambridge: Cambridge University Press, 1997); Stephen Orgel, *Imagining Shakespeare: A History of Texts and Visions* (New York: Palgrave, 2003); David Scott Kastan, *Shakespeare and the Book* (Cambridge: Cambridge University Press, 2001); Lukas Erne, *Shakespeare as Literary Dramatist* (Cambridge: Cambridge University Press, 2003).

power relations."¹⁶ This volume, by contrast, suggests that such a narrative of a Romantic sleep followed by a critical awakening is itself a simplification of a more complex situation. By demonstrating the various ways in which Romantic subjects approached the Shakespearean corpus as *materia*, and not necessarily as the embodiment of an individual, coherent mind, the essays in this volume show that the meaning of Shakespeare—and even the presumption that meaning is the point of Shakespeare—is hardly more stable in the Romantic period than at any other time. Thus, the image of a Romantic culture drunk on the liquor of Bardolatry, while providing a favorite whipping boy for scholars wishing to assert their own critical maturity, may actually be yet another "ghost who continues to haunt our understanding of dramatic authorship."¹⁷

\* \* \*

This last quotation is from Douglas A. Brooks's landmark work on the changing notion of dramatic authorship in Renaissance England. It makes a fitting launching point for the following essays, not least because it was Brooks himself who solicited these essays for an earlier planned volume on Shakespeare and Romanticism. Although Brooks's untimely passing meant that he was not able to see the collection to its publication, it is clear from his original plans for the collection that he felt a Romantic Shakespeare should be studied not only in terms of the history of interpretations of Shakespeare's works, but also in terms of the effects of Shakespearean interpretation on the larger culture around it. In keeping with this sentiment, the following essays have been organized into four sections, each of which complicates and expands our notion of the Romantic Shakespeare from a different perspective. Each section identifies a particular site of contact between Shakespeare and Romantic culture: the critic, the poet, the theater, and the marketplace. While these categories necessarily overlap in myriad ways, they provide a useful set of vantage points for gauging the astonishing complexity of Shakespearean thought and influence in the nineteenth century.

The first section, "Rethinking the Romantic Critic," reconsiders the history of critical attitudes toward Shakespeare in Romantic England. For some time now, the approach to Shakespeare taken by William Hazlitt, the most well-known literary critic in the period, has more or less been taken as representative of the general critical response to Shakespeare in Romantic England. However, David Chandler's lead essay in this volume discusses the presence of other critical voices, particularly those that go against the grain of Romantic idealizations of Shakespeare. Chandler focuses on Walter Savage Landor's *Citation and Examination of William Shakespeare* (1834), which represents the historical Shakespeare as a lover of

---

¹⁶ Edward Pechter, *What Was Shakespeare?: Renaissance Plays and Changing Critical Practice* (Ithaca, NY: Cornell University Press, 1995), 99.

¹⁷ Douglas Brooks, *From Playhouse to Printing House: Drama and Authorship in Early Modern England* (Cambridge: Cambridge University Press, 2000), 4.

festivity and mischief who uses his acting skills to evade civic authority. In this respect, Chandler's essay highlights the political dimensions of Shakespeare criticism in Romantic England, which in its most conservative forms boldly pronounced Shakespeare as a *bona fide* Tory. Karen Gevirtz's essay also expands our understanding of the range of Shakespeare criticism by examining the work of Elizabeth Inchbald. Although Inchbald drew upon criticism by Johnson, Coleridge, and Hazlitt in her essays on Shakespeare in *The British Theatre* (1806–08), her experience as an actress and a playwright profoundly influenced her reading of the plays. In her prefaces, Inchbald authoritatively discusses Shakespeare's plays in terms of their theatrical effects, as well as their status as poetry. Moreover, Inchbald allows her own perspective as a woman to bear upon her interpretation of Shakespeare in productive ways—making the point, for example, that women were much less likely than men to be impressed with Prince Hal's craftiness in *1 Henry IV*. Karen Britland's essay, the last in this section, also demonstrates the potential of female critics and actresses to unsettle Romantic paradigms. Britland focuses specifically on the Romantic idea of "genius"—a concept that since the early nineteenth century has routinely been associated with the character of Hamlet (and, by extension, with Shakespeare). Britland's essay shows that the idea of genius has a much more complicated genealogy, having been applied to theatrical performances of Ophelia in the eighteenth century, particularly those by the acclaimed actress Sarah Siddons. Thus, when the identification of genius with a specifically male poetic subjectivity becomes prevalent in the nineteenth century, it partly does so as a result of a persistent effort (by critics as well as theater directors) to downplay the effect of Ophelia's intelligence and sensibility.

 The essays in the second section, "Shakespeare and the Making of the Romantic Poet," consider the ways in which English poets in the nineteenth century responded to and appropriated Shakespeare in their own works. Jonathan Bate and others have richly traced the far-reaching presence of Shakespearean language and ideas in the works of canonical Romantic writers such as Coleridge, Wordsworth, Blake, and Keats. The essays in this section expand upon this critical project, both by reconsidering canonical poets and by focusing on lesser-known writers and writers who are not always included in discussions of Romantic poetry. Thomas Festa reconsiders Wordsworth's relationship to Shakespeare, which has all too often been represented as an opposition between an egotistical Wordsworth and a timeless Shakespeare. As Festa points out, this kind of opposition has often been used to characterize Romantic poetry generally. In his essay, Festa makes a maverick move in arguing that, far from simply being egotistical or transcendent, Wordsworth becomes keenly aware of the historical situatedness of his imagination precisely through his appropriation of Shakespeare. This approach to Wordsworth allows Festa to develop a "social anthropology" of Shakespeare reception that treats allusion as part of the larger history of the material and philosophical construction of Shakespearean "authorship."

 The other two essays in this section also take novel approaches to the idea of literary allusion. Joy Currie considers the poetry of Charlotte Smith, whose annotations to her own poems made explicit her extensive use of Shakespearean allusion and quotation. Smith's appropriation of Shakespeare, as Currie shows, was doubly strategic. On the one hand, Smith often quoted Shakespeare to lend authority to her political views, such as quoting lines from *Henry V* in her condemnation of war with France. On the other hand, Smith also turned to Shakespeare to claim equality with male writers, emphasizing the popular notion of Shakespeare as a "natural" talent who (like many women) lacked a university education. Smith's ability to conscript Shakespeare in her decidedly nonconservative campaign demonstrates the near infinite lability of Shakespearean allusion in the period. Marianne Noble's essay further expands our sense of this lability by tracing an unexpected network of allusions to Shakespeare's *Hamlet* in Emily Dickinson's "He Fumbles At Your Soul." While Dickinson does not normally figure in discussions of Romantic poets, Noble persuasively shows that, in her early career, Dickinson was a self-proclaimed Bardolater who emulated Romantic proclaimers of Shakespearean genius. For Dickinson, the sublimity of Shakespeare lies particularly in his mingling of sound and sense—an effect that Dickinson attempts to create in her own poetry. In this way, Noble's essay demonstrates that Romantic ideas about Shakespearean sublimity had subtle yet far-reaching effects on the development of English poetry, especially when mediated through the talent of a poet like Dickinson.

The third section, "The Romantic Stage," explores the central role of the theater in producing interpretations of Shakespeare's plays in the period. Just as the essays in the first section of this volume show the myriad ways in which Romantic literary criticism is inflected by theatrical performances, the essays in this section trace the critical dimensions of works by Romantic playwrights and of staged productions of Shakespeare plays. Paola Degli Esposti reconsiders Coleridge's *Zapolya*, a play long recognized as a reworking of elements from *The Winter's Tale* and *Cymbeline*. Esposti argues that *Zapolya* depicts the conflict between an unjust, "jacobinical" government and a rightful, god-fearing government, and that it incorporates Shakespearean elements in order to ground its political commentary in universal truths. In this way, Coleridge sees Shakespeare not as removed from the historical and the particular, but embedded in it. Francesca Saggini's essay focuses on *Fontainville Forest* (1794), the first of James Boaden's theatrical adaptations of Ann Radcliffe's novels, based on *The Romance of the Forest*. Saggini suggests that Boaden's introduction of an on-stage ghost in his play reproduces a set of well-known Romantic visual depictions of Shakespearean plays, thus showing the ability of Shakespeare to mediate the relationship between Romantic painting and Gothic drama. Suddhaseel Sen considers Ambroise Thomas's *Hamlet*, a French opera based on Romantic French adaptations of Shakespeare's play, most notably Jean-François Ducis's 1770 version of *Hamlet* that was written for performance at the Comédie Française. Sen shows how a Romantic French tradition of adapting *Hamlet* for the stage arose in part as a response to debates over neoclassical aesthetics. Thomas's *Hamlet* holds a unique place in these debates, since it adheres to neoclassical theatrical models while drawing on Romantic interpretations of Shakespeare's play, particularly in its musical treatment of Hamlet and Ophelia.

The final section of this volume, "Harnessing the Renaissance: Markets, Religion, Politics," explores the Romantic appropriation of Shakespeare and his contemporaries in areas beyond the spheres of criticism, poetry, and theater. Together these essays demonstrate the diffuseness of Shakespearean thought in Romantic culture, and they show how an approach to Shakespeare could serve as a model for negotiating with the past more generally. Ann Hawkins's essay meticulously traces the changing fortunes of the Shakespeare Boydell Gallery, an ongoing exhibition that was originally intended to show the paintings used for illustrations in Boydell's nine-volume "National Edition" of Shakespeare. Although scholars usually refer to the Boydell Gallery as though it were a static, finished product, Hawkins shows that the contents in the Gallery were remarkably in flux over its fifteen-year period, and that changes and additions to the Gallery stemmed from a changing public market for Shakespeare. In many cases, the public tastes that are reflected by the Gallery's changing form are in stark contrast to traditional Romantic criticism of Shakespeare, as in the overwhelming public preference for *The Merry Wives of Windsor* over *Othello* or *Richard II*. The next essay, by Marjean Purinton and Marliss Desens, explores the religious dimensions of Shakespearean appropriation in the period. Drawing on concepts of the feminine sacred as theorized by Catherine Clèment and Julia Kristeva, Purinton and Desens suggest a shared unorthodox spiritual sensibility between Shakespeare's *Pericles* and two dramas by the Scottish poet and dramatist Joanna Baillie. Finally, Leigh Wetherall-Dickson's essay goes outside the strict bounds of Romantic Shakespearean criticism to consider the relationship between Romantic culture and another English Renaissance dramatist, John Ford. Wetherall-Dickson suggests that Lady Caroline Lamb's *Glenarvon*, a Gothic novel that portrays Lamb's disastrous relationship with Lord Byron, draws extensively on Ford's works in order to criticize the selfishness of Whig aristocracy and to advocate for political reform. While all of the previous essays in this volume significantly expand our understanding of the myriad uses to which Shakespeare was put in the period, this final essay suggests that Romantic appropriations of Shakespeare also helped to foster a culture in which nearly all Renaissance poets and dramatists were available for conscription by individuals of all literary, religious, national, or political persuasions.

# PART I
# Rethinking the Romantic Critic

## Chapter 1
# "Small reverence for station": Walter Savage Landor's Subversive Shakespeare

### David Chandler

Garrick's celebrated description, "the god of our idolatry," established the tone for Romantic appreciation of Shakespeare.[1] With the exception of Byron, a problematic case,[2] the major Romantic writers in Britain were all prepared to declare Shakespeare superhuman, a genius of immeasurable proportions; his "divinity" became a shared article of faith. Thus, to take three examples, to Coleridge "Shakspeare is the Spinozistic Deity, an omnipresent creativeness."[3] To Keats "the Genius of Shakspeare was an in[n]ate universality—wherefore he had the utmost atchievement [*sic*] of human intellect prostrate beneath his indolent and kingly gaze."[4] And to De Quincey Shakespeare was "the sole authentic oracle of truth," a man who "thought more finely and more extensively than all other poets combined."[5] Walter Savage Landor (1775–1864), who grew up in Shakespeare's Warwickshire, was thoroughly at home in this Bardolatrous environment, and contributed his eloquence to the cause. Thus, to take three examples again, in Landor's *Collected Works* there are plenty of statements along the following lines: "all the faults that ever were committed in poetry would be but as air to earth, if we could weigh them against one single thought or image, such as almost every scene exhibits in every drama of this unrivalled genius"; "Glory to thee in the highest, thou confidant of our Creator! who alone hast taught us in every particle

---

[1] For the origins of Romantic Bardolatry see Robert Witbeck Babcock's valuable study, *The Genesis of Shakespeare Idolatry 1766–1799* (Chapel Hill: University of North Carolina Press, 1931).

[2] For Byron's ambiguous response to Shakespeare see Anne Barton, "Byron and Shakespeare," in *The Cambridge Companion to Byron*, ed. Drummond Bone (Cambridge: Cambridge University Press, 2004), 224–35. As Barton shows, Byron liked to insist that "Shakespeare belonged well this side of idolatry" (229), though he was constantly quoting him.

[3] Samuel T. Coleridge, *Table Talk*, ed. Carl Woodring, 2 vols. (Princeton, NJ: Princeton University Press, 1990), 1:125.

[4] R. S. White, *Keats as a Reader of Shakespeare* (London: Athlone Press, 1987), 148.

[5] Thomas De Quincey, *The Works of Thomas De Quincey*, ed. Grevel Lindop et al., 21 vols. (London: Pickering and Chatto, 2000–2003), 13:330, 332.

of the mind how wonderfully and fearfully we are made"; and "[Shakespeare is] the best poet and the wisest man, whom not only England but God's whole world has produced."[6] Such pronouncements prompted Swinburne to rank Landor, with Coleridge and Charles Lamb, as one of "the three who have written of Shakespeare as never man wrote, nor ever man may write again."[7]

If Landor only wrote about Shakespeare in this vein, his could be described as a fairly typical Romantic response to the "unrivalled genius," albeit one armed with an enthusiastic eloquence remarkable even in this culture of overstatement. In fact, though, his attitude to Shakespeare was complicated by the circumstance that, while irresistibly attracted to Romantic Bardolatry, he disliked its tendency to produce an essentially safe, socially conservative version of England's greatest writer. The Romantics' godlike Shakespeare may have been thrillingly imaginative, but in his political attitudes he was a firm supporter of the existing institutions of society—a reflection, this, of the Burkean, antirevolutionary strand in English Romanticism. The classic statement of the case is Hartley Coleridge's, whose 1828 essay "Shakspeare a Tory, and a Gentleman" logically extended many of his father's local criticisms to comfortably maintain that "a strong evidence of Shakspeare's Toryism, is the respect with which he always treats established orders, degrees, institutions, and opinions; never seeking to desecrate what time and the world's consent have sanctified."[8] This conservative Shakespeare is found, too, in the work of critics who would clearly have liked to find a more radical spirit in the plays. Thus Hazlitt, in his famous account of *Coriolanus*, argues that though the play includes arguments both for and against democracy and freedom, yet "Shakespear himself seems to have had a leaning to the arbitrary side of the question."[9] (He continues with the fascinating, though little discussed, speculation: "perhaps from some feeling of contempt for his [Shakespeare's] own origin.") These readings of the plays were, as will be demonstrated, fully supported by the major biographies of the period, which describe Shakespeare as a thoroughly moral man and good citizen.

The depth of Landor's distaste for this conservative consensus can be measured in his most substantial writing on Shakespeare, the (surprisingly) Bardolatry-free *Citation and Examination of William Shakspeare* of 1834. This curious work, the full title of which is *Citation and Examination of William Shakspeare, Euseby Treen, Joseph Carnaby and Silas Gough, Clerk, before the worshipful*

---

[6] Walter Savage Landor, *The Complete Works of Walter Savage Landor*, ed. T. Earle Welby and Stephen Wheeler, 16 vols. (London: Chapman and Hall, 1927–36), 5:150; 7:245; 12:146.

[7] Algernon Charles Swinburne, *A Study of Shakespeare* (London, 1880), 225.

[8] Jonathan Bate, ed., *The Romantics on Shakespeare* (London: Penguin, 1992), 232–3.

[9] William Hazlitt, *The Complete Works of William Hazlitt*, ed. P. P. Howe, 21 vols. (London: Dent, 1930–34), 4:164. Jonathan Bate discusses Hazlitt's statement at length, perhaps too defensively, in *Shakespearean Constitutions: Politics, Theatre, Criticism 1730–1830* (Oxford: Clarendon Press, 1989), 164–75.

*Sir Thomas Lucy, Knight, Touching Deer-Stealing on the 19th day of September in the year of Grace 1582. Now first published from Original Papers*, is rather hard to characterize. It is, in some respects, a greatly extended—38,000 word—version of the *Imaginary Conversations* that established Landor's fame in the 1820s by representing historical figures through wide-ranging dialogues. Unlike the *Conversations*, however, in the *Citation* considerable emphasis is placed on the textuality of the work, a supposed relic of the age of Shakespeare, and it is presented complete with an "Editor's Preface" and notes. In this sense, the *Citation* is a joke directed at Shakespearean scholars, one that can be connected to William Henry Ireland's forgeries of Shakespearean documents in the 1790s and, with more precision, to James White's spoof on Ireland, *Falstaff's Letters* (1796), which Landor had been given by Lamb in 1832.[10] Combating the generally conservative shift in the way Shakespeare had come to be understood in the Romantic era, the *Citation* reinvigorates the traditional stories that had represented Shakespeare as a lusty rogue, a devotee of the pleasures of the flesh, rather than a literary god or superman. The most remarkable of these stories, and the one providing a framing context for the "imaginary conversation" that occupies the main body of Landor's work, concerned the young Shakespeare stealing deer from Sir Thomas Lucy, and being caught and prosecuted. The *Citation* purports to be a legal deposition taken at his trial. It appeared at a time when fictions concerning Shakespeare were just starting to become common; indeed Charles A. Somerset's play, *Shakspeare's Early Days*, which dramatizes the deer-poaching legend, had enjoyed some success in 1829, and possibly provided Landor with a few hints.[11]

The critical neglect of the *Citation* is remarkable. Samuel Schoenbaum included a few characteristically condescending paragraphs on Landor's work in the first edition of his *Shakespeare's Lives* (1970), but removed them from the revised edition. Maurice J. O'Sullivan commented briefly, but more positively, in his article, "Shakespeare's Other Lives" (1987), and included an extract in his similarly titled anthology (1997). But in most books and articles on Shakespeare's reception, and on Romantic readings of Shakespeare, the *Citation* goes wholly unmentioned. Even Landor specialists have had very little to say about it, and what they have said is nearly scathing: Malcolm Elwin classes it "among the least worthy of Landor's writings," while R. H. Super calls it "one of Landor's greatest

---

[10] For Landor's indebtedness to *Falstaff's Letters* and Lamb see David Chandler, "Lamb, *Falstaff's Letters*, and Landor's *Citation and Examination of William Shakspeare*," *Charles Lamb Bulletin* n.s. 131 (2005): 76–85.

[11] For a rather contemptuous survey of the Shakespearean fictions of this period see Samuel Schoenbaum, *Shakespeare's Lives* (Oxford: Clarendon Press, 1970), 365–80. (This section was dropped from the revised 1991 edition of Schoenbaum's work.) See, too, Maurice J. O'Sullivan, "Shakespeare's Other Lives," *Shakespeare Quarterly* 38 (1987): 133–53. A significant early Shakespeare fiction, unmentioned by Schoenbaum and O'Sullivan, is Caspar Johannes Boye's *William Shakespeare* (Copenhagen, 1826).

failures."[12] Much of the critical neglect can be attributed to straightforward ignorance of the *Citation*, but such judgments suggest that those readers who have found their way to the book have found the portrayal of Shakespeare unpalatable. Landor's radical young Shakespeare still provokes more than his author intended, but it is argued here that he is considerably closer to the Shakespeare many of us find fascinating today than the godlike Bard of much Romantic criticism.

The legend of Shakespeare's poaching that Landor decided to treat was first made public, and given its standard form, by Nicholas Rowe in 1709:

> [Shakespeare] had, by a Misfortune common enough to young Fellows, fallen into ill Company; ... some that made a frequent practice of Deer-stealing, engag'd him with them more than once in robbing a Park that belong'd to Sir *Thomas Lucy* of *Cherlecot*, near *Stratford*. For this he was prosecuted by that Gentleman, as he thought, somewhat too severely; and in order to revenge that ill Usage, he made a Ballad upon him. And tho' this, probably the first Essay of his Poetry, be lost, yet it is said to have been so very bitter, that it redoubled the Prosecution against him to that degree, that he was oblig'd to leave his Business and Family in *Warwickshire*, for some time, and shelter himself in *London*.
>
> It is at this Time, and upon this Accident, that he is said to have made his first Acquaintance in the Play-house.[13]

Told thus, the story was repeated over and over again in the eighteenth century, the liveliest episode in the accepted biography of Shakespeare. In his posthumous "Life of William Shakspeare" (1821), however, Edmond Malone rejected the legend with an overwhelming range of evidence. The most damaging aspect of his case was very simple: there was no park to steal from, ergo no deer to steal. Malone's scholarship was superb; his motivation more suspect. His biography of Shakespeare tends to whitewash its subject, just as he had, quite literally, organized the whitewashing of the bust of Shakespeare in Stratford Church. Malone wanted Shakespeare to be respectable, noble, pure. He turned his fierce intelligence on traditional stories that made Shakespeare seem less than these things, and of course such stories, by definition, were not designed to withstand the withering cross-examination that Malone, with his legal training, was able to bring to bear on them. The issues involved in the deer-stealing legend are made clear enough when Malone portentously introduces his discussion as "of the utmost moment." "[I]f it be a mere fiction," he solemnly declares, "it is the bounden duty of the historian ... minutely and explicitly to refute an unfounded calumny." Later, he describes the traditional account of the deer stealing and subsequent prosecution as "degrading

---

[12] Malcolm Elwin, *Landor: A Replevin* (London: Macdonald, 1958), 19; R. H. Super, *Walter Savage Landor: A Biography* (New York: New York University Press, 1954), 246.

[13] Nicholas Rowe, ed., *The Works of Mr. William Shakespear*, 6 vols. (London, 1709), 1:v–vi.

circumstances."[14] James Boswell the younger, Malone's friend and sympathetic editor, made explicit what Malone had largely left implicit when he added the thought that it was a "subject of congratulation" that Malone had "shown, by an examination of the legendary tales which have so long been current respecting Shakspeare's early years, that they are wholly groundless; and that the greatest genius which his country has produced, maintained, from his youth upwards, that respectability of character which unquestionably belonged to him in after life."[15] De Quincey took the same line, condemning the traditional story as a "slanderous and idle tale," an "outrageous calumny upon Shakespeare's memory."[16] William Harvey, who wrote the first biography of Shakespeare subsequent to Malone's, was not wholly convinced that there had been no poaching, but still echoed the sentiment: "For the sake of the poet's memory, we trust that the *deer-stealing* story is fabulous."[17]

When Malone had dismissed the "legendary tales" surrounding "Shakespeare's early years" it became clear that virtually nothing was actually known about them—certainly nothing that would serve to give Shakespeare a distinctive character. But this served the purposes of Romantic idealization, as Malone himself made clear:

> Were our poet's early history accurately known, it would unquestionably furnish us with many proofs ... of his acuteness, facility, and fluency; of the playfulness of his fancy, and his love of pleasantry and humour; of his curiosity, discernment, candour, and liberality; of all those qualities, in a word, which afterwards rendered him the admiration of the age in which he lived.[18]

Landor was too much a rebel, too skeptical of authority and bourgeois morality, to be comfortable with such a sanitized image of the "respectable" genius. In writing the *Citation* he had a number of targets, but the most important is Malone. The *Citation* gives imaginative life to the story the great scholar had taken most pains to refute, and which he considered most offensive to Shakespeare's memory. In his "Editor's Preface" Landor writes, teasingly, "The malignant may doubt, or pretend to doubt, the authenticity of the *Examination* here published. Let us, who are not malignant, be cautious of adding anything to the noisome mass of incredulity that surrounds us."[19] In the context of presenting the public with "Original Papers" connected with Shakespeare, Landor was probably deliberately evoking the Ireland forgeries, and Malone's exposure of them, in the 1790s. But the comment has a more general application: Malone's fundamental approach to *all* the stories

---

[14] Edmond Malone, ed., *The Plays and Poems of William Shakspeare*, 21 vols. (London, 1821), 2:118–19, 484.

[15] Ibid., 472.

[16] De Quincey, *Works*, 13:317, 319.

[17] *The Works of Shakspeare . . . With a Biographical Memoir . . . By W. Harvey, Esq.* (London, 1825), v.

[18] Malone, *Shakspeare*, 2:102.

[19] Landor, *Complete Works*, 10:263.

in the Shakespearean mythos was, as Schoenbaum's was later, to "doubt, or pretend to doubt" them. Schoenbaum's complaint, that Landor relied on "folk notions of Shakespeare," ignoring the "facts" Malone had brought to light, almost comically misses the point.[20] More recently, in any case, such "folk notions" have been powerfully defended by Margreta de Grazia, who argues that the traditional tales, whatever their factual accuracy, preserved important information concerning the way Shakespeare was understood by his contemporaries.[21]

Landor was not just responding to the doubters, however. Nathan Drake, Malone's main rival in the field of Shakespearean biography, was as credulous a man as one could wish, but his sentimental and wholesome approach to Shakespeare is equally rejected in the *Citation*. Drake's major work, *Shakspeare and his Times* (1817), eventually inaugurated a whole new species of Shakespearean biography by showing how the few records of Shakespeare's life could be stretched into a large, book-length work with the introduction of copious background information, speculation, and moralizing. Drake was, in many respects, the opposite of Malone: while Malone was ruthlessly forensic and essentially reductive, Drake was genially accommodating and essentially accretive. Traditional stories of the Bard were, for him, far too precious to be discarded. If they occasionally cast Shakespeare in an unattractive light, then he considered it the biographer's duty to improve, explain, excuse, reposition, or do anything to negate their negative implication. If Malone, in other words, idealized Shakespeare by rejecting the "legendary tales," Drake idealized him by reinterpreting those same tales on the assumption that Shakespeare could never have been less than noble, wise, and gracious.

The deer-stealing "tale" was the biggest challenge for Drake's method. He introduced it with a piece of portentous, Johnsonian moralizing:

> To regulate the workings of an ardent imagination, and to control the effervescence of the passions in early life, experience has uniformly taught us to consider as a task of great difficulty; and seldom, indeed, capable of being achieved without the advice and direction of those, who, under the guidance of similar admonition, have successfully borne up against the numerous temptations to which human frailty is subjected.[22]

---

[20] Schoenbaum, *Shakespeare's Lives*, 370.

[21] Margreta de Grazia, *Shakespeare Verbatim: The Reproduction of Authenticity and the 1790 Apparatus* (Oxford: Clarendon Press, 1991). De Grazia discusses the deer-poaching story in 104–7, and her conclusion is worth quoting here: "The narrative conveyed neither correct information nor 'unfounded calumny', but rather dramatized the critical juncture of his [Shakespeare's] life: his fortuitous conversion from pranks to plays, from wayward 'Extravagance' to motivated 'Genius'—an important reformation for a poet known for his 'extravagance', for his 'unruly' deviations from textual, critical, and biographical norms" (107).

[22] Nathan Drake, *Shakspeare and his Times*, 2 vols. (London, 1817), 1:401.

Shakespeare, Drake proceeds to explain, "possessed powers of fancy greatly beyond the common lot of humanity, and ... with these is almost constantly connected a correspondent fervency of temperament and passion." No surprise, then, that there were "some juvenile irregularities." Drake summarizes Rowe's account of the deer stealing, which he classes as a "reprehensible practice."[23] Having briefly conjured up a picture of the "irregular" and "reprehensible," however, he diverts his reader with a paragraph on Thomas Lucy and his house and park at Fulbroke—which he takes to be the scene of the crime. When Shakespeare reenters the story the taint of criminality has all but vanished:

> That the rich woods, sequestered lawns, and romantic recesses of Fulbroke Park, would very frequently attract the footsteps of our youthful bard, independent of any lure which the capture of its game might afford, we may justly surmise; and still more confidently may we affirm, that his meditations or diversions in this forest laid the foundation of a part of the beautiful scenery which occurs in *As You Like It*.[24]

Drake proceeds to suggest that the "woodland pictures" in *As You Like It* are "faithful transcripts" of Fulbroke, and he implicitly associates the play's banished lords with young Shakespeare. Those lords, it will be recalled, kill deer for their sustenance, but regret having to do so. Jacques, in particular, is moved to lament the suffering of a wounded deer abandoned by its fellows, and Drake quotes the entire speech, suggesting that Shakespeare must have witnessed "such an incident"—and been similarly moved. Such descriptions, Drake argues, "strikingly prove ... that the habits of the chase, though fostered in the morn of youth, had not, even in respect to the objects of their sport, in the smallest degree impaired the native tenderness and humanity of the poet." Biographical sleight of hand has transformed the "reprehensible" act of poaching into the gentle-sounding "habits of the chase." When Shakespeare's crime is next directly named it is called an "adventurous amusement."[25] The "ill company" Shakespeare assorted with, according to Rowe, is completely forgotten. Shakespeare is represented as a solitary, romantic young nature lover, a bit like Wordsworth perhaps—tempted on occasion to release an arrow at a deer, but never without regret for the suffering caused.

But why did Sir Thomas Lucy persecute Shakespeare so harshly for his "adventurous amusement"? Why did Shakespeare write a harsh satire on Sir Thomas? Drake tries hard to put the best gloss on everything. Sir Thomas was certainly in the right in seeking to protect his "property and character," and what we otherwise know of him paints him as an admirable man. Nevertheless, on this occasion resentment must have carried him too far. Here the standard

---

[23] Ibid., 402.
[24] Ibid. For a comparable Romantic account of Shakespeare's poetic "rambles" in the park at Fulbroke see Samuel Ireland, *Picturesque Views on the Upper, or Warwickshire Avon* (London, 1795), 155.
[25] Drake, *Shakspeare*, 1:403.

idealization of Shakespeare is resorted to: given "the known benevolence of the poet's character," Drakes urges, it must be admitted that his sense of injury on this occasion shows Sir Thomas had overstepped the line of prudence.[26] Nevertheless, Drake cannot believe that Shakespeare left Warwickshire merely as a result of this "persecution," and follows George Chalmers in thinking that Shakespeare may have been in debt, too, and was thus tempted to go to London in an attempt to make his fortune.[27]

Somerset's *Shakspeare's Early Days* is worth mentioning here as both a fictional extension of Drake's biographical method and a remarkable attempt to preserve and dignify the deer-poaching legend subsequent to Malone's magisterial demolition. Here, instead of Rowe's "ill company," the youthful Shakespeare spends his time "with young gentles of good degree and spirit."[28] Accused by Sir Thomas, Shakespeare admits to having shot a deer, but explains that he did so having discovered the starving family of a "humble shepherd":

> "Have you no food?" quoth I—
> "None, for the last two days," was their reply;—
> Like one pursued by fiends, forth from the cottage
> I madly rushed, resolved to bring them food!
> My home I could not reach—it was too far;
> I therefore shot the buck I chanc'd to meet,
> And on my shoulders bore it off in triumph,
> To the poor shepherd's dwelling;—there arriv'd,
> I lit a fire—prepared some savoury broth
> For the poor sufferers—tended them myself—
> And when I saw their eyes beam joy again,
> And heard them speak sweet words of gratitude,
> And view'd the smiling infants all around me,
> I thought them angels from the realms of light!—
> Their cottage, paradise! myself in heaven![29]

The fact that the gluttonous, illiterate Sir Thomas proceeds to prosecute Shakespeare, despite recognizing that he did "well to feed the hungry," allows Somerset to introduce a few sharp hints about social inequality and injustice that would doubtless have pleased Landor. Nevertheless, if read as a serious answer to Malone, *Shakspeare's Early Days* was simply a return to Drake's sentimental indulgence, and in a sense it actually reinforces the moral aspect of Malone's

---

[26] Ibid., 407, 408.

[27] In his *Apology for the Believers in the Shakspeare-Papers, which were Exhibited in Norfolk-Street* (London, 1797), Chalmers suggested that Shakespeare was "probably induced to remove to London, in the period, between the years 1585, and 1588; chased from his home, by the terriers of the law, for debt, rather than for deer-stealing, or for libelling" (48).

[28] Charles A. Somerset, *Shakspeare's Early Days* (London, n.d., ca. 1829), 13.

[29] Ibid., 23.

argument, clearly implying that poaching without the good excuse that Somerset's fictional Shakespeare offers would indeed be a "degrading circumstance."

Against both the Malone-Boswell and Drake-Somerset approaches to the old story, Landor's *Citation* proposes that Shakespeare and his scapegrace friends really did poach deer from Charlecote, motivated by a love of venison and adventure. The sentimentalism of the Drake-Somerset approach is answered at numerous points, nowhere more roundly than in a report of Shakespeare sitting astride the dead deer and remarking "I never sat pleasanter in my lifetime ... than upon this carcass."[30] The evening ended not with regrets, or the "heaven" of a benevolent act, but with a jolly venison feast. In Landor's scenario, Shakespeare is tried in Sir Thomas Lucy's house by Lucy himself (as in Somerset) and Silas Gough, the chaplain: that is, by representatives of civil and ecclesiastical authority. It is Silas who leads the prosecution, introducing two witnesses who are prepared to testify against Shakespeare. Shakespeare defends himself, not by denying the crime (his guilt is never in question), but by employing a series of ruses to distract those ranged against him from the matter at hand. Landor's is essentially a comedy of digression, and there is a leisurely rhythm to the book, clearly not to every reader's taste (Schoenbaum finds it "spun out unconscionably"). As the clock slowly turns, Sir Thomas becomes more and more distracted, Silas more and more frustrated, and Ephraim Barnett, the clerk writing everything down, waxes more and more sympathetic to young Willy Shakespeare. Shakespeare appears to be the only person in the room who knows more than a smattering of law: he describes himself as "having more than one year written in the office of an attorney, and having heard and listened to many discourses and questions on law."[31] Landor probably knew that it was Malone who had popularized the theory that Shakespeare, as a young man, had been trained in a law office.

The *Citation* is by no means just about deer stealing. The trial is skillfully used to create a framework for a wider examination of Shakespeare's character and his relation to social codes and structures in his time. Shakespeare's sexual character is also very much at issue. Landor significantly redates the episode of the legendary poaching, as attentive readers will have observed. Tradition placed it sometime subsequent to 1585, immediately prior to Shakespeare's departure for London. Landor pulled it back to September 1582, just after Shakespeare was supposed to have been married. Malone had placed Shakespeare's marriage in "June or July" 1582.[32] Edward Capell, more cautious, thought that it "must have happen'd before he [Shakespeare] was seventeen, or very soon after."[33] These were guesses, as the record of Shakespeare's marriage had not then been discovered. As guesses, they were calculated on the basis of the fact that Shakespeare's eldest child, Susanna, was

---

[30] Landor, *Complete Works*, 10:304.
[31] Ibid., 283.
[32] Malone, *Shakspeare*, 2:112.
[33] Edward Capell, ed., *Mr William Shakespeare, his Comedies, Histories, and Tragedies*, 10 vols. (London, 1768), 1:31.

baptized on May 26, 1583, and they were of course designed to discreetly protect young Shakespeare from suspicion of prenuptial sexual intercourse. Nevertheless, Shakespeare's having married at the tender age of eighteen, if not earlier, was bound to raise speculation not necessarily flattering to his respectability and general saintliness. While Somerset could resort to poetic license and represent his sentimental Shakespeare still unmarried in 1585, Malone and Drake had to accept the known facts and smooth them over as best they could. Malone pointed to "the warmth, the tenderness, and the sensibility of [Shakespeare's] disposition," which he felt had been "the occasion of his wishing, at an early period of life, to participate in 'the sweet silent hours of marriage joys'" (the quotation, rather incongruously, is from Richard III's proposal to Queen Elizabeth, immediately prior to his downfall, that he marry her daughter).[34] Drake took the suspicion of sordid motives more seriously, putting the question "whether convenience, or the attraction of a beautiful form, was the chief promoter of this early connection." But, after some discussion, he was able to conclude, happily, that "the young poet's attachment to Anne Hathaway was ... perfectly disinterested," and though she was twenty-six this was still "an age compatible with youth, and with the most alluring beauty."[35] Drake apparently thought that beauty or property were the only things that might have tempted Shakespeare to enter the marriage state.

One of Landor's obviously subversive moves is to make it clear that as late as September 19, 1582, Shakespeare was *not* married to the woman he calls Hannah Hathaway, though it is reported that he is a regular nocturnal visitor to her "hovel." Hannah Hathaway is described in the *Citation* as the slut of Shottery, a village close to Stratford. Her mother is said to have been "housemaid and sempstress" in the Lucy family,[36] and it is hinted that Hannah had a sexual relationship with Sir Thomas in the past, and with Silas more recently. There are echoes of the Molly Seagrim plot in *Tom Jones*, and Landor's Shakespeare is indeed something like a more intellectual and disingenuous version of Fielding's virile hero. By emphasizing the lowness of the Hathaways, Landor was subverting the biographers' project of aggrandizing Shakespeare's lineage and connections as much as possible. With regard to the date, he was actually right, a fact that must have delighted him when it became known. A record of Shakespeare's marriage came to light in 1836 and showed that the Bard was indeed not married until late November or early December: some six months before the birth of his first child.[37] In the *Citation*, Shakespeare's relationship with Hannah hangs in the background throughout his trial for deer stealing, and Silas shows a prurient and jealous interest in what occurs between the young couple. A description rather in the manner of Sterne gestures amusingly at unspeakable improprieties: "She points

---

[34] Malone, *Shakspeare*, 2:111.
[35] Drake, *Shakspeare*, 1:62, 63.
[36] Landor, *Complete Works*, 10:364.
[37] R. B. Wheler, "Shakspeare's Marriage License Bond," *Gentleman's Magazine* 109 (1836): 266–8.

his [Shakespeare's] young beard for him; persuading him it grows thicker and thicker, blacker and blacker; she washes his ruff, stiffens it, plaits it, tries it upon his neck, removes the hair from under it, pinches it with thumb and forefinger, pretending that he hath moiled it, puts her hand all the way round it, *setting it to rights*, as she calleth it..."[38]

In his treatment of the Shakespeare-Hathaway relationship Landor develops an idea from Capell, who had argued that the connection led Shakespeare into conflict with his father.[39] Sir Thomas, who adopts an increasingly parental attitude to Shakespeare, eventually claims to be acting as a surrogate for John Shakespeare when he insists, as the price of leniency, that Shakespeare "abstain and withhold in future from that idle and silly slut, that sly and scoffing giggler, Hannah Hathaway, with whom, to the heartache of thy poor worthy father, thou wantonly keepest company," and follow his father's profession instead. In an unexpected denouement, Shakespeare is made to swear on the Bible that he will leave Hannah; instead he swears, provocatively, that he will always "worship and cherish" her, flings the Bible into the fireplace, and makes his escape from the hall. As he is seen galloping away, Sir Thomas laments that "a reputable woolstapler's son [has] turned gipsy and poet for life."[40] What Shakespeare's intentions are at the end is left unclear, but a "Post-Scriptum" added to the account of the trial states that in the twelve days after his escape no one in the Stratford area had seen him, not even Hannah. She is described as distraught, and Landor presumably surmised that many of his readers would know she was pregnant with Shakespeare's baby by this juncture.

If Landor's Shakespeare is thus far from the respectable, saintly figure of Malone and Drake's biographies, and quite unlike the omnipresent spirit of creativity that the Romantic writers tended to idealize him as, he is, nevertheless, possessed of great talents as an actor and storyteller, and the way Landor works this into the *Citation* is important. When Shakespeare is put on trial he is already a "known" character, not just because of his relationship with Hannah, but because, as Sir Thomas tells him:

> Thou hast, for these many months, been represented unto me as one dissolute and light, much given unto mummeries and mysteries, wakes and carousals, cudgel-fighters and mountebanks, and wanton women. They do also represent of thee ... that thou enactest the parts, not simply of foresters and fairies, girls in the green-sickness and friars, lawyers and outlaws, but likewise, having small reverence for station, of kings and queens, knights and privy-counsellors, in all their glory.[41]

---

[38] Landor, *Complete Works*, 10:364.

[39] "The displeasure of his father, which was the consequence of this marriage, or else some excesses which he is said to have been guilty of, it is probable, drove him up to town ...." Capell, *Mr William Shakespeare*, 1:31–2. Capell's conjecture was included in later editions of Shakespeare's works.

[40] Landor, *Complete Works*, 10:365, 367.

[41] Ibid., 306.

Arguably, Landor here comes closer than anyone else in the Romantic period to anticipating the main idea of C. L. Barber's classic 1959 study, *Shakespeare's Festive Comedy*, which argued that Shakespeare's earlier comedies were essentially "saturnalian," with a shape and rhythm developed from the festive rituals that Shakespeare, as a countryman, knew well.[42] Sir Thomas's description of young Shakespeare makes him, in Barber's terms, an embodiment of the anarchic spirit of holiday. Although Barber did not claim that Shakespeare used his festive materials in a subversive way, he showed that the potential was there, as traditional holiday activities were increasingly frowned upon by anxious authorities in the late 1500s, and at least one allegedly satirical entertainment became a Star Chamber matter. Landor's Sir Thomas represents such nervous authority; his extreme sensitivity to any disturbance or mockery of the social order makes holiday behavior ipso facto dangerous and subversive.

Landor probably took his ideas about Elizabethan festivity from Drake, whose biography included a long account of "Country-Life during the Age of Shakspeare," with a chapter devoted to "Rural Holydays and Festivals." Drake drew his account from many of the sources later utilized by Barber. He was undoubtedly troubled by some of the more anarchic and irreverent aspects of the Elizabethan holiday, and when quoting Puritan critics of popular festivity sometimes echoes their tone of severe condemnation. Nevertheless, always genial and indulgent, he argues that holidays were, all in all, not only innocent but even pious. The general tone of his account can be gauged from the introductory paragraph:

> The record of rural festivity and amusement, must, as far as it is unaccompanied by any detail of riot or intemperance, be a subject of pleasing contemplation to every good and cheerful mind. Labour, the destined portion of by far the greater part of human beings, requires frequent intervals of relaxation; and the encouragement of innocent diversion at stated periods, may be considered, therefore, both in a moral and political point of view, as essentially useful. The sports and amusements of our ancestors on their holydays and festivals, while they had little tendency to promote either luxury or dissipation, contributed very powerfully to preserve some of the best and most striking features of our national manners and character, and were frequently mingled with that cheerful piety which forms the most heart-felt species of devotion, where religion, mixing with the social rite, offers up the homage of a happy and contented heart.[43]

Drake quotes liberally from the plays to demonstrate Shakespeare's intimate knowledge of the seasonal festivals. But he does not argue, as Barber did, and as Landor anticipated, that the spirit of the festivals actually became an integral part of Shakespeare's imaginative world and writing. His representation of festivals as essentially innocent, even pious, and good for social stability is challenged

---

[42] C. L. Barber, *Shakespeare's Festive Comedy* (Princeton, NJ: Princeton University Press, 1959).

[43] Drake, *Shakspeare*, 1:123.

by Landor's *Citation*, in which festivals mark the battle line between those who would control society, like Sir Thomas, and those who resent and resist control, like Shakespeare.

Landor describes Shakespeare not as writing plays, but as entertaining his companions with stories "in voices" that the reader recognizes as having later developed into plays. One of his deer-stealing companions is reported as having begged Shakespeare to stop his

> strange vagaries; thy Italian girls' nursery sighs; thy Pucks and pinchings, and thy Windsor whimsies. ... We have slept with thee under the oaks in the ancient forest of Arden, and we have wakened from our sleep in the tempest far at sea. Now art thou for frightening us again out of all the senses thou hadst given us, with witches and women more murderous than they.[44]

The references are, presumably, to *Romeo and Juliet*, *A Midsummer Night's Dream*, *The Merry Wives of Windsor*, *As You Like It*, *The Tempest*, and *Macbeth*—three of which, it may be noted, are the kind of festive comedies defined by Barber. In imagining these stories as improvised, Landor represents Shakespeare as an essentially popular playwright, a poet of the people, whose imaginative world is an outgrowth of country festivals and folklore, with all their subversive potential. In part at least, he was surely taking aim at the bookish image of Shakespeare constructed in the second half of the eighteenth century as the plays became steadily encrusted with annotation. Collecting and analyzing Shakespeare's source materials in the early 1750s, Charlotte Lennox saw herself as "attempting what has by some unaccountable Neglect been hitherto omitted."[45] Capell, who thought that Shakespeare had been intended to go to university, took this much further in his "School of Shakespeare," which presents over 500 pages of "extracts ... from books that may properly be call'd—his [Shakespeare's] school; as they are indeed the sources from which he drew the greater part of his knowledge in mythology and classical matters, his fable, his history, and even the seeming peculiarities of his language."[46] This "bookish" image of Shakespeare was eventually given monumental visual form in Ford Madox Brown's imaginary *Portrait of William Shakespeare* (1849). Painted within a decade and a half of the publication of Landor's *Citation*, this image represents a professionally respectable Shakespeare who is the very opposite of Landor's young poacher; Brown's Shakespeare could even do duty as Landor's Sir Thomas.

Festivals were most subversive when the conventional social order was mimicked. Good mimicry requires good acting, and in the *Citation* Shakespeare

---

[44] Landor, *Complete Works*, 1:287.

[45] Charlotte Lennox, *Shakespear Illustrated: or the Novels and Histories, on which the Plays of Shakespear are Founded*, 3 vols. (London, 1753–54), 1:iv.

[46] Capell, *Mr William Shakespeare*, 1:31. "The School of Shakespeare" was eventually published in the third volume of Capell's *Notes and Various Readings to Shakespeare* (1783).

Fig. 1.1　　Ford Madox Brown, *William Shakespeare*, 1849. © Manchester Art Gallery. Reproduced by permission.

threatens Sir Thomas most with his rumored ability as an actor. Sir Thomas lectures him in a wonderfully funny speech:

> To pass over and pretermit the danger of representing the actions of the others, and mainly of lawyers and churchmen, the former of whom do pardon no offences, and the latter those only against God, (having no warrant for more) canst thou believe it innocent to counterfeit kings and queens? Supposest thou that if the impression of their faces on a farthing be felonious and rope-worthy, the imitation of head and body, voice and bearing, plume and strut, crown and mantle, and everything else that maketh them royal and glorious, be aught less? Perpend, young man, perpend! Consider who among inferior mortals shall imitate them becomingly? Dreamest thou they talk and act like cheesemen at Banbury fair? How can thy shallow brain suffice for their vast conceptions? How darest thou say, as they do, hang this fellow, quarter that, flay, mutilate, stab, shoot, press, hook, torture, burn alive? These are royalties.[47]

Much of the humor here comes from obvious contradictions. If it is difficult or impossible to imitate the style of royalty, Sir Thomas need not worry about social order being overthrown. But he *is* afraid, and his fear proceeds from a half-conscious recognition that it is actually rather easy to imitate royalty, which consists of nothing more than pride, ferocity, and inhumanity—or the appearance of those things—dressed in the right clothes. Sir Thomas wants to believe in a world of degree—of innate differences. He tries to explain to Shakespeare, for example, that killing a deer or a swan is much more heinous than killing a goose, and links this to the way human society is organized:

> In a buck there is something so gainly and so grand, he treadeth the earth with such ease and such agility, he abstaineth from all other animals with such punctilious avoidance, one would imagine God created him when he created knighthood. In the swan there is such purity, such coldness is there in the element he inhabiteth, such solitude of station, that verily he doth remind me of the Virgin Queen herself.[48]

Some human lives, to extend the argument, are more expendable than others. Although Sir Thomas is essentially a comic character, there is something chilling about his Falstaffian contempt for the lives of the masses. He speaks nostalgically of the Wars of the Roses a century earlier: "Things are not as they were in our glorious wars of York and Lancaster. The knaves were thinned then; two or three crops a year of that rank squitch-grass which it has become the fashion of late to call the people."[49] But Sir Thomas immediately continues, after this statement, with a recognition that the difference of social rank, and accordingly of expendability, was largely a matter of costume: "There was some difference then between

---

[47] Landor, *Complete Works*, 10:306–7.
[48] Ibid., 308.
[49] Ibid., 278.

buff doublets and iron mail; and the rogues [the people] felt it." In other words, everyone used to go to war together in what is represented as a natural piece of social "thinning": the rich wore armor and the poor did not, and accordingly it was mostly the poor who got cut down. Costume was highly respected. In peacetime, Sir Thomas regrets, costume loses its power to enforce distinction.

There is obviously confusion here. If a knight is superior because of his noble bearing, that is one thing; if he is superior just because he has the economic resources to buy armor and expensive clothes, that is quite another. And it is precisely Sir Thomas's confusion of a belief in innate difference—the buck superior to the rabbit, the swan to the goose—with his recognition that in human society there is a need to rely on external signs and tokens of difference that makes him vulnerable. Shakespeare fully exploits this vulnerability. He deftly acts the part of a pious, docile youth in need of gentle guidance, and after a few initial doubts Sir Thomas swallows the deception. Shakespeare then leads him a merry dance, diverting him from the matter at hand with a long account of the religious lessons he has picked up from Dr. Glaston, "the learnedst clerk in Christendom," on his visits to Oxford.[50] Despite the stories he has heard of Shakespeare's expert acting, Sir Thomas seems absolutely blind to the possibility that Shakespeare may be just putting on a performance: such is his faith in outward appearances. As Landor states in his "Editor's Preface," Sir Thomas "is led by the nose, while he believes that nobody can move him."[51]

Landor's representation of Shakespeare as an excellent role-player who understands the world around him dangerously well allows an illuminating comparison with the most ambitious Elizabethan fiction of the period, Scott's *Kenilworth* (1821). The comparison is especially apt, in fact, for Landor highly admired *Kenilworth*, coming to consider it his favorite among Scott's novels, and "a fine epic."[52] Although the central historical event in the novel is Queen Elizabeth's visit to Kenilworth in 1575, Scott takes considerable liberties with chronology, and Shakespeare is imagined already a well-established playwright, his poetry on everyone's lips. His deer stealing, which is assumed to have really taken place, becomes the subject of royal conversation. The Earl of Sussex, an old soldier, asked his opinion of Shakespeare by the Queen, replies: "'He is a stout man at quarter-staff, and single falchion, as I am told, though a halting fellow; and stood, they say, a tough fight with the rangers of old Sir Thomas Lucy of Charlecot, when he broke his deer-park and kissed his keeper's daughter.'" The Queen, who remembers the Lucy case, denies there was any "'kissing in the matter,'" but alludes generally to Shakespeare's "former errors" in "breaking parks" and "other follies."[53] Shakespeare, Scott suggests, was a young rogue who made good not

---

[50] Ibid., 318.

[51] Ibid., 264.

[52] John Forster, *Walter Savage Landor: A Biography*, 2 vols. (London, 1869), 2:527.

[53] Sir Walter Scott, *Kenilworth*, ed. J. H. Alexander (Edinburgh: Edinburgh University Press, 1993), 174.

just because of extraordinary talent, but because of his willingness to woo the favor of the rich and powerful. On the one occasion he is glimpsed, he is seeking the protection of the Earl of Leicester, and it is the "elegant flattery" addressed to Elizabeth in *A Midsummer Night's Dream* that turns out to be his wisest career move—an interpretation of Shakespeare perhaps to be expected from Scott, the Tory royalist.[54]

It is hard to imagine Landor's Shakespeare addressing anyone with "elegant flattery" not thoroughly underscored with mockery. Scott refrains from speculation on the degree of Shakespeare's sincerity, but the world of *Kenilworth* is a world where imposture is always found out and punished. Landor's Shakespeare actually has a good deal in common with Scott's hard-drinking adventurer, Michael ("Mike") Lambourne, whose "juvenile wildness" is adverted to at the very beginning of the novel, who boasts of "robbing the Abbot's orchard," who ran away as a young man to become a soldier, and who is generally disrespectful and irreverent to those above him—even the Queen herself.[55] But Lambourne's desire to raise himself runs aground on the recognition that it is no easy matter to appear better than he is:

> There is something about the real gentry that few men come up to that are not born and bred to the mystery. I wot not where the trick lies; but although I can enter an ordinary with as much audacity, rebuke the waiters and drawers as loudly, drink as deep a health, swear as round an oath, and fling my gold as freely about as any of the jingling spurs and white feathers that are around me,—yet, hang me if I can ever catch the true grace of it ...[56]

Landor's Sir Thomas would obviously nod cautious approval to this. But Landor's Shakespeare has "the trick" that puzzles Lambourne, and a good few others in reserve. In *Kenilworth* Shakespeare is a very minor character—he does not even speak—presented against an elaborately tiered version of Elizabethan England in which every good man knows his place and those, like Lambourne, with "vaulting ambition" wind up dead. In Landor's *Citation*, by contrast, the focus is on Shakespeare throughout, and the structures and hierarchies of Elizabethan England are essentially seen through him, alternately constructed and deconstructed, respected and disrespected, in his restless, versatile imagination. Scott's Shakespeare, whatever his transcendent talent, fits quietly into Elizabethan society, as Scott, "the Great Unknown" and the most successful writer of his time, fitted into his. Landor's Shakespeare, by contrast, is too big for Elizabethan society, and however well he plays his parts there is ultimately something unruly and uncontainable about him, just as there was about Landor.

This uncontainable side of Landor's Shakespeare is revealed at the end of the *Citation*, when he willfully squanders all the credit he has painstakingly gained

---

[54] Ibid., 176.
[55] Ibid., 6, 7.
[56] Ibid., 20.

with Sir Thomas. His hurling the Bible aside and escape from Charlecote is a blatant defiance of church and secular authority. Nevertheless, he is arguably most subversive not in this final moment of overt rebellion, which Landor could not refrain from including, but in the bulk of the work, where he demonstrates how plausibly he can express those sentiments that authority wants to hear. His real opinions, during the long interview, are expressed in asides and cryptic jokes—marginal comments, as it were, which Sir Thomas generally half understands at best. It is this more subtly subversive representation of Shakespeare that has potentially large consequences for the reading of his plays. It was of course essentially impossible for Landor to maintain, even obliquely, that the plays read as a whole represent some radical, antiauthoritarian view of society, however much he may have liked to have found them espousing such ideas. But by insinuating that Shakespeare was expert at putting on a show of respectful conformity when it suited his interests, or when he was in the mood, Landor upset the cozy relationship between biography and criticism that made Shakespeare a conservative because the plays were, and the plays conservative because Shakespeare was. The *Citation* raises the liberating possibility that Shakespeare should be read against the grain, and that it is in the incidental and seemingly marginal elements that his true sentiments and true self can be located. This might seem a vague reading program, but it is the sort of vagueness that very much works against a securing of the national Bard in the Tory interest. It opens the plays up to new and unsettling readings, such as Terry Eagleton's famous provocation "that positive value in *Macbeth* lies with the three witches. The witches are the heroines of the piece, however little the play itself recognizes the fact, and however much the critics may have set out to defame them."[57] Indeed, though Landor's book has been all but ignored in histories of Shakespeare's reception, his slippery, subversive Shakespeare is easier to spot in modern Shakespeare criticism than the divinely moral Bard worshipped by Coleridge, De Quincey, Keats, and other mainstream Romantic writers.

---

[57] Terry Eagleton, *William Shakespeare* (Oxford: Blackwell, 1986), 2.

Chapter 2
# Peer Reviewed:
# Elizabeth Inchbald's Shakespeare Criticism

Karen Bloom Gevirtz

Acclaimed as a playwright as well as a novelist, Elizabeth Inchbald was both popularly respected and commercially powerful. Small wonder that when the publisher Longman was looking for someone to write prefaces to the plays in the soon-to-be published *The British Theater*, he turned to Inchbald. Her 125 prefaces, composed between 1806 and 1808, covered every play in the repertory of London's theaters, from Restoration comedy to Inchbald's own work. In this context, Inchbald's 24 essays on Shakespeare's plays do not appear at first glance as the carefully considered criticism of Shakespeare's work that they in fact are. They can be read as a bridge between eighteenth-century and Romantic schools of Shakespeare criticism; however, more significant is what Inchbald's prefaces offer on their own. Inchbald was a Catholic, a woman, a playwright, and a retired actress—identities that shaped her work in important ways. In particular, as a fellow theater professional, Inchbald was able to explain how Shakespeare's plays work as foundations for performance and as texts within a genre, following (or not following) certain conventions. When coupled with the sensibility often associated with male Romantic authors of the period, this perspective is remarkable and provocative.

Although Inchbald's prefaces in the *Remarks* have been studied, they have not been understood specifically as part of a tradition of Shakespeare criticism. Francesca Saggini describes ways in which Inchbald's method is both "neoclassical" and Romantic.[1] But while Saggini sees Inchbald as a bridge between one school of drama criticism and the next, she does not consider Inchbald's position as a bridge between one school of Shakespeare criticism and the next, which is an important difference. As Marvin Carlson points out, the conventions of drama criticism were different from those of Shakespeare criticism, which were well established. Carlson observes that Inchbald draws heavily on the conventions of Shakespeare criticism in her Shakespeare essays but not in her other essays, a difference he erroneously attributes to Inchbald's composing the Shakespeare essays first. As Annibel Jenkins has shown, Inchbald composed the prefaces in random order; they were organized later, and by her publisher Longman, not by herself. The

---

[1] Francesca Saggini, "The Art of Fine Drama: Inchbald's *Remarks for The British Theatre* and the Aesthetic Experience of the Late Eighteenth-Century Theatre-Goer," *Textus* 28 (2005): 133–52.

use of Shakespeare criticism in her Shakespeare essays therefore cannot be a chronological issue, but a deliberate choice for those particular prefaces.[2]

It is within the context of Shakespeare criticism that I wish to discuss Inchbald's prefaces to Shakespeare's plays. James Engell points out that differences between eighteenth-century and Romantic criticism have been overstated, since there are similarities as well as differences between the two schools, and the differences are not always very great.[3] Eighteenth-century and Romantic critics alike referred to the work of others, for example, although the earlier critics seem to have deployed more and denser allusions to other authors, and with a greater variety of attitudes towards them. While Samuel Taylor Coleridge "was familiar with the common assumptions of the age," R. A. Foakes explains, he did "not refer to a wide range of works or authors by name in his lectures."[4] William Hazlitt and Charles Lamb were even less scholarly. Critics in both groups tended to use the work of others to establish the uniqueness and importance of their own contribution, although a Romantic critic such as Coleridge "exaggerate[d] his differences" to establish his own critical insights and method as a revolutionary break, not as a development along a continuum of criticism.[5] Eighteenth-century critics did not usually position their own work as a revolutionary break with the past so much as the best version of ideas usually already in circulation.

Elizabeth Inchbald's Shakespeare criticism draws on many of these conventions. She refers to other Shakespeare critics, such as Samuel Johnson, Edmond Malone, and George Steevens, as well as authors such as Joseph Addison and Alexander Pope. She also alludes to sources such as Holinshed, Plutarch, and Geoffrey of Monmouth, giving some scholarly heft to her discussion. Nevertheless, the amount of scholarship in her prefaces is quite limited in comparison with her predecessors. Inchbald also eschews the antagonistic prose that usually characterizes eighteenth-century and Romantic attitudes towards other critics. As she explains in the preface to *Hamlet*, "This tragedy is a work of such intellectual magnitude, that every comment which has been written upon it is too well known to be quoted."[6]

---

[2] Marvin Carlson, "Elizabeth Inchbald: A Woman Critic in Her Theatrical Culture," in *Women in British Romantic Theatre: Drama, Performance, and Society, 1790–1840*, ed. Catherine Burroughs (Cambridge: Cambridge University Press, 2000), 210–11; Annibel Jenkins, *I'll Tell You What: The Life of Elizabeth Inchbald* (Lexington: University Press of Kentucky, 2003), 452.

[3] James Engell, "Coleridge, Johnson, and Shakespeare: A Critical Drama in Five Acts," *Romanticism: The Journal of Romantic Culture and Criticism* 4, no. 1 (1998): 22–39.

[4] R. A. Foakes, ed., *The Collected Works of Samuel Taylor Coleridge, Volume 5: Lectures 1808–1819: On Literature,* 2 vols. (Princeton, NJ: Princeton University Press, 1987), 1:lvii–lviii.

[5] Engell, "Coleridge, Johnson, and Shakespeare," 26, 35–6.

[6] Elizabeth Inchbald, Preface to *Hamlet*, in *Remarks for "The British Theatre"* (1806–9; Delmar, NY: Scholars' Facsimiles and Reprints, 1990), 3. All references to Inchbald's dramatic criticism will be from this edition, a single volume reprinting of Inchbald's prefaces alone. Because each preface in this edition has its own pagination, references will be to the play that corresponds to the preface being quoted.

In fact, Inchbald sometimes hides behind other critics rather than use them to illuminate her own position. For example, she concludes her preface to *King Lear* with a recapitulation of the different views of Nahum Tate's ending of the play, in which Cordelia lives: "[Addison] condemns him for this; Dr. Johnson commends him for it; both showing excellent reasons. Then comes Steevens, who gives a better reason than all, why they are all wrong" (*King Lear*, 4–5). And here the preface ends. She does the same at the end of her preface to *Macbeth*, avoiding a clear conclusion of her own and leaving the reader to extract from the body of the preface what her views might be. This strategy is not a general but a specific one, used by Inchbald when the controversy is too hot. It is possible that Inchbald did not have the resources for a more academic approach to the Bard. Her education had been in modern literature, including French, and with 125 prefaces to churn out in three years, she probably did not have time to do extensive classical reading.[7] It is also likely that neither she nor her publisher thought their target audience would appreciate a heavy dose of academicism, especially since Inchbald's reputation was not for brilliant scholarship, but for brilliant play and novel writing; no doubt she had been hired for her strengths.

In fact, Longman's choice of a theater expert for his prefaces has significant implications when it comes to Inchbald's treatment of Shakespeare's plays in particular. Shakespeare's plays were understood and classified very differently at the beginning of the nineteenth century than they had been during the eighteenth century, starting with the nature of the playtext itself. For eighteenth-century Shakespeare critics, Shakespeare's plays did not possess a definitive text, so commentators felt free, if not obliged, to attempt to establish one, primarily by tracking Shakespeare's sources and editing the manuscripts. Charlotte Lennox's *Shakespear Illustrated* (1753), for example, documents Shakespeare's sources, comparing his plays to the originals. Editors usually sought to clarify meaning or repair meter in search of a permanent, definitive text. Elizabeth Griffith suggests, "Might we not venture to substitute the word *quick*, in this passage, as being the better opposed to the description in the second line following of *low and tardily*—Those who speak *quick*, generally speak *loud* also; which compleats the opposition." Johnson points out that although one of Sir Thomas Hanmer's "emendations" does not clarify the meaning, at least Hanmer "found the metre though he missed the sense."[8] Each edition strove to establish a definitive text but paradoxically, by reproducing disagreements, each edition confirmed the notion that the text required an imposed reliability. The fact that one edition rapidly followed another also perpetuated the idea of an unreliable text.

This view of the texts did not begin to change until Edmond Malone's *Plays and Poems of William Shakespeare* (1790). Peter Holland suggests that Malone's

[7] Jenkins, *I'll Tell You What*, 8–9, 21.

[8] Elizabeth Griffith, *The Morality of Shakespeare's Drama Illustrated* (London: T. Cadell, 1775), 237n; Samuel Johnson, "Notes on Shakespeare's Plays," in *Johnson on Shakespeare*, ed. Arthur Sherbo, vol. 7 (New Haven, CT: Yale University Press, 1968), 275.

meticulous archival work conferred on his edition of Shakespeare an authenticity and authority hitherto unknown, and Thomas Postlewait points out that "Malone tried to confine Shakespeare within documentary records, but in the process supposedly turned him into the isolated genius of bardolatry."[9] By the time the Romantics were writing about them, the plays were as sacred as scripture and Shakespeare was their equally sacred author; changes were heretical. Lamb complains that "Tate has put his hook in the nostrils of" *King Lear*. He calls changes "tamperings" and says of the late, great David Garrick, "I am almost disposed to deny to Garrick the merit of being an admirer of Shakspeare. A true lover of his excellencies he certainly was not; for would any true lover of them have admitted into his matchless scenes such ribald trash as Tate and Cibber, and the rest of them ... have foisted into the acting plays of Shakspeare? I believe it is impossible that he could have had a proper reverence for Shakspeare."[10] Of course, Romantic critics themselves still recognized the value of different editions. When Coleridge put together his lectures, he used "Mrs Milne's Shakespeare" and five other editions from Theobald (1726) to Reed (1803).[11] Nevertheless, these same critics vehemently propounded the notion that the words were immutable. The reality, of course, was that the stability conferred upon the texts by the Romantic critics was illusory, but the attitude preferring textual stability was significant.[12]

One part of the explanation for this attitude lies in the influence of Malone's impressively researched assertion that a great part should be attributed to genre. Eighteenth-century critics viewed the plays as plays, even if they contained poetry. Consequently, Shakespeare's plays were working objects, documents for building a performance. They could be changed to suit the current audience's taste, which often meant "improving" upon the original. Eliza Haywood in 1745 asserted that the plays that have had their "Weeds pluck'd up by the skilful Hands of [Shakespeare's] Successors are much the most elegant Entertainments" and thought that Colley Cibber's production of the full and original *Romeo and Juliet* was far inferior to Thomas Otway's "moderniz'd and clear'd" version, *Caius Marius*. Lewis Theobald also borrowed the garden metaphor from *Hamlet*, calling Shakespeare's plays an

---

[9] Peter Holland, "A History of Histories: From Flecknoe to Nicoll," in *Theorizing Practice: Redefining Theatre History*, ed. W. B. Worthen and Peter Holland (New York: Palgrave Macmillan, 2003), 8–29; Thomas Postlewait, "The Criteria for Evidence: Anecdotes in Shakespearean Biography, 1709–2000," in Worthen and Holland, eds., *Theorizing Practice*, 60.

[10] Charles Lamb, "On the Tragedies of Shakspeare, Considered with Reference to their Fitness for Stage Representation," 1811, in *The Romantics on Shakespeare*, ed. Jonathan Bate (New York: Penguin Books, 1992), 123, 121.

[11] R. A. Foakes, "Editorial Practice, Symbols, and Abbreviations," in *The Collected Works of Samuel Taylor Coleridge, Volume 5*, 1:xvii.

[12] Jonathan Bate, Review of "A Man for All Ages," Books Section, *The Guardian*, April 14, 2007. As Bate observes, "through the 18th, 19th and 20th centuries, there was a major new edition of his Complete Works once every 20 years or so."

"unweeded Garden grown to Seed."[13] Buried in these comments is the idea that members of the theater, such as Colley Cibber, have the knowledge and legitimacy to change the plays to suit audiences and their own views.

Romantic critics, however, viewed the plays as poetry and therefore immutable. Hazlitt's attack on Johnson, for example, is based on the idea that Johnson did not appreciate the poetry that is Shakespeare's work: "We have a high respect for Dr. Johnson's character and understanding, mixed with something like personal attachment: but he was neither a poet nor a judge of poetry. He might in one sense be a judge of poetry as it falls within the limits and rules of prose, but not as it is poetry. Least of all was he qualified to be a judge of Shakespear, who 'alone is high fantastical.'"[14] It is probably not a coincidence that many of the men who treated Shakespeare as a poet (and not a playwright) were failed playwrights but successful poets. As Jeffrey Cox points out, "Wordsworth, Coleridge, Scott, Southey, Byron, Keats, Shelley, and Hunt" either could not get their work staged or when they did, suffered theatrical bombs. Only Coleridge saw any success on the stage—just once, with his play *Remorse*, in 1813.[15] This process seems somewhat borne out by the sequence of ideas in critical writings. Tracing the development of Romantic insights into Hamlet's dealings with Ophelia, Arthur Hudson contends that some of Coleridge's finest insights into Hamlet's psyche arose during Coleridge's work on *Christabel*, after which they were transferred to Coleridge's lectures and, through the poetry and those lectures, to Hazlitt and Lamb.[16]

If the plays were poetry, then they were not to be used for performance. In a review of John Kemble as Hamlet, Hazlitt reports that "Mr. Kemble's voice seemed to faint and stagger, to be strained and cracked, under the weight of this majestic image: but, indeed, we know of no tones deep or full enough to bear along the swelling tide of sentiment it conveys."[17] For Lamb, more extreme, Shakespeare's plays should be kept out of the theater altogether. "It may be a paradox," he concedes, "but I cannot help being of the opinion that the plays of Shakspeare are less calculated for performance on a stage, than those of almost any other dramatist altogether. Their distinguished excellence is a reason that they should be so. There is so much in them, which comes not under the province of

---

[13] Eliza Haywood, from *The Female Spectator*, Book 8 (1745), in *William Shakespeare: The Critical Heritage, Volume 3: 1733–1752*, ed. Brian Vickers (Boston: Routledge & Kegan Paul, 1975), 162–3; Lewis Theobald, *Shakespeare restored ... ever yet publish'd* (London: R. Francklin et al., 1726), ii.

[14] William Hazlitt, Preface to "Characters of Shakespear's Plays," 1817, in Bate, ed., *Romantics on Shakespeare*, 176.

[15] Jeffrey N. Cox, "Baillie, Siddons, Larpent: Gender, Power, and Politics in the Theatre of Romanticism," in *Women in British Romantic Theatre: Drama, Performance, and Society, 1790–1840*, ed. Catherine Burroughs (Cambridge: Cambridge University Press, 2000), 25–6.

[16] Arthur Palmer Hudson, "Romantic Apologiae for Ophelia," *ELH* 9 (1942): 59–70.

[17] William Hazlitt, "On Siddons, Kemble, and Kean," 1816–1820, in Bate, ed., *Romantics on Shakespeare*, 169.

acting, with which eye, and tone, and gesture, have nothing to do."[18] Performance imposes materiality on sublimity, and interpretation on imagination. In contrast, the "reading of a tragedy is a fine abstraction. It presents to the fancy just so much of appearances as to make us feel that we are among flesh and blood, while by far the greater and better part of our imagination is employed upon the thoughts and internal machinery of the character. But in acting, scenery, dress, the most contemptible things, call upon us to judge of their naturalness."[19] Reading shifts the focus from the ridiculous to the sublime. Ultimately, only readers can appreciate the texts' beauty, because only readers can achieve the requisite quiet, solitary contemplation of word and character.

Inchbald's work resembles both eighteenth-century and Romantic criticism, and though she follows eighteenth-century critics by classifying the plays as plays, her perspective on the matter of genre is different. She uses her experience as a playwright and former actress to explain the plays from the perspective of the theater, as objects to be used for performance.[20] Like Shakespeare, she understands that plays are "made things"—things made for performance and for making money as well as edification and pleasure. Overall, the prefaces consider the plays on their own, as they affect viewers and readers, and as they work in the hands and mouths of actors. For Inchbald, the plays are part of a chain linking three different parties with different needs and expectations: playwright, actor, and audience. As a result, she avoids wholesale admiration, since she knows where Shakespeare fails not as an artist, but as a craftsman. She spends two pages repeatedly condemning Shakespeare's adoption of "the incredible occurrences here inserted" in *Measure for Measure* (4). As she explains about *Measure for Measure*:

> Shakspeare displays such genius in the characters, poetry, and incident of his dramas, that it is to be regretted, he ever found materials for a plot, excepting those of history, from any other source than his own invention. Had the plots of old tales been exhausted in his time, as in the present, the world might have had Shakspeare's foundation as well as superstructure, and the whole edifice had been additionally magnificent. (3–4)

Inchbald is fair here, but the repetition of this sentiment gives it its sharpness, as she often expresses this view in this preface and in others. After all, as a fellow actor-turned-playwright she could appreciate, even venerate, his skill, without succumbing to Bardolatry.

---

[18] Lamb, "On the Tragedies," 113–14.

[19] Ibid., 123.

[20] John Keats celebrated Edmund Kean's ability to declaim—"The sensual life of verse springs warm from the lips of Kean"—but Keats prioritizes the verse rather than the play. He also applauds Kean's ability to get lost in a speech instead of acting for a unified effect: "Other actors are continually thinking of their sum-total effect throughout a play. Kean delivers himself up to the instant feeling, without a shadow of a thought about any thing else." John Keats, "Mr Kean," 1817, in Bate, ed., *Romantics on Shakespeare*, 201–2.

Inchbald's comments on *Measure for Measure* also underscore the fact that she well understood another technical aspect of Shakespeare's work: they are adaptations. As a translator and adapter herself, Inchbald knew how to rework an original effectively. She notes in the preface to *Cymbeline* that, although in other plays Shakespeare uses absolutely impossible events, he makes them acceptable because the "improbability is overpowered by the author's art, and his auditors are made to feel, though they cannot believe." Unfortunately, "No such magic presides over the play of 'Cymbeline,' so as to transform reason into imagination" (4). While she praises Shakespeare for creating characters that explore universal human qualities, she also considers those characters as devices in a drama. She criticizes *Cymbeline*'s Posthumus for acting more Italian than English, and Imogen's brothers for being depraved: "Whoever Cloten was, or whatever ill he might threaten, yet, for the author to make this youthful forester lay his foolish enemy dead at his feet, and then be facetious over the horrid act, was sinking him beneath the common bravo, who is ever pourtrayed [*sic*] grim and gloomy, as the good sign that he is still a man, and has a conscience capable of remorse" (*Cymbeline*, 5). Inchbald's complaints at such points have to do with credibility—the idea that the audience will never believe a character or plot because of the flaws in its composition. Implicit in such statements is the question of purpose, since the audience's acceptance would not be so important if the willing suspension of disbelief for education and entertainment were not at issue.

This understanding of Shakespeare's plays as having generic responsibilities naturally includes the idea that a written part must be crafted so an actor can translate it into a representation of a person for an audience. In considering *As You Like It*, Inchbald writes:

> This comedy has high reputation among Shakspeare's works; and yet, on the stage, it is never attractive, except when some actress of very superior skill performs the part of Rosalind.
>
> This character requires peculiar talents in representation, because it has so large a share of the dialogue to deliver; and the dialogue, though excellently written, and interspersed with various points of wit, has still no forcible repartee, or trait of humour, which in themselves would excite mirth, independent of an art in giving them utterance.
>
> Such is the general cast of all the other personages in the play, that each requires a most skillful actor, to give them their proper degree of importance. (*As You Like It*, 3)

The "proper degree of importance" means that everything contributes to the success of the whole. All parts of the drama, not just the obvious ones, thus attract Inchbald's attention. Her extensive analysis of *Henry VIII* points out that there are "interesting" parts of the play that do not involve the main characters, like Buckingham's "final adieu" (*Henry VIII*, 6). Here speaks the playwright, with her experience of assembling words not only to animate characters but also of communicating through someone else—an actor—with an audience.

Inchbald's theatrical perspective also meant that she was comfortable with changing the plays to suit performance and audience standards. These are not sacred documents; they are working documents. As Jenkins observes of Inchbald, "It is this constant attitude toward theatre that sets her apart from many of her friends and contemporaries who thought themselves deserving of seeing their work presented at Drury Lane or Covent Garden and could not understand why they were not accepted or why, when they had a play accepted, it failed by the disapprobation of the audience."[21] When Inchbald criticizes the inclusion of Gloucester's blinding in *King Lear*, for example, she concludes that Johnson's support of the scene "is no apology for the correctors of Shakspeare, who have altered the drama to gratify spectators more refined, and yet have not expunged this savage and improbable act" (*King Lear*, 4–5). Her phrase "the correctors of Shakspeare," so different from Lamb's "tamperings," indicates that, for Inchbald, there were no sacred cows. About *The Tempest* she argues that no matter what "the learned" may think, Shakespeare needed Dryden's adaptation to make it a good play. The humans did not have enough to do, and the supernatural beings "were more wonderful than pleasing" (*The Tempest*, 3, 4). Sometimes changes are necessary to make a play performable, as in the case of *The Comedy of Errors*, which "Mr Hull, in 1779, then deputy manager of Covent Garden theatre, curtailed, and made other judicious alterations and arrangements, by which it was rendered attractive for some nights, and afterwards placed upon the list of plays that are generally performed during every season" (*Comedy of Errors*, 5). Here Inchbald draws a very different conclusion from Hazlitt or Lamb about Shakespeare's work and its performance. For Hazlitt, for example, the fact that the supernatural elements of the drama cannot be staged convincingly means that the play should not be staged. For Inchbald, it means that the play should be adjusted so it can be staged.

It is important to underscore that Inchbald's respect for "performability" did not mean violating the structural and thematic values of the original. When she reports that David Garrick staged *Macbeth* as a contemporary event, with soldiers in red coats and so forth, she concludes, "Garrick had taste, it is said; and so, they say, had his admirers: yet, taste like this would be now exploded" (*Macbeth*, 3–4). Similarly, she criticizes the adaptation of *The Merchant of Venice* performed in 1701, called *The Jew of Venice*, because by making "the Jew a comic character," the adapter "wholly destroyed the moral designed by the original author" (*Merchant of Venice*, 5). For Inchbald, maintaining the art, including not only the theme but also the generic integrity of the text as a play, was paramount.

With this emphasis on performance, it makes sense that, for Inchbald, an introduction to a Shakespeare play should also include the acting history, since that history speaks to a history of interpretation and popular response. Her discussion of the acting history of a role sometimes spans several generations and takes up much of her preface, such as when she considers the genealogy of actors from Garrick to Cooke who acted Richard III (*Richard III*, 4–5). She evaluates not only different men in the same role, but also women. She compares Sarah Siddons

---

[21] Jenkins, *I'll Tell You What*, 443.

and Mrs. Yates in *Measure for Measure*, judges Garrick (weak) and Mrs. Cibber (strong) in *Romeo and Juliet*, and ends a negative review of *A Winter's Tale* by suggesting that Siddons in the statue scene is the only thing that can save the play. Inchbald's views of performance are also positioned to refute certain arguments about the texts, especially the emerging Romantic notion that Shakespeare's plays are inappropriate for performance. After opening her preface to *As You Like It* by enumerating the qualities that make it nearly impossible to perform, Inchbald closes it by praising the performances of "Mrs Jordan" and John Kemble in the primary roles. This placement allows Inchbald to show structurally, rather than directly, the importance of actors to the survival of a play: this praise is not only the last word in the preface, but also bookends the opening claim that only a great actor can bring *As You Like It* to life. Similarly, in describing *King John*, Inchbald notes that "this tragedy is one amongst Shakspeare's dramas, which requires, in representation, such eminent powers of acting, that it is scarcely ever brought upon the stage, but when a theatre has to boast of performers highly gifted in their art" (*King John*, 3); she then goes on to review performances by Garrick, Kemble, Cooke, Charlotte Charke ("Mrs. Cibber"), and Siddons. The prefaces thus demonstrate the value of performance to novice theater-goers, establishing a living history for the plays rather than a scriptural one. Even the ephemeral nature of acting, seemingly a liability, is itself an important aspect of plays. She points out that acting cannot be "preserved ... for the inspection of critics of the present era," then notes, "On this impossibility the actor's art triumphs over, yet sinks beneath, every other. He has no rivals to vanquish, but contemporaries. He has no former artists to excel, but such as cannot come forth to claim the preference, or to crouch to superior skill" (*Macbeth*, 4). For Inchbald, the plays are unstable documents: they can be adapted and changed, and they can sustain a variety of interpretations by actors and audiences. This instability is a positive, crucial component of the plays' value and of Shakespeare's cultural legacy.

This rejection of a hyper-refined view of the plays also appears in the prefaces' acceptance of popular as well as critical perspectives. "Garrick, Henderson, Kemble, and Cooke, have all in their turn been favoured with the love, as well as the admiration, of the town, for acting Richard," Inchbald recounts in the preface to *Richard III*, adding later, "Cooke holds, at present, the possession of the part, and has popular favour in it, to the highest degree. That he is a very fine actor, all, who see him, acknowledge" (*Richard III*, 4). But, she continues, Cooke is not as good a Richard as the others who have interpreted the role. She has no problems with Cooke himself—she praises him lavishly as Falstaff in *The Merry Wives of Windsor* (*Merry Wives*, 4–5)—but she acknowledges that "all, who see him" have their own, possibly less intellectual or informed view. Her recognition of popular views and experience, however, is much more judgment-free than that of critics like Lamb or Coleridge. By suggesting that everyone who sees Cooke act agrees that he is a fine actor, and that he "holds popular favour" without impugning the acumen of "all" and whoever confers "popular favour," Inchbald acknowledges these entities and their judgment, even accepting it as her own. Very different indeed from the idea that Shakespeare should be savored in silence and solitude.

The issues of adaptation and performance come together in Inchbald's prefaces to the history plays. Adapting English history for performance on the stage is considerably more fraught than making use of a story from a foreign, dead author unknown to many in the audience, to say the least. Whether literate or not, Shakespeare's audience as well as Inchbald's could be relied upon to know something of Richard II and Henry IV, for example, and a play on the subject would resonate for English audiences of any period. Inchbald's interest in Shakespeare's use of history went well beyond his use of the material for plot. Certainly, she uses Malone in the preface to *Cymbeline* to tell her readers that the names are from English history, and adds that the "fable" is from "an Italian novel" (*Cymbeline*, 3). She rejects Lennox's claims regarding the origin of *Macbeth* and points out in the preface to *Henry V* that a number of sources agree on the figures for British casualties at Agincourt (*Henry V*, 5). But for Inchbald, history in Shakespeare's hands primarily served as a vehicle for telling the audiences who they were and are. Twice, in prefaces to both parts of *Henry IV*, Inchbald emphasizes the temporal distance to excuse the events, but the events, the facts of history, merely anchor the plays in reality, providing authenticity for their portraits of humanity. When she discusses the satire of the French in *Henry V*, Inchbald notes that "a dramatist, who had feigned occurrences, or who had not closely adhered to facts, as Shakspeare in this play has done, might have been charged with burlesquing the human character in the vainglory which is here given to France, and her consequent humiliation" (*Henry V*, 4). Facts are not the substance of the history plays, she readily acknowledges:

> Fiction, from the pen of genius, will often appear more like nature, than nature will appear like herself. The admired speech invented by the author for King Henry, in a beautiful soliloquy just before battle, seems the exact effect of the place and circumstances with which he was then surrounded, and to be, as his very mind stamped on the dramatic page; and yet his majesty, in his meditations, had no such thoughts as are here provided for him. (*Henry V*, 5)

As this passage suggests, part of the function of history in Shakespeare's plays is to help reveal the realities of human nature. Similarly, Inchbald declares in the preface to *Richard III*, "Shakspeare's historical plays are particularly valuable, wherein faithful history is combined with transcendant poetry" (*Richard III*, 3). This combination moves the plays into dramatic art, making them "particularly valuable." History is therefore not the end but part of the means by which the plays provide insight. Inchbald's dramatic experience did not preclude her from treating the plays as objects to be read as well, although it did inflect her reasons for reading the plays. She was not the first critic to appreciate the plays' power as viewed as well as read objects—as early as 1726, Lewis Theobald was celebrating the introduction of Shakespeare to the closet—but given her contemporaries' views, her ambidextrous critical approach is surprising.[22] Certainly, she admired

---

[22] Lewis Theobald, Dedication, *Shakespeare Restored* (London, 1726).

the beauties of Shakespeare's language. In her preface to *Hamlet* she calls him "the great poet" (3), and she celebrates Shakespeare's verse in *The Tempest* (4). Such linguistic skill demands reading, or at least has the best effect when read. As Inchbald declares of *The Winter's Tale*, "Although the reader of the following play may have read it frequently, he will dwell upon many of its beauties with a new delight; and, if the work is wholly unknown to him, or its fable, incidents, and poetry, have been but slightly impressed upon his memory, he will sometimes be surprised into a degree of enthusiastic admiration!" (*The Winter's Tale*, 3). The quality of Shakespeare's poetry is so great, in fact, that it alone offers evidence of Shakespeare's authorship. For example, *The Comedy of Errors* can be only partly written by Shakespeare because it is not good poetry—though as for the parts of the play he did write, "not even in these parts are there any very powerful marks of his genius" (*Comedy of Errors*, 4). Like the Romantic critics, Inchbald thinks that the plays are valuable to read; unlike the Romantic critics, she does not prefer reading the plays to seeing them performed.

Shakespeare's language is only one element of the drama to be examined, however. Great language, she points out, can compensate for other flaws. *The Winter's Tale* works better "in the closet" than "in performance" partly because the plot is strained, and partly because "some of the poetry is less calculated for that energetic delivery which the stage requires, than for the quiet contemplation of one who reads. The conversations of Florizel and Perdita have more of the tenderness, than the fervour, of love; and consequently their passion has not the force of expression to animate a multitude, though it is properly adapted to steal upon the heart of an individual" (*The Winter's Tale*, 3–4). Regarding *As You Like It*, Inchbald writes, "The reader will, in general, be more charmed than the auditor; for he gains all the poet, which neither the scene nor action much adorn, except under particular circumstances" (*As You Like It*, 3). Inchbald understood that reading and viewing could have different effects on the comprehension of and emotional response to a play, and she did not rate reading or viewing as superior to the other. As she explains about *Antony and Cleopatra*, "There are things so diminutive, they cannot be perceived in a theatre; whilst in a closet, their very smallness constitutes their value" (*Antony and Cleopatra*, 4–5). Instead, at specific moments and particularly when taken all together, Inchbald's prefaces argue for different types of encounters depending on the play and its strengths.

This conflict between reading and viewing also involved questions of morality. For Inchbald's predecessors, Shakespeare's brilliance partly lay in his ability to represent real people in unusual circumstances. Johnson explains that "Shakespear's excellence is not the fiction of a tale, but the representation of life; and his reputation is therefore safe till human nature shall be changed."[23] Throughout the eighteenth century critics claimed that the plays showed real

---

[23] Samuel Johnson, Dedication to *Shakespear Illustrated* by Charlotte Lennox, 1753, in *Samuel Johnson on Shakespeare*, ed. W. K. Wimsatt, Jr. (New York: Hill and Wang, 1965), 14.

human beings in action, thus helping the audience to understand themselves more deeply and to make better choices as a result. Romantic critics generally were concerned with the psychology of specific characters, however. Lamb's view of Lear as an "intellectual" rather than "corporal" entity also characterizes his treatments of Othello, Macbeth, and Hamlet.[24] Coleridge's lectures reflect how his understanding of the plays increasingly centered on extraordinary protagonists. In the 1811–12 lectures, he combined his discussions of *Richard II* and *Hamlet* into one lecture, in which he talked almost exclusively about Hamlet. In 1813, he gave one whole lecture to Hamlet alone.[25] This fascination with Macbeth, Othello, and Hamlet reflects the Romantic fascination with extraordinary men—the "transcendental ego standing alone," i.e., the Romantic poet himself.[26] Someone like Macbeth thus seems absolutely realistic: he is an extraordinary man reacting to circumstances. As Hazlitt puts it in his critique of Johnson's method, "But he could not quit his hold of the common-place and mechanical, and apply the general rule to the particular exception, or shew how the nature of man was modified by the workings of passion, or the infinite fluctuations of thought and accident."[27] In other words, while Johnson kept his focus on the common elements of humanity, for Romantic critics Shakespeare is about the uncommon element. In moral terms, the eighteenth-century interest in common humanity is an aspect of sensibility in its earlier stages, the idea that all people can be socialized by learning through exposure to events. The Romantic interest in isolated humanity is a manifestation of sensibility's degradation by the early nineteenth century into the personal performance of feeling to display one's own extraordinariness.

Carlson and Saggini have argued that Inchbald moves between eighteenth-century and Romantic aesthetics, and certainly Inchbald balances different views of human nature—and therefore of Shakespeare's plays. Like Romantic critics, she is interested in the inner workings of extraordinary individuals. In her preface to *Coriolanus*, she examines the protagonist's character for signs of his mother's influence, then analyzes Volumnia's character to expand that analysis (3–4). Nevertheless, in the end, Inchbald maintains that Shakespeare's art represents general human nature: "After the first three acts have displayed the comic persons of the drama, with all the modes and manners annexed to 1400," she writes in

---

[24] Lamb, "On the Tragedies," 117, 122–3, 115.

[25] Foakes, ed., *Collected Works*, 1:lxxiv. Jonathan Bate points out that what Coleridge did to *Hamlet* exemplifies the Romantic treatment of Shakespeare's plays. Coleridge read *Hamlet* as "removed from the troubling public sphere" and instead "an intensely personal meditation on the feelings. The essence of the play is found in Hamlet's soliloquies, and the rights of feeling become an alternative to the Rights of Man." Jonathan Bate, "The Politics of Romantic Shakespearean Criticism: Germany, England, France," *European Romantic Review* 1, no. 1 (1990): 15.

[26] Anne K. Mellor, "A Criticism of Their Own: Romantic Women Literary Critics," in *Questioning Romanticism,* ed. John Beer (Baltimore: Johns Hopkins University Press, 1995), 31.

[27] Hazlitt, Preface, 177.

the preface to *2 Henry IV*. For Inchbald, the play culminates "with such personas and fashions, minds, characters, and propensities, which belong to every age" (*2 Henry IV*, 4). Inchbald extends the eighteenth-century notion of common humanity beyond Christian, upper-class men, however. "The reader will, in the following pages, contemplate the Triumvirs of Rome as men, as well as emperors," she writes of *Antony and Cleopatra*, adding, "The reader will also be introduced to the queen of Egypt, in her undress, as well as in her royal robes; he will be, as it were, admitted to her toilet, where, in converse with her waiting-woman, she will suffer him to arrive at her most secret thoughts and designs; and he will quickly perceive, that the arts of a queen with her lover, are just the same as those practised by any other beauty" (*Antony and Cleopatra*, 3–4).

In fact, Inchbald's analyses of Shakespeare's characters often point out that Shakespeare deliberately guards against the tendency to view people in extraordinary circumstances as unusual beings. When she examines the mutual passion of Desdemona and Othello, Inchbald underscores Shakespeare's ability to render what would seem astonishing, dangerously transgressive, and psychologically aberrant as psychologically logical and coherent:

> So vast is the power of the author's skill in delineating the rise and progress of sensations in the human breast, that a young and elegant female is here represented, by his magic pen, as deeply in love with a Moor,—a man different in complexion and features from her and her whole race,—and yet without the slightest imputation of indelicacy resting upon her taste:—whilst the Moor, in his turn, dotes on her with all the transport of the most impassioned lover, yet without the smallest abatement of the rough and rigid cast of his nature. (*Othello*, 3–4)

In this respect, Inchbald's project is opposed to the Romantic project as it emerged to celebrate the remarkable, exceptional protagonist. According to her analysis, Shakespeare's protagonists might experience unusual events, but they are not unusual specimens of humanity. Such an approach is certainly consistent with her purpose, to help regular people better understand the literary and cultural significance of specific plays and of the theater.

Such an approach is also the result of a distinctive morality visible in a variety of ways throughout the prefaces. Inchbald's interest in women characters, especially as they are recognizable people, reveals a genuine interest in female experience that goes beyond selling books, a compassion for populations that are not well cared for in English society. In her preface to *The Merchant of Venice*, Inchbald makes sense of Jessica's character by concluding that "gentle Jessica" must have been very like Shylock, "or though she had deserted, she never would have robbed him." In other words, she was a thief because she was like him in "her disposition" (4–5). Likewise, Inchbald finds the key to Coriolanus's character in Volumnia's:

> Volumnia, too, for all her seeming heroism, so dazzling to common eyes, is woman to the very heart. One, whose understanding is by no means ordinary, but which extends no further than the customary point of woman's sense—to do

mischief. She taught her son to love glory, but to hate his neighbours; and thus made his skill in arms a scourge to his own country. But, happily, her feminine spirit did not stop here; for, terrified at the peril which threatened Rome from the hand of this darling son, she averted the frightful danger of a city in flames, by the careless sacrifice of his life to the enemy. (*Coriolanus*, 4–5)

Her discussions of the female characters thus makes her different from the major Shakespeareans, who rarely if ever were interested in the representation of authentic female experience in Shakespeare's work. Similarly, Inchbald was sensitive to the different impact of the plays on the different genders. This view appears vividly in her preface to *1 Henry IV*: "This is a play which all men admire, and which most women dislike. Many revolting expressions in the comic parts, much boisterous courage in some of the graver scenes, together with Falstaff's unwieldy person, offend every female auditor; and whilst a facetious Prince of Wales is employed in taking purses on the highway, a lady would rather see him stealing hearts at a ball, though the event might produce more fatal consequences" (3). These kinds of observations grant validity to female experience and, taken with her emphasis on women's issues throughout the prefaces, set Inchbald apart from almost all of the other eighteenth- and nineteenth-century Shakespeare critics.

This interest in female as well as male experience of the plays, either in reading or in performance, applies to the female experience represented by the plays themselves. Inchbald is sympathetic to Henry VIII's wives, especially as they were women suffering at the hands of male power, ego, and caprice. Describing Henry VIII's adulthood, she writes, "[H]e would divorce four virtuous wives, and behead two of them!" (*Henry VIII*, 4). Here "virtuous" applies to all four of the divorced wives, and could apply to the two who are beheaded, which distributes her sympathy for the wives equally among them, and offers none to the king. Inchbald has lost count—only two wives were divorced—but the mistake, whether accidental or deliberate, works to heighten her readers' sympathy for the wives. This interest in women's issues and perspectives characterizes the work of eighteenth-century female Shakespeare critics such as Charlotte Lennox and Elizabeth Montagu more than it does the work of nineteenth-century male Shakespeare critics. It also indicates ways in which Inchbald shares interests with female critics of her day, even if there were almost no women writing about Shakespeare the way Inchbald was.[28] Inchbald's concern with women's experience is a crucial component of the ethical and moral framework that combined with Inchbald's theatrical expertise to shape Inchbald's critical views.

---

[28] Susan Wolfson points out that although Shakespeare had enormous cultural influence during the early nineteenth century, and that women Romantics such as Mary Lamb, Mary Wollstonecraft, and Felicia Hemans were influenced by his work, women were and are still not regarded as significant Shakespeare critics. Susan Wolfson, "Shakespeare and the Romantic Girl Reader," *Nineteenth-Century Contexts* 21, no. 2 (1999): 191. For a discussion of the exclusion of eighteenth-century female critics from the development of Shakespeare criticism, see Karen Bloom Gevirtz, "Ladies Reading and Writing: Eighteenth-Century Women Writers and the Gendering of Critical Discourse," *Modern Language Studies* 33 (2003): 60–72.

Inchbald's critical approach also contained distinctive political and religious leanings. Inchbald viewed the ingratitude of King Lear's daughters as a political metaphor for more recent events in English history. After surveying other scholars' views to conclude that the events in *Lear* never happened, Inchbald continues, "But, if it never did before the time of Shakspeare, certainly something very like it has taken place since. Lear is not represented much more affectionate to his daughters by Shakspeare, than James the Second by Hume" (*King Lear*, 4). The preface then vividly evokes the pathos of King James II after his daughters side with the "revolutionaries" of 1688. This discussion of the connections between Lear and James II suggests Jacobin leanings, but it also hints at Catholic sympathies (we know that Inchbald was Catholic, although the degree of her devotion varied).

Inchbald's views of the historical and Shakespearean Katherine of Aragon are similarly suggestive. In terms of size, Inchbald's analysis of Katherine is almost as long as her most detailed examinations of other, more obviously central figures in other plays, or her lengthy complaints about Shakespeare's failings, such as in *Measure for Measure* or *Cymbeline*. This analysis repeatedly puts Katherine at the center of virtue in the play. Shakespeare "has made her the most prominent, as well as the most amiable sufferer in his drama." Just as in other history plays, Inchbald asserts Shakespeare's fidelity to facts. She writes that he "thus closely adher[es] to the truth of history," and explains that "Katharine's first speech, in that excellent part of the play, her trial, is taken from history, with but trivial variation; and likewise the king's reply to it. Her dying scene, particularly her letter and message to the king, have also the sanction of history for their most pathetic passages." This approach to the play allows her to acknowledge Shakespeare's talents and Elizabeth I's good qualities—"in thus closely adhering to the truth of history," she writes, Shakespeare "pays a silent tribute to the liberality of Elizabeth, more worth than all his warmest eulogiums." But the extensive discussion, punctuated with warm approbation for "good Queen Katharine," is designed to focus on the historical Katherine just as much as Shakespeare's Katherine. She had "virtues," she suffered "injuries," and she was forced out of her nature: "perhaps, a mild and submissive woman, such as Katharine is described, can never be considered so much an object of pity as when bitter provocation has impelled her to assume the deportment of haughtiness and the language of anger" (*Henry VIII*, 4–5). Katherine of Aragon does not exemplify an unusual brand of morality. She is the gentle, domestic female driven by circumstances to behave in an uncharacteristic, an unfeminine, manner. Inchbald's use of Katherine here suggests that capricious power, certainly male power, can disrupt even gender roles, even if a woman can respond to that disruption with dignity. The use of Katherine in this analysis, however, is a different matter.

For eighteenth- and nineteenth-century historians, Inchbald's sympathy for Katherine of Aragon is not unusual. They too considered Katherine a noble, virtuous, wronged lady, and Henry a terrible person. Charles Alfred Ashburton called Henry a "tyrant" in his *A New and Complete History of England* (1795) and Charles Allen was unremittingly negative about him in *A New and Improved*

*History of England* (1793). Oliver Goldsmith in his *History of England* (1783), which is otherwise viciously anti-Catholic, described Katherine as kind and virtuous.[29] The scope of the discussion in Inchbald's work is unusual, however. Historians usually wrote very briefly about Katherine, tending to concentrate on Elizabeth I, about whom they (and Inchbald) were ambivalent.[30] Furthermore, the existence of such a discussion is unusual for Shakespeare criticism. Such an extended focus on Katherine is thus a departure from the history and criticism Inchbald would have known, and it suggests not just her independence of thought, something signaled by plenty of other attributes in her criticism as well, but a particular political and religious interest.

Nevertheless, such comments are oblique at best. Parliamentary Acts in 1778 and 1791 permitted social and legal freedom for Catholics, and historians consider the first Relief Act of 1778 a watershed in English Catholic history after the Reformation.[31] W. J. Shiels and John Bossy agree that following 1778, English Catholicism began to grow into a vibrant community that would eventually, more than a century later, become a significant and accepted part of English life.[32] Inchbald's showing a hint of ankle, a hint of her religious views in such a public way, seems to confirm this view. That she was indirect also confirms what Bossy, Shiels, and Nicholas Rogers point out: that the Gordon Riots in 1780 revealed a still-healthy vein of anti-Catholic feeling, and that the final emancipation for Catholics, ensuring them full liberty, would not come until 1829.[33] In light of these aspects of history, Inchbald's careful indication of religious and political ideology in her

---

[29] Charles Alfred Ashburton, *A New and Complete History of England ...* (London, 1795); Charles Allen, *A New and Improved History of England ... Designed for the Use of Schools* **(London, 1793);** Oliver Goldsmith, *An History of England, in a series of letters from a Nobleman to his Son*, vol. 1 (London, 1783).

[30] For a more extensive discussion of views of Elizabeth I, see Pam Perkins, "Sixteenth-Century Queens in Eighteenth-Century Literature," *Eighteenth-Century Women* 2 (2002): 109–35.

[31] For a more extensive review of historians' views of this period, see W. J. Shiels, "Catholicism from the Reformation to the Relief Acts," in *A History of Religion in Britain: Practice and Belief from Pre-Roman Times to the Present*, ed. Sheridan Gilley and W. J. Shiels (Oxford: Blackwell, 1994), 237–8.

[32] Shiels considers the anti-Catholic harassment in London between 1767 and 1771 as the "last major disruption faced by the community before the Relief Act of 1778," pointing out that although the Relief Act itself triggered the Gordon Riots, these "marked an end rather than a beginning, and were expressive of social antagonism against wealthy Catholics and the embassy chapels as much as of religious bigotry." Shiels, "Catholicism," 251. See also John Bossy, *The English Catholic Community, 1570–1850* (New York: Oxford University Press, 1976).

[33] Shiels, "Catholicism"; Bossy, *English Catholic Community*; Nicholas Rogers, "The Gordon Riots Revisited," *Historical Papers* 16 (1988): 16–34.

comments on Shakespeare seem even more striking.[34] These utterances also show how, as always, Inchbald understood her cultural moment and could write for it.

Regardless of the influence of her Catholicism on her literary analysis, however, one thing is certain: for Inchbald, literary issues were moral issues. She warns her readers that although Henry V was very great in the play, in history he endured "the catastrophe of his life" and "the final event of all his actions, may convey, to many a youthful debauchee, as good a moral as his total abandonment of his early associates." She goes on to say he was ill at Agincourt, died only three years later, and "left no more than one child, who was dethroned and murdered" (*Henry V*, 6). But unlike her contemporaries such as Hannah More and Charles and Mary Lamb, Inchbald is comfortable with mixed virtue. In the preface to *1 Henry IV* she argues that it is better art and better morality to represent mixed virtue than pure virtue, because the former is recognizable but the latter is not (3–4). Charles Lamb clearly recognized the importance of the closeted reading experience in shaping male character, but he also clearly recognized the danger that this experience could pose to women's characters. Early nineteenth-century editions of Shakespeare were designed to limit only women's imaginative experience, Susan Wolfson points out.[35] Although Inchbald was working with editions that had already been revised, her prefaces demonstrate no such concern for women. The passage from her preface to *1 Henry IV*, which recognizes that men and women will have different reactions to the same material, reveals that she is writing for both men and women. The closet is not a dangerous place for women when accompanied by Shakespeare, precisely because Shakespeare's brand of morality is mixed, and therefore right.

Inchbald's morality derives from a branch of sensibility that proved particularly fruitful to women authors from the 1750s on: the idea that literature made people feel properly, thus educating and socializing people at the same time. Her concern with the morality of the plays therefore is not, as Saggini suggests, subordinate to her aesthetics but part of it. Anne Mellor notes that Inchbald's prefaces are strongly didactic, and Carlson points out that her didacticism cleverly "could draw authority from traditional gender expectations" to support her critical contentions.[36] It is not the histrionic sensitivity exemplified by Henry Mackenzie's *Man of Feeling* (1777), Elizabeth Griffith's *Delicate Distress* (1769), or Charlotte Smith's *Emmeline* (1788). Inchbald's brand of sentiment looks back to Adam Smith's idea in *The Theory of Moral Sentiments* that we watch others and learn

---

[34] The last ten years in particular have yielded many studies of Shakespeare's affiliation with Catholicism. For example, Peter Milward reissued *The Catholicism of Shakespeare's Plays* (1997) in 2000, and Claire Asquith's expose of the plays' Catholic codes, *Shadowplay*, appeared in 2005. There is no indication in the prefaces, however, that Inchbald regarded Shakespeare as Catholic.

[35] Wolfson, "Shakespeare," 191–214.

[36] Saggini, "Art of Fine Drama," 139; Mellor, "A Criticism of their Own," 39; Carlson, "Elizabeth Inchbald," 219.

how to respond emotionally and appropriately so we fit into society. Sympathy, what Smith called "fellow feeling"—or literally, "feeling with" another person—thus holds society together. Writers had long used this idea to shape and justify their narratives; Inchbald did so in her drama, and her criticism of Shakespeare's plays shows how important it was to her.

Inchbald's application of sympathy is much less elitist than that of her male peers. Hazlitt may have been profoundly concerned with the sympathetic response of readers to Shakespeare, but his criticism was aimed at readers who already knew the plays.[37] Although cheaper editions and the rise of popular lectures on the Bard made it easier for a growing population of people to encounter Shakespeare's work over the course of the eighteenth century, the notion that Shakespeare's impact ought to be felt in private and through careful study meant that only people with privacy, time, and the training to undertake literary analysis should approach Shakespeare.[38] Lamb's contention that "those delicacies which are so delightful in the reading ... by the inherent fault of stage representation, how are these things sullied and turned from their very nature by being exposed to a large assembly" criticizes the theater's conversion of imaginative text into material reality and attacks the public nature of this conversion.[39] The beauties of poetry are "turned from their very nature" by entering into the common realm, "being exposed to a large assembly." Access to Shakespeare's heroes therefore should be limited to those who can feel that sympathy—who have the emotional resources, but also who have the physical, financial, and temporal resources to achieve that sympathy as well. That meant men. As Wolfson notes, women were certainly not supposed to identify with a Macbeth or a Hamlet.[40] The fact that Hazlitt and other similarly minded critics did not attend to women characters or readers, for example, only underscores the narrowness of their approach and the breadth of Inchbald's.

Inchbald's handling of sentiment in general and its application to Shakespeare's plays puts her among what Anne Mellor calls the female Romanticists. Female Romanticism was simultaneous with what is usually called Romanticism, but its aesthetic and ideology, in fact its moral framework, were considerably different. The self, the individual, was not the "transcendental ego standing alone"—that is, not Hamlet—but "a subjectivity constructed in relation to other subjectivities, hence a self that is fluid, absorptive, responsive, with permeable ego boundaries"—

---

[37] Janet Ruth Heller, "Hazlitt's Appeal to Readers in His Dramatic Criticism," *Charles Lamb Bulletin* 57 (1987): 7–9.

[38] The price of editions of Shakespeare's plays fell during the eighteenth century. The first lectures on Shakespeare took place at universities, such as William Hawkins's lectures at Oxford in 1750. By 1808, however, public lecture series like Coleridge's were common and profitable. J. W. Binns, "Some Lectures on Shakespeare in Eighteenth-Century Oxford: The *Praelectiones poeticae* of William Hawkins," in *Shakespeare: Text, Language, Criticism. Essays in Honour of Marvin Spevack*, ed. Bernhard Fabian and Kurt Tezeli von Rosador (New York: Olms-Weidmann, 1987), 19–33.

[39] Lamb, "On the Tragedies," 114–15.

[40] Wolfson, "Shakespeare," 211–12.

that is, a Cleopatra who behaves like other beauties. As Mellor explains of female Romantics, "In their writings, this self typically locates its identity in its connections with a larger human group, whether the family or a social community." Consequently, female Romantic authors recognized the importance of didactic literature in teaching the self, and works like Inchbald's prefaces are determinedly, overtly didactic.[41]

Female Romanticism thus offers an alternative school of thought for Inchbald's Shakespeare criticism than either eighteenth-century ideology, Romanticism, or the canonical Shakespeare genealogy comprised mostly of men. Her particular ideas, such as concern with the community—of readers, viewers, actors—is a moral and social concern, demonstrating an awareness of the larger impact of texts and an endorsement of that larger impact. This morality itself might not seem so very radical to us today—Henry V was punished for his dissolute life by dying young, virtuous women should behave modestly, and so forth—but the use of this morality, including its interest in social responsibility and a broad definition of society, in understanding Shakespeare's plays is more distinctive and extraordinary. It also suggests a philosophical explanation for Inchbald's inclusion of all populations, even long-dead actors, to accompany the empirical one. Lastly, while Mellor contends that female Romanticism is ultimately tied to the novel, Inchbald's prefaces suggest ways in which it worked effectively in more discursive forms.

Susan Bennett argues that it is time not simply to recover female writers, especially female critics, but to remake theater history altogether, using male and female authors to do so.[42] Certainly the history of Shakespeare criticism deserves some reconsideration, given the contributions of women to the development of its conventions and ideas. In light of her work and her part in an alternative approach to the relationship between text and its consumers, Elizabeth Inchbald should have her own place in the pantheon. Her prefaces certainly demonstrate facility with the expected conventions and familiarity with the ideas of her contemporaries and literary forebears, but her perspective as a woman, an actress, and a playwright give her work a significance and richness of their own. As the work of a female Romantic who was the inheritor of eighteenth-century sensibility in its emerging form, Inchbald's prefaces also merit serious consideration. They present far more than a chronological bridge between two schools. They enlarge our view of how early nineteenth-century women writers synthesized experience and intellect—performance and reading—in an inclusive, socially minded ideology and aesthetic.

---

[41] Mellor, "A Criticism of their Own," 31.

[42] Susan Bennett, "Decomposing History (Why Are There So Few Women in Theater History?)," in Worthen and Holland, *Theorizing Practice*, 71–87.

## Chapter 3
# "My God! Madam, there must be only *one* black figure in this play": *Hamlet*, Ophelia, and the Romantic Hero

### Karen Britland

In early 2001, at Leeds University's Brotherton Library in West Yorkshire, I stumbled across the beginnings of this project. While checking something up in the reference section, I became aware of an undergraduate student, clad in a black hat and a long black coat, standing in the center of the reading room, looking intently at a book. He was there for about ten or fifteen minutes, and then he put the book down and went away. I had a private bet with myself and wandered over to see what he had been reading. It was, to my delight, a copy of *Hamlet*, and I began to wonder about the accumulated cultural assumptions that underpinned this highly theatrical moment—a moment of which, I have to admit, I was slightly envious. What allowed this young, male student to pose with *Hamlet*? Or *as* Hamlet? And why did I (an increasingly decrepit, female academic) feel excluded by his performance? This essay is a first, and somewhat tardy, attempt to untangle some of the assumptions that subtended that moment.

Margreta de Grazia has most recently explored the cultural phenomenon of *Hamlet*, noting that "no work in the English canon has been so closely identified with the beginning of the modern age" and outlining the ways in which late eighteenth-century and nineteenth-century literary criticism began to represent Hamlet as "'modern' in its present sense: that is, in possession of interiority or subjectivity, whether imagined in terms of Coleridge's psychology or Hegel's consciousness."[1] The notion of interiority, developing over time, de Grazia says, has led to Hamlet being hailed variously as "the Western hero of consciousness," an "icon of pure consciousness," and "a distinctly modern hero" who provides "the premier Western performance of consciousness."[2] Developing concomitantly with

---

[1] Margreta de Grazia, *"Hamlet" Without Hamlet* (Cambridge: Cambridge University Press, 2007), 7, 18.

[2] Harold Bloom, *Shakespeare: The Invention of the Human* (New York: Riverhead, 1998), 409; Jonathan Bate, *The Genius of Shakespeare* (London: Picador, 1997), 261; Alexander Welsh, *Hamlet in His Modern Guises* (Princeton, NJ: Princeton University Press, 2001), x; Marjorie Garber, *Shakespeare After All* (New York, Pantheon, 2004), 4. All quoted in de Grazia, *Hamlet*, 7.

the rise of the question "Why does Hamlet delay?", Hamlet's modern character has its origins, de Grazia proposes, "around the turn of the eighteenth century."[3]

Jonathan Bate similarly places the rise of the concept of Shakespeare as a national genius in the eighteenth century, observing that "the first book with a title asserting the genius of its subject was *An Essay on the Genius and Writings of Shakespear* by John Denis," published in 1712. This was followed by such defenses of the national poet as Elizabeth Montagu's *An Essay on the Writings and Genius of Shakespear* (1769), which defended Shakespeare's work against the charges of barbarism leveled at it by the French critic Voltaire. In sum, Bate proposes that "*'genius' was a category invented in order to account for what was peculiar about Shakespeare.*"[4] This notion of "genius," as David Farley-Hills has observed, quickly became transferred to *Hamlet*, which, by the late eighteenth century, he says, was generally perceived to be Shakespeare's "outstanding creation." In his words, it "paves the way for the Romantic view of Hamlet as poet and philosopher, [and] anticipates the Romantic tendency to see the playwright in the hero."[5] Shakespeare and Hamlet become prototypical men of genius: pensive, introspective, troubled and profound.

I think Van Dyck's 1632 portrait of the poet John Suckling holding a copy of Shakespeare's First Folio open at the title page of *Hamlet* might complicate this historical narrative. However, it is fair to say that the association of the renowned playwright with the character of Hamlet has led other artists (with Suckling perhaps in the vanguard) to identify themselves with Shakespeare and his Danish prince. Coleridge, observing that "Hamlet's character is the prevalence of the abstracting and generalizing habit over the practical," famously concluded that he had "a smack of Hamlet, myself, if I may say so," provoking A. C. Bradley, equally famously, to note that Coleridge's version of Hamlet was "a man in certain respects like Coleridge himself, on one side a man of genius, on the other side, the side of will, deplorably weak, always procrastinating and avoiding unpleasant duties."[6] At the close of the nineteenth century, Edward Gordon Craig, the theater-designer son of the actress Ellen Terry, noted that he "somehow or other lived Hamlet day by day," adding: "Since I was so much like Hamlet myself I *had* to—not only were my weaknesses his, but his situation was almost mine."[7] More

---

[3] De Grazia, *Hamlet*, 158.

[4] Bate, *The Genius of Shakespeare*, 166, 165, 163.

[5] David Farley-Hills, ed., *Critical Responses to Hamlet 1600–1900*, 4 vols. (New York: AMS Press, 1996), 2:xiv. Farley-Hills's comments here are given in the context of the writings of the Scottish critic, Thomas Robertson.

[6] Samuel Taylor Coleridge, *The Table Talk and Omniana of Samuel Taylor Coleridge*, ed. T. Ashe (London: G. Bell and Sons, 1888), 47; A. C. Bradley, *Shakespearean Tragedy*, 4th ed. (Palgrave: Basingstoke, 2007), 77–8. See also Barbara Hardy, "'I Have a Smack of Hamlet': Coleridge and Shakespeare's Characters," *Essays in Criticism* 8, no. 3 (1958): 238–55.

[7] Edward Gordon Craig, *Index to the Story of My Days: Some Memoirs of Edward Gordon Craig 1872–1907*, intro. Peter Holland (Cambridge: Cambridge University Press, 1981), 162.

recently, the actor and director Steven Berkoff has commented: "Hamlet is a feast for an actor since there is something naturally of Hamlet in us all … I *am* Hamlet since when you *play* Hamlet he becomes *you*."[8] The figure of Hamlet (implicitly endowed with his creator's genius) underpins many of our modern conceptions of artistic greatness and creative struggle.

This does not immediately mean that women are precluded from this kind of identification. From as early as 1741, as Tony Howard's recent book *Women as Hamlet* has elegantly demonstrated, female performers took on the role of the Danish prince. Howard notes:

> It was in the eighteenth century that Shakespeare's emergence as the embodiment of Genius first encouraged actresses to aspire to be the protagonist of the "master's masterpiece"—as, on a practical level, did Hamlet's commercial appeal. Determined to offer a personal vision, several classical actresses of extraordinary ability, most notably Sarah Siddons and fifty years later Charlotte Cushman, laid claim to the role and to equality of intellectual opportunity. For women had few tailor-made chances to play "Genius."[9]

In this essay, I want particularly to consider the notion of "intellectual opportunity" and "Genius" as it applied to theatrical productions of *Hamlet* in the Romantic period. How did Hamlet's "Genius" develop, and was it connected in any way to the representation of the female characters in the play?

Much modern criticism has seen Ophelia as indissolubly linked to the character of Hamlet, less a character herself than a vehicle through which Hamlet's character is brought into focus. Elaine Showalter begins her seminal essay on Ophelia by drawing attention to this phenomenon and invoking Lacan's description of her as a "piece of bait" who is "linked forever, for centuries, to the figure of Hamlet."[10] More recently, Carol Thomas Neely has commented that "perhaps the most important aspect of her role is the contrast with Hamlet that it introduces. Ophelia in her mad scenes serves as a double for Hamlet during his absence from Denmark and from the play."[11] Similarly, and perhaps most tellingly, Marvin Rosenberg has noted of theatrical portrayals of the pair:

> This intellectual, passionate, poetic, philosophic, puritanical, religious Prince has chosen [Ophelia] for a love-object … If he is to be the noble (though flawed) youth, Ophelia must be worthy of his love. If she is silly, cheap, stupid or tartish

---

[8] Steven Berkoff, *I Am Hamlet* (London: Faber and Faber, 1989), vii–viii.

[9] Tony Howard, *Women As Hamlet: Performance and Interpretation in Theatre, Film and Fiction* (Cambridge: Cambridge University Press, 2007), 36.

[10] Elaine Showalter, "Representing Ophelia: Women, Madness, and the Responsibilities of Feminist Criticism," in *Shakespeare and the Question of Theory*, ed. Patricia Parker and Geoffrey Hartman (London: Methuen, 1985), 77.

[11] Carol Thomas Neely, *Distracted Subjects: Madness and Gender in Shakespeare and Early Modern Culture* (Ithaca, NY: Cornell University Press, 2004), 53.

(as, on stage, she has been) a statement is made about his taste that diminishes his quality.[12]

Ophelia's character seems to be important only in how it reflects on Hamlet and his choice of a love object. At best, her actions serve to illuminate those of the Prince; at worst, she is unworthy of his attention and demeans him.

Rosenberg's comment about the second kind of Ophelia (the "silly, cheap, stupid or tartish" woman) taps into an overtly misogynist view of the character that (while it is obviously present in the play itself) I thought I would find in Romantic commentaries on the play. I was surprised to discover that this was not so, and further investigation revealed that such derogatory criticism becomes more readily apparent a century later, particularly in psychoanalytic interpretations of the text.[13] In similar fashion, Elaine Showalter has suggested that, by the turn of the twentieth century, "there was both a male and a female discourse on Ophelia." A. C. Bradley, she says, "spoke for the Victorian male tradition when he noted ... that 'a large number of readers feel a kind of personal irritation against Ophelia; they seem unable to forgive her for not having been a heroine.'" The feminine view, Showalter continues, was represented by such works as *The True Ophelia*, "written by an anonymous actress in 1914, which protested against the 'insipid little creature' of criticism, and advocated a strong and intelligent woman destroyed by the heartlessness of men."[14] Showalter identifies a critical tradition that finds Hamlet's female characters somehow lacking, and opposes against this a "feminist counterview" that seeks to redeem Ophelia as an "emblem of righteousness."[15]

Showalter's distinction here might not, though, be simply a gendered one. It is notable that she opposes the views of a literary critic against those of an actress, potentially invoking two distinct worlds and two different versions of Shakespeare's play. Bradley's theatrically sensitive, but nonetheless academic, version located Ophelia as "merely one of [*Hamlet*'s] subordinate characters," while the theatrical alternative, inflected by memories of performances by famous actresses such as Sarah Siddons, could posit a strong and central role for her character.[16]

---

[12] Marvin Rosenberg, *The Masks of Hamlet* (Newark: University of Delaware Press, 1992), 237–8.

[13] Jacqueline Rose identifies a similar trend in early twentieth-century criticism that, she suggests, locates responsibility for the play's aesthetic failings in the character of Gertrude. See Jacqueline Rose, "Sexuality in the Reading of Shakespeare: *Hamlet* and *Measure for Measure*," in *Alternative Shakespeares*, ed. John Drakakis, 2nd ed. (London: Routledge, 2002), 97–120.

[14] Showalter, "Representing Ophelia," 89. Showalter's categories are somewhat manipulated here: she omits the final part of Bradley's sentence, which, in its entirety, reads: "They seem unable to forgive her for not having been a heroine, and they fancy her much weaker than she was." However, this only underlines the point that early twentieth-century commentators represented Ophelia as fragile. See Bradley, *Shakespearean Tragedy*, 117.

[15] Showalter, "Representing Ophelia," 89.

[16] Bradley, *Shakespearean Tragedy*, 118.

Edward Gordon Craig's views are interesting in this regard as they blend the literary critical view with the view of a theater practitioner whose own mother had enacted Ophelia. In a periodical article in *The Mask* in 1908, he famously wrote:

> Cut the passage between Ophelia and Hamlet in Act III, scene ii, when he is lying at her feet, and you rob the character of Hamlet of very much of its force. Ophelia, instead of being a woman of intelligence, becomes an early Victorian *débutante*; and Hamlet, instead of being a man of his time and suggesting a period which was more than a period of manners, becomes a kind of preaching curate.[17]

While reinforcing the view that sees Ophelia as a foil to Hamlet's character, Craig nevertheless posits that the weakening of her role common in the nineteenth century undermines the play's suggestion that she is actually intelligent. However, in 1909, during preliminary preparations for his own production of *Hamlet* with the Moscow Arts Theater, he is recorded as observing: "Though I have seen many performances of *Hamlet*, I have never seen a good rendering of the Queen. Both the women in *Hamlet*, both the Queen and Ophelia, are as a matter of fact very bad women, very worthless."[18] In Craig's own production, he made concerted efforts to convince his collaborator, the actor-director Konstantin Stanislavsky, that Ophelia should not be presented as "beautiful, pure, noble, as is generally done," but should be "stupid and beautiful at the same time." "Only when she begins to go mad," he added, "does she become more definite."[19] Although Stanislavsky was obviously concerned by what he saw as the departure from a tradition that saw Ophelia as "poetical" and "incapable of any sort of protest or active measure," Craig's notion of Ophelia is less radical than perhaps either one of them thought.[20] Although there is a marked difference between the way Ophelia is represented in early nineteenth-century productions and the way she comes to be represented a century later, the seeds of her later incarnation are present in those earlier performances, and it is this development that I wish to investigate.

Tony Howard has noted that the 1603 so-called "bad" quarto of *Hamlet* "gave more scope to the woman's voice" than either the second quarto or the folio versions of the text. In Q1, he says, Ophelia's speeches have "an animation that she later loses," and both women (she and Gertrude) are, after 1603, reduced to "objectified figures unable to articulate ethical understanding or even their own distress."[21] This can be demonstrated in the "nunnery scene" that, in Q1, comes before the entrance of the players. The King cues Hamlet's entrance with the

---

[17] Quoted in Laurence Senelick, "The Craig-Stanislavsky *Hamlet* at the Moscow Art Theatre," *Theatre Quarterly* 6, no. 22 (1976): 59. Craig reprinted this paragraph in *On the Art of the Theatre* (London: W. Heinemann, 1912), 282–3.
[18] Senelick, "The Craig-Stanislavsky *Hamlet*," 74.
[19] Ibid., 76–7.
[20] Ibid., 77.
[21] Howard, *Women as Hamlet*, 19–20.

words, "See where he comes, poring upon a book," and Corambis (Q1's Polonius) places a book in his daughter's hands with the instructions, "here, Ofelia, read you on this book / And walk aloof."[22] Hamlet enters, declaiming Q1's version of the "To be, or not to be" speech, which, in this situation, becomes less an autonomous philosophical disquisition on the nature of death and suicide than a quasi-theological train of thought provoked by what he is reading.

Ann Thompson and Neil Taylor have noted that "several scholars have commented on the awkwardness of *both* Hamlet and Ofelia reading books [in this scene] and have used it in their arguments about the 'displacement' of this sequence in Q1."[23] However, if it does nothing else, the fact that both characters are reading makes a visual equation on stage between Q1's Ofelia and Hamlet that does not necessarily reduce her to the prince's mirror image, and which, bolstered by the less subservient language she then uses, helps to render her a less pitiable character when she is subsequently vilified by him.[24]

Q2's version of the scene sees Ophelia given a book by her father with the extended exhortation:

> Read on this book
> That show of such an exercise may colour
> Your loneliness. We are oft too blame in this—
> 'Tis too much proved that with devotion's visage
> And pious action we do sugar o'er
> The devil himself.[25]

Polonius's words, particularly his invocation of "devotion's visage" and "pious action," combined with Hamlet's later request to Ophelia ("Nymph, in thy orisons / Be all my sins remembered," 3.1.88–89), have made subsequent editors and actors gloss Ophelia's book, not unreasonably, as a prayer book. However, interestingly, the Restoration version of the acting text saw Ophelia's book

---

[22] Shakespeare, *Hamlet: The Texts of 1603 and 1623*, ed. Ann Thompson and Neil Taylor (London: Arden, 2007), Q1, scene 7, lines 110 and 113–14. References to the Q1 and F texts of *Hamlet* will be to this edition.

[23] Ibid., 113n.

[24] Q2 omits Ophelia's tentative salutation ("Good my lord, / How does your honour for this many a day?"), and peppers her speech with deferential phrases. For example, in response to the Q1 Hamlet's "I never loved you," Ofelia replies baldly, "You made me believe you did." Q2 softens this on both sides, translating Hamlet's words to "I did love you once," while Ophelia deferentially concurs: "Indeed, my lord, you made me believe so." Hamlet is then able to contradict her with, "You should not have believed me," and finally to assert, "I did not love you." In other words, Q2 undermines Ophelia here, both emotionally and intellectually, much more effectively than does Q1.

[25] Shakespeare, *Hamlet*, ed. Ann Thompson and Neil Taylor (London: Arden, 2006), 3.1.43–48. References to the Q2 text of *Hamlet* will be to this edition. Q2 actually reads "lowlines" for "loneliness," but most editors follow F's reading.

entirely removed, a cut that was also maintained in Garrick's version.[26] John Philip Kemble's Drury Lane *Hamlet* in 1796 restored the book, and edited the more overtly religious parts of Polonius's speech, while his later Covent Garden version retained both, adding a manuscript stage direction into the acting text that read: "*Gives her a Prayer-book.*"[27] Charles Kean's 1859 Princess Theater production, like Kemble's 1804 performance, retained both the book and the speech.[28] This retention, combined with the overt description of the book as religious, has the effect of increasing the sense of Ophelia's piety, although it must be noted that in the two cases where Polonius's words were fully restored, some part of the King's reaction to them was also kept, thus shifting the moment's focus away from Ophelia to the monarch's guilt.

My point here is not that Ophelia should be regarded as a second, scholarly Hamlet, but that the stage tradition tells us something about a culture's attitude to women and their intellects, as well as about Ophelia's relationship to Hamlet. Erased entirely until the late 1700s, Ophelia's book then progressively became a sign of her religious devotion and obedience to her father, reflecting and bolstering the eighteenth-century critical idea of her character as young, beautiful, harmless, and pious.[29] Although later critics would implicitly blame her for her part in Polonius's deception, critics in the long eighteenth century overlooked the possibility that her reading was strategic, taking her obedience as a sign of her innocent virtue, and her book as indicative of devotion.[30]

As Ophelia became more malleable and vulnerable, so Hamlet's gentility in the scene became a focus of scholarly and theatrical commentary, with Thomas Davies summing up prevailing attitudes when he wrote:

> [Hamlet's] assumed madness with Ophelia was, by Garrick, in my opinion, made too boisterous. He should have remembered, that he was reasoning with a

---

[26] See *The Tragedy of Hamlet ... As it is now Acted at his Highness the Duke of York's Theatre* (London: Andrew Clark, 1676), 38; *Hamlet, Prince of Denmark: A Tragedy. As it is now acted at the Theatres Royal, in Drury-Lane, and Covent-Garden* (London: Hawes and Co., 1763), 33.

[27] *John Philip Kemble Promptbooks*, ed. Charles H. Shattuck, 11 vols. (Charlottesville: University of Virginia Press, 1974), 2:37. Shattuck notes that Kemble's prompts were marked on an 1804 edition of the text, but "were doubtless written up after the 1808 fire" (2:iii).

[28] See *Hamlet, Prince of Denmark ... Altered from Shakspeare, by J. P. Kemble* (London: C. Lowndes, 1796); *Hamlet ... arranged for representation at the Princess's Theatre with explanatory notes by Charles Kean ... ; as performed on Monday, January, 1859* (London: John K. Chapman and Co., 1859).

[29] The adjectives are Samuel Johnson's. See Samuel Johnson, "Hamlet," in *Johnson On Shakespeare*, ed. R. W. Desai (Oxford: Oxford University Press, 1929), 196.

[30] Bradley, in 1904, was concerned to correct the critical perception of Ophelia's duplicity, explaining, in his fourth lecture, that her part in the "plot" was "a sign not of weakness, but of unselfishness and strength." Bradley, *Shakespearean Tragedy*, 120.

young lady, to whom he had professed the tenderness of passion. Wilks retained enough of disguised madness; but, at the same time, preserved the feelings of a lover and the delicacy of a gentleman. Barry was not so violent as Garrick, and was consequently nearer to the intention of the author. Sheridan, Smith, and Henderson, have all, in this scene, avoided a manner too outrageous.[31]

Cumulatively, then, the characters of both Ophelia and Hamlet underwent a certain amount of sanitization as the eighteenth century progressed: while Hamlet became more considerate and gentlemanly, Ophelia became younger, more helpless and, arguably, less interesting.[32]

This is most evident in the *Murder of Gonzago* scene, which, as has often been discussed, was severely cut in performance in the eighteenth and nineteenth centuries. Susan Lamb draws attention to this practice, noting that feminist critics have argued that the cuts were part of a campaign to "de-sexualize Ophelia because she is female," but pointing out that "Shakespeare adaptors cut sexually explicit language in general, not just in the mouths of women."[33] Although this is certainly the case, the cuts to Ophelia's part in the Gonzago scene reduce the opportunity for repartee between her and Hamlet and limit her knowingness, not only about sexual matters, but about linguistic play and double entendre. For example, Kemble's nineteenth-century Covent Garden productions cut Hamlet's potentially lewd insinuation that Ophelia should ask the Prologue to explain "any show that [she] will show him" (3.2.137). It also deleted her response: "You are naught, you are naught. I'll mark the play." This was a response that not only demonstrated her awareness of the off-color nature of Hamlet's remark, but which could also be seen obliquely and slyly to return back to him his own smutty comments about "nothing" (3.2.111–4). Rendering her more seemly, Kemble's cuts also rendered her less intelligent and witty.

I want to argue, with Lamb, that the characterization of Ophelia subtly changed in the last few decades of the eighteenth and the first few decades of the nineteenth centuries; that is, between Sarah Siddons's performances of the character in the

---

[31] Thomas Davies, *Dramatic Micellanies* [sic]: *consisting of critical observations on several plays of Shakespeare: with a review of his principal characters*, 3 vols. (London, 1783–84), 3:79–80.

[32] The cultural phenomenon of female mindlessness in this period is dealt with more extensively in Julie A. Carson, *In the Theatre of Romanticism: Cambridge, Nationalism, Women* (Cambridge: Cambridge University Press, 1994), especially 144ff. See also her essay, "Remaking Love: Remorse in the Theatre of Baillie and Inchbald," in *Women in British Romantic Theatre: Drama, Performance, and Society, 1790–1840*, ed. Catherine Burroughs (Cambridge: Cambridge University Press, 2000), 285–310.

[33] Susan Lamb, "Applauding Shakespeare's Ophelia in the Eighteenth Century: Sexual Desire, Politics, and the Good Woman," in *Women as Sites of Culture: Women's Roles in Cultural Formation from the Renaissance to the Twentieth Century*, ed. Susan Shifrin (Aldershot, UK: Ashgate, 2002), 110. Lamb notes that Showalter and Floyd-Wilson interpret the cuts in this manner (118n15).

1780s, and Harriet Smithson's in 1827. I suggest that the "feminine" view of Ophelia, identified by Showalter in early twentieth-century writing, is the direct descendant of Siddons's version of the character, while the more "masculine" viewpoint Showalter identifies is inflected by later developments in literary criticism. I also propose that Siddons's early acting style has been largely misrepresented by critics (including Showalter), and should not be allied, as it so often is, with her brother J. P. Kemble's so-called neo-classicism. Instead, it can be linked with the eighteenth-century fashion for "sensibility" and, as such (despite marked physical differences) was the direct forebear of Smithson's so-called Romantic Ophelia. Where Showalter takes Harriet Smithson's Parisian Ophelia as indicative of the Romantic conception of the character, contrasting what she calls Smithson's "intensely visual performance" of "picturesque madness" with Sarah Siddons's more traditional "stately and classical dignity," I suggest that both performances, in different ways, drew on the notion of sensibility.[34] As Lamb has pointed out in a corrective to Showalter, "Smithson's Ophelia was not innovative," but, through its use of music and miming, a white dress and straw in the hair, was "directly eighteenth century in character" and ended, rather than began, the "Romantic" portrayal of the character.[35] Sarah Siddons was the sister of John Philip Kemble and played Ophelia to his Hamlet at Drury Lane in 1786. She also played Hamlet herself (although she was notoriously uncomfortable in masculine costume and, as Tony Howard notes, only ever undertook the role in the provinces).[36] Her entry onto the London stage in 1782 was hailed by Thomas Davies as that of "a great and admirable genius," and, as Shearer West has pointed out, contemporary commentators often employed the language of masculinity to describe her performances, extolling her "powers of almost masculine declamation," the "masculine firmness" of her performance, and her portrayal of "strong heroic virtues."[37] In her professional demeanor, she was often perceived as equal to the male actors of her age: even the king reputedly announced, "There was never any player in my time so excellent—not Garrick himself, I own it."[38] For a moment, then, at the close of the eighteenth century, a professional actress was endowed with the attributes of genius and the capacity for depicting heroism.

---

[34] Showalter, "Representing Ophelia," 82–3.

[35] Lamb, "Applauding Shakespeare's Ophelia," 107.

[36] See Howard, *Women As Hamlet*, 40, 48.

[37] Shearer West, "The Public and Private Roles of Sarah Siddons," in *A Passion for Performance: Sarah Siddons and her Portraitists*, ed. Robyn Asleson et al. (Los Angeles: J. Paul Getty Museum, 1999), 9. James Boaden, too, uses the word "genius" to describe Siddons's talent. See James Boaden, *Memoirs of the Life of John Philip Kemble* (Philadelphia: Wilder & Campbell, 1825), 69.

[38] See Philip H. Highfill Jr., Kalman A. Burnim, and Edward A. Langhans, eds., *A Biographical Dictionary of Actors, Actresses, Musicians, Dancers, Managers and Other Stage Personnel in London, 1660–1800*, vol. 14 (Carbondale: Southern Illinois University Press, 1991), *sub.* Sarah Siddons. See also Carlson, *Theatre of Romanticism*, 162, 252, 56n.

Siddons was not alone in this. Her predecessor on the stage, the famous Mrs. Pritchard, also drew the appellation of "genius." For example, comparing Pritchard to Siddons in 1788, Fanny Burney noted, "For Versatility of Genius, or Comprehension of various Characters, Pritchard was greatly her Superior ... what a *Mind* she had!"[39] Here the actress's art is linked to her intellectual understanding of character in a manner compatible with Paul Goring's very interesting investigation into the "rhetoric of sensibility" on the eighteenth-century stage. Noting that the eighteenth century saw an attempt to turn the theater into a polite and respectable institution, Goring suggests that assumptions began to be made that "actors' performances would influence the conduct of those who witnessed them."[40] Modern polite society could be edified and rowdy audiences restrained by the example of actors displaying "good breeding," and "soft" and "delicate" forms of expression.[41] An actor's responsibility lay in closely studying a part and then playing it with carefully modulated feeling, using the body to convey emotion, rather than having recourse to the static declamatory poses of former times.

Pritchard's facility in performance led Thomas Davies, retrospectively, to note of her Lady Macbeth that her "acting resembled those sudden flashes of lightning, which more accurately discover the horrors of surrounding darkness."[42] This phrase was later, consciously or unconsciously, taken up by Samuel Taylor Coleridge and applied to the actor Edmund Kean in a manner that has famously been taken as a description of a "Romantic" style of acting. In the words of Tracy C. Davis:

> Most students of theater history know the phrase from Alois M. Nagler's *Source Book*, where in an introduction to a passage from Leigh Hunt the editor writes: "Coleridge said that to see him [Kean] 'was to read Shakespeare by flashes of lightning.' This was the Romantic way to read Shakespeare, in contrast to the classical reading of [John Philip] Kemble."[43]

"Kean's galvanizing physicality," Davis continues, "constituted a new distinctly masculinized school of acting so exclusive to him that it was sometimes called genius."[44]

Although I dispute Davis's claim that Kean's school of acting was "new," believing (as I will show) that it bore a strong resemblance to Siddons's early performances, I would like to suggest that the notion of "genius," which could

---

[39] Quoted in Roger Manvell, *Sarah Siddons: Portrait of an Actress* (New York: G. P. Putnam's Sons, 1971), 131.

[40] Paul Goring, *The Rhetoric of Sensibility in Eighteenth-Century Culture* (Cambridge: Cambridge University Press, 2005), 117.

[41] Ibid., 129.

[42] Thomas Davies, *Memoirs of the Life of David Garrick*, 2 vols. (London, 1780), 2:184.

[43] Tracy C. Davis, "'Reading Shakespeare by Flashes of Lightning': Challenging the Foundations of Romantic Acting Theory," *ELH* 62, no. 4 (1995): 937.

[44] Ibid.

relatively easily be applied to actresses during the eighteenth century, was progressively masculinized; and, by the time Kean arrived on the London stage in 1814, it could stand for a kind of acting suitable mainly for men. Kean's acting was not, as Davis believes, "exclusive to him": it bore the traces of earlier acting styles. However, although an actress like Pritchard or Siddons could be seen to generate the enlightening and intense emotions so prized in Kean's performances, by the time Harriet Smithson took to the stage as Ophelia in 1827 this was starting to be forgotten. Rather than embodying genius herself, an actress might only inspire it.

Writing in 1783, Thomas Davies could not help but interpret Ophelia in the light of the notion of sensibility. She was not, he said, "a personage of insensibility," but

> rather resembles that to which she compares Hamlet's madness, "sweet bells out of tune:" the sound is still preserved in them, though irregularly played upon. It is rather, I think, sensibility deranged, and deserted by reason. She seems, at times, to recollect her scattered senses; and throws out, though disorderly, truths, solemn and affecting, in the most pathetic expression.[45]

This passage upholds Goring's contention that dramatic sensibility involved "innate propriety," providing a model of "sentimental decorum" that could be appreciated by "spectators whose own refinement could be assayed through their appreciation of sentimental acting."[46] Although Ophelia is deranged, she (unlike her lewder early modern counterpart) is "solemn" and "pathetic." Davies's passage also, it should be noted, appropriates Ophelia's description of Hamlet's madness in order to return it to the young woman. This has two effects: on one level, it serves to load the play's depictions of madness on to Ophelia, making *her* into an affecting but discordant bell instead of the Danish prince; on another, in its emphasis on sound, it draws attention to the increasingly musical component of Ophelia's part on the eighteenth-century stage.

Writing of eighteenth-century Ophelias, John Boaden, J. P. Kemble's posthumous biographer, noted, "Ophelia had usually been consigned to the mere vocalist, who could, in addition to the snatches of old tunes, whine out the coherent and incoherent ravings of her lunacy, and not utterly in her manners discredit the declared partiality of the Prince of Denmark."[47] Boaden, prefiguring Rosenberg by making Ophelia's personality into an index of Hamlet's good taste, also bears witness here to the increasing fashion for musical Ophelias. Once the play's songs were stripped of their bawdy elements, the part became a showcase for an actress's virtuosity in a manner deemed respectable for young ladies. Boaden proceeds to note, however, with approbation and some surprise that "we had not been accustomed to see such a part sustained … by the great actress of the time."

The "great actress" in Boaden's mind was Sarah Siddons, who, in 1786, played Ophelia opposite J. P. Kemble's Drury Lane Hamlet. For Boaden at least, Siddons's

---

[45] Davies, *Dramatic Micellanies*, 3:127.
[46] Goring, *The Rhetoric of Sensibility*, 139–40.
[47] Boaden, *Kemble*, 186.

performance was out of the ordinary: her own greatness seems to have colored the character of Ophelia who, as he reports, was portrayed listening to the counsel of Laertes with "affectionate intelligence" in a manner that distinguished her from the Ophelias of other actresses. Just as Siddons herself was credited with remarkable, scholarly diligence in the preparation of her roles, so her Ophelia, for Boaden, was marked by the "strong sense and passion" of the woman who performed her.[48] As such, both actress and character rose beyond the commonplace, evincing delicate sensibility but also a certain amount of intellectual strength. In this, Siddons's Ophelia seems to correspond closely with Goring's contention that the theatrical manifestation of sensibility involved "innate propriety."

However, although eighteenth-century critics could hail Sarah Siddons as a discriminating genius, her portrayal of Ophelia still participated in a tradition that juxtaposed the heroine's "real" insanity against Hamlet's "feigned distraction." Writing of her mad scene, the *Public Advertiser* of May 17, 1786, noted that, until Mrs. Siddons acted Ophelia, "there never was, in sensible discrimination, as there ought to be, the real madness of Ophelia from the feigned distraction of Hamlet. Till then, the dignity, the love, even the pathos of the part [were] but poorly, if at all administered."[49] Siddons's theatrical sensibility allowed her to create an Ophelia whose excessive sensibility had an ecstatic effect—literally carrying her beyond herself. Hamlet's madness, on the other hand, although colored by his propensity for brooding and deep, intellectual thought, remained here a piece of misdirection.

The distinction between the madnesses of Hamlet and Ophelia is instructive, for it marks out a gendered trend in the discourse of sensibility. For Davies, Hamlet's madness was undoubtedly feigned (he variously calls it "assumed," "disguised," and "personated").[50] However, for Samuel Taylor Coleridge, Hamlet was unbalanced because his sensibility and propensity for thought made him vacillate and procrastinate.[51] It was precisely this sensibility, though, that marked the prince out as a man of "genius," whose "senses are in a state of trance" and who is beset by a "craving after the indefinite."[52] Hamlet's genius, although profoundly pensive, remains, even for Coleridge, intrinsically masculine, in stark contrast to Ophelia's feminized and excessive displays of emotion.

At the risk of gross generalization, this marked a cultural trend: although men, in the period, could defer to women's aesthetic judgment (as J. G. Lockhart did,

---

[48] Boaden, *Kemble*, 186. Shearer West notes that "Siddons's close and continual study of her parts, through which she thoroughly analyzed characters' motivations, was fully consonant with late-eighteenth-century debates about women's education that saw learning as a way of improving women's virtue as well as exercising their minds." West, "Sarah Siddons," 13.

[49] Quoted in Highfill et al., *A Biographical Dictionary*, sub. Sarah Siddons, 14:17.

[50] Davies, *Dramatic Micellanies*, 3.36, 3.79, 3.90.

[51] Samuel Taylor Coleridge, *The Complete Works of Samuel Taylor Coleridge*, ed. W. G. T. Shedd, 7 vols. (New York: Harper & Brothers, 1853), 4:145.

[52] Ibid., 4:146.

when, in a letter to Lord Meadowbank about Charles Kean's 1838 *Hamlet*, he conceded that ladies were "the most delicate of all critics on matters of deportment and gesture"), the very sensitivity that gave women this authority also compromised them.[53] This can be seen to great advantage in Denis Diderot's comments about the display of sensibility in the theater. He notes:

> Think of women ... They are miles beyond us in sensibility; there is no sort of comparison between their passion and ours. But as much as we are below them in action, so much are they below us in imitation. If a man who is really manly drops a tear, it touches us more nearly than a storm of weeping from a woman.[54]

Diderot exemplifies a trend that sees sensibility becoming progressively masculinized (just as Davies's comments about Mrs. Pritchard's acting were transferred to Edmund Kean and have come to stand as the archetypal description of a "Romantic," *male* actor).[55] Displays of emotion by a man are more affecting because, paradoxically, they demonstrate that he has experienced emotion more deeply than a woman who feels everything to excess. By extension, Hamlet's madness is distinguished from that of Ophelia by the latter's excesses of sensibility; what Davies called her "sensibility deranged, and deserted by reason." Hamlet can be affected by sensibility and retain his faculties; Ophelia's sensibility strips her of her mind.

Siddons, the professional actress, sits uneasily in this moment. In her autobiographical writings, she emphasized her intellectual care in analyzing her parts (and thus manifested the kind of theatrical sensibility identified by Goring).[56] She was also known for her propriety, both on stage and off. For example, Julie A. Carlson carefully details the ways in which the actress attempted to reform the character of Lady Macbeth, transforming her from an unsexed fiend into a woman who, in the words of Siddons's biographer, gives "striking indications of sensibility, nay, tenderness and sympathy."[57] Siddons herself claimed that Lady

---

[53] Letter from J. G. Lockhart, esq., to Lord Meadowbank, London, January 17, 1838. Quoted in John William Cole, *The Life and Theatrical Times of Charles Kean, F.S.A.*, 2 vols. (London: Richard Bentley, 1859), 1:271.

[54] Denis Diderot, "The Paradox of Acting," trans. Walter Herries Pollock, in *The Paradox of Acting by Denis Diderot and Masks or Faces? by William Archer* (New York: Hill and Wang, 1957), 18.

[55] This trend is examined in much greater detail in Christine Battersby, *Gender and Genius: Towards a Feminist Aesthetics* (Bloomington: Indiana University Press, 1990).

[56] See for example Sarah Siddons, *The Reminiscences of Sarah Kemble Siddons 1773–1785*, ed. William van Lennep (Cambridge: Widener Library, 1942), 16.

[57] Carlson, *In the Theatre of Romanticism*, 166. Carlson also notes here that Siddons recognized how much she was taking liberties with Shakespeare. For a contrasting view of Siddons's Lady Macbeth, see Jane A. Bernstein, "'Bewitched, bothered and bewildered': Lady Macbeth, Sleepwalking, and the Demonic in Verdi's Scottish Opera," *Cambridge Opera Journal* 14 (2002): 31–46.

Macbeth should be seen to be "of that character which ... is generally allowed to be most captivating to the other sex—fair, feminine, nay, perhaps even fragile," and, breaking with costume tradition, played the sleepwalking scene not in a traditional black dress, but in white satin.[58] Commenting on this change, the *Public Advertiser* of February 1785 noted that the innovation could be excused because Lady Macbeth was wearing her nightdress, and thus it demonstrated a contemporary concern for natural veracity in theatrical productions (Lady Macbeth was sleepwalking in her night attire). It also indicated that the new color symbolically allied Lady Macbeth with madness when it observed that there was no reason but custom for "a *mad* heroine" to appear in white.[59] Siddons's careful choice of costume indicated that her heroine had lost her mind, associating her with other white-clad, mad characters, such as Ophelia.[60] Lady Macbeth became, for Siddons, less fiendish and more closely allied to the characters the actress habitually played to critical acclaim, such as the wronged wife, Belvidera, in Thomas Otway's *Venice Preserv'd*, and the abandoned royal mistress, Jane Shore, in Nicholas Rowe's play of the same name.

Despite this apparent concern for propriety, though, Siddons was renowned for her emotive acting and her complete emotional absorption in her roles.[61] Rather than being informed by J. P. Kemble's more formal techniques, her performances can be seen as the forerunners of Edmund Kean's so-called Romantic style.[62] Indeed, distinguishing her performances from those of Kemble, Siddons herself noted: "My brother John, in his most impetuous bursts, is always careful to avoid any discomposure of his dress or deportment; but in the whirlwind of passion, I lose all thought of such matters."[63] Siddons was acclaimed for her abilities to depict extremes of passion, just as Edmund Kean would later be lauded for his

---

[58] For a discussion of Siddons's performance and of the preference for a blonde or dark-haired Lady Macbeth, see *Blackwood's Edinburgh Magazine* 36 (September 1834): 355–72, especially 359.

[59] See the *Public Advertiser* (February 7, 1785). See also Charles Beecher Hogan, ed., *The London Stage 1660–1800, Part 5: 1776–1800*, 3 vols. (Carbondale: Southern Illinois University Press, 1968), 2:796.

[60] For evidence that Belvidera traditionally wore a white dress for her mad scenes, see Hogan, ed., *The London Stage, Part 5*, 1:579.

[61] Diderot criticized this kind of emotional absorption, describing it as the mark of the "middling" actor. See Diderot, "Paradox," 20.

[62] Interestingly, Benjamin Robert Haydon (1786–1846) compared Edmund Kean and Sarah Siddons (rather than associating Siddons with J. P. Kemble), when he noted that Edmund Kean "never played the same part twice in the same way" and asserted that "the same thing was true ... of Mrs. Siddons." Quoted in William Archer, "Masks or Faces?", in *The Paradox of Acting by Denis Diderot and Masks or Faces? by William Archer* (New York: Hill and Wang, 1957), 212.

[63] Quoted in Archer, "Masks or Faces?", 197–8.

"natural passion" and the "agony of his soul, showing itself in looks and tones of voice."[64] Thomas Davies, for example, notes of her acting:

> Her modulation of grief, in her plaintive pronunciation of the interjection, oh! is sweetly moving and reaches to the heart. Her madness, in Belvidera, is terribly affecting. The many accidents, of spectators falling into fainting-fits in the time of her acting, bear testimony to her effects of her exertions.[65]

William Russell's 1783 poem similarly praised Siddons for her "affecting style" and for her "unconscious[ness] of the crowds" that watched her.[66] He contrasted her performances with the overt sexuality of former actresses, suggesting that her appeal lay in the fact that she became so absorbed in her roles she appeared unaware that anyone was watching. Many biographical and autobiographical anecdotes support this view of her acting, cumulatively implying that she identified intimately with her characters.[67] For many, tragic acting when Siddons did it somehow became more truthful: it was a natural act (Davies called her "the great ornament of Nature's school"), and displayed the actress's admirable capacity for empathy and feeling.

Siddons could therefore be acclaimed as a theatrical "genius" who, as Davies noted, approached her profession "in *downright earnest*," at the same time as she displayed on stage what might be seen as feminized excesses of emotion.[68] While this emotional capacity was admired, it could also verge on the dangerous. Untempered by the masculinity that attended male actors, her passions ran the risk of getting out of control. Various witnesses attest to the draining effect her acting had on her, at the same time as they suggest she asserted a fascinating, and equally unhealthy, power over her audiences.[69] Indeed, Judith W. Fisher has gone so far as to propose that Siddons's capacity to create affect in her audience not only invoked the eighteenth-century notion of "sensibility," but was endowed with a sense of the gothic. Quoting from Ann Radcliffe's description of Siddons's Lady Macbeth, she notes:

---

[64] Quoted in William Hazlitt, *The Collected Works of William Hazlitt*, ed. A. R. Waller and Arnold Glover, 12 vols. (London: J. M. Dent & Co., 1903), 8:414.

[65] Davies, *Dramatic Micellanies*, 3:249.

[66] William Russell, *The Tragic Muse: A Poem Addressed to Mrs. Siddons* (London: G. Kearsley, 1783), 9.

[67] See, for example, her daughter's description of Siddons becoming ill with weeping when performing Mrs. Haller in Kotzebue's *The Stranger*, or Siddons's own description of how she became frightened when preparing for Lady Macbeth. Judith W. Fisher, "The Stage on the Page: Sarah Siddons and Ann Radcliffe," *Eighteenth-Century Women* 2 (2002): 243–63.

[68] Davies, *Dramatic Micellanies*, 3:250.

[69] For examples of Siddons's enervation and her effect on her audiences, see Fisher, "The Stage on the Page," especially 255.

In her "Supernatural in Poetry," Mrs. Radcliffe mentions how she would have quitted the theater after the witches' appearance in *Macbeth*, because their effect on her mind was "so vexatious[,] ... had not the fascination of Mrs. Siddons's influence so spread itself over the whole play, as to overcome [her] disgust, and to make [her] forget even Shakspeare [*sic*] himself; while all consciousness of fiction was lost, and his thoughts lived and breathed before [her] in the very form of truth."[70]

For Radcliffe, Siddons's performance as Lady Macbeth is hypnotizing; it binds her to the theater, almost against her will, creating an illusion that seems unbreakable. Siddons becomes like a supernatural force: her intense sensibility and her capacity to convey emotion affect her audience and hold them spellbound. Fainting fits were common among spectators, who, overcome by her performances, could not restrain their emotions. In James Boaden's words, "The nerves of many a gentle being gave way before the intensity of such appeals" while "manhood" struggled to suppress its tears.[71] Boaden represents such emotional excesses as cathartic, but he also notes that they "alarmed the decorum of the house," registering an anxiety about the unstable nature of large crowds, and about Siddons's power to unleash violent passions.[72]

The power of a Siddons's performance was not, furthermore, just confined to the theater. Like a terrifying secret in a gothic novel, it could make an impression in the mind that would linger for years afterwards. Lord Byron, for instance, was haunted by the recollection of her Lady Macbeth, and observed, "When I read Lady Macbeth's part, I have Mrs. Siddons before me; and imagination even supplies her voice, whose tones were superhuman, and power over the heart supernatural."[73] Siddons's performance becomes part of Byron's mind: her genius affects the way he perceives Shakespeare's play for all time. Even her Ophelia, as I will show, had the capacity to live in the memories of her contemporaries for years after the event.

In the nineteenth century, Siddons's friend, the actress Elizabeth Inchbald, drafted a letter in which she described her impressions of John Philip Kemble's latest *Hamlet*. Of the production's Ophelia, she wrote:

> Ophelia, ~~properly~~ ^[exquisitely acted ~~by~~ ^[siddons]] is more ^[tender], more pathetic than julliet, for she Loves with proper maiden concealment: her ^[timid] restrictions ^[with her lover] breathe more of ^[real] passion than the warmest language: and the loss of her reason evinces more powerfuly than sighs & groans the excess of her sufferings.[74]

---

[70] Fisher, "The Stage on the Page," 246.

[71] James Boaden, *Memoirs of Mrs. Siddons* (Philadelphia: J. B. Lippincott Co., 1893), 195. See also Davies, *Dramatic Micellanies*, 3:249.

[72] The Kembles were to suffer the wrath of the theatrical crowd when, in 1809, the Old Price Riots severely damaged the newly refurbished Covent Garden theater.

[73] Quoted in Fisher, "The Stage on the Page," 249.

[74] Elizabeth Inchbald, "Essay on J. P. Kemble's portrayal of Hamlet" [1805?], MS HM 63342, 6, Huntington Library.

Like Radcliffe's view of Siddons's Lady Macbeth, this Ophelia, for Inchbald, was inherently natural: she displayed "*proper* maiden concealment," breathed "*real* passion," and her suffering was powerfully felt. However, even though the letter bears witness to Siddons's power as Ophelia, Inchbald's recollection of the production was inherently *false*.

This *Hamlet* almost certainly took place at Covent Garden after Kemble's move there in 1803, and was probably the elaborate production he mounted in 1804–5. Inchbald mentions that the Covent Garden actor, Joseph Munden, was the play's Polonius, so the Huntington Library cataloguers are probably correct when they tentatively date her manuscript to 1805. Kemble's printed text of *Hamlet* in 1804 listed a certain Miss Mortimer as Ophelia, and the holograph insertions and deletions in Inchbald's letter seem to indicate confusion about the actress who played her: the name "Siddons" is inserted into the text, and then crossed through, leaving the performer's identity uncertain. It seems that Inchbald unconsciously associated J. P. Kemble's Hamlet with his sister's Ophelia, and then had to correct her mistake. It is Siddons who is memorable, and her emotive style of acting affects the way Inchbald thinks about the character, whatever actress played her.[75] Even in a part that was usually the preserve of minor actresses and not, as Boaden noted, generally undertaken by "the great actress of the time," Siddons's genius left its mark.

Inchbald's description of this nineteenth-century Ophelia is striking in another way, for it draws attention to the physical nature of the performance of her madness in the Covent Garden production. Her remark that "the loss of [Ophelia's] reason evinces more powerfuly than sighs & groans the excess of her sufferings" indicates that the focus of the performance had moved away from the vocal and towards the pictorial: Ophelia no longer expressed her distress in sounds, but in gestures. Showalter identifies this "picturesque madness" as a feature of Harriet Smithson's 1827 Parisian performance, observing that it "quickly influenced English productions" and "became the dominant international acting style for the next 150 years."[76] However, this pictorial approach was apparent much earlier and, although it could be linked to philosophical debates about aesthetics and the nature of beauty, its roots were much more mundane and practical.[77]

The Drury Lane theater in which Sarah Siddons performed Ophelia in 1786 was rebuilt in the 1790s with seating for an extra 1,500 spectators. By the time Kemble performed his 1804–5 *Hamlet* at Covent Garden, both of the London theaters seated around 3,000 people. When Siddons returned to the Drury Lane stage in 1796, the difference in size was made immediately apparent: reporting on her performance of Isabella in Thomas Southerne's *The Fatal Marriage*, the *Oracle* noted that she could not be heard in all parts of the house, adding: "To

---

[75] James Boaden, for example, described Siddons's acting in the nunnery scene as "exquisitely simple." Boaden, *Kemble*, 186.
[76] Showalter, "Representing Ophelia," 83.
[77] On Siddons's acting and debates about aesthetics, see West, "Sarah Siddons," 27.

be so she would strain her voice unnaturally. She does not choose to make the sacrifice, and preserved her excellence with the near, whatever she may lose to the remote."[78] The huge capacity of the new theaters facilitated a change in acting style that was particularly noticeable in the female performers. Where Siddons had previously relied on her ability to transmit emotion through her voice and intimate facial expressions, large physical gestures gradually became more predominant. Indeed, Shearer West has noted that "when mapping the effect of Siddons's acting, it becomes clear that by the early years of the nineteenth century, her performance was more frequently viewed as if it were a work of art rather than an exhibition of nature."[79] Rather than being an intensely felt, emotional performance, Siddons's acting style gradually evolved into "a broader, more operatic use of gesture and picturesque posing to convey meaning" that became associated with J. P. Kemble's "neo-classical" performance style.[80]

When Siddons played Ophelia in 1786, the part was already associated with musical adornment, and, because of the architectural developments in the London theaters in the 1790s and early 1800s, its musical aspects were progressively intensified. Young women, who suffered on these stages because they could not make themselves heard, turned to displaying their virtuosity in singing and so necessarily became little more than attractive adjuncts to their male colleagues.[81] The intellectual elements that Davies perceived in Siddons's portrayal of Ophelia gave way to a mimetic style of acting, performed within big, elaborate stage sets. On this broader canvas, Ophelia could no longer respond to Laertes' counsel with "affectionate intelligence," not least because the larger theaters required a declamatory style that prohibited this kind of intimacy. As Peter Raby has observed, "'Henceforward theatres for spectators rather than playhouses for hearers,' had been Richard Cumberland's reaction to Holland's Drury Lane."[82] Thus, at Covent Garden in November 1821, Ellen Tree (future wife of the actor Charles Kean) was praised, as Raby notes, "not so much for her acting but because she 'sang the airs in [the part of] Ophelia with great feeling and sweetness.'"[83] Similarly, the *Globe* reviewer of Charles Kean's own *Hamlet* at Drury Lane in 1838 observed, "The scene with Ophelia was well worked out, though he received but little support

---

[78] *The Oracle*, September 27, 1796, quoted in Highfill et al., *A Biographical Dictionary*, *sub*. Sarah Siddons, 22.

[79] West, "Sarah Siddons," 22.

[80] Ibid., 21–2.

[81] This was not just a problem for actresses. In 1819, as Peter Raby notes, the *Examiner* commented that "a great part of the house [Drury Lane] can neither see nor hear [Edmund Kean] to any purpose, especially when his voice is exhausted." Peter Raby, *"Fair Ophelia": A Life of Harriet Smithson Berlioz* (Cambridge: Cambridge University Press, 1982), 18.

[82] Ibid., 18.

[83] Ibid., 55–6.

from her fair representative, whose excellence was confined to the musical part of her character."[84]

Harriet Smithson's Ophelia, characterized by the use of music and miming, was, then, as Lamb points out, intrinsically a late eighteenth-century one, and it was precisely what Showalter calls her "intensely visual performance" that excited non-English-speaking spectators when she took the role to Paris. Her Ophelia, in Raby's words, "was made markedly subsidiary by a text cut even more heavily than usual," in part because of concessions to French taste; but, nevertheless, it had a profound impact on the French audience.[85] Raby describes this impact, noting:

> Without perhaps being fully in control of what she was doing, keyed up by the atmosphere and the sensitive reactions of the audience, she unleashed an almost overwhelming emotional force. This was achieved partly by using her extensive command of mime to depict in precise detail the state of Ophelia's confused mind; partly, as she had so often observed in Kean, by conveying the impression of an absolute identification with the role which was totally at variance with French classic acting.[86]

In her "absolute identification" with the part and the emphasis on forceful emotion, Smithson's Ophelia can be seen not only to have been influenced by Kean's style of acting, but also by Siddons's tragic heroines. Notably, though, unlike that of Siddons, Smithson's performance was deemed by French observers to be largely instinctive (and this is a sentiment duplicated by Raby when he notes that she was perhaps not "fully in control of what she was doing"). Siddons's performances, however powerful and potentially dangerous their emotional excesses might be, were counterbalanced by a sense of the intellectual endeavors that informed the actress's choices. However, the most striking elements of the 1827 production exacerbated the split that saw Hamlet inhabit the realm of mind and Ophelia that of frail physicality. Observers were fascinated by the passions evoked by Smithson's mad Ophelia, commenting, for example, that she "offers flowers to those around her, whom she no longer recognises, and sings, without being aware that she is singing."[87] While making evident the extent to which the part had become mimetic and musical, these remarks also reveal a fascination with a certain kind of femininity. Smithson's performance of Ophelia was less about her analysis of the role and delivery of the lines, and more about her ability to convey emotion through her physical actions. Her Ophelia ultimately became an abstract figure of beauty: pathetic, attractive, and entirely devoid of mind.

---

[84] Cole, *Charles Kean*, 1:261.
[85] Showalter, "Representing Ophelia," 83. For example, the King and Queen of Denmark became the Duke and Duchess, and the discussion of the burial of suicides was cut. See Raby, *"Fair Ophelia"*, 56, 59.
[86] Raby, *"Fair Ophelia"*, 63.
[87] Quoted in ibid., 66.

Famously, the composer Hector Berlioz saw Smithson's Ophelia, and, in a telling conflation, fell in love with the actress and eventually married her. Writing retrospectively, as Raby reports, he bore witness to her "extraordinary talent," which he says "was equalled only by the havoc wrought in me by the poet she so nobly interpreted."[88] Although Smithson, for Berlioz, displayed a kind of "dramatic genius," it was Shakespeare, "coming upon [him] unawares" who struck him "like a thunderbolt."[89] In a manner that recalls earlier Romantic effusions about the power of the theater, Berlioz continues: "The lightning flash of that discovery revealed to me at a stroke the whole heaven of art, illuminating it to its remotest corners. I recognised the meaning of grandeur, beauty, dramatic truth."[90] Berlioz's metaphor here is subtly different from that of Davies in the 1780s. Where, for Davies, Mrs. Pritchard's acting *itself* resembled "sudden flashes of lightning" and therefore partook of her genius, for Berlioz, the lightning is internal to him. Coleridge, perhaps, stood between these positions when he said that "to see [Kean] was to *read* Shakespeare by flashes of lightning" (my emphasis).[91] For Coleridge, communion with the poet was intrinsically textual, but was facilitated by the actor's talents. For Berlioz, the communion seems to be between two poetic souls: Smithson becomes no more than a vehicle through which Shakespeare inspires the composer with art, beauty, and truth.

This process is strikingly similar to a theatrical analogy used by Diderot in "The Paradox of Acting" to describe his relationship to "the play of the world." He writes:

> In the great play, the play of the world, the play to which I am constantly recurring, the stage is held by the fiery souls, and the pit is filled with men of genius. The actors are in other words madmen; the spectators, whose business it is to paint their madness, are sages.[92]

Some men, he suggests, inhabit the world as spectators whose task is to comment upon "the absurdity of the motley crowd." Genius inheres in these men and slips away from those who are moved by excessive sensibility. Ophelia, perhaps, stands in the vanguard of these theatrical "madmen": overwhelmed by feeling, she loses her mind, and her insanity serves to inspire genius in onlookers. In effect, she becomes a kind of Yorick's skull for spectators: white and without thought, she allows them to see themselves thinking. Indeed, by the end of the nineteenth century, even in the work of a female poet, she had become simply "a sweet incarnate revelation / Of the great Master's mind."[93] Where, for Violet Fane,

---

[88] Quoted in ibid., 76.
[89] Ibid.
[90] Ibid.
[91] Davis, "Reading Shakespeare," 937.
[92] Diderot, "Paradox," 18.
[93] Violet Fane, "The Silent Player. At 'Hamlet,' December 30, 1878," in *Collected Verses by Violet Fane* (London: Smith, Elder & Co., 1880), 35.

Shakespeare's intentions in the character of Hamlet were complex and unclear, providing many interpretive choices for an actor, Ophelia was "like a saint" or the "essence of a dream"—pious, sad, and insubstantial.

My titular quotation comes from Ellen Terry's theatrical memoirs and describes her first appearance as Ophelia alongside Henry Irving's Hamlet at the Lyceum in London. Rehearsals for the production began in November, and it was probably a performance of this run that Fane saw on December 30, 1878. Her impressions of Terry's Ophelia are instructive, both for their conventionality and for her obvious enthusiasm for the actress, whom, she asserts, she would have "praised, / And more than praised, nor nearly praised enough" if she hadn't been abashed by the presence of a "serried line of critics" who made her opinions feel too "raw."[94]

Fane's self-effacing, but obliquely ironic, poetic persona strangely mirrors Terry's presentation of her early professional relationship with Irving. This seems to have blended a kind of deference, verging on hero worship, with a desire for artistic integrity, even when this meant standing up to the master.[95] Terry, like Siddons before her, was convinced of the value of studying her parts, and conceived of an Ophelia who wore a pink dress in her first scenes because, as she noted, "It's all rose-colored with her. Her father and brother love her. The Prince loves her—and so she wears pink." For the "nunnery scene" she had a "pale, gold, amber dress" which Terry, mindful of the stage picture, believed would "tone down" the color of her hair. And, for the mad scenes, she intended to wear black because she perceived it to be "more interesting" than white.[96] Famously, Irving objected to Terry's choice, which provoked Walter Lacy, his Shakespeare adviser, incredulously to comment: "My God! Madam, there must be only one black figure in this play, and that's Hamlet!" Terry, eventually castigating herself as a "blundering donkey," agreed to switch to white and, despite the obvious attention she had already paid to the stage picture, admitted Irving's superiority, recognizing that he had "a finer sense of what was right for the *scene*."[97]

This episode is not just fascinating for the insight it gives into a stage tradition; it also throws a light on Irving's attitudes to the role of Ophelia. Plucked from the provincial stages to participate in the London production, the young Terry was anxious to rehearse her role with Irving, but found him more interested in the music and stage lighting for her role.[98] It is possible that this was indicative of his confidence in the young actress's abilities, but other evidence seems to indicate that he simply did not see Ophelia's part as that important. For example, during their exchanges about her proposed final costume, Irving reputedly headed off an explosion from the irascible Lacy, by asking: "They generally wear *white*, don't

---

[94] Fane, *Collected Verses*, 34–5.
[95] See, for example, her criticism of his Lyceum Hamlet, in Ellen Terry, *The Story of My Life: Recollections and Reflections* (New York: McClure, 1908), 169–70.
[96] Ibid., 170–71.
[97] Terry, *The Story of My Life*, 172.
[98] Ibid., 167.

they?" The use of "they" here, rather than "other Ophelias" or "other actresses," is dismissive of former interpretations of the role: everyone gets lumped together namelessly under a carapace of white. Similarly, as Terry reports, on the first night of rehearsals, Irving personally read out every part in the play except Ophelia's, which he skipped.[99] This has to be less a compliment to the young actress, inexperienced on the London stage, than an indication that Irving believed her part was conventional and unimportant.

Clad in white, Ophelia in the Lyceum production became part of a tradition that had lost its raison d'être. As the *Public Advertiser*'s comments about Siddons's Lady Macbeth made clear, by 1785 the reasons why stage madwomen wore white had been forgotten (the paper, as I have noted, commented simply that mad heroines wore white out of *custom*). By 1878, when Irving and Lacy (who had worked with Charles Kean) objected to an Ophelia dressed in black, the association of white with more general feminine stage madness seems to have been completely lost: for Irving, the mad Ophelia wore white just as Hamlet habitually wore black. *His* costume illustrated his melancholic and pensive disposition; *hers*, rather than associating her with other unfortunate heroines, underlined her innocence, her virtue, and the weakness of her love-torn mind. Ophelia's whiteness, though, did not originally belong just to the stage tradition of *Hamlet*: it was a whiteness that had been attached to the majority of suffering, insane heroines on the eighteenth-century stage. Rather than portraying "an absence that took on the colours of Hamlet's moods," this earlier tradition marked Ophelia's excessive sensibility, the intensity of feeling that "untuned" her and drove her to distraction. As such, it contrasted her mental composition with that of Hamlet, marking her out as truly distracted in opposition to his "antic," and black-clad, performance of madness.[100] As this tradition was forgotten, however, and as Ophelia's character was progressively sanitized, her white dress became indicative of her purity and served the stage picture through the contrast it made with Hamlet's black. Thus, although Harriet Smithson would arrive on stage for the Parisian mad scene with a black veil over her white dress, it was the whiteness, as Showalter makes clear, that was remembered by the poets in her audience.[101] This impression of whiteness was, moreover, exacerbated by a profusion of black-and-white engravings of Ophelia, and later, by black-and-white photography of actresses playing the part. We know, for example, that Terry undertook the nunnery scene in a gold dress, yet the popular black-and-white engraving of the scene, based on a painting by Edward Bell, necessarily propagates the impression that she wore white.

What is most interesting about the Lyceum episode, however, is that Irving and Lacy saw black as Hamlet's preserve. Their objections to a black-clad Ophelia were not made because they perceived black to be indicative of villainy (as it was when Siddons's rejected it for Lady Macbeth), but, presumably, because black was

---

[99] Ibid.
[100] The quoted phrase is Showalter's. See "Representing Ophelia," 89.
[101] Ibid.

associated with Hamlet's melancholy abstraction and was therefore a part of his genius. Where a later Ophelia might wear black in mourning for her father, and therefore establish a connection between Hamlet's mourning and her own, Irving's Hamlet seems to have been designed to emphasize the Danish prince (and Irving himself) above all others.[102]

This is certainly borne out by Terry's recollections of Irving's first entrance onstage in an 1878 Birmingham performance of the play. She notes that the "lights were turned down ... to help the effect that the figure [of Hamlet] was spirit rather than man," and remembers that he entered "to music so apt that it was not remarkable in itself, but merely a contribution to the general excited anticipation."[103] Irving's attention to music and lightning (to the detriment of rehearsals with Terry) were directed to enhancing his own performance, and contributed to producing a Hamlet, in Terry's opinion, that was "translated into life by Irving's own genius"; a Hamlet who was a "visionary," but "sharp as a needle" and "blaz[ing] with intelligence." In other words, when Hamlet took center stage in Irving's productions he bore witness both to his own brilliance, and to the actor's. For Terry, at least, Hamlet was Irving's greatest triumph. She writes: "It was the only part that was big enough for him ... it was more difficult, and he had more scope in it than in any other. If there had been a finer part than Hamlet, that particular part would have been his finest."[104] Irving's genius, Hamlet's genius, and Shakespeare's genius all here become conflated in a celebration of masculine creativity.

This was a creativity that was not readily available to women, even when they did have the audacity to attempt to play Hamlet themselves. As Tony Howard has pointed out, when Sarah Bernhardt took the role to England in 1899 she found herself the subject of an attack by Max Beerbohm who termed her performance "preposterous" and castigated her for her "unreasoning vanity."[105] "Creative power," Beerbohm said later, "the power to conceive ideas and execute them, is an attribute of virility: women are denied it. In so far as they practise art at all, they are aping virility, exceeding their natural sphere."[106] Indeed, as Andrew Elfenbein has noted, the "central objection to female genius was that it was an oxymoron: genius supposedly belonged to men, and women who tried to assume it were trying to masculinize themselves."[107] Bernhardt's Hamlet was, from this perspective, quite

---

[102] Mrs. Patrick Campbell played Ophelia in 1897 wearing a black veil over her traditional white dress. Gertrude Elliot, in 1902 and 1913, wore a costume of complete black. See Raymond Mander and Joe Mitchenson, *Hamlet Through the Ages: A Pictorial Record from 1709*, 2nd ed. (London: Rockliff, 1955), 111.

[103] Terry, *The Story of My Life*, 138.

[104] Ibid., 191.

[105] Quoted in Howard, *Women As Hamlet*, 113.

[106] Ibid.

[107] Andrew Elfenbein, *Romantic Genius: The Prehistory of a Homosexual Role* (New York: Columbia University Press, 1999), 127.

literally "preposterous" in that it turned the gender binaries upside down. The link between Hamlet and Ophelia, which saw the prince increasingly associated with poetic inspiration and the woman with deranged physicality, both contributed to and was influenced by this conception of genius: the progressive sanitization and infantilization of theatrical representations of Ophelia undoubtedly aided in the valorization of Hamlet as the prototype of modern subjectivity and the tortured scholar-poet. Although works such as *The True Ophelia* showed that the theatrical tradition held memories of other Ophelias who could promise strength and intelligence, the overwhelming image of Hamlet at the end of the nineteenth century was one of a young man, in black, with a book in his hand.

# PART II
# Shakespeare and the Making of the Romantic Poet

# Chapter 4
# The State of Unfeigned Nature: Poetic Imagination from Shakespeare to Wordsworth

Thomas Festa

> The presence of nature, of objects existing without our intervention and controul, disarms the will of its restless activity, and disposes us to submit to accidents that we cannot help, and the course of outward events, without repining. We are thrown into the hands of nature, and become converts to her power. Thus the idea of the artificial, the conventional, the voluntary, is fatal to the romantic and imaginary. To us it seems, that the free spirit of nature rushes through the soul, like a stream with a murmuring sound, the echo of which is poetry.
> —William Hazlitt, "Pope, Lord Byron, and Mr. Bowles"[1]

Literary history owes the commonplace distinction between the talents of Wordsworth and Shakespeare, like so many of its operating assumptions, to criticism written during the Romantic age. In his *Table Talk* (1821), William Hazlitt seized upon the difference in the second of his essays "On Genius and Common Sense": Shakespeare and Wordsworth present opposite yet exemplary gifts, the one "the Proteus of human intellect," the other "the greatest, that is, the most original poet of the present day, only because he is the greatest egotist."[2] This early differentiation has led some modern critics to accept blindly a pejorative view not merely of Wordsworth, but of the English Romantics altogether, who of course lose out in the comparison to Shakespeare. A gang of egotists, they engage not Shakespeare but themselves while reading the plays and poems. "By their failure to confront Shakespeare directly," claims Gary Taylor, "the English

---

[1] Hazlitt's essay originally appeared in, and is quoted from, the *London Magazine* 3, no. 18 (1821): 593–607 (at 605n).

[2] William Hazlitt, "The Same Subject Continued," Essay 5, *Table Talk* (1821), in *The Selected Writings of William Hazlitt*, ed. Duncan Wu, 9 vols. (London: Pickering and Chatto, 1998), 6:36, 37. For a persuasive argument that Hazlitt's thought underlies Keats's more famous diagnoses of "the wordsworthian or egotistical sublime" (which I discuss below) and Shakespearean "negative capability," see Jonathan Bate's seminal study, *Shakespeare and the English Romantic Imagination* (1986; repr., Oxford: Clarendon Press, 1989), 157–74, esp. 164 and 171. A. W. von Schlegel had earlier deemed Shakespeare "a very Proteus" in his *Lectures on Dramatic Art and Literature* (1808–11), in *The Romantics on Shakespeare*, ed. Jonathan Bate (London: Penguin, 1992), 109.

Romantics marginalized themselves; their own work became a set of scribblings on the periphery of past literary history."[3]

Quite apart from the theoretical faith such formulations express about the authenticity of "direct" access to any literary work—an assumption that needs more rigorous scrutiny—the reception of Shakespeare in particular demands a social anthropology. This endeavor, powerfully underway in the recent work of Michael Dobson, Simon Jarvis, and Péter Dávidházi, locates the foundational moment of the Romantic cult of Shakespeare squarely in the eighteenth century, above all in the creation of edited texts, literary commentaries, and theatrical events such as those that surrounded David Garrick's celebration of the 1769 Shakespeare "Jubilee" at Stratford.[4] By revisiting the material conditions within which Shakespeare's reception during the Romantic age became possible, these critics have given us a more complex picture of the origins of the modern conception of Shakespeare's authorship.

This essay seeks to complement these recent developments in social anthropology with philosophical historicism.[5] Thinking through Wordsworth's use of Shakespeare ought to make the idea of Shakespeare's "aesthetic" more historically intelligible, particularly as this reception history reveals what is at stake in treating the relationship between Wordsworth's poetry and Shakespeare's as an emblem of Romantic epistemology. In the effort to deduce aesthetic principles from the way one poet figures the achievement of another, a further point comes into critical focus: the adaptation of Wordsworth's poetry that is required to make it available for today's uses. What if, instead of treating poetic allusion as a species of anachronism, we consider reception history as a form of literary evolution?[6] This is not to suggest a linear progression of literary technique, so much as to situate the texts, in Hegel's terms, as "moments of an organic unity in which they not only do not conflict, but in which each is as necessary as the other; and this mutual necessity alone constitutes the life of the whole."[7]

---

[3] Gary Taylor, *Reinventing Shakespeare* (1989; repr., London: Hogarth Press, 1990), 151.

[4] Michael Dobson, *The Making of the National Poet: Shakespeare, Adaptation and Authorship, 1660–1792* (Oxford: Clarendon Press, 1992); Simon Jarvis, *Scholars and Gentlemen: Shakespearean Textual Criticism and Representations of Scholarly Labour, 1725–1765* (Oxford: Clarendon Press, 1995); Péter Dávidházi, *The Romantic Cult of Shakespeare: Literary Reception in Anthropological Perspective* (London: Macmillan, 1998), 34–107.

[5] Kenneth Haynes, "Text, Theory, and Reception," in *Classics and the Uses of Reception*, ed. Charles Martindale and Richard F. Thomas (Oxford: Blackwell, 2006), 44–54, sketches out the implicit assumptions and the interrelations of these theoretical avenues.

[6] See Franco Moretti, *Modern Epic*, trans. Quintin Hoare (London: Verso, 1996), esp. 5–6, 19–22, 37–41, 48, which employs the term "literary evolution" to describe the emergence and mutation of a genre of flawed masterpieces.

[7] G.W.F. Hegel, *Phenomenology of Spirit*, trans. A. V. Miller (Oxford: Oxford University Press, 1977), 2.

Put differently, each moment in the reception history may be seen, in retrospect, as prefiguring the next. Thus, for Wordsworth, Shakespeare prefigures something crucial about Wordsworth's own approach to writing poetry, just as for certain readers Wordsworth's construction of subjectivity prefigures their own autobiographical experience. The aim of this essay, therefore, is not skeptically to dismiss such "prefigurations" as less legitimate or authoritative than approaches positing the universality of historicism's appeal—though, indeed, the presupposition of universality and autonomy in aesthetic judgment emerges at the outset of English Romanticism in the 1790s with the transmission of Kant's ideas. Instead, the emphasis will fall on the way in which reception of Shakespeare becomes an enabling—or better, an "authorizing"—condition of Wordsworth's poetic imagination. Such an investigation of the aesthetic cannot properly be anachronistic, though this critical task may demonstrate a mode of appropriation against which current historicist scholarship fervently seeks to define itself.[8] How, this essay will ask, does this imaginative reordering of Shakespearean texts produce its own genealogy of the imagination as an emergent phenomenon at once historically bound and particular to Wordsworth's autobiography? And further, how do the conditions of Romantic authorship legible in Wordsworth's appropriation of Shakespeare affect Wordsworth's own poetic project?

Take Hazlitt's description of Wordsworth. Wordsworth's genius strikes Hazlitt in a peculiar way, which the critic first expresses through a surprising comparison: "I am afraid I shall hardly write so satisfactory a character of Mr. Wordsworth, though he, too, like Rembrandt, has a faculty of making something out of nothing, that is, out of himself, by the medium through which he sees and with which he clothes the barrenest subject."[9] Deprecating rhetoric aside, the juxtaposition of Wordsworth with Rembrandt, who probably represents the highest attainment of mimetic realism in European painting, is especially striking given the interpretation of Wordsworth it implies. After all, "Rembrandt's conquests were not over the *ideal*, but the real," says Hazlitt.[10] From this conceptual vocabulary, an enigma emerges: Wordsworth, "like Rembrandt," has invented a new view of nature through introversion, "by the medium through which he sees." The genesis of this form of creation is not mimetic representation but "making something out of nothing"—a phrase that would seem to describe just the opposite of realism according to today's critical lexicon.

---

[8]  See for example Margreta de Grazia, "*Hamlet* Before Its Time," *Modern Language Quarterly* 62 (2001): 355–75.

[9]  Hazlitt, *Selected Writings*, 6:37. Earlier, Hazlitt had compared Wordsworth's poems and Rembrandt's landscape paintings in "Observations on Mr. Wordsworth's Poem, 'The Excursion,'" *Round Table* (1815–17), in *Selected Writings*, 2:121. Later, he employs the same phrase ("that artist works something out of nothing") when again comparing the two. "Mr. Wordsworth," *The Spirit of the Age* (1825), in *Selected Writings*, 7:167. Duncan Wu reminds us that Wordsworth had given high praise to Rembrandt in a letter to Sir George Beaumont on April 8, 1808. *Selected Writings*, 7:301n37.

[10]  Hazlitt, *Selected Writings*, 6:37.

Yet Goethe gives voice to just such an antinomy when describing Wilhelm Meister's first encounter with Shakespeare's plays:

> "Yes indeed," said Wilhelm, "I cannot remember a book, a person, or an event that has affected me as deeply as these wonderful plays. ... They seem to be the work of some spirit from heaven that comes down to men and gently makes them acquainted with themselves. They are not fictions! ... The few glances that I have cast into Shakespeare's world have impelled me more than anything else to take more resolute steps into the real world, to plunge into the flood of destinies that hangs over the world and someday, if fortune favors me, to cull several drafts from the great ocean of living nature and distribute these from the stage to the thirsting public of my native land."[11]

The effect of Shakespeare's plays (especially *Hamlet*) is to lead the character toward necessary and expansive introspection and is thus integral to the work of the novel as *Bildungsroman*. Indeed, to the actors in Serlo's troupe who will perform Wilhelm's adaptation of the play, *Hamlet* "has something of the breadth of a novel."[12] Wilhelm experiences Shakespeare as a tutelary spirit who "makes [him] more acquainted with [himself]." At the same time, Shakespeare's works "are not fictions [*Gedichte*]" and so impel the fledgling artist toward greater experience of "the real world" and ultimately his own artistic creation taken "from the great ocean of living [*wahren*] nature."

How, then, can a work of art be mimetic and, at the same time, created as "something out of nothing," in Hazlitt's phrase? Can artists imitate nature and themselves, or are these mutually exclusive options? Although Hazlitt associates Wordsworth with a high order of mimetic art, many other Romantic critics portray Wordsworth as an egotist who imitates his own process of thought rather than external reality, therefore producing art antithetical to Shakespeare's. I argue the reverse. Shakespeare brings Wordsworth back to mimesis, indeed brings the world and history into the poetic text, sometimes through contrast and sometimes through sympathetic allusion and appropriation. Wordsworth's poetry becomes counterintuitively *untranscendental* or not idealizing but, conversely, "realistic" and historical in its comprehension of the mind's imaginative disappointment as Wordsworth exhibits consciousness of Shakespeare's verse. At times, Shakespeare represents for Wordsworth a destabilizing reminder of what was once, but may no longer be, possible in the human imagination, not in Wordsworth's present.

---

[11] J. W. von Goethe, *Wilhelm Meister's Apprenticeship*, bk. 3., chap. 11, trans. E. A. Blackall (New York: Suhrkamp, 1989), 112–13. The novel was written 1776–96, published 1795–96.

[12] Ibid., bk. 5, chap. 7, 186. Compare, at a further extreme, Charles Lamb's argument against the performance of Shakespeare's tragedies—that "Hamlet is made another thing by being acted" and that "the Lear of Shakspeare cannot be acted"—whereas "the reading of a tragedy is a fine abstraction." See "On the Tragedies of Shakspeare, Considered with Reference to their Fitness for Stage Representation," 1812, in *The Works of Charles and Mary Lamb*, ed. E. V. Lucas, 7 vols. (London: Methuen, 1903), 1:101, 107, 111.

## Natural Selection: Wordsworth's Allusions to Shakespeare and Milton

Wordsworth's relationship to Shakespeare's works runs much deeper than was once recognized, a powerful countercurrent to the more obvious and direct influence exerted by Milton. Since Milton is openly revered throughout Wordsworth's writings as a philosophical poet of unique political depth, he frequently appears when Wordsworth needs a defense against attacks on his moral idealism, when not just England but Wordsworth "hath need of thee": "Oh! raise us up, return to us again; / And give us manners, virtue, freedom, power."[13] Wordsworth hopes in sublimity, grandeur, and political commitment to stand with Milton, who speaks righteously and authoritatively from a position of unmatched learnedness. Milton provides Wordsworth with his tone and his attitude toward at times unconscionable tradition.

There is no doubt that Wordsworth inherited from his eighteenth-century predecessors a conception of Shakespeare as the poet of nature. Just as Hamlet said that the end of playing is "to hold as 'twere the mirror up to nature" (3.2.20),[14] so Dr. Johnson had proclaimed that Shakespeare's "drama is the mirror of life."[15] Nature takes a literary form in Shakespeare's poetic creations, according to the traditions of neoclassical criticism from Jonson, Milton, and Dryden in the seventeenth century, to Rowe, Pope, Johnson, and countless others in the eighteenth. Yet both these terms—poet and nature—undergo a critical shift in Wordsworth's writings toward new philosophical and, above all, affective significance. Even as Shakespeare provokes thought about nature, Wordsworth often invokes Shakespeare as a protective ward against *unreflective* imitation, as if Shakespeare not only represented nature, but also an analytical attitude toward nature. If, that is, "Wordsworth is an environmental historicist" ever sensitive to the intertwined histories of mind and earth, then Shakespeare evinces for Wordsworth an earlier stratum of human imagination comparable to those sublime features visible in a landscape, such as rocky outcrops and mountains, that give evidence of revolutionary geological upheaval.[16] Or, to take the metaphor in the direction

---

[13] William Wordsworth, "London, 1802," *The Major Works*, ed. Stephen Gill, rev. ed. (Oxford: Oxford University Press, 2000), 7–8. All references to Wordsworth's writings will be from this edition unless otherwise noted, and will be cited in the text by page (prose) or line (poetry) number.

[14] William Shakespeare, *The Norton Shakespeare*, ed. Stephen Greenblatt et al., 2nd ed. (New York: W. W. Norton, 2008). All references to Shakespeare will be from this edition.

[15] Samuel Johnson, *Samuel Johnson on Shakespeare*, ed. H. R. Woudhuysen (Harmondsworth, UK: Penguin, 1989), 124. A. D. Nuttall endorses the neoclassical perspective: "The eighteenth-century critics were right. The poet of glorious, licentious imagination was also the poet of reverent and attentive perception." *A New Mimesis: Shakespeare and the Representation of Reality* (London: Methuen, 1983), 100.

[16] Alan Bewell, *Wordsworth and the Enlightenment: Nature, Man, and Society in the Experimental Poetry* (New Haven, CT: Yale University Press, 1989), 240ff.

of psychology, Shakespeare stands for a literary correspondence to youth, with all that this implies for a poet to whom "the Child is Father of the Man."[17]

The "Ode. Composed upon an Evening of Extraordinary Splendor and Beauty" of 1817 (published 1820) demonstrates the nature of Wordsworthian allusion by showing what I am calling the "mimetic" function of Wordsworth's allusions to Shakespeare. Allusion is particularly rife with significance in a poem that advertises its allusiveness by revisiting the "Ode: Intimations of Immortality"; as Wordsworth's note at the end of the 1820 text says, "The reader, who is acquainted with the Author's Ode, intitled 'Intimations of Immortality, etc.' will recognize the allusion to it that pervades the last stanza of the foregoing Poem."[18] The second stanza of the Evening Ode resonates with evocative rhetoric:

> No sound is uttered,—but a deep
> And solemn harmony pervades
> The hollow vale from steep to steep,
> And penetrates the glades.
> Far-distant images draw nigh,
> Called forth by wond'rous potency
> Of beamy radiance, that imbues
> Whate'er it strikes, with gem-like hues! (21–8)

The intertext here is *Hamlet*. In Gertrude's private chamber, the prince implores his mother to refrain from sleeping with Claudius: "For use almost can change the stamp of nature— / And either in the devil, or throw him out / With wondrous potency" (3.4.151.8–10). Wordsworth has almost changed the stamp of Shakespeare, so to speak, by recollecting Hamlet's "gem-like" phrase and rendering the recontextualized language the equivalent of a "solemn harmony" that silently pervades the visual scene of the vale. Shakespeare is thus "called forth" like the "far-distant images" that draw near the poet in his reflection upon the natural setting. The distance covered is, of course, both spatial and temporal. Shakespeare's "wond'rous potency" figures memory, such that the appearance of Shakespeare's text functions as a surrogate for the poet's recollection as memory overlays the scene with its "far-distant images." Memory mediates the visual sensation, and so, by the trick of light and the silent memory of an unspoken phrase, the scene is ineluctably changed and the viewer brought into harmony

---

[17] Wordsworth, "My heart leaps up," 7. Jonathan Bate remains the critical point of departure for thinking about these relationships. See Bate, *Shakespeare*, 71–116, esp. 81. Lucy Newlyn illustrates Wordsworth's complex appropriations of Milton in *The Prelude* in *"Paradise Lost" and the Romantic Reader* (Oxford: Clarendon Press, 1993), 85–6, 211–13, 239–41. For an analysis that weighs the relative claims of Shakespearean and Miltonic classicism, and an excellent discussion of Shakespeare in relation to classical allusion more generally, see Sarah Annes Brown, "'There Is No End but Addition': The Later Reception of Shakespeare's Classicism," in *Shakespeare and the Classics*, ed. Charles Martindale and A. B. Taylor (Cambridge: Cambridge University Press, 2004), 277–93, esp. 278–82.

[18] Quoted in Gill, ed., *The Major Works*, 722–3.

with it. The embedded quotation imbues literary memory with an analogous experience of the "wond'rous potency" of recollection. Wordsworth's allusion to the ghost of Old Hamlet at the turn in one of his sonnets on the Chapel at King's College, Cambridge—like the appropriation of *Hamlet* (1.5.22) in the Evening Ode—induces through music a visual "ecstasy," as the "sound, or ghost of sound" kisses every stone: "from the arms of silence—list! O list! / The music bursteth into second life."[19]

The "beamy radiance" Wordsworth refers to in the Evening Ode is the "effulgence" observed in the ode's first line, and, by means of this recollection of Hamlet's words, it is the poetic equivalent of the last light of day, the visual cue that triggers the recognition and begins the poem's meditation. The afterlife of Shakespeare's text radiates from Wordsworth's like the afterglow of the setting sun. But the effulgent radiance also recollects another poetic antecedent in Wordsworth's twilit diction. The poem begins by alluding to the description of the Son of God in Book 3 of *Paradise Lost*: "Had this effulgence disappeared / With flying haste" (Evening Ode, 1–2). The allusion places readers in a position to compare Wordsworth's vision of transcendence with Milton's and to understand that Wordsworth rewrites Milton's supernatural description from within the psychology of natural experience.[20] Whereas Wordsworth reflects impressionistically upon the effects of the sun, in *Paradise Lost* a multitude of angels sings the glories of the Son: "on thee / Impressed the effulgence of his glory abides, / Transfused on thee his ample Spirit rests."[21] The context as a whole recalls its Miltonic forebear in an agonistic relation: pushing against the invocation to "holy light" that begins Book 3 of *Paradise Lost*, Wordsworth meditates upon the last infusion of daylight as a means of contemplating the impossibility of writing in Milton's idiom. He mourns,

> Time was when field and watery cove
> With modulated echoes rang,
> While choirs of fervent Angels sang
> Their vespers in the grove;
> Or, ranged like stars along some sovereign height,
> Warbled, for heaven above and earth below,
> Strains suitable to both.... (Evening Ode, 9–15)

It is as though Milton recalls a worldview no longer available, despite its sublimity and grandeur, to the Romantic poet, whereas Shakespeare remains as present and necessary as the luminous air at twilight, or the memory of childhood. Wordsworth contests the authority of Milton, who is himself consigned to his own echo of

---

[19] Ecclesiastical Sonnet 44, lines 9–14, *The Poems of William Wordsworth* (London, 1851), 334.

[20] Compare this assertion with the magisterial thesis of M. H. Abrams, *Natural Supernaturalism* (New York: W. W. Norton, 1971).

[21] John Milton, *Paradise Lost*, ed. Alastair Fowler, 2nd ed. (London: Longman, 1998), 3.387–9. All references to *Paradise Lost* are from this edition.

Shakespeare in the diction of this passage, even as he draws upon the "wond'rous potency" of Shakespeare's enduring radiance. While implicitly agreeing with Milton's representation of "sweetest Shakespeare fancy's child" who "warbles his native wood-notes wild" in "L'Allegro," Wordsworth brings Milton down to earth by contrasting him with Shakespeare.[22] Time and again, Wordsworth tries to strike a middle ground between the two by finding the cosmic in the natural and not needing more than "the low and wren-like warblings" celebrated in contrast to the loftier strain of Miltonic prophecy in *The Prelude* (5.208) or the arrested traveler in the opening of *The Ruined Cottage*:

> some huge oak whose aged branches make
> A twilight of their own, a dewy shade
> Where the wren warbles while the dreaming man,
> Half-conscious of that soothing melody,
> With side-long eye looks out upon the scene. (12–16)

In the Evening Ode, Wordsworth evokes *Hamlet* when the poet seeks to grasp the significance of a fleeting reminder of his "blissful infancy" (64). In the Intimations Ode (composed 1802–1804), the "obstinate questionings / Of sense and outward things, / Fallings from us, vanishings" (144–6) call forth the ghost of Old Hamlet in Horatio's words to Barnardo, "And then it started like a guilty thing / Upon a fearful summons" (1.1.129–30):

> Blank misgivings of a Creature
> Moving about in worlds not realized,
> High instincts, before which our mortal Nature
> Did tremble like a guilty Thing surprised. (Intimations Ode, 144–7)

Where in the Intimations Ode, the injunction of the ghost, "Remember me," represents the retention of immortal instincts in our "mortal Nature," in the Evening Ode Wordsworth himself becomes like the ghost, a "soul, though yet confined to earth" (77).[23] In this, Wordsworth's appropriation looks forward to Tennyson's borrowing of the same line to depict his haunting grief for Hallam: "Behold me, for I cannot sleep, / And like a guilty thing I creep / At earliest morning to the door."[24] Like Coleridge claiming, "I have a smack of Hamlet myself," Romantic mourners read themselves into the ghost of Old Hamlet.[25] Allusion to *Hamlet* in the Evening

---

[22] John Milton, *Complete Shorter Poems*, ed. John Carey, 2nd ed. (London: Longman, 1997), 143.

[23] Thus, in the concluding lines of the Evening Ode—when the "second birth" of the "visionary splendour fades, / And Night approaches with her shades" (78–80)—Wordsworth represents himself as a spirit who is, as the ghost of Old Hamlet says, "Doomed for a certain term to walk the night, / And for the day confined to fast in fires" (1.5.10–11).

[24] Tennyson, *In Memoriam*, 7.7, ed. Erik Gray (New York: W. W. Norton, 2004), 11.

[25] Coleridge, *Table Talk*, June 24, 1827, in Bate, ed., *The Romantics on Shakespeare*, 161.

Ode functions as an allusion to the operations of memory, the "wondrous potency" that when habituated "almost can change the stamp of nature," as Hamlet says.

In his use of Shakespeare, Wordsworth makes good on his promise to document the "language really used by men," but not at the expense of a richly symbolic expansiveness (Preface to *Lyrical Ballads*, 597). This dynamic allusive context at once evokes Shakespeare's characters at particular moments in their plays and manages to dislodge the poetry from its Shakespearean setting, so that the symbolic application of the verse to Wordsworth's new context generates a greater expressive potential through its clearly signaled modification of Shakespeare. Alluding to the language of Shakespeare's characters, Wordsworth interprets the philosophical content of poetic lines from the plays and finds in their phrasing the inspiration for his own philosophizing. This is precisely the liberating energy Coleridge drew from Hamlet in particular: "*Hamlet* was the play, or rather Hamlet himself was the character, in the intuition and exposition of which I first made my turn for philosophical criticism...."[26]

In the Preface to *Lyrical Ballads*, Wordsworth reframes a line from one of Hamlet's soliloquies to make just this turn and applies the words polemically in support of his claim that poetry humanizes knowledge. At the same time as he pursues Coleridge's kind of abstract, philosophical criticism, then, Wordsworth makes Hamlet's words a bridge between the poet and the rest of humanity akin to the "primal sympathy" that unites people beyond the particularity of their suffering in the Intimations Ode (184). The passage in the Preface works by returning the concept of inspiration to its etymological and physiological origins, a motive that, as we shall see, comes to be identified with Shakespeare in Wordsworth's writings. Poetry is

> the breath and finer spirit of all knowledge; it is the impassioned expression which is in the countenance of all Science. Emphatically may it be said of the Poet, as Shakespeare hath said of man, "that he looks before and after." He is the rock of defence of human nature; an upholder and preserver, carrying every where with him relationship and love. (606)

The quotation is not exact—Hamlet's line reads "he that made us with such large discourse, / Looking before and after" (4.4.9.26–7)—but quotation marks nonetheless signal the borrowing as an allusion, as if Wordsworth were trying to say by means of the inexactness of his adaptation that he possessed the phrase in memory. Lending Wordsworth's scientific countenance the expression of passion, Hamlet's soliloquy ("How all occasions do inform against me") does not bear directly upon Wordsworth's context except as a generalized statement of the dignity of human beings. The interconnectedness of poet and common man, the bond between the poem and its audience as much as that between the poet and his subject, derives from their shared thoughts and feelings. Wordsworth himself becomes "an upholder and preserver" as he merges his thought with Hamlet's, just

---

[26] Coleridge, Lecture of 1818, in Bate, ed., *The Romantics on Shakespeare*, 311.

as, in the expression of "relationship and love," he shows himself to be "carrying with him" that humanizing sympathy which he attributes to Shakespeare. Sensitivity to human feeling allows the inspired poet to step away from the particularity of his context in order to defend human nature, and it is Shakespeare who comes immediately to Wordsworth in defense of his point. Again, according to Coleridge, Shakespeare authorizes this expansion: "Hamlet's character is the prevalence of the abstracting and generalizing habit over the practical."[27] Ironically, two of the most influential commentators on Wordsworth from the last century, Geoffrey Hartman and M. H. Abrams, employ this same borrowed phrase without placing quotation marks around Hamlet's words. Through this doubly allusive, buried quotation, they assent to Wordsworth's amplification of its significance in the Preface to *Lyrical Ballads* and implicitly apply to Wordsworth his own description of the poet by quoting Shakespeare's phrase.[28]

Allusion, too, "looks before and after," as Christopher Ricks maintains, opening a new prospect through retrospection.[29] The 1798 volume of *Lyrical Ballads* concludes with "Tintern Abbey," a poem rife with just this kind of Shakespearean allusion. Wordsworth gestures toward a passage in which Hamlet says of his father: "'A was a man, take him for all in all, / I shall not look upon his like again" (1.2.187–8). Taking the Shakespearean phrase symbolically, Wordsworth's speaker places nature in the paternal role, even as he separates himself in the present moment of composition from the youthful consciousness that enjoyed "courser pleasures": "For nature then / … To me was all in all" ("Tintern Abbey," 73–6). Jonathan Bate observes that "Wordsworth flees, perhaps from the memory of his father's death, only to find himself haunted by nature," and asks suggestively, "Has nature become a substitute for his father?"[30] Not only has nature become *a* father to the youthful Wordsworth, but, the context of the borrowing implies, a surrogate for *the* Father. Indeed, through the further mediation of a Miltonic allusion to the Shakespearean phrase in *Paradise Lost*—where God pronounces the Last Judgment before the Heavenly Host, "For regal scepter then no more shall need, / God shall be all in all" (3.340–41)—Wordsworth reinvests their shared intertext with a newfound sense from its primary source, 1 Corinthians 15:28: "And when all things shall be subdued unto him, then shall the Son also himself become subject unto him that put all things under him, that God may be all in all." One wonders, furthermore, whether Wordsworth has learned from Shakespeare a particular mode of allusion here, since Shakespeare ironically employs a scriptural

---

[27] Coleridge, *Table Talk*, June 24, 1827, in Bate, ed., *The Romantics on Shakespeare*, 160.

[28] Geoffrey H. Hartman, *Wordsworth's Poetry 1787–1814* (New Haven, CT: Yale University Press, 1964), 48; Abrams, *Natural Supernaturalism*, 14.

[29] Christopher Ricks, *Allusion to the Poets* (Oxford: Oxford University Press, 2002), 86.

[30] Bate, *Shakespeare*, 98.

text to describe Hamlet's father that features centrally in the ceremony for the Burial of the Dead in the Elizabethan *Book of Common Prayer*.[31]

In Wordsworth's youth, nature stood not merely as a God to him, but as a source of the outermost bound of meaning, the *telos* toward which he, like all things, directed his being, and through which his life took what form it had. For Wordsworth, this was not the result of meditation on the Last Judgment, so much as life's first semiconscious judgment. In the first instance, the allusion to Corinthians, by way of *Paradise Lost* and *Hamlet*, bespeaks the dissolution of the self, the loss of the principle of individuation in the overwhelming sublimity of nature. But in retrospect, through the revisionary glance of allusion, the individuality of Wordsworth's mature reflection acquires its particular moral cast. The sustaining sympathy induced by natural phenomena must have a greater human application if it is to be a guarantor of the poet's consciousness.[32] For Wordsworth, a deep and at times unmarked recollection of Shakespeare's verse, mediated by a more overt Miltonic presence, was as natural as the saving grace of memory.

## Nature, Imagination, and Mutability in Wordsworth's Use of Shakespeare

In "Mutability" (written 1821, published 1822), a fundamental property of the material universe has become a Shakespearean character—a tragic being whose *peripeteia* has sufficient grandeur to signify the universal principle of decay: "From low to high doth dissolution climb / And sinks from high to low" (1–2). Throughout the sonnet Wordsworth makes the poetic form embody this tragic recognition, just as the poem humanizes the concept of natural reversal: "crime" (5) dissolves as the eye descends the page to meet its partner, "rime" (8), in a "musical but melancholy" concord of notes sounded along the scale of dissolution and revealing the underlying truth of change. Echoing the description of Lear at Dover, the "outward forms" of truth "drop like the tower sublime / Of yesterday, which royally did wear / Its crown of weeds ..." (10–12). One way of seeing this appropriation is to imagine that Wordsworth reads the character of Lear as concealing in his outward form the inner truth of mutability. The borrowed phrase becomes so resonant precisely as a result of the filiations of "relationship and love," which as he says in the 1802 Preface to *Lyrical Ballads* the poet must carry with him. It is after all Cordelia who, in the depth of her care for Lear, brings the pathos of the image into the play telling the Doctor that Lear is "crowned with rank

---

[31] See Thomas Festa, "'All in All': The *Book of Common Prayer* and *Hamlet*, I.ii.186," *Notes and Queries* 54, no. 3 (2007): 289–90.

[32] My formulation here owes its main point to Paul Hamilton: "Wordsworth makes it his poem's subject to show that the Romantic sublime grows out of Enlightenment materialism and the spiritual indeterminacies lying at the far end of materialism's comprehensive claims to generate all experience from sensuous grounds." Paul Hamilton, "Wordsworth and Romanticism," in *The Cambridge Companion to Wordsworth*, ed. Stephen Gill (Cambridge: Cambridge University Press, 2003), 222ff.

fumiter and furrow-weeds" (conflated text, 4.4.3).[33] Indeed, the rending ironies of the encounter with Gloucester at Dover emerge most fully in the equivocal symbol of the man stripped of authority wearing his "crown of weeds" and proclaiming ironically that he is "every inch a king." Wordsworth accentuates the *volta* of the sonnet through the allusion to Lear in his catastrophic fall, an allusion that in turn universalizes and carries into "Mutability" the tragic failings of "relationship and love" in *King Lear*.

If "Mutability" shows the way Wordsworth could translate the pathos of a Shakespearean character into a more generalized philosophical idiom by applying human attributes to a principle of nature, then *The Prelude* opens this representational strategy up to rigorous scrutiny in its investigation of the powers of imagination. Will the imagination hold such power as to carry forth into the poem the "relationship and love" that is the poet's obligation? Recalling his early residence at Cambridge, Wordsworth describes how, despite the initial sluggishness of his studies, his imagination has endowed him with a power to create mental pictures of a more ideal place of learning. Having been "trained up in paradise" and "accustomed in my loneliness to walk / With nature magisterially" throughout his childhood and adolescence, the young poet

> could shape the image of a place
> Which with its aspect should have bent me down
> To instantaneous service, should at once
> Have made me pay to science and to arts
> And written lore—acknowledged my liege lord—
> A homage frankly offered up, like that
> Which I had paid to nature. Toil and pains
> In this recess which I have bodied forth
> Should spread from heart to heart, and stately groves,
> Majestic edifices, should not want
> A corresponding dignity within.[34]

Responding to Hippolyta's prompt in *A Midsummer Night's Dream*, "'Tis strange, my Theseus, that these lovers speak of" (5.1.1), the duke of Athens, as if

---

[33] Hence the modern editorial tradition of introducing a stage direction after Lear's statement, "I will preach to thee": "LEAR *takes off his crown of weeds and flowers*" (4.6.174 s.d.). In Malone's edition, which Wordsworth owned, a note (attributed to Steevens) connects the stage tradition of Lear removing his headdress, there imagined as a "hat," and "turning it and feeling it" as he speaks, "in the attitude of the preachers of those times" on entering the pulpit. See *The Plays and Poems of William Shakespeare*, ed. Edmond Malone, 10 vols. (London, 1790), 8:647. According to a note in the Arden Third Series edition, the tradition of Lear removing the crown here is said to have begun with Garrick. See *King Lear*, ed. R. A. Foakes (Walton-on-Thames, UK: Thomas Nelson and Sons, 1997), 340.

[34] William Wordsworth, *The Prelude: The Four Texts (1798, 1799, 1805, 1850)*, ed. Jonathan Wordsworth (Harmondsworth, UK: Penguin, 1995), 3.375–91. All references to *The Prelude* are from this edition and follow the 1805 text unless otherwise noted.

following Socrates in Plato's *Ion*, sounds a skeptical note of caution against the *furor poeticus*:

> The poet's eye, in a fine frenzy rolling,
> Doth glance from heaven to earth, from earth to heaven,
> And as imagination bodies forth
> The forms of things unknown, the poet's pen
> Turns them to shapes, and gives to airy nothing
> A local habitation and a name. (5.1.12–17)

Wordsworth's allusion to Shakespeare is "bodied forth" in an invocation of Theseus's ironic *resistance* to the inventive powers of the imagination. Through his focused appropriation of the content, Wordsworth actually manages to reverse the direction of Theseus's argument. Wordsworth echoes Theseus on the imagination when picturing a place in which "book-mindedness" (3.405) should not be relegated to nature but should rather emulate it through "a corresponding dignity within" the hearts of poet and audience. Imagination, "bodied forth" in the allusion to Shakespeare as a way of figuring an alternative to conventional university education, is in this passage both idealizing and mimetic of nature—a venerable if backhanded compliment to Shakespeare that goes back to Francis Beaumont's 1615 manuscript verses to Ben Jonson.[35]

In the passage in Book 3 of *The Prelude* where he alludes to Theseus's speech, then, Wordsworth's awe takes the form of "service" (3.383) and subservience to an aristocratic authority, there personified as his "liege lord" (3.385). It is as if the medieval institution of the university imposes feudal relations upon those who pay homage and offer fealty to its academic aims. Yet Wordsworth escapes the constraints of the place as it is through the naturalizing force of imagination, an action of the mind upon the object of its contemplation that is infused with the alternative authority of Shakespeare as the uneducated imaginative genius. After alluding to Theseus's words as a corrective, adding to them his own poetic "toil and pains" (3.387) the imagined place, until now depicted in the conditional tense, becomes an actuality—the literary place of the poem. He *has* "bodied forth" the

---

[35] In his commendatory poem for the First Folio of 1623, Ben Jonson set the stage for subsequent efforts to come to terms with Shakespeare's gifts by associating him with natural genius untamed by scholarly labor. Francis Beaumont may have some claim to have initiated this line of praise in connection with Shakespeare, however, in the poem to Jonson mentioned above, where he celebrated "how farr sometimes a morall man may goe / by the dimme light of Nature." Beaumont would let "schollershippe" slip "And from all Learning keepe these lines as [cl]eere / as Shakespeares best are," as if imitating the manner of Shakespeare's verse implied a coarsening of rhetoric to render it less artificially. But Beaumont's categories were only to have an influence on the thought of later readers of Shakespeare through their possible influence on Jonson's more famous commendatory poem. Beaumont's poem was first printed in full in E. K. Chambers, *William Shakespeare: A Study of Facts and Problems*, vol. 2 (Oxford: Clarendon Press, 1930) and is excerpted in *The Norton Shakespeare*, ed. Greenblatt et al., 3341.

toil and pains to create a grammatical, imagistic, and conceptual parallel between the "stately groves" (3.389) in which he was accustomed "to walk / With nature magisterially" (3.379–80) and the "majestic edifices" (3.390) of the university. The poem, embodying the synthesis of natural and cultural forces, sublimates and transcends the dialectical opposition of "groves" and "edifices." In composing these lines, Wordsworth calls upon Shakespeare's language to claim the poem as proof of the imagination's power. He wrests the peripatetic tradition of the academic grove away from its institutional site and locates it within his own corresponding experience of hiking, and it is Shakespeare who authorizes this down-to-earth literalizing. As the "recess" formed in the imaginative space of the poem "should spread from heart to heart," so the "congregating temper which pervades / Our unripe years" (3.392–3) should not be wasted but, instead, come to fruition in that "corresponding dignity within" his readers. Such dignity keeps the poet from subservience to the authority of intellectual tradition as symbolized by the "liege lord" of the university. Wordsworth allows that the implications of this "healthy sound simplicity, / A seemly plainness," will be social and political, whether "republican, or pious" (3.407).

As late as his Preface to *Poems* (1815), Wordsworth would persist in characterizing this passage from *A Midsummer Night's Dream* as a defense of his own view of the imagination. There he rejects the definitions of fancy and imagination by William Taylor, who in his *English Synonyms Discriminated* (1813) had employed the associative, imagistic notion of the imagination "formed by patient observation."[36] Against this definition, Wordsworth inveighs with Theseus that "the lunatic, the lover, and the poet / Are of imagination all compact" (*A Midsummer Night's Dream* 5.1.7–8):

> What term is left to designate that Faculty of which the Poet is "all compact"; he whose eye glances from earth to heaven, whose spiritual attributes body-forth what his pen is prompt in turning to shape; or what is left to characterize fancy, as insinuating herself into the heart of objects with creative activity?—Imagination, in the sense of the word as giving title to a Class of the following Poems, has no reference to images that are a merely faithful copy, existing in the mind, of absent external objects, but is a word of higher import, denoting operations of the mind upon those objects, and processes of creation or of composition ... (Preface to *Poems*, 630–31)

Crucially Wordsworth argues for the interaction of mind and object instead of "a merely faithful copy." Imagination, as he argues in *The Prelude*, is but another name for "Reason in her most exalted mood" (13.170). Thus Wordsworth is consistent in the way he disparages what he calls the "rules of mimic art," which produce the picturesque but not the sublime experience of aesthetic consciousness (11.154). "A cogent justification of mimesis," as Stephen Halliwell has argued, "must appeal to something *more* than verisimilitude.... Verisimilitude, the look of

---

[36] Quoted in Wordsworth, Preface to *Poems*, 630.

the real, should not be confused with veracity, the grasp of the real itself."[37] In the 1815 Preface, the hybrid formula for the poetic imagination dissolves the binary of mimesis and expression by showing how the mind synthesizes the two in the creative act—an aesthetic power that Wordsworth, early and late, attributes to and derives from Shakespeare.

Wordsworth places Shakespeare at the center of a theory of representational art that is, in some crucial respects, diametrically opposed to the theory that Wordsworth has been made to represent in influential treatments of Romanticism that emphasize "expressive aesthetics."[38] As opposed to a theory of mimetic representation, the expressive mode represents a subjective experience, rather than a process imitative of external reality. Although such critics have recognized the continuities between Wordsworth and the aesthetic theories of the eighteenth century, they persistently distort Wordsworth's writings in the claim that Wordsworth leaves behind mimesis and history.

## Mimesis and Historical Imagination: Shakespeare in *The Prelude*

Imagination does not consist in a direct relationship of mind to matter in *The Prelude*. "Marvellous things / My fancy had shaped forth," he says of his childhood fantasies of London, which he mocks in his revision of 1850 by changing "fancy" to "vanity" (1805, 7.108–9; 1850, 7.104). Wordsworth gives up not only on his youthful faith in the imagination, but also on the power of this allusion to Theseus's speech as a figure for it. But the deflationary reaction of the mind when forced to confront reality allows a clearer insight into the truth of the imagination after the faltering anticipation.[39] In one vivid instance, the contrast

---

[37] Stephen Halliwell, *The Aesthetics of Mimesis: Ancient Texts and Modern Problems* (Princeton, NJ: Princeton University Press, 2002), 58–9.

[38] Andrew Bennett, "Expressivity: The Romantic Theory of Authorship," in *Literary Theory and Criticism: An Oxford Guide*, ed. Patricia Waugh (Oxford: Oxford University Press, 2006), 48–58, tries to reassert these categories. Halliwell, *The Aesthetics of Mimesis*, 8–9 and 344–69, undoes the opposition between mimeticism and Romantic theory. This theory receives its most influential formulation in M. H. Abrams, *The Mirror and the Lamp: Romantic Theory and the Critical Tradition* (New York: Oxford University Press, 1953), 22–6, 100–101, 113–14. Abrams's view of Wordsworth's theory is persuasively refuted in James A. W. Heffernan, *Wordsworth's Theory of Poetry: The Transforming Imagination* (Ithaca, NY: Cornell University Press, 1969), 54–7; see also James Engell, *The Creative Imagination: Enlightenment to Romanticism* (Cambridge, MA: Harvard University Press, 1981), 265–76. For a useful assessment of the return to aesthetic criticism in Shakespeare studies, see the review essay by Jeff Dolven, "Shakespeare and the New Aestheticism," *Literary Imagination* 5, no. 1 (2003): 95–109. For an effort to urge a reflective materialist aestheticism into the field, see John J. Joughin, "Shakespeare, Modernity and the Aesthetic: Art, Truth, and Judgement in *The Winter's Tale*," in *Shakespeare and Modernity: Early Modern to Millenium*, ed. Hugh Grady (London: Routledge, 2000), 62–84, esp. 65.

[39] See Hartman, *Wordsworth's Poetry*, 33–69.

between real and literary shepherds grounds Wordsworth's attempt at the pastoral mode. The episode highlights the self-reflexive quality of the imagination without dismissing the problem of mimetic representation of reality. In fact, the space that opens up between the thing itself and its traditional representations again becomes the condition of possibility for Wordsworth to participate in the creative act. The falsity of traditional pastoral stands in stark relief against the hard realities of rural life in the Lake District, yet in the 1850 *Prelude* the space of pastoral assumes its own dimensions as a result of the presence of "Shakespeare's genius":

> And shepherds were the men that pleased me first;
> Not such as Saturn ruled 'mid Latian wilds,
> With arts and laws so tempered, that their lives
> Left, even to us toiling in this late day,
> A bright tradition of the golden age;
> Not such as, 'mid Arcadian fastnesses
> Sequestered, handed down among themselves
> Felicity, in Grecian song renowned;
> Nor such as, when an adverse fate had driven,
> From house and home, the courtly band whose fortunes
> Entered, with Shakespeare's genius, the wild woods
> Of Arden, amid sunshine or in shade,
> Culled the best fruits of Time's uncounted hours,
> Ere Phoebe sighed for the false Ganymede. (1805, 8.128–41)

Just as Wordsworth depicts his own "toil and pains" in the passage recounting the disappointment of his actual experience at Cambridge (1805, 3.381)—fusing the imagined ideal of education in nature and the actual experience of education in the university to forge the imaginative space of the poem itself—so here Wordsworth's inclusion of poetic labor in the phrase "even to us toiling in this late day" establishes a continuity with the pastoral "golden age" that it seemingly rejects.

In comparison with the poets' re-creation of the innocent golden age, Wordsworth recalls "the unluxuriant produce of a life / Intent on little but substantial needs / Yet rich in beauty, beauty that was felt" (1850 *Prelude*, 8.161–3). The poem measures the lived reality against the literary version, so that it creates a genuinely pastoral effect of doubleness. As Paul Alpers says, "It is full of idyllic feeling and at the same time true to reality. ... In representing Shakespeare's shepherdess, Wordsworth's genius takes us *out* of the woods of Arden and into the world of the modern shepherd and, perhaps, of a modern pastoral."[40] Wordsworth does not merely rehearse the plot of *As You Like It* but rather participates in the pastoral world through an imitation of the tensions endemic to the play from

---

[40] Paul Alpers, *What Is Pastoral?* (Chicago: University of Chicago Press, 1996), 21. My discussion here is indebted to Alpers's interpretation of this passage. For a brilliant and more extensive reading of Wordsworth's poetry in the light of the "materialism of the beautiful" than lies within the scope of my argument, see Simon Jarvis, *Wordsworth's Philosophic Song* (Cambridge: Cambridge University Press, 2007), 7–8, 24–7, 84–107.

within—as if from the vantage of Phoebe herself, who would see Ganymede as "false." Wordsworth's line, "Culled the best fruits of Time's uncounted hours," emulates and compresses the exchange between Orlando and Rosalind disguised as Ganymede, before Phoebe falls for "false Ganymede" in Act 3:

> ROSALIND.
> I pray you, what is't o'clock?
>
> ORLANDO.
> You should ask me what time o' day. There is no clock in the forest.
>
> ROSALIND.
> Then there is no true lover in the forest, else sighing every minute and groaning every hour would detect the lazy foot of time as well as a clock. (3.2.274–9)

In his confrontation with Shakespearean pastoral and its limits as a mimetic mode, Wordsworth first feels the disappointment that life has not lived up to the ideal represented in Shakespeare's art, what he deems "the great nature that exists in works / Of mighty poets" (1805 *Prelude*, 5.618–19). He then employs a thoroughly Miltonic rhetorical scheme to reduce the "golden age" representations of English pastoral life in Shakespeare and Spenser to delusive fictions. Just as Milton extensively catalogues, gorgeously describes, and ultimately disavows classical points of comparison through which he establishes representations in Eden, Heaven, and Hell, Wordsworth includes earlier depictions of the pastoral in order to make his art by exploiting the earlier poets' inexactitude or unreality as compared to his own experience. It is telling that in such moments when he draws closer to an unmediated imitation of natural life—albeit from a later, reflective maturity—Wordsworth recurs to the cluster of ideas he associates with Shakespeare. As when he recounts the origin of the pastoral poem *Michael* (1800), he clearly tries to exemplify the theoretical ideals of the Preface to *Lyrical Ballads*:

> And hence this Tale, while I was yet a boy
> Careless of books, yet having felt the power
> Of Nature, by the gentle agency
> Of natural objects led me on to feel
> For passions that were not my own, and think
> At random and imperfectly indeed
> On man; the heart of man and human life.
> Therefore, although it be a history
> Homely and rude, I will relate the same
> For the delight of a few natural hearts,
> And with yet fonder feeling, for the sake
> Of youthful Poets, who among these Hills
> Will be my second self when I am gone. (27–39)

The thought of his own relationship to posterity provides Wordsworth with a device for conceiving his break with tradition as an aesthetic of intensified liberty and expansiveness. He speculates of the stranger addressed in the early poem "Lines Left upon a Seat in a Yew-Tree": "If thou be one whose heart the holy forms / Of young imagination have kept pure" (44–5). This formulation commonly becomes a means of expressing a wishful correspondence between his own state of consciousness and that of an idealized future audience, much as his sister figures into the ending of "Tintern Abbey" as at once a reflection of Wordsworth's earlier self and an implicit anticipation of his audience's empathy with him. To "feel / For passions that are not my own" is to come very close to the ideal that Keats defined as Shakespearean and distinguished from "the wordsworthian or egotistical sublime; which is a thing per se and stands alone."[41] But it is worth recalling that Keats employs allusions to Shakespeare both in his parenthetical description of this Wordsworthian attribute ("They say he is a very man *per se*, / And stands alone," *Troilus and Cressida*, 1.2.15–16) *and* in offering up the counterexample of his own desire to embody a Shakespearean imagination, which, Keats writes, "has as much delight in conceiving an Iago as an Imogen."

In the passage in *Michael*, the reconstruction of Wordsworth's personal past, in which he was "careless of books" and therefore closer himself to that state of nature represented by Luke and his parents, the "natural objects" of the poem, proceeds by way of an oblique reference to the conception of Shakespeare as, in Dryden's words, "naturally learn'd; he needed not the spectacles of books to read Nature; he looked inwards, and found her there."[42] In other words, when Wordsworth represents himself as a boy uncorrupted in his natural sympathies and sharing in the fellow feeling of local people and their stories, he represents himself as the neoclassical tradition had represented Shakespeare. In Pope's phrase, Shakespeare "is not so much an Imitator, as an Instrument, of Nature ... His Characters are so much Nature her self, that 'tis a sort of injury to call them by so distant a name as Copies of her."[43]

As much as Wordsworth, in line with the critical commonplaces of eighteenth-century readers of Shakespeare, fantasized about the inward and capacious amalgamation of life that granted Shakespeare the ability to represent human nature effortlessly, he nonetheless recognized that Shakespeare's time, like Wordsworth's own idyllic youth, had passed. History has marred Wordsworth's ability to idealize, as he makes clear in displacing the trauma of the French Revolution and its failures onto the lovers Vaudracour and Julia, *The Prelude*'s surrogates for himself and Annette Vallon. As if to abase his tale's subject, Wordsworth likens their plight to the star-crossed lovers:

---

[41] John Keats, Letter to Richard Woodhouse, October 27, 1818, in *The Letters of John Keats 1814–1821*, ed. Hyder E. Rollins, 2 vols. (Cambridge, MA: Harvard University Press, 1958), 1:386–8. The subsequent quotation from Keats is also from this letter.

[42] John Dryden, *An Essay of Dramatic Poesy*, 1668, in *Essays*, ed. W. P. Ker, 2 vols. (Oxford: Clarendon Press, 1900), 1:80.

[43] Alexander Pope, ed., *The Works of Shakespear*, 6 vols. (London, 1723–25), 1:ii.

> I pass the raptures of the pair; such theme
> Hath by a hundred poets been set forth
> In more delightful verse than skill of mine
> Could fashion—chiefly by that darling bard
> Who told of Juliet and her Romeo,
> And of the lark's note heard before its time,
> And of the streaks that laced the severing clouds
> In the unrelenting east. 'Tis mine to tread
> The humbler province of plain history,
> And, without choice of circumstance, submissively
> Relate what I have heard. (9.635–45)

To bid farewell to his own imaginative representational powers, Wordsworth imports the comparison to *Romeo and Juliet*, in which Romeo bids farewell to Juliet for one last time in the play: "Look, love, what envious streaks / Do lace the severing clouds in yonder east" (3.5.7–8). As in the passage from Book 8 in which the actual shepherds of the Lake District call into question the veracity of traditional pastoral as exemplified in *As You Like It* (and *The Winter's Tale*), so here a reference to Shakespeare illuminates "the humbler province of plain history" by way of contrast.

If Shakespeare stands at the apex of human imaginative powers, his presence in Wordsworth's poetry allows the later poet access to what he calls the "homely and rude" history of his own time and place (*Michael*, 35). Shakespeare, at times by example and at others by contrast, authorizes the return to history, which becomes a means of demystification through allusion. Wordsworth draws upon Shakespeare's plays to make his own subject seem less transcendental, even as he alludes to Shakespeare as a way to figure imaginative failure and the traumatic disruption of historical verisimilitude imposed upon poetic creativity. The result of the comparison is that Wordsworth conceives his own poetic powers as derived from historical necessity, "without choice of circumstance," though his pretense "submissively" to "relate what I have heard," must ultimately appear as a mimetic strategy. At the end of the episode, when explaining the silence of Vaudracour in his father's house after the deaths of Julia (by "self-slaughter," 9.694; a usage borrowed from *Hamlet*, 1.2.132) and their child, Wordsworth says, "From that time forth he never uttered word / To any living" (9.912–13), an allusion to Iago's final lines in *Othello*: "Demand me nothing. What you know, you know. / From this time forth I never will speak word" (5.2.309–10). The poet's loss of his own voice, as it were, when he employs Iago's words to express the unspeakable horror mimics Vaudracour's loss of speech. Wordsworth gains an imaginative voice, but only through a kind of ventriloquism, as he gives over the words of his poem to allusion and thereby makes Shakespeare's language, instead of his own, expressive of Vaudracour's tragedy.

The mind's joy at its generative powers of imagination usurps reality from the senses and lifts itself up "like an unfathered vapour," though Wordsworth, facing his disappointment at the actual crossing of the Alps at Simplon Pass, finds himself initially "lost as in a cloud, / Halted without a struggle to break through" (6.525–30). Again, where Wordsworth seeks to describe the sublime power of the imagination over nature, he evokes a Shakespearean context as a poetic correlative. The phrase "unfathered vapour"—suggesting autochthonic genius unbound by tradition—employs a Shakespearean usage. In *2 Henry IV* Gloucester calls the portents observed by the people "unfathered heirs and loathly births of nature" (4.3.122).[44] Overtaken by the recollection of Shakespeare's verse, Wordsworth himself is at once *unfathered* by Shakespeare—a displaced progenitor of his own verse, uprooted from patriarchal systems of power and signification—and *fathered* or engendered as a poet by means of the allusion.

The "visitings / Of awful promise" that accompany the failure of "the light of sense" at Simplon Pass shows us "our destiny, our nature, and our home," which is pure immanence—"something ever more about to be" (*Prelude*, 6.533–4, 542). This passage on the sublime power of the imagination then activates a further Shakespearean allusion: the mind, "blest in thoughts / That are their own perfection and reward," does not think of spoils or trophies but knows it is "strong in itself, and in the access of joy / Which hides it like the overflowing Nile" (6.545–8). This is the mind not tricked by "strong imagination" (*A Midsummer Night's Dream*, 5.1.18), as Theseus has it, but rather "in the access of joy" that swells with recognition of imagination's creative independence. In the imaginative acts that bracket the actual experience on either side, both in anticipation and reflection, the retrospective pleasure is likened to "the overflowing Nile," and as Antony says, "The higher Nilus swells / The more it promises" (*Antony and Cleopatra*, 2.7.19–20); or, as Charmian ironically relates, "the o'erflowing Nilus presageth famine" (1.2.43). The structure of Wordsworth's poetic experience at Simplon Pass, like Charmian's ironic reversal of the commonplace, conveys first disappointment at the famine of experience when measured against the fecundity of anticipation, only to invert itself into an ironic celebration of imaginative bounty and fertility.

Wordsworth understands his poetic identity by grappling with the limitations of his imagination and the historical embeddedness that this self-consciousness discloses. The poetic predecessor whose works give Wordsworth the clearest access to this aspect of his identity is Shakespeare. As we saw in the first pages of this essay, Hazlitt's accusation of egotism in Wordsworth's art also, paradoxically, lays the foundation for articulating its particular genius, a trait Wordsworth shares with Rembrandt in that each "invented a new view of nature" and pointed out "what is before our eyes and under our feet."[45] To represent nature mimetically while, at the same time, expressing the self is to comprehend that there are within the subject two natures: "the mind / Learns from such timely exercise to keep /

---

[44] *OED* 1 cites this occurrence as a coinage of the term meaning "Having no (known or acknowledged) father; illegitimate." But *OED* 2 gives an earlier instance from Sidney's *Arcadia* 3.17 for the term meaning "deprived of a father," although this usage, too, has a more likely origin for Wordsworth in Shakespeare's Sonnet 124, line 2.

[45] Hazlitt, *Selected Writings*, 6:37.

In wholesome separation the two natures: / The one that feels, the other that observes" (*Prelude*, 13.328–31). Wordsworth thus frames the issue of mimeticism in the *Essay, Supplementary to the Preface* (1815): the duty of poetry "is to treat of things not as they *are*, but as they *appear*, as they *seem* to exist to the *senses* and the *passions*" (641).

I want to close by recalling the philosophical basis for this approach to aesthetic representation, a treatment of the object of aesthetic contemplation that insists that there is no such thing as unmediated access to "things ... as they *are*." In section 49 of the *Critique of the Power of Judgment*, Kant explains the operations of the "faculties of the mind that constitute genius." Genius is not a conceptual or theoretical extension of reason, but rather a harmonization of all the powers of the mind made possible by the capacity of the imagination to attune itself to the understanding in an absence of rules. Aesthetic ideas, "which no science can teach and no diligence can learn," appear as intuitions, communicable dispositions of the mind according to the free play of the genius's cognitive powers upon an object. Although the product of an earlier genius may provide an example for a later genius, the later genius may succeed only by emulating the earlier genius's liberation from artistic conventions, not by dutifully imitating what might seem to be rules set by the example. In emulating the attitude, instead of imitating the aesthetic technique, of an earlier artist, the later genius's treatment of things "as they *appear*" will yield a more authentic (because historically contingent) representation, a work that embraces the distinct subjectivity of the belated genius's vision. Recognizing the achievement of an earlier genius, according to Kant, will therefore entail that the one who recognizes a predecessor honestly acknowledge the distance that separates his own situated consciousness from that earlier genius's equally particular subjectivity. To translate this structure of relation into the language of reception theory: the later poet is aroused by the works of the earlier poet "to the feeling of his own originality, to exercise freedom from coercion in his art in such a way that the latter [i.e., art] thereby itself acquires a new rule," as if "nature gave the rule through a genius."[46] To Wordsworth, Shakespeare stands for—in Polixenes' enigmatic phrase from *The Winter's Tale*—"an art / Which does mend nature—change it rather; but / The art itself is nature" (4.4.95–7). The very terms of Kant's argument suggest Wordsworth's interpretive shock at recollecting the imaginative sympathy of Shakespeare's verse, and the contrary yet productive dislocation of self-consciousness that charged Wordsworth's imagination and at the same time grounded it in history.

---

[46] Immanuel Kant, *Critique of the Power of Judgment*, ed. Paul Guyer, trans. Paul Guyer and Eric Matthews (Cambridge: Cambridge University Press, 2000), 317–8. For a very different but compatible approach to the relation between the thought of Kant and that of Wordsworth, with special emphasis on "originality" as the vocation of a genius's exemplarity, see Timothy Gould, "The Audience of Originality: Kant and Wordsworth on The Reception of Genius," in *Essays in Kant's Aesthetics*, ed. Ted Cohen and Paul Guyer (Chicago: University of Chicago Press, 1982), 179–93.

## Chapter 5
# "Mature Poets Steal": Charlotte Smith's Appropriations of Shakespeare

### Joy Currie

In one of her final volumes, *Beachy Head, with other Poems* (1807), Charlotte Smith rewrites La Fontaine's fable "The Two Pigeons" as "The Truant Dove from Pilpay." To forestall criticism for "translating" a fable or for creating a talking bird, Smith calls upon several well-known literary names. Since her female dove "talks from Shakspeare," she explains in her preface, "I must take refuge under the authority of Chaucer; or rather his polisher Dryden; who makes his Dame Partlet quote Galen and Cato, while Chanticleer explains Latin sentences."[1] With these references, Smith displays the fact that she has read and learned from Dryden's translation of Chaucer into modern English (he claimed to be Chaucer's "polisher"),[2] while inviting her readers to consider her poetry in the same class as the works of these eminent male writers.[3]

While these allusions in *Beachy Head* appeared late in Smith's career (the volume was published posthumously), she began annotating her poetry in her very first volume, increasing the number and length of notes for particular poems as her career progressed. For example, she identifies quotations from Shakespeare and Milton in *Elegiac Sonnets* (1784), and affixes longer notes to Sonnet 77, "To the insect of the gossamer," and Sonnet 79, "To the goddess of botany," in Volume 2 (1797). Critics have noted Shakespearean allusions in the works of male poets of the Romantic period; however, no similarly extensive study of such allusive

---

[1] Charlotte Smith, *The Poems of Charlotte Smith*, ed. Stuart Curran (New York: Oxford University Press, 1993), 251. All references to Smith's poetry will be from this edition, with page numbers for prefaces and notes, and line numbers for poems.

[2] John Dryden, Preface to *Fables: Ancient and Modern*, in *The Poems and Fables of John Dryden*, ed. James Kinsley (London: Oxford University Press, 1962), 533.

[3] See Jacqueline M. Labbe, *Charlotte Smith: Romanticism, Poetry and the Culture of Gender* (Manchester, UK: Manchester University Press, 2003), 47–8. Judith Hawley, "Charlotte Smith's *Elegiac Sonnets*: Losses and Gains," in *Women's Poetry in the Enlightenment: The Making of the Canon, 1730–1820*, ed. Isobel Armstrong and Virginia Blain (London: Macmillan, 1999), 194, sees less confidence in Smith's identification with male writers.

practices in the poetry of Romantic women writers yet exists.[4] This essay seeks to begin such a study by examining Smith's appropriations of Shakespeare. Through allusions and quotations, she creates moments of shared emotion between her speakers, Shakespeare, and herself; appropriates his language and metaphors; claims authority for her use of natural history; claims equality with male writers; claims authority for her expression of political views; and develops extended analogies between Shakespeare's themes and characters and her own.

Good poets have long participated in a centuries-old practice of "stealing" from earlier writers.[5] Eighteenth-century poets, male and female, from Dryden to Erasmus Darwin, and from Lady Mary Wortley Montagu to Mary Robinson, often allude to and appropriate other writers, most frequently classical Latin writers, as well as Shakespeare, Milton, and Pope. Smith's female contemporaries, such as Frances Burney, Helen Maria Williams, Mary Robinson, and Ann Radcliffe, enhance their poetry and prose with literary references. For example, Radcliffe's "Titania to Her Love" and Robinson's "Oberon's Invitation to Titania" and "Titania's Answer to Oberon" all draw on Shakespeare's *A Midsummer Night's Dream*, while Williams incorporates uncited lines from Shakespeare and others in her poems and *Letters Written in France*.[6] Yet no other poet of the early Romantic period engages with Shakespeare at quite the same level as Smith, who refers to his plays more than to any other body of work, including Milton's.[7]

Shakespeare himself, of course, constantly borrows from other writers. He reworks Golding's translation of Ovid's *Metamorphoses*, Holinshed's *Chronicles*, and North's translation of Plutarch's *Lives*—adapting, for example, Golding's longer verse lines into iambic pentameter. Smith adopts a similar interpretive and adaptive model of appropriation. Her borrowings include the use and transformation of Shakespeare's lyric expressions, blank verse, prose, and song in her own various genres, much like the kind of generic crossing identified by G. Gabrielle Starr in her examination of the absorption of the lyric into the novel during the eighteenth century.[8] Smith draws on Shakespeare's dramatic lines for her own poetic

---

[4] See Jonathan Bate, *Shakespeare and the English Romantic Imagination* (Oxford: Clarendon, 1986).

[5] T. S. Eliot, "Philip Massinger," *The Sacred Wood: Essays on Poetry and Criticism* (New York: Knopf, 1930), 125. See also Robert Burton, *The Anatomy of Melancholy*, ed. Thomas C. Faulkner, Nicholas K. Kiessling, and Rhonda L. Blair (Oxford: Clarendon, 1989), 11.

[6] See Ann Radcliffe, *Romance of the Forest*, vol. 3 (London: Hookman and Carpenter, 1792), 150–51; Mary Robinson, *The Poetical Works*, vol. 3 (London: Routledge, 1996), 149–52; Helen Maria Williams, *Letters Written in France, In the Summer of 1790, to a Friend in England, Containing Various Anecdotes Relative to the French Revolution*, ed. Neil Fraistat and Susan L. Lanser (Peterborough, Canada: Broadview, 2001).

[7] In the Curran edition of the poems, I count 33 references to Shakespeare and 14 to Milton. There are many more references to Shakespeare in Smith's novels.

[8] G. Gabrielle Starr, *Lyric Generations: Poetry in the Novel in the Long Eighteenth Century* (Baltimore: John Hopkins University Press, 2004).

expressions. Other forms of generic crossing in Smith's works include the insertion of dramatic lines and phrases in prefaces and explanatory notes attached to poems, the placement of poems within her novels, and allusions to Shakespeare's dramatic characters as a means of developing her own poetic ones.

By the time Smith began writing, Shakespeare was firmly established as the national bard, the Homeric-like poet of the English people. In this capacity, both he and his works were adapted or appropriated variously as a symbol for the monarchy, the opposition, women, and middle-class morality, among other things.[9] Writers increasingly appropriated the playwright's words and characters for purposes other than that of dramatic adaptation. Lingering notions of Shakespeare as a "natural" and undisciplined writer offered women a model for achieving success without the credentials of a university education.[10] The plays, as well as the author, became a source of authority from which other writers could draw. As Jane Austen's character in *Mansfield Park* explains, Shakespeare's "celebrated passages are quoted by everybody; they are in half the books we open, and we all talk Shakespeare, use his similes, and describe with his descriptions."[11] Given Shakespeare's cultural status in the late eighteenth century, it is not surprising that Smith draws from Shakespeare's plays when creating intertextual moments in her work, since this practice would increase both her literary authority and her cultural capital.

Critics are increasingly aware of the care with which Smith controlled the production of her texts.[12] Others have noted her skillful use of male voices. Susan Wolfson, for example, observes Smith's ability to "write across gender," using, in *The Emigrants*, "men's texts and their traditions—sometimes in affiliation,

---

[9] See Jonathan Bate, *Shakespearean Constitutions: Politics, Theatre, Criticism 1730–1830* (Oxford: Clarendon, 1989); Michael Dobson, *The Making of the National Poet: Shakespeare, Adaptation and Authorship, 1660–1769* (Oxford: Clarendon, 1992); and Jonathan Brody Kramnick, *Making the English Canon, Print-Capitalism and the Cultural Past, 1700–1770* (Cambridge: Cambridge University Press, 1998).

[10] See Marianne Novy, "Women's Re-Visions of Shakespeare 1664–1988," in *Women's Re-Visions of Shakespeare* (Urbana: University of Illinois Press, 1990), 2–4.

[11] Jane Austen, *Mansfield Park*, in *The Novels of Jane Austen*, ed. R. W. Chapman, vol. 3 (London: Oxford University Press, 1933), 338. Quoted in Gary Taylor, *Reinventing Shakespeare: A Cultural History, from the Restoration to the Present* (New York: Weidenfeld & Nicolson, 1989), 110–11.

[12] See Judith Phillips Stanton, "Charlotte Smith's 'Literary Business': Income, Patronage, and Indigence," *The Age of Johnson* 1 (1987): 375–401; Sarah Zimmerman, "Charlotte Smith's Letters and the Practice of Self Presentation," *Princeton University Library Chronicle* 53 (1991): 50–77; Stuart Curran, "Charlotte Smith and British Romanticism," *South Central Review* 11, no. 2 (1994): 66–78; and Stuart Curran, "Romantic Poetry: Why and Wherefore?", in *The Cambridge Companion to British Romanticism*, ed. Stuart Curran (Cambridge: Cambridge University Press, 1996), 222.

sometimes in opposition."[13] In her investigation of the manipulation of gender in Smith's prefaces, notes, and verse, Jacqueline Labbe explains that the poet is "'self-aware' about her use of personae and voice."[14] In this essay, I argue that Smith was equally aware of the power of her appropriations and allusions. In particular, Smith's references, especially those to Shakespeare, function in two ways: claiming authority and deepening the impact of her verse. First, Smith sometimes makes in her prefaces the conventional disclaimer of women as inferior writers or unwilling participants in the field of letters (i.e., they must publish to support their families). Other times, she defends her methods in notes: she justifies her right to include scientific terminology, political ideas, and others' words in quotation. Her defensive practices suggest to me an authorial insecurity—not from the anxiety of influence, but from the anxiety of gender. Society has urged her to stay away from the public sphere, or at least from certain topics.[15] Smith needed approval for her work and thus continued to defend her literary practices throughout her career. Even more significant are the allusions and phrases she deliberately incorporates for artistic purposes: she finds words in the writings of others exactly suited to the feelings and thoughts she wishes to express in her verse.

While Smith's allusions and quotations act rhetorically to add variety and eloquence to her diction, as well as to evoke her sources and adapt their meaning, her allusions to esteemed, male writers also raise her own literary stature by situating her as an equal among them. In essence, Smith implies that her poetry can be associated with that of the greats of English poetry: Chaucer, Shakespeare, Milton, and Pope. References to such figures demonstrate both courage and pride on Smith's part—courage to create and publish in a male-dominated literary world, and pride in the quality of her poetry. This essay is concerned with both aspects of Smith's allusive practice—the hesitant and self-defensive, and the bold and self-promoting.

Smith's defensiveness surfaces most prominently in her prefaces and notes. In 1785, she was accused of plagiarism by "Scourge" (probably George Steevens) in

---

[13] Susan Wolfson, "Charlotte Smith's *Emigrants*: Forging Connections at the Borders of a Female Tradition," in *Forging Connections: Women's Poetry from the Renaissance to Romanticism*, ed. Anne K. Mellor, Felicity Nussbaum, and Jonathan F. S. Post (San Marino, CA: Huntington Library, 2002): 82, 118.

[14] Labbe, *Charlotte Smith*, 5. Labbe also argues that Smith's poetic personae present a series of artificial poses, poses that include her "complicated self-representation as grieving mother and needful woman" (75).

[15] Recent scholars note conflicting evidence as to the restrictions on women writers. See Sandra M. Gilbert and Susan Gubar, *The Madwoman in the Attic: The Woman Writer and the Nineteenth-Century Imagination* (New Haven, CT: Yale University Press, 1979), 64; Judith Pascoe, "Female Botanists and the Poetry of Charlotte Smith," in *Re-Visioning Romanticism: British Women Writers 1776–1837*, ed. Carol Shiner Wilson and Joel Haefner (Philadelphia: University of Pennsylvania Press, 1994), 198–201; William Stafford, *English Feminists and their Opponents in the 1790s: Unsex'd and Proper Females* (Manchester, UK: Manchester University Press, 2002).

the *Public Advertiser* for her translation of Prévost's *Manon Lescaut*, since two earlier English translations already existed. In response, Smith defends her work by writing that she "never pretended it was otherwise than a translation."[16] The real objection was the perceived immorality of the tale, and perhaps the fact that Smith was female.[17] However, she names more of her sources after this rebuke, writing self-consciously about her attributions in the preface to the third edition of *Elegiac Sonnets* (1786): "I have there quoted such lines as I have borrowed; and even where I am conscious the ideas were not my own, I have restored them to the original possessors" (*Poems* 4). She continued to reference other writers even after she had established herself in the field of letters, most likely due to the fear of literary censure. Anna Seward, for example, complains that Smith's sonnets are "made up of hackneyed scraps of dismality, with which her memory furnished her from our various poets."[18] Moreover, though she quickly reacted to such charges of "hackneyed" writing, Smith was aware that her politics may have been the real target, as when reviewers condemned her representation of adultery in *Desmond*.[19] In the preface to Volume 2 of *Elegiac Sonnets*, Smith ironically suggests that it was her political views that contributed to a considerably shortened subscription list: "As party can raise prejudice ... there are [some] who can never forgive an author that has, in the story of a Novel, or the composition of a Sonnet, ventured to hint at any opinions different from those which these liberal-minded personages are determined to find the best" (10). She must have been particularly sensitive to harsh reviews, such as the one in *The Critical Review* in which the writer observes a "decline in [her] genius."[20]

**Shared Emotions**

Many of Smith's sonnets, nearly half of which are written in the Shakespearean form, transform the Renaissance lament for an unattainable or lost love into an

---

[16] Quoted in Sir Walter Scott, *The Miscellaneous Prose Works of Sir Walter Scott, Bart.*, vol. 1 (Edinburgh: Cadell, 1847), 353–4.

[17] Smith to unnamed recipient, ca. September 1785, *The Collected Letters of Charlotte Smith*, ed. Judith Phillips Stanton (Bloomington: Indiana University Press, 2003), 7. See also Loraine Fletcher, *Charlotte Smith: A Critical Biography* (Basingstoke, UK: Palgrave, 2001), 82–4.

[18] Quoted in Stanton, *Letters*, 743n4. For examples of critics who praised Smith's poetry, see J. T., "An Essay on the English Sonnet; illustrated by a Comparison between the Sonnets of Milton and those of Charlotte Smith," *Universal Magazine* 91 (1792): 409; Samuel Coleridge, Introduction to *Sonnets from Various Authors*, in *The Complete Poetical Works of Samuel Taylor Coleridge*, vol. 2 (Oxford: Clarendon, 1912), 1139; William Wordsworth, *The Poetical Works of William Wordsworth*, vol. 4, ed. Ernest de Selincourt and Helen Darbishire (Oxford: Clarendon, 1947), 403.

[19] *The Critical Review* n.s. 6 (1792): 100; *The Monthly Review* n.s. 9 (1792): 412.

[20] *The Critical Review* 32 (May 1801): 35.

elegy for personal anxiety or loss. Perhaps because her own life was filled with worry over finances and grief over the deaths of children, Smith seems particularly attracted to Shakespeare's suffering characters and often incorporates their emotions into her speakers' expressions of sorrow. For example, she borrows the words of Constance in Shakespeare's *King John* in the final couplet of Sonnet 6, "To Hope," to help demonstrate her speaker's despair: "pale Misery's love!" (13). Before examining Smith's sonnet, however, let us look at the scene in Shakespeare's play, where Constance calls on Death much like a poet calls on a muse:

> Death, death. O amiable lovely death!
> .............................
> Come, grin on me, and I will think thou smil'st,
> And buss thee as thy wife. Misery's love,
> O, come to me! (*King John*, 3.4.24, 34–6)[21]

Constance is distraught for a specific reason: the King has taken her son Arthur away to prison, and she fears she will never see him again. Her intuition is correct; Arthur dies while trying to escape. In essence, Constance's words are *lyrical*—they express the personal emotion of the speaker. Shakespeare "absorbs" the lyric into his dramatic storytelling to increase our knowledge of his character and her situation. Constance blames the peace between King Philip of France and King John for Arthur's capture. Although spoken to an audience that includes Philip of France, the lyricism of her expression makes it nearly a soliloquy.

In the first two quatrains of Sonnet 6, Smith's speaker seeks to displace her emotional pain:

> O Hope! thou soother sweet of human woes!
> How shall I lure thee to my haunts forlorn?
> For me wilt thou renew the wither'd rose,
> And clear my painful path of pointed thorns?
> Ah, come, sweet nymph! In smiles and softness drest,
> Like the young Hours that lead the tender Year,
> Enchantress! come, and charm my cares to rest:—
> Alas! The flatterer flies, and will not hear! (1–8)

Finding no one to listen to her woes, and with Hope failing to respond, the speaker invokes another form of solace in the final couplet: "Come then, 'pale Misery's love!' be thou my cure, / And I will bless thee, who, tho' slow, art sure" (13–14). Smith relies on her readers' memory of the Shakespearean context where death is invoked, enhancing (or misremembering) the phrase "Misery's love" by adding the adjective "pale" to fill out the blank verse line. It is possible that Smith misremembers the Shakespearean passage, since she did not always have access to

---

[21] William Shakespeare, *The Riverside Shakespeare*, ed. G. Blakemore Evans, 2nd ed. (Boston: Houghton, 1997). All references to Shakespeare will be from this edition.

her books. Her letters indicate that she frequently asked her publishers for books so as to check her quotations, especially when she was away from her library.[22]

Smith usually expected her readers to be familiar with the lines she borrowed. However, in Sonnet 6, first published in *Elegiac Sonnets* in 1784, she identifies her source, perhaps to remind readers of this lesser-known play.[23] She undoubtedly wants us to think of Constance, yet she adapts Shakespeare's sense when she generalizes the terms of her speaker's neglect, thereby allowing readers to insert their own pain into the poem. Like Constance, her speaker feels betrayed by those who promised her aid, but we do not learn the specifics of this betrayal, as we do in the play. Smith also adapts the playwright's text by reversing his form of generic crossing: she absorbs his dramatic lines (although lyrical ones) into the emotional outpouring of her sonnet's speaker. Just as Starr recognizes that early novels incorporate forms of the lyric, I see Smith and Shakespeare each employing the lyric "for constructing shared emotional experience between characters and from character to reader,"[24] or from character to auditor. And finally, in adopting Constance's words and emotions for her sonnet, Smith transforms Shakespeare's dramatic line by reversing the Petrarchan practice in which the male speaks of, or for, the female, while using the dramatist to identify the gender of her speaker as female. In her sonnets, she speaks of, and for, her speakers, who are at various times male, female, and genderless. Smith also encourages us to believe that the speakers represent her, as Labbe notes in several other instances, but sometimes their femininity is merely "implied, hinted at, or suggested through allusion."[25] The same is true for Sonnet 6.

Often when Smith alludes to Shakespeare to express her speakers' emotions, she also intends that her readers equate their sorrows with her own. One significant example of this kind of self-reflective writing occurs in Sonnet 79, "To the goddess of botany." Smith's poetic speaker seeks a retreat from sorrow in nature, desiring an escape from the "Violence and Fraud" (2) of society. Instead, she would live with the goddess addressed in the title. In her note to this poem, Smith points

---

[22] Smith to William Davies, June 25, 1794, *Letters*, 131. Smith never says which editions of Shakespeare she read, but she asked her publishers to find her a concordance of his works. See Smith to Thomas Cadell, Jr., and William Davies, September 24, 1794, *Letters*, 165. It is possible that she consulted William Dodd, *Beauties of Shakespeare* (1752; New York: Augustus M. Kelley, 1971); *Bell's Edition of Shakespeare's Plays*, ed. Francis Gentleman, 8 vols. (1773; London: Cornmarket, 1969); Samuel Johnson, *The Plays of William Shakespeare* (London: Tonson, 1765); or Edmond Malone, *The Plays and Poems of William Shakespeare* (London: Rivington, 1821). These editions exhibit a similar kind of interest in the emotion of Shakespeare's characters that I find in Smith.

[23] Smith also attributes line 12 to Pope's "Imitation of the first Ode of the fourth Book of Horace."

[24] Starr, *Lyric Generations*, 8.

[25] Labbe, *Charlotte Smith*, 3, 102. On Smith's mixing of genders see also Adele Pinch, *Strange Fits of Passion: Epistemologies of Emotion, Hume to Austen* (Stanford, CA: Stanford University Press, 1996), 60–63.

out the existence of similar ideas in the writings of several other writers, aptly bringing together three unsociable figures, the young man in Milton's *Il Penseroso*, Shakespeare's Imogen from *Cymbeline*, and Rousseau himself, all of whom find healing in the company of plants: "'Rightly to spell,' as Milton wishes, in *Il Penseroso*, 'Of every herb that sips the dew' seems to be a resource for the sick at heart—for those who from sorrow or disgust may without affectation say 'Society is nothing to one not sociable!'" (*Poems* 68).[26] The last, uncited quotation here is from Shakespeare's *Cymbeline*, and with it Smith again adapts Shakespeare's context. Her speaker seeks a long-term removal from society for vaguely defined reasons, whereas Imogen's desire for solitude is specific and short lived. The latter seeks it because Posthumus thinks she is unfaithful, and because she can tell no one the reason for her sadness. Once they are reconciled, she will feel sociable again.

In the same note to Sonnet 79, Smith compares her own "real calamities" to that which "drove [Rousseau] from the society of men" with the following disclaimer: "Without any pretensions to those talents which were in him so heavily taxed with that excessive irritability, too often if not always the attendant on genius" (*Poems* 68). Smith affects the typical self-deprecating strategy for female writers of the time, when in fact she considers her work equal to that of these male writers.[27] At the end of her note, she compares her kind of suffering (presumably from the financial, social, and medical conditions that have driven her from society[28]) to Rousseau's through an allusion to another Shakespearean episode—the scene where Lear speaks to Cordelia of his anguish after she awakens him to the memory of his abuse:

> Perhaps, if any situation is more pitiable than that which compels us to wish to escape from the common business and forms of life, it is that ... where the sufferer, chained down to the discharge of duties from which the wearied spirit recoils, feels like the wretched Lear, when Shakespeare makes him exclaim "Oh! I am bound upon a wheel of fire, / Which my own tears do scald like melted lead." (68)[29]

---

[26] The Milton quotation is from *Il Penseroso*, 170–72, though slightly misquoted. The other quotation is from Shakespeare, *Cymbeline*, 4.2.12–13.

[27] For a discussion of Smith's note to Sonnet 79, see Labbe, *Charlotte Smith*, 47–8.

[28] Smith began publishing her poetry in 1784 to pay her husband's debts. He was imprisoned that year for several months. After suffering years of emotional and probably physical abuse, she separated from him in 1787 (not a legal separation). Hereafter, she was the breadwinner for her nine children, while they all waited for her father-in-law Richard Smith's will to be settled. The children who were living when he died were to receive the bulk of his estate. Unfortunately, other legatees were able to challenge the will, tying up the settlement in Chancery Court for years. For Smith's biography, see Florence May Anna Hilbish, *Charlotte Smith, Poet and Novelist* (Philadelphia: University of Pennsylvania Press, 1941); Carrol L. Fry, *Charlotte Smith* (New York: Twayne, 1996); and Fletcher, *Critical Biography*.

[29] See *King Lear*, 4.7.47–8.

Here and elsewhere, Smith deliberately dramatizes her plight by referencing dramatic scenes in order to highlight her personal dilemma and to evoke sympathetic feelings in her readers.

In both *Cymbeline* and *King Lear*, Shakespeare allows his characters to express their grief to others, though in different ways. Lear speaks to his daughter and the audience, Imogen speaks to her brothers. Imogen's brothers, however, do not understand the reason for her grief, and thus see her as unsociable. Like Constance's speech in King John, Imogen's words are lyrical and are directed primarily toward the audience, as if they were more part of a soliloquy than a piece of dialogue. Smith, too, speaks to her audience, appropriating Shakespeare's lyrical dramatic language for the prose expansion of Sonnet 79 in another form of generic crossing. Her collection of source materials as an aggregate whole, in the sonnet and its note, creates a mythology for her speaker's situation (which we are meant to see as Smith's own), by linking it to these real and fictional characters.[30]

**Shared Language and Metaphors**

As in Sonnet 6, the moods of anxiety and sorrow permeate Smith's verse, and she frequently appropriates other poets' words to help establish it. For example, her identification with Petrarch, whose poems she rewrites as Sonnets 13 through 16, and whose lines she borrows for the epigraph to the second volume of her poems, signals her melancholy subject and justifies it by demonstrating that she is not alone in writing of sorrow. In Sonnet 7, "On the departure of the nightingale," Smith's speaker longs for the bird to pour out her song on "the Night's dull ear" (4), a phrase from *Henry V*, and looks for the bird's return because it can offer relief: it moves the sorrowful as well as the lover through the beauty of its song. Both Smith and Shakespeare use the phrase as part of the atmosphere surrounding their respective characters.[31]

In *Henry V*, the Chorus sets the scene. As an actor and playwright, Shakespeare was aware of the purposes of the different features of drama, and his characters frequently comment on acting techniques and functions. For example, Ophelia tells Hamlet he is "as good as a chorus," when he explains the plot of "The Mousetrap" (*Hamlet*, 3.2.245). Shakespeare may have drawn on Senecan tragedy for the Chorus's role of describing the location and summarizing a portion of the plot, as when the Chorus in *Henry V* describes the physical and emotional atmosphere on the night before the defining battle at Agincourt: "Steed threatens steed, in

---

[30] Smith's ultimate act of self-mythologizing occurs in the frontispiece to Volume 2 of *Elegiac Sonnets*, where she identifies herself with Shakespeare's Egeon by metaphorically inscribing lines from *The Comedy of Errors* (they are printed in cursive) under her portrait, "as if the poet had written them herself." Zimmerman, *Romanticism*, 44.

[31] Smith also adapts lines from Milton's Sonnet 1—"Whether the Muse, or Love call thee his mate. / Both them I serve, and of their train am I" (13–14)—in her Sonnet 6: "The pensive Muse shall own thee for her mate" (7).

high and boastful neighs / Piercing the night's dull ear" (*Henry V*, 4.0.10–11).[32] The Chorus is able to evoke the mood of anticipation as experienced by various portions of the army on the night before the battle of Agincourt, briefly, without having to set up an elaborate dialogue. In her sonnet 7, Smith (as elsewhere) adapts Shakespeare's metaphoric language for a different circumstance (her speaker misses the song of her muse); she appropriates his descriptive dramatic language not as a reminder of his particular context, but as part of the setting in which her speaker lyrically expresses her relationship to the bird, to love, and to sorrow. This time for her attribution, she mentions only the playwright's name. As Bate points out in reference to canonical male poets of the Romantic period, writers at this time quoted Shakespeare "with the expectation that the original will be recognized and the felicity of its adaptation noticed."[33] Smith also expects readers to know the origin of quoted passages and to equate her speakers and contexts with Shakespeare's and, by implication, her lyric expressions with his dramatic ones, whether her uses of these passages are similar or widely different from the playwright's. Her acknowledgement of her source lets the reader know that Shakespeare, and not she, coined the personification, perhaps to deflect criticism for her choice of words. Later, for example, Smith claims that a reader had objected to her use of an obscure word in "Saint Monica" (*Poems*, 301n).

On occasion, Smith borrows a metaphor from Shakespeare to validate one of her own insights. For example, her speakers often find that the nurturing aspect of sleep helps some but not others. She appropriates the phrase "Nature's soft nurse" from *2 Henry IV* (3.1.6) in Sonnet 66, "Written in a tempestuous night on the coast of Sussex."[34] This poem originally appeared in *Montalbert: A Novel*. Her speaker F. Walsingham (who is neither named in the sonnet, where the speaker could be either male or female, nor given a complete first name in the novel) is not royalty, but he refers to his inability to sleep, just as King Henry does in Shakespeare's play.[35] The King cannot sleep because he is worried about the war he is currently waging and the irresponsible behavior of his son Prince Hal, the future king. The circumstances, however, are very different in Smith's poem and novel, where Walsingham writes the lines in a fit of despair over his lost love. The natural conditions provide the perfect atmosphere for the melancholy lover to reflect on his unhappiness:

> The night-flood rakes upon the stony shore;
> Along the rugged cliffs and chalky caves
> Mourns the hoarse Ocean, seeming to deplore

---

[32] See R. F. Hill, "Shakespeare's Early Tragic Mode," *Shakespeare Quarterly* 9 (1958): 456–7; Victoria Tietze Larson, *The Role of Description in Senecan Tragedy* (Frankfurt am Main: Peter Lang, 1994), 56, 70.

[33] Bate, *Shakespeare*, 34.

[34] See also Smith's Sonnet 9, "To Sleep," and Sonnet 74, "The Winter Night."

[35] Curran, ed., *Poems*, 58, and Labbe, *Charlotte Smith*, 97, incorrectly identify the "author" of Sonnet 66, as it appears in Smith's novel, as Sommers Walshingham.

All that are buried in his restless waves—
Mined by corrosive tides, the hollow rock
Falls prone, and rushing from its turfy height,
Shakes the broad beach with long-resounding shock,
Loud thundering on the ear of sullen Night;
Above the desolate and stormy deep,
Gleams the wan Moon, by floating mist opprest;
Yet here while youth, and health, and labour sleep,
Alone I wander—Calm untroubled rest,
"Nature's soft nurse," deserts the sigh-swoln breast,
And shuns the eyes, that only wake to weep![36]

As in the drama, the speaker in the poem cannot sleep well because he is troubled. Smith conveys Walsingham's emotion, in part, by the mixing of genres—both appropriating a phrase from a dramatic soliloquy for her lyric poem and placing a lyric poem inside a novel. This "inter-generic" exchange might also be seen as a challenge to ideas of literary decorum, perhaps another move away from standard critical opinion toward a proto-Romantic stance.

**Authority for Natural History**

Smith undoubtedly found in male writers a reliable means of self-authorizing. At the time she was writing, some readers thought it unseemly for a woman to study natural history. Richard Polwhele, for example, calls the study of botany "forbidden fruit" for women, since he wonders "how the study of the sexual system of plants can accord with female modesty."[37] Yet, Smith's letters and notes display her confidence to write about what she knew well, regardless of contemporary strictures against women. She justifies her "improper" incursion into the male territory of natural history by citing male authorities to verify her information, much as she alludes to male poets for other aspects of her poetry.[38] From close observation and instruction in painting, she developed an artist's skill of describing, which enabled her to particularize the natural settings in which her poetic speakers tell their stories. Since Smith found solace and a source of artistic inspiration in nature, incorporating her love of the countryside and the flora and fauna of her native Sussex came easily. For example, in Sonnet 5, "To the South

---

[36] See also Charlotte Smith, *Montalbert: A Novel*, vol. 3 (London: Sampson Low, 1795), 165.

[37] Richard Polwhele, *The Unsex'd Females: A Poem*, 1798, ed. Gina Luria (New York: Garland, 1974), 8. Polwhele cites Smith specifically for her "Gallic mania," not her botany, which is most evident in her poetry published after 1798. See Pascoe, "Botanists," 197–8, on the eighteenth-century debate over women's study of botany.

[38] Curran writes that Smith "annotates her generically different *Elegiac Sonnets* with knowing citations of Petrarch as a shorthand substitute for the learned disquisition she implies she could write on the subject." Curran, "Why and Wherefore," 222.

Downs," she describes her attraction to nature: "Ah! Hills belov'd!—where once a happy child ... I wove your blue-bells into garlands wild, / And woke your echoes with my artless song" (1–4). From the first edition of *Elegaic Sonnets*, she provides in her notes the Latin names of plants. Later, she seeks "authority" by referring to Erasmus Darwin and works of natural history in order to establish the accuracy of her knowledge, while also justifying her transgression of societal expectations. Such notes are a part of the overall conception of her poetry. She explains to publisher Joseph Johnson that *Beachy Head* needs "numerous [notes] because of historical, biographal & local facts relative to Beechy & the Coast. ... The [other] poems too which relate to natural history will want notes" as well.[39]

Allusions to Shakespeare that are interspersed with scientific references function for Smith as a means of equating herself with men. A telling example occurs in Sonnet 77, "To the insect of the gossamer," where her speaker expresses her sorrow. The poem begins:

> Small, viewless Æronaut, that by the line
> Of Gossamer suspended, in mid air
> Float'st on a sun beam—Living Atom, where
> Ends thy breeze-guided voyage;—with what design
> In Æther dost thou launch thy form minute
> Mocking the eye? (1–6)

In a note to line 1, Smith acknowledges Dr. Lister and Erasmus Darwin for information about the spider that produces the gossamer. Smith then exploits Shakespeare as the "natural" poet when she describes the mechanism of the spider's thread and identifies it as the variety he writes of in *Romeo and Juliet*: "These filmy threads form a part of the equipage of Mab: 'Her waggon spokes are made of spiders legs, / The cover of the wings of grasshoppers, / The traces of the smallest spider's web'" (*Poems* 66).[40] In the poem itself, Smith's speaker expresses the notion that "the young and visionary Poet leaves / Life's dull realities" (11–12) by writing poetry. However, the solace the speaker finds is as vulnerable as the spider is to the "Swift" (8), a bird Smith describes as "a kind of swallow that feeds on insects" (67n). The interplay between the poem, its note, and Shakespeare's play sets up an analogy between the action of the insect and the poet's craft. In *Romeo and Juliet*, Mercutio speaks of lovers' and others' dreams of desire, not the escape Smith's speaker seeks. Shakespeare envisions the imaginary world of dreams, which is like the fictional world of creation; Smith's speaker seeks a dream-like fictional world as a means of escaping an unpleasant reality, while referencing both the dream of the play and the insect that attempts to hide from its prey.

Later in her note to Sonnet 77, Smith compares Juliet's waiting for Romeo to her speaker's (and by implication the author's own) waiting for "the golden

---

[39] Smith to Joseph Johnson, July 12, 1806, *Letters*, 741.
[40] See *Romeo and Juliet*, 1.4.62–4. Smith slightly misquotes the passage here.

thread that Fancy weaves" (9) and "Hope's illusive flattery" (10): "Juliet, too, in anxiously waiting for the silent arrival of her lover, exclaims, 'Oh! So light of foot / Will ne'er wear out the everlasting flint; / A lover may bestride the Gossamer / That idles in the wanton Summer air, / And yet not fall'" (66).[41] Although Smith omits Shakespeare's final phrase in the speech, "so light is vanity," her substitution of Juliet as speaker rather than Friar Laurence rightly makes Romeo, not Juliet, the vulnerable one; Romeo, after all, shows his cowardice when he thinks of taking his life in Laurence's cell. The change in gender and speaker (which is perhaps necessary to make her point) takes nothing away from Smith's analogy, but rather intensifies the meaning she creates in her reinterpretation of the play. It solidifies the relationship she wants to construct between Shakespeare's characters, the spider, and her own precarious existence as an author.

Two more instances in which Smith seeks to establish her ability to use scientific terminology occur in her long poem *Beachy Head*. In one section, she describes the location of a ruined mansion, where a rustic lives nearby. In the night air, he hears, among other things, a "night jar, chasing fern-flies" (514). To point out the originality of her usage, Smith's note refers to a pamphlet written by Dr. John Aikin, *An Essay on the Application of Natural History to Poetry*. Aikin lists the examples of the cockchafer in poetry, the insect or beetle found in Shakespeare's *Macbeth*, Milton's *Lycidas*, Gray's "Elegy written in a Country Church-Yard," and Collins's "Ode to Evening." Although he finds quality in their imagery, he is critical of a "propensity to imitation" and a lack of "original observations of nature."[42] Shakespeare, for example, "paints the approach of night," when Macbeth tells Lady Macbeth not to fear Banquo:

> be thou jocund; ere the bat hath flown
> His cloister'd flight, ere to black Hecate's summons
> The shard-borne beetle with his drowsy hums
> Hath rung night's yawning peal, there shall be done
> A deed of dreadful note. (3.2.40–44)

Macbeth has ordered the murder of Banquo and Fleance to be carried out before night. The image of the humming beetle may be commonplace, but Shakespeare's reminder of the witches' involvement in Macbeth's evil dealings through his reference to Hecate goes beyond mere repetition. His piling up of details vividly creates the mood for a bloody night when a bell should peal, or toll, for Banquo. Although Aikin fails to appreciate Shakespeare's originality in his use of the figure (or perhaps he gives him more credit for being the first cited to use it), on this occasion Smith takes the doctor's assessment as valid:

---

[41] See *Romeo and Juliet*, 2.6.16–20.

[42] Dr. John Aikin, *An Essay on the Application of Natural History to Poetry* (London: Warrington, 1777), 7, 9.

> I remember only one instance in which the more remarkable, though by no means uncommon noise, of the Fern Owl, or Goatsucker, is mentioned. It is called the Night Hawk, the Jar Bird, the Churn Owl, and the Fern Owl ... It was this bird that was intended to be described in the Forty-second Sonnet [Smith's sonnet]. I was mistaken in supposing it as visible in November; it is a migrant, and leaves this country in August. I had often seen and heard it, but I did not then know its name or history. (*Poems* 239)

Smith uses this opportunity to correct her earlier error in Sonnet 42, while subtly pointing out the fact that she seeks scientifically accurate information and directing attention to her images, which she feels are superior to those Aikin finds hackneyed.

Later in *Beachy Head*, in a more obvious effort toward equating herself to, and even surpassing, well-known male writers by "correcting" a past master, Smith informs the reader of Shakespeare's error by naming the color of the cuckoo flower in a song (another genre) from *Love's Labour's Lost* (5.2.894). Even as she corrects, however, she is aware of the relationship between Shakespeare's context and her own. Her rustic, who lives in a ruined "mansion" (506), lists this flower in one of his verses (within Smith's longer poem) as a variety "strewn" (591) along the ground. In this pastoral setting, he imagines his beloved, a woman who may not love him in return. His final lines give evidence of his anxiety:

> "Ye phantoms of unreal delight,"
> ........................
> ... leave me drooping and forlorn
> To know such bliss can never be,
> Unless Amanda love like me. (649, 652–4)

Similarly, Spring claims, in a song at the end of *Love's Labour's Lost*, that the cuckoo's song is a "word of fear, / Unpleasing to a married ear!" (5.2.901–2), an idea derived from the auditory relationship between the cuckoo's call and the word "cuckold."[43] After identifying the playwright's error, Smith speculates on the reason for it: "Shakespeare describes the Cuckoo buds as being yellow. He probably meant the numerous Ranunculi, or March marigolds (*Caltha palustris*) which so gild the meadows in Spring; but poets have never been botanists. The Cuckoo flower's scientific name is *Lychnis floscuculi*" (242).[44] Later, Shakespeare might have learned the correct color, since the caption in John Gerard's *Herbal* (1597) points out that the cuckoo flower is white, not yellow. According to J.

---

[43]  Ibid., 246n901.

[44]  Two species known as cuckoo flowers are *Lychnis* and *Cardamine pratensis*, or Lady's Smock. Neither is yellow. For Smith's "ironic self-reference," see Jacqueline Labbe, "'Transplanted into More Congenial Soil': Footnoting the Self in the Poetry of Charlotte Smith," in *Ma(r)king the Text: The Presentation of Meaning on the Literary Page*, ed. Joe Bray, Miriam Handley, and Anne C. Henry (Aldershot, UK: Ashgate, 2000), 84.

W. Lever, Gerard was often Shakespeare's source for the names of the flowers;[45] however, *Love's Labour's Lost* probably predates Gerard. Smith gives no source for her more accurate botanical information; however, earlier in the poem she cites standard works of botany and geology: Sowerby and Smith's *English Botany*, Thomas Martyn's edition of Philip Miller's botanical dictionary, and Gilbert White's *The History of Selbourne* (1789).[46] Whatever her sources, her critique of Shakespeare's lyrical reference to this flower is direct, purposeful, and it is included to inform the reader of her own superior botanical skill.

**Authority for Political Views**

Although Smith "corrects" Shakespeare in the previous example, she usually quotes from his plays or mentions his name or his characters to lend prestige and credibility to her work. Absorbing his blank verse lines into her own in *The Emigrants*, she "describe[s] with his descriptions" the conditions for French emigrants and Britons, locating her expressions in a particular time (April 1793) and setting (the Southern coast, where emigrants were frequently seen, some of whom lived for a while in her home).[47] During the height of the war with France, she borrowed other writers' words to make political statements, often gleaning phrases and ideas from Milton rather than Shakespeare.[48] However, in *The Emigrants*, she also appropriates lines from Shakespeare's history plays to express the horror of war a few months after the execution of Louis XVI. In the opening of section of Book 2, Smith describes how she wishes the land looked on "the brow of May" (2.35). Instead, however, she sees the headless corpse of a king, a population fearful and in disarray, and a land "blasted" (2.76) by war. Of the war between Britain and France, which began in February, she writes:

> There, taunting in the van
> Of vengeance-breathing armies, Insult stalks;
> And, in the ranks, "Famine, and Sword, and Fire,
> Crouch for employment." (2.76–9)

In the opening of *Henry V*, Shakespeare's Chorus claims that, if "a Muse of fire" (1) can be summoned to invent a stage and various princely characters,

---

[45] For Gerard's illustration and description of the cuckoo flower, see *The Riverside Shakespeare*, 212.

[46] James Sowerby and Sir James Edward Smith, *English Botany* (1790–1814). Curran, *Poems*, 236, identifies the second text as Thomas Martyn, *The Gardener's and Botanist's Dictionary ... by the late Philip Miller ... To Which Are Now Added a Complete Enumeration and Description of All Plants* (1797–1807).

[47] Smith to Joseph Cooper Walker, February 20, 1793, *Letters*, 62.

[48] Not only does *The Emigrants* contain Miltonic echoes, Smith's attitude toward the failings of the French clergy is reminiscent of Milton's, in his own time, toward those who favored the monarchy over a republican form of government.

the King will appear as he was: a fierce, destructive warrior ready to control the traditional instruments of battle, an image perhaps borrowed from Henry's speech in Holinshed. The Chorus looks forward to a successful reclamation of part of France for England, although not without describing the horrors of battle. Later the Duke of Burgundy relates to the French king the devastation that the war has brought: France's "vine, the merry cheerer of the heart, / Unpruned dies" (5.2.41–2). Smith recalls these lines when describing a similar devastation in her own time in her novel *The Banished Man* (3:68), similar to the way that she uses Shakespeare in *The Emigrants*. In *Henry V*, Shakespeare resists giving us a single opinion on the King's war; instead, as is his usual method, he "fills the play with competing, critical voices."[49] Smith's commentary is also multivocal, although perhaps more obviously political. She encourages her readers to question the actions of those who have sought their "liberty" through the violence of war, while also condemning those who would give up the principles of liberty because of that violence. Thus, her appropriation of Shakespeare in *The Emigrants* and *The Banished Man* exhibits her ability to adapt a source while retaining the context of the original.[50] Although Smith credits Shakespeare for the borrowed lines about Henry, she reminds us of the death of a later king and how "Freedom's name" has been "usurp'd and misapplied" by the revolutionaries (81).

Smith turns Shakespeare's context around in a second reference to *2 Henry IV* just a few lines later in *The Emigrants*, by making the victims of kings and tyrants her subject. Her narrator reminds those who would have the world return to "the purple Tyrant's rod" (2:82) to remember the victims of "regal crimes / Committed to destroy" human freedom (88–9):

>                rather count
> The hecatombs of victims who have fallen
> Beneath a single despot; or who gave
> Their wasted lives for some disputed claim
> Between anointed robbers: Monsters both!
> "Oh! Polish'd perturbation—golden care!"
> So strangely coveted by feeble Man
> To lift him o'er his fellows. (2:90–96)

Smith quotes Shakespeare's Prince Hal, who contemplates the notion that kings have trouble sleeping because of their responsibilities. Henry IV's earlier musings in Act 3 prepares us for the Prince's thoughts as he watches his sleeping and dying father: the cares of state bring "polished perturbations, golden care! / That keeps the ports of slumber open wide / To many a watchful night!" (4.5.23–5). A few lines later, Hal observes another sort of port or portal: "By the gates of breath / There lies a downy feather which stirs not" (31–2), a piece of evidence that

---

[49] James Shapiro, *A Year in the Life of William Shakespeare, 1599* (New York: Harper, 2006), 92.

[50] See Bate, *Shakespeare*, 88–9, who comments on the Shakespearean context in Wordsworth's appropriation of the same passage.

convinces him that his father is dead. Even though he recognizes the burdens of kingship, Hal places the crown on his own head, an act that incurs a severe reprimand when his father awakes.

Transferring "Prince Hal's ambivalent regard of his destined crown" to her own verse, as Wolfson puts it, Smith speaks of those who suffer at the hands of those in power, whereas Hal thinks of his or his father's anxiety of office.[51] She is disgusted with those in her own country as well as in France who feel that liberty might not be worth the price—those "Deluded Men" (2:83)—and those in France who have turned violent after gaining power. Smith never wavered in her belief in the principles of the Revolution; however, she condemned war and its consequences. She most likely had in mind the latter part of Shakespeare's scene, where the king scolds his son. However, she connects the familial quarrel of Shakespeare's scene with another familial quarrel that caused misery for the innocent as well as the powerful, in a note accompanying the phrase "Monsters both" (*Poems* 152). Although Smith omits any direct references to her own suffering in this part of the poem (see instead 2:5-8, 347-63), she suffered her own "disputed claim" in the long delay of the legal settlement of Richard Smith's will. Her children's claim was challenged by other branches of the family, and, in fact, some of the trustees, who frequently denied her funds, were also relatives. In this way, her implicit analogy between political and familial conflicts suggests that those who are oppressed suffer the same, whether political or legal victims.

**Extended Analogies**

Smith's appropriations are the most powerfully executed when she borrows from Shakespeare for longer passages or an entire poem to develop a theme. Her references do what Bate observes of the "most sophisticated form of imitation" in the male Romantic poets: they "establish creative tension between the original and new contexts."[52] Smith seems to have Shakespeare's Macduff (whose wife and children are killed on Macbeth's order) in mind when she describes the personal cost of political unrest in *The Emigrants*. Her French "feudal Chief" (2:292) returns home, where "at the vacant gate, no Porter sits / To wait his lord's admittance" (296–7) from "distant lands" (294), to find his family all dead (although in Shakespeare's play the porter who is present works for Macbeth, not Macduff).[53] Like Shakespeare's noble Scotsman, Smith's Chief returns to an empty castle:

> He sees that devastation has been there:
> Then, while each hideous image to his mind
> Rises terrific, o'er a bleeding corse

---

[51] Wolfson, "Smith's *Emigrants*," 109.
[52] Bate, *Romantic Imagination*, 31.
[53] Smith also borrows Macduff's words "such things were" to express her speaker's inability to forget the loss of a loved one in Sonnet 90, "To Oblivion." See *Macbeth*, 4.2.222.

> Stumbling he falls; another interrupts
> His staggering feet—all, all who us'd to rush
> With joy to meet him—all his family
> Lie murder'd in his way! (2:302–8)

Although Macduff does not see his slaughtered family (Rosse tells him of it), both he and Smith's Chief lose their families for fighting for what they believed is right: Macduff for the recovery of Scotland from a tyrant, and the Frenchman for resisting the changes to his country. Smith's poem points out one of the worst miseries of war—the loss of loved ones—yet she changes Shakespeare's outcome. Macduff, upon the counsel of Malcolm, channels his grief into the courage to seek out his enemy, though he still "feel[s] it as a man" (*Macbeth*, 4.3.221). Smith's chief, however, who has no single enemy, succumbs to madness from his loss: "the day dawns / On a wild raving Maniac" (2:308–9). Shakespeare emphasizes the need to set aside the personal for the good of the nation: Rosse says to Macduff, "your eye in Scotland / would create soldiers, make our women fight, / To doff their distresses" (4.3.186–8) and Malcolm says of Macduff's grief, "Be this the whetstone of your sword, let grief / Convert to anger; blunt not the heart, enrage it" (4.3.228–9). Smith's poem, by contrast, represents the experience of grief almost entirely in terms of personal sorrow.

In another extended analogy, in Book 1 of *The Emigrants*, Smith considers the emigrants and her country's politicians as generalized groups. Using a form of soliloquy and blank verse, as Shakespeare does in *King Lear*, Smith develops an unidentified echo, along with an antipastoral statement that contradicts ideas common to romance about prosperous and poetic shepherds:

> Poor *wand'ring wretches!* Whoso'er ye are,
> That hopeless, *houseless*, friendless, travel wide
> O'er these bleak russet downs; where, dimly seen,
> The solitary Shepherd shiv'ring tends
> His dun discolour'd flock (Shepherd, unlike
> Him, whom in song the Poet's fancy crowns
> With garlands, and his crook with vi'lets binds);
> *Poor vagrant wretches!* Outcasts of the world!
> Whom no abode receives, no parish owns;
> Roving, like Nature's commoners, the land
> That boasts such general plenty. (296–306, my emphasis)

Similarly, Shakespeare's Lear views his wretches in realistic terms, realizing his errors of omission:

> *Poor naked wretches*, wheresoe'er you are,
> That bide the pelting of this pitiless storm,
> How shall your *houseless* heads and unfed sides,
> Your loop'd and window'd raggedness defend you
> From seasons such as these? O, I have ta'en
> Too little care of this!" (*King Lear*, 3.4.28–33, my emphasis)

In deliberately echoing Shakespeare's lines, Smith allegorizes the French emigrants, although not without judging their previous lives of extravagance in France.[54] Many emigrants were formerly wealthy but carried little with them or lost it while escaping from France. Smith draws a direct parallel between the failings of Shakespeare's Lear and these people. Like Lear, some of them brought their woes upon themselves, and some were also blind to the sufferings of *their* poor. Nevertheless, her poem also condemns leaders and citizens of England and France. She cultivates sympathy for the French as victims of war when she criticizes their treatment at the hands of those in government, those "worthless hirelings of a Court" (1:329), blaming her prejudiced leaders and other countrymen and women, who only want the emigrants (especially the Catholic ones) to go away. Wolfson believes that writing this Lear-like passage was "to court a political risk by evoking the British king whose madness in 1788 had made him politically vulnerable."[55] Interestingly enough, however, Smith's contemporary reviewers paid little attention to the political tenor of her poem. Perhaps it seemed, in 1793, a more loyalist poem than it actually is. Only the *Critical Review* notes her description of the horrors of war in connection with the passage on the Dauphin, and it omits any mention of her "wand'ring wretches."[56]

Like her allusions in *The Emigrants*, Smith's appropriations from Shakespeare help her develop the character of the female dove in "The Truant Dove, from Pilpay," the poem mentioned at the beginning of this essay. In her version of the poem, which is longer and more detailed than La Fontaine's, the truant dove wishes to leave his home in order to learn more about the wider world and to find new topics for conversation. Even before he informs his female mate about his intentions, the female dove knows that "all was not right" and attempts to smooth things out: "She with dissembled cheerfulness 'beguiled / The thing she was,' and gaily coo'd and smiled" (68–9). Like Desdemona, the dove dissembles her true feelings in an attempt to charm her mate into staying at home. In *Othello*, Desdemona describes her feelings while listening to Iago engage in suggestive wordplay. As Francis Gentleman argues in *Bell's Edition of Shakespeare's Plays* (1773), "through the whole of this scene, Iago expresses himself most indecently to his wife, and barefacedly impudent to Desdemona."[57] Iago has just jokingly slandered his wife's character. To divert her thoughts (although unsuccessfully), Desdemona plays along. However, she anxiously awaits the arrival of her husband, whose ship was delayed by weather and possibly a skirmish with the Turks: "I am not merry; but I do beguile / The thing I am by seeming otherwise" (*Othello*, 2.2.32–3). Although in different contexts, both Smith's Dove and Desdemona exhibit anxiety about their mates.

---

[54] See Labbe, *Charlotte Smith*, 118.
[55] Wolfson, "Smith's *Emigrants*," 105.
[56] *Critical Review* 9 (1793): 301.
[57] Gentleman, ed., *Bell's Shakespeare*, 1:175.

Smith adapts another line in "The Truant Dove," this time from *Macbeth*, to further describe the female Dove's concern about her mate's intended excursion:

> "If it be so," exclaim'd his hapless wife,
> "It is my fate, to pass my days in pain,
> To mourn your love estrang'd, and mourn in vain;
> Here in our once dear hut to wake and weep,
> When your unkindness shall have 'murder'd sleep.'" (83–7)

In Shakespeare's play, after killing Duncan, Macbeth thinks he "heard a voice cry 'Sleep no more! / Macbeth does murther sleep'" (*Macbeth*, 2.2.32–3). He speaks these lines to his wife, who criticizes him for giving in to his fears. However, Smith's female dove is no murderer. Instead, she alludes to the sleepless nights she anticipates during her mate's absence. In both the play and Smith's poem, the speakers contemplate insomnia for different reasons: Macbeth's guilt causes his own sleeplessness, while Smith's female dove worries that her mate will find "some new love" (91), perhaps a veiled reference to Smith's own unfaithful husband. While away from home, the truant dove avoids several near-disasters, but ultimately he is shot down by a hunter. His mate finds him lying by the bank of a stream, and she and their "feather'd young" (244) carry him to a high rock to nurse him back to health. Smith's strategy for developing characters in her novels, which includes allusions and quotations, carries over into this poem and enriches the female dove's character by providing her with intelligence and sensitivity.[58] Consequently, the absorption of dramatic forms within Smith's lyrics not only indicates a sophisticated handling of different forms and generic crossings between Shakespeare's plays and her poetry, but also the adaptation of dramatic techniques in her own poetry and novels.

\* \* \*

The variety of Smith's references to Shakespeare is impressive: she borrows from eleven plays—nearly a third of the canon—just in the examples given here. Among Romantic poets, only her later contemporaries Wordsworth and Keats engage with Shakespeare more often. Smith's appropriations take the form both of quotation, as in "Verses intended to have been prefixed to the novel of *Emmeline*, but then suppressed": "The proud man's contumely, th' oppressor's wrong" (2),[59] and of allusion, as in "Written for the benefit of a distressed player, detained at Brighthelmstone for debt, November 1792," which contains an acknowledged reference to Portia's "quality of mercy":[60]

---

[58] Stuart Curran observes Smith's novelistic technique in her sonnets. See *Poetic Form and British Romanticism* (New York: Oxford University Press, 1989), 30.

[59] See *Hamlet*, 3.1.70. Smith reverses the two phrases.

[60] See *The Merchant of Venice*, 4.1.186–7.

> Oh! ye, whose timely bounty deigns to shed
> Compassion's balm upon my luckless head
> Benevolence, with warm and glowing breast,
> And soft, celestial mercy, doubly blest! (66–9)

Here, Smith compares the blessings her own benefactors have received to what will come to those who assist the distressed players. She crosses genres when she imports Shakespeare's dramatic lines into verse and prose apparatuses. When she incorporates his lines in instances of shared emotions, language, and metaphor, when she seeks authority for writing about natural history and politics, and when she creates extended metaphors to support her poetical themes and characterizations, Smith consciously and deliberately reminds readers of the his characters and plots. These reminders establish a continuity, which situates her as a poet in an historic mainstream, not in a female periphery. Like Smith, who is grateful for her supporters, we too are "doubly blest" when we pay attentions to her references, for they increase our understanding of, and appreciation for, her verse, while allowing us to find additional pleasure in the richness of what she borrows from Shakespeare.

# Chapter 6
# The Sublimity of *Hamlet* in Emily Dickinson's Poem, "He Fumbles at Your Soul"

## Marianne Noble

While all eyes in America were on the Civil War, Emily Dickinson turned her eyes inward in a battle of her own. She spent four months in 1864 and again six months in 1865 in Boston undergoing treatment for eye problems. The treatment required her to remain in a dark room for much of the time, avoiding bright light and eye-straining tasks in order to cure what was most likely a case of anterior uveitis, or inflamed iris.[1] In a later letter to her friend Joseph Lyman, she called this period "eight months of Siberia" because the doctor had shut out "all her dearest ones of time, the strongest friends of the soul—BOOKS."

> Well do I remember the music of the welcome home. It was at his office. He whistled up the fox hounds. He clapped and said "Sesame." How my blood bounded! Shakespear [sic] was the first; Antony & Cleopatra where Enobarbus laments the amorous lapse of his master. Here is the ring of it.
>
> "heart that in the scuffles of
> great fights hath burst the
> buck[l]e on his breast"
>
> then I thought why ~~touch~~ clasp any hand but this. Give me ever to drink of this wine. Going home I flew to the shelves and devoured the luscious passages. I thought I should tear the leaves out as I turned them. Then I settled down to a willingness for all the rest to go but William Shakespeare. Why need we Joseph read anything else but him.[2]

---

[1] Alfred Habegger, *My Wars Are Laid Away in Books: The Life of Emily Dickinson* (New York: Random House, 2001), 487.

[2] Richard B. Sewall, *The Lyman Letters: New Light on Emily Dickinson and Her Family* (Amherst, MA: University of Massachusetts Press, 1965), 76. Following Lawrence Levine, we could posit that the Bardolatry here may be part of Dickinson's unconscious effort to construct a middle-class or elite subjectivity. Lawrence W. Levine, *Highbrow/Lowbrow: The Emergence of Cultural Hierarchy in America* (Cambridge, MA: Harvard University Press, 1988).

This letter illuminates Dickinson's priorities as a reader and as a writer.[3] The Shakespearean passage that so affects her is remarkable for its mirrored pairing of rich sound with an arresting visual image. She emphasizes the "ring of it"; the fifteen words quoted feature alliteration, internal rhyme, and vigorous iambs interrupted by a strong spondee. It has two particularly rich words: "scuffle" and "buckle." Bursting with sound, this passage aurally mirrors the image it portrays: the heart of a valiant fighter bursting the buckle on his breast plate. Evidently, for Dickinson, excellent poetry masterfully arranges sound and sense so that they reinforce and intensify each other.

This passage not only impressed Dickinson; it also inspired her to attempt a similar virtuosity of language in her own letter. Ecstatic metaphors tumble forth as she strives to describe the effect of these "luscious" lines; she clasps hands with Shakespeare's poetry; it is like wine; she flies to the shelves and devours the pages, practically tearing the pages out. Reading *Antony and Cleopatra* is like returning home and like discovering an Aladdin's cave of treasures. She also feels as if she were on a fox hunt, her blood bounding like a dog in pursuit of its prey. As full of artistic effects as its source, Dickinson's letter is self-reflexive; it describes the overwhelming effects of reading *Antony and Cleopatra* and it simultaneously attempts to produce such effects for Joseph. She *could* have said, "The doctor says I can read now." But by saying he "whistled up the fox hounds. He clapped and said 'Sesame,'" Dickinson attempts to create for Joseph an equally luscious literary wine, an equally magical Aladdin's cave, and an equally exciting fox hunt. Her letter also strives to create rich sonic effects. "Give me ever to drink of this wine" alters conventional syntax, creating an anapestic meter that has the galloping effect suggested by the image of a fox hunt. And one is tempted to speculate that she misattributed the passage to Enobarbus rather than Philo because of the luscious sound of that name, particularly when it is situated in the anapestic and alliterative clause "Enobarbus laments the amorous lapse." This letter models a pattern that Dickinson followed in the many responses to Shakespeare that characterize her career. Her famous poem "He Fumbles at Your Soul," written in late 1862, can also be read as an encomium to, and imitation of, Shakespeare's sophisticated union of form and content. As in the letter to Joseph Lyman, in "He Fumbles at Your Soul" Shakespeare's virtuosity is represented as a source of inspiration, a subject of discussion, and a model to be imitated and possibly surpassed. This poem, which I will refer to by its number in Ralph Franklin's variorum edition of Dickinson's poetry, 477, is a familiar and admired poem, but scholars have

---

[3] Her quotation is not quite accurate. The passage, which is from the opening speech of Antony and Cleopatra, is spoken by Philo, not Enobarbus, and it reads as follows: "His captain's heart, / Which in the scuffles of great fights hath burst / The buckles on his breast, reneges all temper, / And is become the bellows and the fan / To cool a gipsy's lust" (1.1.6–10). Dickinson's lineation of this passage makes the first line seem trochaic, but it is not. All references to Shakespeare are from *The Norton Shakespeare*, gen ed. Stephen Greenblatt (New York: W. W. Norton, 1997).

not fully appreciated its masterful artistry because they have not recognized its complex intertextuality. The poem not only comments upon and epitomizes the sublime effects of poetry, but it does so by alluding to and competitively imitating the sublimity of Shakespeare's dazzling interplay of sound and sense in *Hamlet*.

The source for Dickinson's poem is the Player's soliloquy in *Hamlet*, which describes the hesitation Pyrrhus feels before killing Priam and his successful act of regicide. The speech epitomizes what the Romantics—and many others too—admire in Shakespeare, which is his masterful creation of dramatic scenes that portray universal psychological states. Many of us know the experience of wavering in the face of decisive action, the uncertainty or inability to take a decisive action that has momentous consequences, and the story of Pyrrhus wavering before Priam creates an arresting visual image of that vacillation, thereby making our interior psychological state dramatic, vivid, and concrete. Moreover, the speech displays a technical mastery of poetic effects that reinforce the exterior image aurally and somatically. As a result, the Player's auditors feel the dramatic scene in their bodies. I propose that Dickinson's poem 477 is about the sublimity of great poetry in general, and about the Player's monologue in particular. The dazzling intertwining of sound and sense in the Shakespearean passage promotes the sublime feeling of being overwhelmed by the poet's artistry, particularly since the passage describes an act of slaying, thereby powerfully suggesting the daunting check that is the first phase of the sublime. Not surprisingly, Dickinson's lyric shifts the point of view from Pyrrhus to Priam, since her concern is not, like Hamlet's, with the problem of indecision, but with the painful and pleasurable experience of waiting to receive that fatal blow. In general, Dickinson's verse does not, like Shakespeare's, exteriorize psychological states; instead it focuses directly upon interior experiences themselves. Shakespeare describes a man about to commit regicide; Dickinson uses that image as a metaphor for a reader's experience of the poetic sublime.

Reading the poem as an engagement with *Hamlet* challenges an oft-held belief that Dickinson's engagements with Shakespeare appear most frequently not in poems but in letters, and mostly in letters written after the experience following her eye treatments, which is viewed as a turning point for her. In *Emily Dickinson's Shakespeare*, Parraic Finnerty writes:

> Her recorded public engagement with Shakespeare, and much of her praise of him, comes after her eye trouble in the mid-1860s. It also follows the period when she wrote the majority of her poems. ... Moreover, she largely excluded reference to Shakespeare ... from her poetry; to the extent that critics find her indebtedness to him insignificant or irrecoverable.[4]

Finnerty does discuss several allusions to Shakespeare in the poems, but the broad impression of his study concurs that her poetic engagements with Shakespeare

---

[4] Pàraic Finnerty, *Emily Dickinson's* Shakespeare (Amherst: University of Massachusetts Press, 2006), 132.

are largely insignificant or irrecoverable. Alfred Habegger insists that the relative absence of Shakespeare in the early work is no accident:

> Certain at age twenty that Shakespeare could write nothing "wicked," Dickinson had to do a great deal of growing up before he could become an invigorating presence for her. ... [A]pparently listening to [her cousins] Louisa and Frances's own recitations [of Shakespeare during the Boston eye treatments], she seems to have had her ears opened, and to have left Cambridge with a voracious desire to read for herself.

Habegger also writes that "prior to that, there is little or no evidence of enthusiasm" for Shakespeare on Dickinson's part.[5]

These critics may deem the allusions to Shakespeare in Dickinson's poetry "irrecoverable" or simply not there at all because Dickinson does not allude directly, as she does in letters. But the allusions are there, and recoverable, as several critics have observed. Jack Capps, for example, writes, "Shakespeare's influence on Emily Dickinson was an absorption that took place over a long period, leaving marks that can be best discerned by careful scrutiny in bright light."[6] He was indeed "an invigorating presence for her," even in the years of her most intense poetic creation. As Paula Bennett recognizes, his influence was "deep and pervasive, a matter of identification as well as apprenticeship"; Bennett claims that it "must be teased out of brief allusions and felt in the complicated patterns of imagery which encode Dickinson's thought. It is not there for the asking."[7] Richard B. Sewall writes:

> Sometimes a single word in one of the plays startled her with its enormous, implied drama. She wrote Judge Lord five years after the death of his wife: "Antony's remark to a friend, 'since Cleopatra died' is said to be the saddest ever lain in Language—That engulfing 'Since'—"[8]

To recognize the weight of the word "since" requires an immersion in the worlds of both Dickinson and *Antony and Cleopatra*. Although Sewall claims that "the few verbal echoes [of Shakespeare] in her poems are insignificant," he believes that "the tone and spirit, the exhilaration and encouragement, were everything."[9] But it is not just a question of tone and spirit; the "verbal echoes" are both

---

[5] Habegger, *My Wars Are Laid Away in Books*, 490, 255.

[6] Jack L. Capps, *Emily Dickinson's Reading: 1836–1886* (Cambridge, MA: Harvard University Press, 1966), 66.

[7] Paula Bennett, "'The Orient is in the West': Emily Dickinson's Reading of Antony and Cleopatra," in *Women's Re-Visions of Shakespeare*, ed. Marianne Novy (Urbana: University of Illinois Press, 1990): 108.

[8] Richard B. Sewall, *The Life of Emily Dickinson* (New York: Farrar, Straus and Giroux, 1980), 703.

[9] Ibid., 704.

recoverable and significant.[10] Indeed, Joan Kirkby persuasively argues that Dickinson's intertextuality in general may be the key that unlocks the mystery of the unique vitality of her poetry. It "breathes" because allusions infuse it with cultural *energia* (a term Kirkby borrows from Stephen Greenblatt). There is no good reason for scholars to perpetuate the notion that Shakespeare was primarily a late-in-life passion for Dickinson. The influence is present in the poetry, just not as directly as it is in her later correspondence. In her early twenties, at the same time that she was committing herself to her vocation as a poet, she attended a Shakespeare Club, from September 1850 to June 1852.[11] We know that the family circle studied *Hamlet* in anticipation of a lecture by Richard Henry Dana; a cousin spent a whole morning at the Dickinsons' reading Shakespeare; and the whole group attended "An Evening with Shakespeare: An Elocutionary Entertainment" by Miss Lizzie Johnson.[12] In 1859, Dickinson wrote to a cousin, "I have heard many notedly *bad* readers [of Shakespeare], and a fine one would be almost a fairy surprise."[13] These incidental anecdotes imply a pattern of early and lifelong engagement with Shakespeare. We just need to understand how she used him in her poetry.

Dan Manheim offers a valuable theory for understanding some of Dickinson's use of allusions. He argues that the beginning poet found her unique voice through competitive revision of other poets. He labels her process of engagement "signifying," borrowing Henry Louis Gates's term to describe "critical parody through repetition and difference," or what Ralph Ellison calls "a technical assault against the styles which have gone before" in order "to create a new narrative space."[14] Dickinson "had to clear her literary voice of some of the styles which had gone before, and she did so through creatively parodying, or signifying upon,

---

[10] For good relatively recent examples of nuanced and comprehensive analyses of particular Shakespearean passages, see Kristin M. Comment, "Dickinson's Bawdy: Shakespeare and Sexual Symbolism in Emily Dickinson's Writing to Susan Dickinson" *Legacy* 18, no. 2 (2001): 167–81; Bennett, "The Orient"; Vivian R. Pollak, "Emily Dickinson's Literary Allusions," *Essays in Literature* 1 (1974): 54–68; Benjamin Lease, *Emily Dickinson's Readings of Men and Books: Sacred Soundings* (New York: St. Martin's Press, 1990); Judith Farr, "Emily Dickinson's 'Engulfing' Play: Antony and Cleopatra," *Tulsa Studies in Women's Literature* 9, no. 2 (1990): 231–50; Eleanor Heginbotham, "Dickinson's 'What If I Say I Shall Not Wait!'," *Explicator* 54, no. 3 (1996): 154–60; and Finnerty, *Emily Dickinson's Shakespeare*. Elizabeth Petrino advances the term "echo" (borrowed from John Hollander) to characterize Dickinson's allusions to Keats and Shakespeare. "Allusion, Echo, and Literary Influence in Emily Dickinson," *Emily Dickinson Journal* 19, no. 1 (2010): 80–102. Jack Capps's book is an indispensable resource for all source studies of Dickinson. Capps, *Emily Dickinson's Reading*.

[11] Sewall, *Life*, 701.

[12] Ibid.

[13] Ibid.

[14] Daniel Manheim, "The Signifying Spinster: How Emily Dickinson Found Her Voice" *ESQ* 51, no. 4 (2005): 215–16.

popular authors of her day."[15] Manheim focuses upon Dickinson's revisions of popular poets, such as Longfellow, Bryant, and several sentimental poets. However, although Dickinson does engage in competitive revision of Shakespeare, "critical parody" is not the right way to think about her engagements with him. Rather, I would describe them as respectful and competitive imitations. As Jack Capps writes, "Dickinson considered Shakespeare as material to be admired, quoted, and absorbed, but not presumed upon. Although she could be impudent with the deity, she displayed remarkable reverence for mortal Shakespeare."[16] Moved by the sublimity of Shakespeare, Dickinson strove to achieve similar sublimity, though clearly within her own voice. In 477, for example, she loosely imitates the Shakespearean sonnet form in writing fourteen lines but jettisons the blank verse in favor of her own terse and compact style. Likewise, while images flow smoothly from one to another in Shakespeare, Dickinson's transitions are more abrupt and disorienting. Her imitation and appropriation, as is the case for all of her formal and imagistic allusions to Shakespeare, function as a springboard that inspires and enlarges her own writing, rather than as the somewhat contemptuous revision that Manheim discusses with regard to lesser poets. Her goal is not to show what can rightly be done with the same material (as it is with lesser poets) but to allow her own emotional responses to formulate themselves in invention. Her allusions are a flowering of her own ideas and phrases that is inspired by and grounded in the original act of reading.

The allusions to *Hamlet* in 477 must, as Bennett puts it, "be felt in the complicated patterns of imagery."[17] In the scene from *Hamlet* that influenced 477, the Players have just arrived at Elsinore Castle, and Hamlet requests that the Player recite one of his favorite speeches—one that Polonius finds too long, but that Hamlet insists is "caviare to the general" (2.2.418), exquisite but too subtle to be appreciated by the average playgoer. The speech narrates the slaying of Priam by Pyrrhus, the son of Achilles, who is seeking revenge for the death of his father. The Player begins by describing Pyrrhus hunting for Priam:

>                     Anon he finds him,
> Striking too short at Greeks. His antique sword,
> Rebellious to his arm, lies where it falls,
> Repugnant to command. Unequal match,
> Pyrrhus at Priam drives, in rage strikes wide;
> But with the whiff and wind of his fell sword
> Th'unnervèd father falls. Then senseless Ilium,
> Seeming to feel his blow, with flaming top
> Stoops to his base, and with a hideous crash
> Takes prisoner Pyrrhus' ear. For lo, his sword,
> Which was declining on the milky head

---

[15] Ibid., 216.
[16] Capps, *Emily Dickinson's Reading*, 65.
[17] Bennett, "Orient," 108.

> Of reverend Priam, seem'd i'th'air to stick.
> So, as a painted tyrant, Pyrrhus stood,
> And, like a neutral to his will and matter,
> Did nothing.
> But as we often see against some storm
> A silence in the heavens, the rack stand still,
> The bold winds speechless, and the orb below
> As hush as death, anon the dreadful thunder
> Doth rend the region: so, after Pyrrhus' pause,
> A rousèd vengeance sets him new a-work;
> And never did the Cyclops' hammers fall
> On Mars his armour, forged for proof eterne,
> With less remorse than Pyrrhus' bleeding sword
> Now falls on Priam. (2.2.448–72)

Dickinson's invention in 477 is grounded in the total effect of the Player's speech, and her debt is most palpably felt in her repetition of a few words within the context of her repetition of a few intertwined metaphors and images.[18] A central image in both poems is the preternatural "calm before the storm," a natural image that both poets use to characterize a scene in which a man is about to inflict a mortal blow upon an utterly helpless and passive victim, and then delivers it. In both cases, the victims are stunned into a paralyzed stillness, breathlessly anticipating the devastating blow, which—in the climax of both—descends with deadly force upon their heads. The allusion in 477 is perhaps most evident in a comparison of the following passages:

> But as we often see against some storm
> A silence in the heavens, the rack stand still,
> The bold winds speechless, and the orb below
> As hush as death. (*Hamlet*, 2.2.463–6)

> When Winds take Forests in their Paws –
> The Universe – is still – (477, 13–14) [19]

---

[18] Dickinson's poems often offer variant words, which she indicates with a plus sign next to the word and a variant listed below the poem. There are two manuscript versions of poem 477. The earlier, which is the version used here, was sent to Susan Dickinson in or around late 1862. The other version appears in Fascicle 22, one of the handmade books into which Dickinson copied the majority of her poems. This latter version incorporates in the poem the choices I list as alternatives and it lists as alternatives the choices incorporated in the body of the variant I present. Thus, for example, the fascicle copy presents the final couplet thusly: "When Winds hold Forests in their Paws – / The Firmaments – are still – ."

[19] Lines from 477 "He fumbles at your soul" and 348 "I would not paint a picture" in this chapter reprinted by permission of the publishers and the Trustees of Amherst College from THE POEMS OF EMILY DICKINSON: VARIORUM EDITION, edited by Ralph W. Franklin, Cambridge, Mass.: The Belknap Press of Harvard University Press, Copyright © 1951, 1955, 1979, 1983 by the President and Fellows of Harvard College.

The only words common to both are "still" and "winds." Nonetheless, the two passages achieve similar effects. Both portray the stillness of the natural world right before a storm, looking at the entire natural world from a lofty perspective that reduces it to a small thing. In Shakespeare, the entire planet is reduced to a hushed "orb" below the rack of clouds. In Dickinson, the winds take control of forests just as a cat takes a mouse in its "Paws," a word that cleverly creates an aural pun on the word "pause." In both cases, the natural world is still, silent, frozen before the impending deathly blow. In both cases another natural image, a thunderbolt, is used to describe the cataclysmic blow descending upon a head:

> anon the dreadful thunder
> Doth rend the region....
> Pyrrhus' bleeding sword
> Now falls on Priam. (*Hamlet*, 2.2.466–72)

> One – imperial – Thunderbolt –
> That scalps your naked Soul – (477, 11–12)

The dramatic pause is shattered by the violent crack that unleashes all of the devastating force of fury that had been pending. Many readers have expressed confusion about the closing couplet of 477, and in fact the poem has often been published without it.[20] But that is a mistake. The poem is a variation upon the Shakespearean sonnet, and as in that tradition, the couplet succinctly sums up the meaning of the poem as a whole.[21] The relation of the couplet to the poem as a whole is clearer when we recognize it as part of a coherent juxtaposition of images that first appear in the Player's soliloquy. It comments upon the significance of the pause before a thunderbolt strikes, the central image in both poems.

This pause and the subsequent cataclysm is the key to the sublimity of both works. One of the most persuasive and insightful readings of 477 is Dominic Luxford's essay, which interprets the poem as Dickinson's description of the sublime force of poetic inspiration.[22] Dickinson famously told Thomas Wentworth Higginson, "If I read a book [and] it makes my whole body so cold no fire ever can warm me I know *that* is poetry. If I feel physically *as if the top of my head were taken off*, I know *that* is poetry. These are the only way I know it" (L342, a second emphasis added). Poetry is recognizable through an overwhelming physical effect that produces the negative pleasure that Romantic poets often referred to as "the sublime." In this respect, the poem reiterates one of the central ideas of her poem 348, which explicitly advances an affective, sublime understanding of poetry by calling it "the Art to stun [readers] / With Bolts – of Melody." This phrase is

---

[20]  Franklin notes that the poem was first published in 1896, using the fascicle version with the alternatives for lines 9 and 12 adopted and the final couplet omitted.

[21]  Wolff discusses it in relation to the Shakespearean sonnet of courtship. Cynthia Griffin Wolff, *Emily Dickinson* (Reading, MA: Perseus Books, 1988), 280.

[22]  Dominic Luxford, "Sounding the Sublime: The 'Full Music' of Dickinson's Inspiration," *Emily Dickinson Journal* 13, no. 1 (2004): 51–75.

strongly echoed in 477, which similarly uses images of thunderbolts and stunned readers, as well as an image of taking off the top of the head:

> He stuns you by degrees –
> … the Ethereal Blow …
> Deals – One – imperial – Thunderbolt –
> That scalps your naked Soul – (4–12)

To be scalped is to "feel physically as if the top of [one's] head were taken off." Luxford suggests that the central message of 477 is that the act of reading and writing poetry is a violent yet sublime experience of being overwhelmed by an external force. The poem actualizes this idea in a series of metaphorical variations, using images of being struck by lightning, scalped, peeled open, hammered, and played upon. Luxford argues that the poem describes Dickinson's own sublime encounter with the abstract force of poetic inspiration, named "He" in the poem. Luxford further argues that the poem does to readers what inspiration did to its author: it fumbles at *our* souls, dealing "bolts of melody" in the form of powerfully patterned sounds. Luxford suggests that the alliterations emphasize sensuality. Clever rhymes lull us into a hypnotic trance. The metrical patterning makes readers experience in their bodies an initial tentativeness, an approaching feeling, a building crescendo, and then a direct hit: "Deals – One – imperial – Thunderbolt –" (11). Physically engaged by the poem's musicality even as we are mentally destabilized by our inability to make sense of it, we are in the author's power. Weakened and overwhelmed, we have been prepared to experience the elated expansion of being associated with the aesthetic sublime.

Luxford's analysis of the ways the prosody of 477 creates a physical and emotional experience of the very thing the poem describes is masterful and persuasive. However, I disagree with his claim that the "He" in the poem is poetic inspiration. The argument is simplified and improved if we assume that the "He" in the poem is the poet, the maker of the sublime object (the poem). Dickinson describes the effects of reading a sublime poem; readers experience the effects of a sublime poem. (This reading poses little threat to Luxford's interpretation since, as we saw in Dickinson's discussion of "Enobarbus," the act of reading is itself inspiring for Dickinson. There is no reason to rule out inspiration as one of the important consequences of reading a sublime poem.) Luxford's strong reading is enhanced if we recognize that the "He" in this poem is not any poet, but Shakespeare. The Player's soliloquy narrates the slaying of a king, and that slaying is a good image of what Shakespeare does to his auditors. It is also a good image of what Dickinson does to her readers, also through a masterful blend of images and musical effects.

Dickinson's emotional response to the Player's speech flowered into 477 in response both to focuses on its patterns of images and its prosody. Let us consider the speech's imagery. When Pyrrhus first comes upon him, Priam is fighting poorly because he is so old. Pyrrhus swings but misses because he is so enraged. Priam, however, is so weak that the wind of the passing sword is enough to topple him over.

Pyrrhus is about to strike the deadly blow, but the fall of Priam magically induces the fall of Troy, and Pyrrhus is distracted by the "hideous crash." The soliloquy goes on to present four increasingly complex images all striving to characterize Pyrrhus's inability to take action. (Hamlet's passion for this particular speech now makes sense.) First, his sword seems to "stick" in the air. Second, he is compared to a tyrant in a painting, poised to strike but perpetually unable to complete his action. Third, he is compared to "a neutral to his will and matter," passive with regard both to his "will"—his determination to kill—and his "matter," the physical enactment of that determination. The fourth simile for Pyrrhus's inaction, the most elaborately developed of the four, is the one we have already encountered:

> But as we often see against some storm
> A silence in the heavens, the rack stand still,
> The bold winds speechless, and the orb below
> As hush as death, anon the dreadful thunder
> Doth rend the region ... (2.2.463–7)

This is the grandest of the four similes, comparing Pyrrhus's indecision to the momentary silencing of the entire natural world before a violent storm.

Hamlet of course would have been miserable if the speech had ended there, for he craves the reassurance that pauses of indecision are followed by decisive debacles, both in nature and in human lives. He receives this reassurance as the Player continues:

> so, after Pyrrhus' pause,
> A rousèd vengeance sets him new a-work;
> And never did the Cyclops' hammers fall
> On Mars his armour, forged for proof eterne,
> With less remorse than Pyrrhus' bleeding sword
> Now falls on Priam. (2.2.467–72)

Just as the stillness before a storm is inevitably rent by thunder, so too Pyrrhus inevitably takes vengeance on his father's killer. Two comparisons—thunderstorms and blacksmithing—interweave to communicate Pyrrhus's slaying of Priam. Actually, these two similes are natural counterparts of each other. Roman and Greek cultures imagined that thunder is the sound of God's hammering at a forge, making the lightning bolts that Jupiter hurls. And according to Roman mythology, the Cyclops not only helped Vulcan make the bolts of lightning that Jupiter threw, but they also fashioned the armor that Mars wore. And because the soliloquy draws upon this mythology, the blacksmith image duplicates the actual scene that the Player is describing, for Priam is himself wearing armor during this scene, so that the image of the Cyclops' hammers falling on armor, like their hammers falling to make thunderbolts, mirrors the image of Pyrrhus's sword falling upon Priam. However, the armor is of no avail for Priam, for "after Pyrrhus's pause, / A rousèd vengeance sets him new a-work," and Pyrrhus hacks away at Priam's milky head with no more remorse than the Cyclops might feel hammering on armor.

Critics of Dickinson's 477 often fail to point out that the poem develops imagery of blacksmithing to describe the preparation of our soul for divine assault. The phrase "prepares your brittle nature" refers directly to blacksmithing, a comparison that is more evident in the alternative word choice, "brittle substance." In this respect, it is akin to her poem "Dare you see a soul at the white heat?" Both poems build upon the fact that blacksmiths cannot immediately do what they want with a metal—in its usual state, it is too brittle and will break. Blacksmiths steadily hammer hot iron in order to beat out carbon and other impurities. So, when you see a blacksmith at work, you notice pieces flaking off while he's hammering; those are the impurities being worked out. When he is done the iron becomes less brittle and more pliable. Dickinson's blacksmith follows this process; he "prepares your brittle substance" for the heavy-duty blow to come, using first soft hammer blows ("fainter hammers"), then more aggressive blows ("nearer" ones) which he combines with increasing heat, until the brittle substance has achieved its maximum heat. This is an important image for the preparation of our souls to receive God, and for the preparation that readers undergo before feeling the sublime effects of poetry. A great part of the aesthetic pleasure in this poem lies in the sophisticated intertwining of the blacksmithing and thunderstorm similes—the way that the hammers have duple meanings. In fact, in the Dickinson poem, the hammers have triple meanings, for they are also associated with the hammers of the piano upon which "the player at the keys" is playing, first "faint[ly]," "then nearer." And "the player" itself is a significant word. The fact that she calls her pianist a "player" is not coincidental; it is the name of the character who recites the passage to which she alludes.

The piano imagery encourages us to read 477 as a commentary upon the musical aspects of Shakespeare's "stunning" virtuosity. The lightning bolts in the poem are also bolts of melody, piano melodies. As we have seen, Luxford demonstrates the remarkably melodic aspects of 477, its "pause – crescendo – assault" metrical pattern culminating in "One – imperial – Thunderbolt" and its lulling effects of alliteration and rhyme. But it is important to recognize that her prosodic work is a variation on the musicality of her Shakespearean source. The prosody of the Player's speech modeled for Dickinson how to mirror visual images with aural effects that dramatically enhance the sublime effect of the poem.

The Player's speech epitomizes the possibilities for sonic mastery in poetry. It emphasizes deliberate sound patterning in its use of alliteration throughout: Pyrrhus and Priam; "whiff and wind"; "father falls"; "senseless ... seeming ... stoops"; "prisoner Pyrrhus." These alliterations emphasize the words' material rather than semantic capacities. The musicality of the Player's speech also appears in the lines after the dramatic, all-important half-line, "Did nothing." They feature a "pause, crescendo, and assault" pattern (to adapt Luxford's phrase) that might have been the model that inspired Dickinson's own realization of that pattern in 477:

> But as we often see against some storm
> A silence in the heavens, the rack stand still,
> The bold winds speechless, and the orb below

> As hush as death, anon the dreadful thunder
> Doth rend the region: so, after Pyrrhus' pause,
> A rousèd vengeance sets him new a-work (*Hamlet*, 2.2.463–8)

The passage opens with repeated "s" and "sh" sounds, which create a feeling of whispering—"see, storm, silence, stand still, speechless, hush"; a hushed feeling is encouraged by the fact that the subject itself is silence. This sibilance yields to a pattern of repeated "d" sounds: "death, dreadful thunder doth rend." This is a more pronounced thudding sound. It is followed by "rend the region," and "Pyrrhus' pause," which are still more vigorous, since paired initial consonants have a more staccato effect; the alliterations are increasing in intensity. The first five lines of the passage also have a number of metrical variations that create a pause. The phrase "the rack stand still" places three strong stresses side-by-side, a strong variation that stops forward momentum. The lines "Doth rend the region, so, after Pyrrhus' pause" and "As hush as death, anon the dreadful thunder" both have eleven syllables; and the former has a pronounced caesura that interrupts the flow of an already uncomfortable line. The first five lines are broken up with commas and parenthetical, explanatory phrases that prevent a flowing rhythm from developing and keep it at a slow pace.

All of this pausing and postponing contrasts with the unusual regularity, the unremitting beating, of the next lines, which speed up the tempo:

> And never did the Cyclops' hammers fall
> On Mars his armour, forged for proof eterne,
> With less remorse than Pyrrhus' bleeding sword
> Now falls on Priam. (2.2.469–72)

These lines are metrically unvarying, enjambed so that there is no pause from line to line, uninterrupted by syntactical vagaries. They have a steady and pulsing meter, created by a heavy preponderance of falling phrases. (Falling sounds arise when a passage uses many trochaic words). In a falling rhythm, the meter is regular, even in tempo, though the stresses of intensity are very strong, creating a strong, steady beat. You might march to "And never did the Cyclops hammers fall on Mars's armour forged for proof eterne," but never to a line with a rising rhythm such as "But with the whiff and wind of his fell sword," even though both are iambic. Shakespeare uses these falling phrases precisely at the moment when he describes the steady hammering of Cyclops on Mars's armor, and that meter anticipates the blows that Pyrrhus is about to rain down. Virtuoso writing like this allows us to visualize the falling of the blows as well as feel them in the meter. Having brought us to the brink, Shakespeare then deals the imperial blow: "Now falls on Priam." The climactic action is briefly stated in a line that feels incomplete. The Player's speech is virtually all build-up, dealing its climax with understatement and matter-of-factness. Readers are startled by the abruptness of this climax.

The Player's speech does to readers precisely what Pyrrhus does to Priam: it overwhelms them with its convergence of physical, imagistic, and emotional power. The aural effects of its metrical pacing, falling phrases, and alliteration render readers physically vulnerable, like Priam with his head bowed before the wrath of Achilles' son. The effects upon readers are physical: the body is made cold, the top of the head is lifted off. Dickinson seems to have been fascinated by the way the readers experience what the passage describes, and she imitates precisely this effect in 477. Her passage describes a great poet playing upon us, working upon our souls and bodies through an overwhelming artistry whose intricate interweaving is so dazzling that as our understanding of it grows increasingly subtle, we are increasingly like a mouse held in the paws of a cat, like a piece of metal being transformed at the will of a blacksmith, like a forest subjected before a sublime wind. Finally, we cannot take it anymore, and the poet takes off the tops of our heads, "Deals – One – imperial – Thunderbolt." She takes her place with Shakespeare as the divine, all-powerful wind; we are the forest through which it blows; the Poet is the Player and we are the played upon; the Poet is the Indian and we are the scalped victims, slain by his mastery.[23] (The variant "peels your naked soul" heightens the feeling of savagery.)

But if that is the case—if Shakespeare is a supreme master of such sublime effects, then why would Dickinson describe what he does with the word "fumbles," a word suggesting a bungler, an amateur, someone who drops the ball? The poem does not go on to develop a tone of amateurishness; words like "prepare" and "deal" suggest deliberateness and mastery. The second trope in the poem invites us to cluster different associations with the word "fumble," suggesting that it is less about amateurishness than indifference. Players fumble at the keys before they begin playing not because they cannot play but because they have not begun to play in full earnest. But if they are great artists, the poem suggests, the simple fact of their warming up begins to touch our souls, hinting at a sublimity that will only be fully achieved when they really get down to it. This Player is sublimely indifferent to any trauma his slight effects might be having on our souls. He does not care about our small egos, and we feel that he is fumbling at our souls. His indifference cannot help but feel offensive to us. The word "fumble" reminds us to resent the sublimity of reading Shakespeare, the invasion and domination of the self by alterity. We need to bear in mind: this resentment is a necessary part of the sublime, which is a *negative* pleasure. According to Kant in the *Critique of Judgment*, the sublime is first an encounter with something vastly larger than

---

[23] My claim that Dickinson admires the sound and technical mastery of Shakespeare, particularly as it mirrors sense, challenges Gary Lee Stonum's claim that with regard to Shakespeare, Dickinson refers "primarily to characters and dramatic speeches rather than to theme or style. Dickinson may thus have admired Shakespeare most for what Keats called his negative capability, the art coming from the embodiment of character more than sheer verbal skill or a capacity to express the poet's own thoughts and feelings." Gary Lee Stonum, "Dickinson's Literary Background," in *The Emily Dickinson Handbook*, ed. Gudrun Grabher et al. (Amherst: University of Massachusetts Press, 1998), 54. The letter to Joseph Lyman quoted in the beginning of this essay directly emphasizes "the ring" of Shakespeare rather than character or negative capability.

the self; second, a momentary check, feeling humbled and impotent; and third, a rebounding exhilaration of one's soul taking flight. In order to experience the expansion beyond our limited self, we had to endure the unpleasant recognition of our own smallness and insignificance. That humiliating subjection is a necessary precursor to our encounter with the immortal divinity that is our nature and our destiny. Before Shakespeare can slay us with immortal beauty, he must humble us with no more respect for our autonomy than Pyrrhus had for Priam's.

There is an important difference between *Hamlet* and 477. In *Hamlet*, the Player is so moved by his own narration that he bursts into tears. Hamlet is astounded and envious that

> this player here,
> But in a fiction, in a dream of passion,
> Could force his soul so to his own conceit
> That from her working all his visage wanned,
> Tears in his eyes, distraction in 's aspect,
> A broken voice … (2.2.528–33)

Dickinson might have shared Hamlet's amazement and envy at the ability of the Player to "force his soul so to his own conceit" that he is physically subdued by it. We do not expect artists to be subdued by their own art. Dickinson describes something similar but uses the subjunctive—suggesting impossibility—when she writes in another poem:

> Nor would I be a Poet –
> It's finer – Own the Ear –
> Enamored – impotent – content –
> The License to revere,
> A privilege so awful
> What would the Dower be,
> Had I the Art to stun myself
> With Bolts – of Melody! (Fr 348)

Here Dickinson expresses the desire both to create and receive sublime effects. Usually, reverence and being stunned are experiences enjoyed by auditors, not by poets themselves. It is expected that Players will "force" the souls of their audiences to their conceits, but not that they will themselves be overcome by their conceits. Dickinson does experience both effects, but separately. Before Shakespeare's mastery, she is merely a mouse; but before her own readers, she is the autonomous, all-powerful wind. Shakespeare's Player epitomizes an artist who is both, who "stun[s him]self / With Bolts – of Melody."

Dickinson may not be able to feel the sublime effects of her own virtuosity, but she is able both to stun and to be stunned. While the average auditor of poetry may only be stunned, as an impotent and content Ear, such an image does not characterize Dickinson's experience with Shakespeare. For Dickinson, the impotence of being stunned and slain is followed by the rebounding desire to do the same, competitively and respectfully. This vaulting response is part of the pleasure of the poetic sublime. According to Kant, the sublime does not leave a reader in the state of humiliated consciousness of his own impotence. Instead, the "momentary check" is followed by a rebounding leap. The confrontations of Dickinson's "enamor'd ear" with Shakespeare's "bolts of melody" do not simply leave her envious and impotent. While Shakespeare "fumbles" at her soul, the experience does not end with that feeling of belittlement; it does not entitle her merely to the "ceaseless poverty" of mute subjection (Poem 446). Instead, the experience typifies the Romantic sublime; it shatters her petty ego, preparing her brittle nature so that she can receive the influent influx of totality, oneness. The result is enormously empowering, inspiring her to try her own hand at authorial mastery in the effort to describe her experience. Just as the brief passage from *Antony and Cleopatra* caused Dickinson to pour forth luscious encomiums that stake her own claim to artistry, so too in 477 she pays homage to Shakespeare while leaping deliberately into his ranks, staking her own claim for immortality. No longer Priam beneath the remorseless sword of Shakespeare, she picks up the sword of Pyrrhus and swings straight at our own soon-to-be-naked scalps.

How intentional and conscious are the links between 477 and the Player's speech? Dickinson explicitly stated that she avoided all reference to other authors in her own poetry. In an August 1862 letter to Higginson, she wrote, "I marked a line in One Verse—because I met it after I made it—and never consciously touch a paint, mixed by another person—I do not let go it, because it is mine" (L271). She claims the verse is hers, but, as she herself acknowledges, she has unintentionally quoted another author. One wonders what Dickinson would have thought about the following poem after reencountering its likely source in *Jane Eyre*:

> My River runs to Thee –
> Blue Sea – Wilt welcome me?
> My River waits reply.
> Oh Sea – look graciously!
> I'll fetch thee Brooks
> From spotted nooks –
> *Say* Sea – take me? (219)

A similar sentiment is spoken by Jane the night before her wedding to Rochester: "I thought of the life that lay before me—*your* life, sir—and existence more expansive and stirring than my own: as much more so as the depths of the sea to which the brook runs are than the shallows of its own strait channel" (285). Is this echo a verse she would have "marked"? Is the resemblance merely coincidental? Or is it a deliberate engagement with Bronte? If we take Dickinson at her word, we rule out the possibility of direct engagement. But in the absence of any firm knowledge, I find it most plausible to suggest that Dickinson's mind was porous, unusually receptive to the striking language in the books she read. We all think in language, and the vocabulary of Dickinson's thought is more literary than most people's. She lived in literature, experienced life through the filters of the books she was reading. Their ways of framing issues informed her own speech, helping her express specific ideas and also resonating broadly and symbolically. Dickinson, like many readers, inhabited a psychological space opened up by someone else's work; words and rhythms from that work would come to her to characterize not only the mood of that space but the questions she considered while she was in it. Thus, for example, "My River Runs to Thee" is infused with the atmosphere of erotic sublime that characterizes *Jane Eyre* in general. It is a flowering invention upon Bronte's passage. Likewise, 477 is characterized by the same central idea, image cluster, and prosodic patterning as is the Player's soliloquy in *Hamlet*. Dickinson left no words about her process of composition, leaving us free to speculate. It seems plausible to imagine that she read and marveled over the soliloquy, above all at the way its prosody mirrors its content, and the way the scene exteriorizes the interior effect it produces. Perhaps sometime later the phrase "he fumbles at your soul" came to her, suggesting to her the discomforting feeling of being mastered by poetic virtuosity, with the provocative religious and erotic overtones that so many readers find in the poem. Out of that experience, she invented a poem that captured the ambivalent discomfort and thrill of being mastered, and images of blacksmithing, approaching thunderstorms, and the paralyzed calm before a storm developed into their own pattern as she fleshed out that image. The result is a dazzling flowering of Dickinson's own artistry, inspired by and indebted to Shakespeare, but equally the product of her own creative genius.

# PART III
# The Romantic Stage

# Chapter 7
# "The Translucence of Eternity in Time": Shakespeare and Coleridge's *Zapolya*

Paola Degli Esposti

**Shakespeare in Coleridge's Dramatic Reform Plan**

The year 1816 represented a landmark in Coleridge's theatrical career both as a dramatist and as a theorist. It marked the completion of his last attempt to compose a play upon a "reformed" dramatic plan, *Zapolya*, as well as his most violent attack against contemporary stage practice.[1] By this date his lectures, articles, and letters had already clarified his basic ideas on drama and theatrical representation, although further explanations were still to come in 1818.

Coleridge's reflections highlight a conception of the theater as the place where political, moral, metaphysical, and aesthetical issues interlace.[2] Such a privileged position is due to the extraordinary educational potential Coleridge perceives in this medium: once the staging of a piece is correctly conceived, and the piece itself is of the highest order, the stage can communicate concepts, emotions, and ideas (which would otherwise be confined to a very small elite) to a vast audience. It can allow such an "inexhaustible Mine of virgin Treasure"[3] as Shakespearean drama to "be sent into the ... Heads and Hearts, into the very souls, of the Mass of Mankind

---

[1] Samuel Taylor Coleridge, *The Collected Works of Samuel Taylor Coleridge*, vol. 7: *Biographia Literaria, or, Biographical Sketches of My Literary Life and Opinions*, ed. James Engell and W. Jackson Bate, 2 vols. (Princeton, NJ: Princeton University Press, 1983), 2:257–9. *Biographia Literaria* is abbreviated henceforth as BL. *The Collected Works* are abbreviated henceforth as CCW.

[2] On the connections between politics and the theater in Coleridge, see John David Moore, "Coleridge and the 'Modern Jacobinical Drama': Osorio, Remorse, and the Development of Coleridge's Critique of the Stage, 1797–1816," *Bulletin of Research in the Humanities* 4 (1982): 443–64, and Julie Ann Carlson, "An Active Imagination: Coleridge and the Politics of Dramatic Reform," *Modern Philology* 1 (1988): 22–33, which connects Coleridge's dramatic and political ideas with his metaphysical conception. On the relation between politics and metaphysics in Coleridge see also Raimonda Modiano, "Metaphysical Debate in Coleridge's Political Theory," *Studies in Romanticism* 3 (1982): 465–74.

[3] CCW, vol. 5: *Lectures 1808–1819: On Literature*, ed. Reginald A. Foakes, 2 vols. (Princeton, NJ: Princeton University Press, 1987), 1:429. *Lectures 1808–1819 on Literature* are abbreviated henceforth as Lectures. The lecture on drama quoted here took place in London on May 19, 1812. This edition of the lectures prints all of Coleridge's autograph deletions, which I omit in my quotations.

to whom except by this living Comment & Interpretation it must remain for ever a sealed up ... Volume."[4]

The problem Coleridge is here addressing is not just aesthetic. What is needed is not only an improvement in taste, but in morals. In his 1812 lecture on European drama he shows his anxiety about the inability of British society to extricate itself from its utilitarian and material thoughts and feelings in order to obtain a higher spirituality, but he also points at the theater as the ideal tool to arouse his countrymen from the mental paralysis they are afflicted by—to make up for their lack of imagination, moral reflection, and creative and inquiring spirit.[5]

For such effect to take place a radical reform is needed, both in the style of stage representation and in the policy ruling the selection of plays at the patent theaters—i.e., the theaters holding a monopoly on spoken drama. The works acted at Drury Lane and Covent Garden are largely immoral and debased, from Coleridge's point of view. One of the reasons for this degradation lies in the spectacular excess of contemporary performance, which damages any moral content the works may have. Coleridge argues that even a masterpiece like *The Tempest* can be seriously injured, in his 1818 lecture on the play:

> [*The Tempest*] addresses itself entirely to the imaginative faculty; and although the illusion may be assisted by the effect on the senses of the complicated scenery and decorations of modern times, yet this sort of assistance is dangerous. For the principal and only genuine excitement ought to come from within,—from the moved and sympathetic imagination; whereas, where so much is addressed to the more external senses of seeing and hearing, the spiritual vision is apt to languish, and the attraction from without will withdraw the mind from the proper and only legitimate interest which is intended to spring from within.[6]

If based on stage display, the *mise-en-scène* will prove essentially anti-imaginative, especially in the case of a Shakespearean play. It is a crucial defect, because imagination is a cornerstone in Coleridge's dramatic and educational plan. In the artistic process the imaginative faculty, enlightened by divine light, produces forms imitating the universal. In other words, an intermediary between the universal and the particular, imagination is the creative principle allowing ideal forms to be perceptible in material reality. After the completion of the work of art, the faculty of imagination also becomes the key factor in the transmission of its universal content to the spectator. The imaginative quality of the artwork affects the imagination of the audience, connecting it to the universal. A lack of imagination, therefore, is much more than a superficial flaw, being the visible sign of an inability to get in touch with a higher sphere of being; from a practical point of view, such deficiency implies a degradation of the principles on which the moral, social, and political

---

[4] Ibid., 1:430.
[5] Ibid., 1:429.
[6] Ibid., 2:268–9.

life of the nation should be based.⁷ What is needed is a dramatic model allowing a reactivation of the imagination. If, in religious literature, Coleridge conceives the Holy Writings as "the living *educts* of the Imagination"⁸—i.e., as the highest example of an imaginative (and therefore educational) work—then Shakespeare is conceived as the supreme ideal as far as dramatic art is concerned.

For Coleridge, one of the consequences of Shakespeare's superiority is that the ideal stage setting for his plays should be almost bare, as it was in the original Elizabethan and early Stuart productions of his plays, in order for his quality to be fully expressed.⁹ In less imaginative pieces by other dramatists a larger amount of carefully balanced stage effect is necessary, in order to make up for their deficiency, an obvious sign of their inferiority. This is due to the nature of theatrical representation:

> The most important and dignified Species of this Genus [theater] is, doubtless, the STAGE (Res Theatralis Histrionica) which [...] may be characterized (in its *Idea*, or according to what it does, or ought to, *aim* at) as a Combination of several, or of all the Fine Arts to an harmonious Whole having a distinct end of its own, to which the peculiar End of each of the component Arts, taken separately … is made subordinate and subservient.¹⁰

An organic balance in staging is essential, in other terms. Such balance implies a different quantity of spectacle in different plays; the less imaginative they are, the more stage display is required for a proper fruition of the piece. Excess in stage effect, however, is never to be allowed, since, as Coleridge asserts in his lecture on *The Tempest*, "where so much is addressed to the more external senses of seeing and hearing, the spiritual vision is apt to languish."¹¹ The less that decoration is used, the better it is for the drama. Hence Coleridge's preference for Shakespearean plays, where, imagination being at its highest, the quality of the texts is almost self-sufficient, and decoration is hardly necessary.

The superiority of Shakespeare's plays as models, in Coleridge's theory of the drama, doesn't merely stem from their independence from spectacular aids in performance, but from their outstanding imaginative quality as texts. Such a conclusion can be drawn, for instance, from Coleridge's reflections on the distinction between classic and romantic drama. Romantic drama, which is implicitly considered superior to its classic predecessor, not only begins

---

⁷ See Carlson, "Active Imagination," 23–7.

⁸ Coleridge, *The Statesman's Manual*, in CCW, vol. 6: *Lay Sermons*, ed. Reginald James White (Princeton, NJ: Princeton University Press, 1972), 29. *The Statesman's Manual* is abbreviated henceforth as SM.

⁹ See J. Tomalin's transcription of the November 25, 1811, lecture on Shakespeare. Lectures, 1:228

¹⁰ Lectures, 1:133.

¹¹ Lectures, 2:269.

with Shakespeare, but coincides with his plays.[12] Ancient Greeks based their productions on Aristotelian unities, thus betraying their essential sensuality and detachment from the universal: Coleridge maintains that time and place are eminently human coordinates, while the "rational" principle underlying the action and characterization of Greek drama is pragmatic, contaminated by the material world. The logic underlying these plays, "was a Reason which must strictly accomodate [sic] itself to the Senses, & so far became a sort of more elevated Understanding"[13]; it was unconnected to the eternal, the divine. The words Coleridge employs are significant: in his vocabulary, "understanding" signifies a pragmatic sort of reason, steeped into material reality, largely inferior to "reason," that is to say a pure faculty strictly connected with the universal.[14] On the other hand, he argues that Romantic—i.e., Shakespearean—drama is ruled by imagination and "reason" (as opposed to "understanding"), to which time, place, and action are made subservient.[15] And, as we have seen in Coleridge's writing, imagination is the faculty connecting humanity with the universal sphere. Hence the superiority of Shakespearean drama.

Given Coleridge's conception of drama, his sharp criticism of contemporary productions can hardly be surprising. Early nineteenth-century stage practice induced dramatists to surrender to spectacular display instead of conceiving spectacle as a tool to highlight the imaginative quality of their pieces. The playwrights' effort to imbue their works with stage effects is evidence of such an approach; the result is a "diseased sensibility of the assimilating power,"[16]—i.e., a paralysis of the imagination that brings on a debasement of drama, leading farther and farther from the superior, metaphysical sphere. In other terms, playwrights tended to produce merely marketable plays, addressing the basest, coarsest tastes instead of promoting a spiritual enhancement. For Coleridge, such artistic policy was furthered by the "national," or patent, theaters, which staged plays that, while emotionally affecting, were harmful where private and public morals were concerned.

Coleridge's preoccupation in this regard dates back to the first decade of the nineteenth century. The second *Satyrane Letter* (1809) includes a detailed analysis of the fashionable drama, highlighting its major faults in a dialogue between a Plaintiff (Coleridge's alter ego) and a Defendant (a "member of the crowd").[17] The poet here criticizes contemporary productions, pointing at their amorality, at their predilection for the trivial representation of everyday episodes and of common people instead of events and characters connoted by universal characteristics. The

---

[12] Ibid., 1:465–7.
[13] Ibid., 1:467.
[14] The difference between "reason" and "understanding" is explained in SM, 60–61n.
[15] See Lectures, 1:467.
[16] Ibid., 1:427.
[17] References to the letter, which was published in *The Friend* on December 7, 1809, and afterwards in BL, are from the 1809 text in CCW, vol. 4: *The Friend*, ed. Barbara E. Rooke, 2 vols. (Princeton, NJ: Princeton University Press, 1969), 2:209–21.

"artistic" choices in contemporary productions were a response to the widespread taste for surprising theatrical effects, for novelty for the sake of novelty, and the spectators' desire to see their everyday, material preoccupations on stage (their "pettifogging nature"[18]) instead of universal issues; at the same time, essentially subversive acted plays, both in a political and in a moral sense, have taken the place of pieces addressing metaphysical issues:

> For the whole System of your Drama is a moral and intellectual *Jacobinism* of the most dangerous kind, and those common-place rants of Loyalty are no better than hypocrisy in your Play-wrights, and your own sympathy with them a gross self-delusion. For the whole secret of dramatic popularity with you, consists in the confusion and subversion of the natural order of things in their causes and effects, in the excitement of surprize, by representing the qualities of liberality, refined feeling, and a nice sense of honour (those things rather, which pass among you for such) in persons and in classes of life where experience teaches us the least to expect them; and by rewarding with all the sympathies that are the dues of virtue, those criminals whom Law, Reason, and Religion, have excommunicated from our esteem![19]

Every ethical principle is subverted by this repertoire, which is significantly accused of "Jacobinism." Although being a "Jacobin" wasn't always a sin in Coleridge's opinion, at this stage of his career his position had turned radically hostile. As the terrible, bloody developments of the French Revolution become manifest, the term *Jacobin* carries a darker meaning in his mind. In this new sense a Jacobin is someone who opposes the divine order, higher morality, or, at any rate, someone acting or propounding ideas contrasting with the divine rule. In a short time Jacobinism comes to coincide with an irrational (irrational also meaning "lacking *nous*")[20] rule of the masses, an ever-growing source of concern for the poet, who is assuming an increasingly conservatory position (possibly also as a reaction to violent episodes such as the Luddist unrest of the 1810s). When dealing with theatrical matters, Coleridge's anxiety takes the shape of a deep aversion to the influence of the public taste in the choice of the texts to be acted, which is probably why he ends up associating Jacobinism with fashionable plays.

For Coleridge, a different sort of drama is needed in order to heal society—a moral drama that deals with metaphysical issues under the mask of historical events. In order to qualify as such, plays should prove to be much closer to the imaginative and therefore universal quality of original Romantic productions. As a consequence, Shakespeare, the highest Romantic model, turns out to be the reference point.

---

[18] Ibid., 2:220.

[19] Ibid.

[20] "Reason" often means *nous* in Coleridge: in SM for instance, where the main expression of nous—i.e., the Bible—is considered the "Statesman's Manual" (hence the title of the work).

## The Triumph of the Divine Rule

That Shakespeare can be identified as the major "authority" underlying the composition of *Zapolya*—Coleridge's attempt to create a reformed drama—is hardly surprising. Before exploring the ways in which Coleridge employs the Elizabethan source in the text, however, some preliminary considerations are needed.

In order to understand the main argument of the play, we must focus our attention on the well-known Coleridgean distinction between "absolute genius" and "commanding genius":

> While the former [men of absolute genius] rest content between thought and reality, as it were in an intermundium of which their own living spirit supplies the *substance*, and their imagination the ever-varying *form*; the latter [men of commanding genius] must impress their preconceptions on the world without, in order to present them back to their own view with the satisfying degree of clearness, distinctness and individuality. ... In times of tumult they [men of commanding genius] are the men destined to come forth as the shaping spirit of Ruin.[21]

While men of absolute genius are satisfied with their contemplative condition "between thought and reality," in which the connection with the spiritual world still holds, men of commanding genius feel the need to act in human reality, being strictly linked with the material world. Such material linking and the weakness of the connection with the superior sphere make men of commanding genius extremely dangerous, to the point of being identified with Milton's Satan.[22] Engaged as they are in acting in a human context, in asserting themselves in the material world, they lose sight of the universal import of their actions, losing touch with the divine plan.[23] This is why in politics they represent "the Masters of Mischief, the Liberticides, and mighty Hunters of Mankind from NIMROD to

---

[21] BL, 1:32–3.

[22] SM, 65.

[23] The mechanism implicitly suggested here is expounded by John Beer, whose analysis is useful in order to understand what lies behind the actions of the characters in *Zapolya*. Beer believes that the distinction between commanding genius and absolute genius mirrors the Coleridgean distinction between primary and secondary imagination, the former being essentially unconscious and contemplative and the latter being conscious and active. The latter, however, must keep in touch with the former to be effective. Beer argues that in Coleridge's theory the actions performed by men of commanding genius, who want to act in the phenomenal world, are not linked with the primary, but only with the secondary imagination; they will therefore be determined by the spirit of the time, not by a universal principle. John Bernard Beer, "Coleridge's Originality as a Critic of Shakespeare," *Studies in the Literary Imagination* 2 (1986): 54–5.

NAPOLEON."²⁴ The connection between Napoleon and commanding genius is particularly interesting because, as some critics have noticed, the French emperor is alluded to in *Zapolya*²⁵ (which was written only a few months after his defeat at Waterloo and his final exile in St. Helena), more specifically in the depiction of Emerick, the usurper. In this respect, Casimir's words in the play's Prelude, while he is still one of Emerick's followers, are significant:

> What better claim can sovereign wish or need,
> Than the free voice of men who love their country?
> Those chiefly who have fought for 't? Who by right
> Claim for their monarch one, who having obeyed,
> So hath best learnt to govern: who, having suffered,
> Can feel for each brave sufferer and reward him?
> Whence sprang the name of Emperor? Was it not
> By nature's fiat? In the storm of triumph,
> 'Mid warriors' shouts, did her oracular voice
> Make itself heard: Let the commanding spirit
> Possess the station of command!²⁶

The lines are meaningful for different reasons. First of all Bonaparte is clearly alluded to, both by the term *Emperor* (which at the time necessarily evoked the image of the French leader), and by the reference to the legitimacy of a government elected by popular acclamation. Moreover, the first two lines point out how Emerick and his allies consider popular (or rather, military) consent as the ideal basis on which power may be granted, while there seems to be no need of or reference to legitimacy from a divine source. Unsurprisingly, Casimir refers to the usurper as "the commanding spirit": Napoleon's alter ego, Emerick, is a representative of commanding genius, which, in politics, is a destructive force.

Bethlen—the heir apparent—on the other hand, possesses superior moral qualities, which he shows when he shields the young girls harassed by the usurper's followers, when he defends Sarolta from Emerick's attack, and when he expresses an instinctive aversion to the usurper.²⁷ Moreover, he is gifted with an aptitude to expand his thoughts beyond his present condition,²⁸ while his ability to act in the material world is somewhat limited; such characteristics seem to allow

---

²⁴ SM, 66. On Napoleon in Romantic criticism and ideology see Simon Bainbridge, *Napoleon and English Romanticism* (Cambridge: Cambridge University Press, 1995).

²⁵ See Julie Ann Carlson, "Command Performances: Burke, Coleridge, and Schiller's Dramatic Reflections on the Revolution in France," *The Wordsworth Circle* 23, no. 2 (1992): 117, 125–6, and *In the Theater of Romanticism: Coleridge, Nationalism and Women* (Cambridge: Cambridge University Press, 1994), 105.

²⁶ Coleridge, *Zapolya*, in CCW, vol. 16: *Poetical Works*: Part 3, *Plays*, ed. James C. C. Mays, 2 vols. (Princeton, NJ: Princeton University Press, 2001), vol. 1, Prelude, 1.1.315–25. All references to *Zapolya* will be to this edition.

²⁷ See *Zapolya*, Sequel, 1.1.112–22, 3.2.82–120, 1.1.255–7.

²⁸ *Zapolya*, Sequel, 1.1.404–5.

for his inclusion in the category of absolute genius, whose representatives are better qualified to reflect on abstract principles than to apply them in contingent reality. Not that the prince is totally inactive; his actions, however, are dictated by an instinctive adherence to superior ethical principles, not by a meditated plan leading to the assumption of power. In other terms, he doesn't *choose* to be the claimant to the throne, but *is chosen* by the divine will; acting within the rules dictated by Heaven, Bethlen can't help following their lead. This explains why he never takes any decisive step as far as politics is concerned: all crucial actions, such as Emerick's killing, are performed by other characters.[29] What may appear as ineptitude is in fact due to a specific reason. His mother's words reveal what this may be:

> "Ask not my son;" said she, "our name or thine.
> The shadow of the eclipse is passing off
> The full orb of thy destiny! Already
> The victor Crescent glitters forth and sheds
> O'er the yet lingering haze a phantom light.
> Thou canst not hasten it! Leave then to Heaven
> The work of Heaven: and with a silent spirit
> Sympathize with the powers that work in silence!"
> Thus spake she, and she looked, as she were then
> Fresh from some heavenly vision![30]

The reason for her reticence in telling her son about his royal origins is the same preventing him from acting: in order to behave according to the divine will, Bethlen must "Leave then to Heaven / The work of Heaven." Divine Providence will determine the fate of the reign, not man and individual initiative. In other words, in order to be worthy of his royal status, the heir must wait for the divine plan to develop without trying to assert his own individuality, an act that would turn him into a representative of commanding genius such as Emerick, and would disqualify him for the throne.[31]

While Bethlen's behavior is pure and virtuous, Emerick's is explicitly portrayed as Satanic. Sarolta calls him a monster, a blasphemous creature, a devil who belongs to the night of "fiends and damned spirits."[32] His actions and ambitions are seen as a stain, a gangrene contaminating the reign. Chef Ragozzi, old king

---

[29] For instance, the revolt is started by Kiuprili and Casimir: this can be inferred by the dialogue in the Sequel, 3.1.83–5, which alludes to Kiuprili telling Bethlen to perform the symbolic act that marks a return of the legitimate divine rule, i.e., fetching his sword and armor. Moreover, Casimir announces the revolt, not Bethlen. Even more significant, it is surprisingly Casimir who kills Emerick, and not the heir to the throne.

[30] *Zapolya*, Sequel, 3.1.95–104.

[31] This is one of reasons most characters keep shielding him: their protective actions denote the "work of Heaven" on which Bethlen should silently rely. This is also why all of Bethlen's acts are defensive (see ibid., 1.1.112–22, 3.2.76–86, 4.2.49–81).

[32] Ibid., 3.2.91. The other epithets are used in lines 90–94, 100–101.

Andreas's loyal soldier, for instance, expresses his anxiety employing a significant vocabulary:

> The mystery, that struggles in my looks,
> Betrayed my whole tale to thee, if it told thee
> That I am ignorant; but fear the worst.
> And mystery is contagious. All things here
> Are full of motion: and yet all is silent:
> And bad men's hopes infect the good with fears.[33]

Emerick's influence spreads as if by contagion. Like the plague, he affects whoever is already apt to follow him, and infects those opposing him. Zapolya's words substantiate the feeling of contamination now haunting the royal palace. The disease will quickly spread from the palace to the whole nation:

> Then as going off, she [Zapolya] looks back on the palace.
> Thou tyrant's den, be called no more a palace!
> The orphan's angel at the throne of heaven
> Stands up against thee, and there hover o'er thee
> A Queen's, a Mother's, and a Widow's curse.
> Henceforth a dragon's haunt, fear and suspicion
> Stand sentry at thy portals! Faith and honour,
> Driven from the throne, shall leave the attainted nation:
> And for the iniquity that houses in thee,
> False glory, thirst of blood, and lust of rapine,
> (Fateful conjunction of malignant planets)
> Shall shoot their blastments on the land. The fathers
> Henceforth shall have no joy in their young men,
> And when they cry: Lo! a male child is born!
> The mother shall make answer with a groan.
> .....
> Till Vengeance hath her fill.—And thou, snatched hence,
> .....
> Offspring of Royal Andreas, shalt return
> With trump and timbrel-clang, and popular shout
> In triumph to the palace of thy fathers![34]

Zapolya's curse has a biblical overtone, confirming that the palace, Emerick's residence, is bound to be the center from which evil will spread. The queen's invective, however, ends in hope: however dark the present may be, the future will show the reestablishment of the divine order.

The journey leading to such a happy outcome begins in the first scene of the Prelude. Emerick's plan to ascend the throne proves to be faulty from the very moment in which Ragozzi, who should prevent Andreas's loyal subjects from

---

[33] *Zapolya*, Prelude, 1.1.24–9.
[34] Ibid., 1.2.83–107.

entering the palace, doesn't answer the usurper's expectations. A faithful supporter of the royal family, he counteracts Emerick's moves employing the same tool the usurper uses: deceit, a strategy that in his case doesn't bear an evil connotation. The ability to act in the contingent reality, in fact, isn't evil in itself, but rather only when it is unconnected to a higher order of history—that is, history as part of the divine plan.[35]

From this moment on, signs of the divine intention to protect whoever supports the legitimate heir to the throne keep turning up. In the second scene of the Prelude, centered on Zapolya's flight, the queen and Ragozzi, who is helping her, repeatedly remark that Heaven is assisting them. As if answering Zapolya's prayer at the beginning of the scene, Chef Ragozzi arrives. As soon as he comes on stage he asserts that the heavenly powers are helping him and allowing him to rescue Kiuprili; when he sees the queen, his conviction gets even stronger. Zapolya's words relating her escape reveal a similar belief in the intervention of Providence. The woman says that while everyone else was celebrating Emerick, she entered her dead husband's room. She let her child kiss the king, while the monarch still held the royal seal in his hand. As she took the seal, Providence intervened:

> As I removed the seal, the heavy arm
> Dropt from the couch aslant, and the stiff finger
> Seemed pointing at my feet. Provident Heaven!
> Lo, I was standing on the secret door,
> Which, through a long descent where all sound perishes,
> Led out beyond the palace. Well I knew it—
>
> But *Andreas* framed it not! *He* was no tyrant![36]

Heaven moved the king's forefinger so as to show the queen how to escape, ironically pointing at a passage that was probably built by the usurper himself.

Divine protection attends the fugitives in every moment of their exile. If a supernatural intervention takes place offstage between the Prelude and the Sequel—that is to say when Bathory, a mountaineer who will afterwards foster the prince, saves baby Bethlen (here, in fact, Zapolya points at the sky)[37]—the second part of the play opens with saintly Sarolta saving Bethlen. In the same scene the heir to the throne appears to be in a sort of trance, as if he was perceiving signs he cannot fully comprehend:

> But in good truth I know not what I speak.
> This luckless morning I have been so haunted

---

[35] See Coleridge's note regarding the notion of "prudence" (a term the author employs, together with "expediency" or "expedience," to define man's wisdom in worldly actions) in CCW, vol. 6: *Lay Sermons*, 129. A Lay Sermon was published in 1817, a few months before *Zapolya*.

[36] *Zapolya*, Prelude, 1.2.73–9.

[37] *Zapolya*, Sequel, 1.1.357.

> With my own fancies, starting up like omens,
> That I feel like one, who waking from a dream
> Both asks and answers wildly.[38]

A prey to visions—or omens—he cannot control, he alludes to a dreaming state that significantly parallels the visionary state Kiuprili will talk about in the next scene—that is, the dream God sent Zapolya to induce the chieftain and the queen to return to the forest where she last saw her child. The following meeting between Bethlen and the two exiles turns out to be another consequence of divine will, since the prince explicitly asserts that Heaven guided him towards his birthplace, where he meets Zapolya and her guardian.

References to the action of heavenly forces are more and more frequent in Acts 3 and 4 of the Sequel[39]; more important, Heaven promptly intervenes—frequently at the very last moment—whenever servants faithful to the divine plan are in danger or when they explicitly pray for help, directing them towards the preordained end. In the first scene of the final act the divine even seems to send a spectacular sign alluding to the battle that is about to be fought (and won) by the entire creatural world:

> RUDOLPH.
> See the sky lowers! the cross-winds waywardly
> Chase the fantastic masses of the clouds
> With a wild mockery of the coming hunt!
>
> CASIMIR.
> Mark too, the edges of yon lurid mass!
> Restless and vext, as if some angering hand,
> With fitful, tetchy snatch, unrolled and plucked
> The jetting ringlets of the vapourous fleece!
> These are sure signs of the conflict nigh at hand,
> And elemental war![40]

While the divine plan unfolds, the signs of Emerick's coming defeat increase. After the earlier indications of Emerick's fundamental weakness (Ragozzi's insubordination and Zapolya's flight), the usurper seems to be winning, since his twenty-year regime ensues. But his victory is just an illusion. As soon as the legitimate heir is ready to regain his ruling power, Emerick's earthly actions are consistently foiled. In the first act Laska (the usurper's inferior doppelganger), who is accusing Bethlen of treason, isn't able to have him imprisoned. In the third act Sarolta's attempted rape is prevented; Bethlen and Bathory, who should be arrested by Emerick's orders, are in fact released; and Casimir, the usurper's

---

[38] Ibid., 1.1.267–71.
[39] Ibid., 3.1.83–5, 212–13; 3.2.31–46, 69, 83–5, 112–20, 143; 4.1.41–9; 4.2.165, 171–3; 4.3.24, 26–9, 45, 64–5.
[40] Ibid., 4.1.41–9.

former supporter, repents his misplaced loyalty and joins the "divine" forces. Civil war breaks out in the final act, and again none of Emerick's and his allies' actions succeed. While trying to murder Bethlen, Laska is killed by Glycine, and Casimir takes Emerick's life in a final combat.

Once the usurper is dead, the divine rule of the state is quickly reestablished. In the short final scene, Bethlen's coronation, the new royal court, now cleansed of Emerick's tainting influence, is shown as a celestial meeting: Zapolya is greeted as a Heaven-sent being, Kiuprili as a gift of Providence, and Sarolta as an angel. And, significantly, in this scene the dowager queen, Zapolya, states that "Heaven's work of grace is full!"[41]

## The Translucence of Shakespeare's Eternity in Time

The printed version of the play (1817) opens with a brief Advertisement by the author. Aware of his unconventional treatment of the Aristotelian unity of time, he feels the need to justify his choice:

> The form of the following dramatic poem is in humble imitation of the Winter's Tale of Shakespeare, except that I have called the first part a Prelude instead of a first Act, as a somewhat nearer resemblance to the plan of the ancients, of which one specimen is left us in the Æschylian Trilogy of the Agamemnon, the Orestes and the Eumenides. Though a matter of *form* merely, yet two plays, on different periods of the same tale, might seem less bold, than an interval of twenty years between a first and a second act.[42]

Classic drama, Aeschylus above all, is here evoked to defend the breach of the rule, which at first seems to embarrass Coleridge; however, the poet doesn't recede from his choice, although by employing the same stratagem he uses in the Prelude he somewhat masks his infringement.[43] As a matter of fact, his justification is a matter of form rather than of substance. If he chooses to assuage the effect of the breach, it is "in mere obedience to custom," and in any case he believes that in some plays "an interval of twenty hours between the acts would have a worse effect (i.e., render the imagination less disposed to take the position required) than twenty years in other cases"[44]—a statement that is in line with the concepts expounded in

---

[41] Ibid., 4.3.24.

[42] CCW, *Plays*, 2:1338.

[43] Although Coleridge states that Prelude and Sequel are two plays, the two are inevitably dependent one on the other. The Prelude, dealing with the circumstances of Emerick's usurpation, sets the premises from which the ensuing events proceed; it is therefore necessary to understand the Sequel, the moral impulse behind the character's actions, and the metaphysical issues underlying the text. As the Advertisement implies, the distinction is just a matter of form, aimed at defending the text from possible criticism.

[44] CCW, *Plays*, 2:1338.

his 1812 lecture on classic and Romantic drama.[45] As we have seen, in his opinion Aristotelian unities do not rule on Romantic drama, whose higher representative is Shakespeare: governed by a "unity of imagination" instead, it is absolutely independent from time or space. Significantly, when justifying his unconventional use of time in *Zapolya*, Coleridge implicitly alludes to Time's soliloquy in *The Winter's Tale* justifying the chronological leap between the third and fourth act: "It is in my pow'r / To o'erthrow law, and in one self-born hour / To plant and o'erwhelm custom."[46] Although Coleridge may seem to choose a compromise to safeguard the traditional rule—which he calls "custom," the same term used by Shakespeare's Time—in actuality he deals with the unity of time as freely as his Elizabethan model. Therefore, mentioning Shakespeare in the Advertisement to *Zapolya* doesn't seem a mere matter of form. But his presence here as an *auctoritas* has wider implications: he is the "tutelary deity," the necessary reference point for a play that aims at being considered not only as a piece of valuable poetry but also as a model of morality and social values for the audience it addresses.[47]

Statements asserting the deep morality permeating Shakespeare's texts are scattered throughout Coleridge's Shakespearean lectures. According to Coleridge, Shakespeare's plays are characterized by a "sublime morality ... [which] pervades all his great characters."[48] Moreover, according to an anonymous report of a 1813 lecture, Coleridge believes that, notwithstanding the accusations levelled against him, the Elizabethan author was the best inspirer of virtue and wisdom:

> If a man speak injuriously of a friend, our vindication of him is naturally warm; Shakespear had been accused of profaneness, he (Mr. C[oleridge]) from the perusal of him, had acquired a habit of looking into his own heart, and perceived the goings on of his nature, and confident he was, Shakespear was a writer of all others the most calculated to make his readers better as well as wiser.[49]

Not only is Shakespeare a moral writer, therefore, but his works engender an ethical improvement in his audience.

---

[45] Lectures, 1:465–7.

[46] William Shakespeare, *The Winter's Tale*, 4.1.7–9. All references to Shakespeare are from *The Riverside Shakespeare*, ed. Gwynne Blakemore Evans (Boston: Houghton Mifflin, 1974).

[47] On this topic, see Carlson, "Active Imagination," 22–33.

[48] Lectures, 1:573. The statement can be found in Coleridge's notes for a lecture on Shakespeare held in Bristol on November 16, 1813.

[49] Ibid., 1:522. The quotation is taken from the anonymous report of a lecture on Shakespeare held in Bristol on October 28, 1813, published in the *Bristol Gazette*, November 4, 1813. Similar observations were expressed in Coleridge's "Lecture on the principles of poetry" (1808), as a letter from Henry Crabb Robinson testifies (see Lectures, 1:116–17), and in the "Lecture on Shakespeare" given in London on December 17, 1818 (Lectures, 2:271).

The Shakespearean influence on the composition of *Zapolya* doesn't simply lie in the intertextual relationship with *The Winter's Tale* and the corresponding time gap in the Coleridgean plot, as the Advertisement seems to imply. At least two more Shakespeare plays are alluded to in *Zapolya*: *Cymbeline* and *Twelfth Night*.[50] The only explicit instance of Shakespearean intertextuality, however, concerns the similar treatment of the unity of time in *The Winter's Tale* and *Zapolya*. In both cases the breach of Aristotelian unity is quite obvious, since there is a sixteen-year gap in the former and a twenty-year gap in the latter;[51] although the interval takes place between different acts—right after the first virtual act (the Prelude) in Coleridge's text and between the third and fourth act in Shakespeare's play—its function is in fact the same. In order for the lost children in both plays to regain the identity and social status of which they were deprived when, as newborn babies, they had no chance to prevent it, they have to develop an ability to act—that is, to reach adulthood; moreover, the interval is necessary to allow them to grow up far from the royal court, in a sort of "state of nature." Here, however, the texts differ, creating a sort of intertextual tension that is crucially important for understanding Coleridge's piece, because it highlights the different ways in which human will and its political and moral implications are portrayed. Bethlen's moral and political choices are extremely significant because he makes them while he is in a "state of nature"; his very birthright is validated only because, when still unaware of his royal parentage, he proves to be worthy of ascending the throne by his noble behavior and by his ability of making choices that morally fit in the divine plan. Like Perdita in *The Winter's Tale*, Bethlen unconsciously shows the signs of his nobility, but in *Zapolya* all this doesn't simply reveal the royal nature of the character, being rather the essential evidence of his fitness to carry out the divine plan, whose fulfilment lies at the core of the text.[52]

Further similarities can be noticed between the two youths. The obvious fact that both are "lost children" is a significant common feature of the two plays that allows us to notice several correspondences between them. Although the circumstances are different, the same atmosphere characterizes Perdita's and Bethlen's disappearance and reappearance. Both are driven from home under a death threat as soon as they are born; they are both saved by a woman (her mother's friend and his mother, respectively), finding shelter in a distant land (the former in Bohemia, the latter in the mountains near Casimir's country residence). While everyone mistakenly believes them to be dead, they are raised by humble inhabitants of the place (a shepherd and a mountaineer, respectively) as if they were their own children, and they are unaware of their origins until late in the

---

[50] In his introduction to *Zapolya*, Mays mentions *The Winter's Tale* and *Cymbeline* as sources for the play, but doesn't elaborate the point. See CCW, *Plays*, 2:1335.

[51] In the draft for the unwritten connecting scene between the Prelude and the Sequel, Coleridge mentions an eighteen-year interval; in the published text, however, the gap is twenty years long. CCW, *Plays*, 2:1426, 1362.

[52] See for instance *The Winter's Tale*, 4.2.62–4, 156–9, and *Zapolya*, Prelude, 1.1.403–9.

plays.⁵³ The characters are only partly similar, however. Perdita is a lost child (hence her name) who is eventually found again, and who functions as the peacemaker between two divided houses: her return to Sicily determines the end of Leontes' long period of expiation, allowing for the reconciliation with Polixenes, and Hermione's reappearance. In *Zapolya*, on the other hand, it is the reappearance of the eponymous character, not Bethlen's, that stirs the characters into action; the heir, moreover, doesn't at all reconcile the forces that came to a clash during the Prelude. The intertextual relationship, however, thanks to the very difference between the texts, discloses a significant level of meaning. The substitution of a solution to the conflict in the form of reconciliation (*The Winter's Tale*) with one in the form of victory or defeat (*Zapolya*) highlights the impossibility of a peaceful compromise in the Coleridgean text. In *The Winter's Tale*, Leontes promptly repents once he recognizes his mistake; by contrast, the malicious betrayal represented in Coleridge's play can't be peacefully redressed because it is the result of a conscious and willing decision that the villain (Emerick) never regrets. In other terms, while the human intellect portrayed in the Shakespearean text is just temporarily clouded by overwhelming passions, in *Zapolya* we are presented with the opposition between two different kinds of reason: on the one hand a purely human "rational" mind, cut off from the ideal world it should mirror; on the other an intellect closely connected with divine law and eager to be the means of its fulfilment.⁵⁴

The intertextual relationship here described works on a deeper level, while on a more immediate level the allusions to *The Winter's Tale* are employed so as to create an overall Shakespearian atmosphere in *Zapolya*. Coleridge's efforts to produce such atmosphere can be seen in the network of references he establishes between his characters and those in Shakespeare's play, first of all in connection with mother figures. In *The Winter's Tale* Hermione seemingly dies of a broken heart in the third act, only to come back on stage in a celebrated *coup de théâtre* in the fifth act. Similarly, at the beginning of Coleridge's Sequel everyone believes Zapolya to be dead, but she unexpectedly reappears in the second act. Both leading a clandestine life for a long time and slandered due to excessive jealousy

---

⁵³ There are further correspondences between them. Both start a relationship (although not at the same level of intimacy) with someone of seemingly superior social status, but who in fact is of the same (prince Florizel) or even of an inferior rank (Glycine). There might also be a further similarity in the illegitimacy theme. Perdita is disowned because Leontes mistakenly believes her to be the fruit of Hermione's supposed unfaithfulness; in Bethlen's case there is no explicit reference to his possible illegitimacy; however, Casimir's doubts that Zapolya is really pregnant together with Emerick's allegations against her seem to allude to *The Winter's Tale*. See *Zapolya*, Prelude, 1.1.392–401.

⁵⁴ As regards the "idealistic" conception of reason see, for instance, J. D. Coates, "Coleridge's Debt to Harrington: A Discussion of Zapolya," *Journal of the History of Ideas* 3 (1977): 501–8. As regards Coleridge's definition of reason, its connection with the divine, and its various meanings, see SM, 60–61n. On the notions of reason, religion, and will, see Appendix C in SM, 59–93.

(Hermione) or thirst for power (Zapolya), the two mothers seem in many ways to mirror each other. The similarity between them is not absolute, just as it is not in Bethlen's and Perdita's case, because the model must be imitated, not copied—in accordance with Coleridge's aesthetic theory[55]—and most of all because what counts here is the creation of an atmosphere that re-creates the aegis of the Shakespearean model, rather than a precise reproduction of the source.[56]

The allusions to Shakespeare are reinforced by the implicit intertextual relationship with another play, *Cymbeline*, which seems to be particularly significant for its focus on the mythical origins of Britain. Holinshed's chronicles and Geoffrey of Monmouth's *History of the Kings of Britain*, on which Shakespeare's play is based, maintain that Cymbeline's reign started between 23 B.C. and 17 A.D.; this confers on *Cymbeline* a sacred aura, since it would mean that Cymbeline's reign coincided with the beginning of the Christian era.[57] It is therefore unsurprising that the play should be chosen as a reference point in the composition of *Zapolya*, a play centered on the victory of a "heavenly" government over a purely human leadership, by an author who is persuaded that the perfect rule for the state should conform to divine law.[58]

A similarity seems to be apparent, in the first place, between Shakespeare's prince Cloten and Coleridge's Laska. Both villainous figures are described as vainglorious, bungling fools. The characters around them often mock them, sometimes voicing merciless judgements about them.[59] But there are further

---

[55] In Coleridge's theory an imitation is different from a copy, in that the latter is an identical exterior reproduction, without any difference, of the model, while an imitation shows a difference due to the intervention of the creative imagination. Moreover, while a copy aims at reproducing the external shape of the model, an imitation aims at reproducing its universal essence. See "Lecture on European literature," 1818, Lectures, 2:217–25, and "Lecture on Shakespeare," 1818, Lectures, 2:264–5.

[56] The "failed" brotherly couple in *Zapolya* can be interpreted in the same sense. On the one hand the relationship between Leontes and Polixenes—who, although not related, are bound by brotherly love—comes to a crisis because of the former's unreasonable jealousy, so much so that Leontes orders Polixenes' death; on the other, the bond between old king Andreas and Emerick, brothers by blood, is broken because of the latter's ambition, and in this case a fratricide seems also to be hinted at. In both cases a bond of affection is broken and a murder is attempted or supposed.

[57] See Frances A. Yates, *Shakespeare's Last Plays: A New Approach* (London: Routledge & Kegan Paul, 1975), 39–61.

[58] See, in addition to SM in its entirety, John Morrow, *Coleridge's Political Thought* (London: Macmillan, 1990), 103–4, and Reginald James White's introduction to CCW, vol. 6, *Lay Sermons*, xxix–xlvii.

[59] There are countless examples of this. For instance, compare the Second Lord's lines in *Cymbeline*, 1.3 and 2.1 or Imogen's in 2.3.87–155; or again Arviragus's and Guiderius's in 4.2.72–290, with the dialogues between Sarolta and Laska, and between Glycine and Laska, in *Zapolya*, Sequel, 1.1, or Emerick's lines and the dialogue between Bethlen and Laska in Sequel, 3.1; or again, the exchange between Laska and Pestalutz in Sequel, 4.2.

echoes between them. Both give vent to their purpose to possess a desired woman (Imogen in Cloten's case, Glycine in Laska's) whatever she may wish, and in spite of the fact that she is in love with someone else (Posthumus and Bethlen respectively).[60] Moreover, they both die a rather humiliating death: Cloten is beheaded by Guiderius, who not only mutilates but also mocks his corpse; Laska is killed by Glycine, who ironically employs his own bow and arrows against him and doesn't refrain from insulting him even after his death.

More complex echoes seem to appear in the second act of *Zapolya*, which in many ways alludes to Act 3 of *Cymbeline*. In the Shakespearean play, we see a tired and hungry Imogen arriving at the cavern where the king's sons—who are mistakenly supposed to be dead—and Belarius live. The occupants of the "savage hold," as Imogen calls it,[61] live as outlaws. While they are gone, Imogen enters their cave and eats their food. With a sort of chiasmus, in the second act of Coleridge's Sequel we find two characters—Zapolya and Kiuprili—who are supposed to be dead, in a cavern; in this case it is they who are tired and hungry, and who take the food Glycine leaves for Bethlen in front of the cave. In both texts the cavern is the abode of royal characters who live as outlaws; in both texts we find major characters who, exhausted and hungry, find and eat the food meant for the heir to the throne—although their roles are somehow inverted, since Kiuprili and Zapolya stay in the cavern and eat the food for a character who has never been there before, while Imogen, who is totally unfamiliar with the cave, eats the food kept there by its inhabitants. Unsurprisingly, therefore, it is near these very caverns—in both cases offstage—that the mirror figures of Cloten and Laska are killed.

In the two plays the cave is the place where or around which the fate of the kingdom is determined—that is to say, where each royal family reassembles (or start to reassemble), marking the beginning of a new course. In *Cymbeline*, the pretender to throne and usurper, Cloten, dies near the cavern, and just outside it the king's sons—still unaware of their parentage—choose to fight the Roman invasion; the Romans' defeat will mark the mythic Holinshedian start of British history, surrounded by the sacral aura deriving from its coincidence with the beginnings of Christianity. In *Zapolya*, on the other hand, the cave is the place where Bethlen meets his mother (incidentally, Arviragus and Guiderius also first meet their sister in the cavern), and where the first steps towards reestablishing the divine order are taken; and in its surroundings the final battle takes place and the usurper is killed.

As before, the complex references to the Shakespearean source are the result of imitation (in Coleridge's sense)—that is to say, a reproduction of some of its elements with a difference. While the beginning of the new order portrayed in *Cymbeline* is mainly the result of the legitimate heir's (Guiderius's) *actions*— Cloten's killing, the fight against the Romans—in *Zapolya* the prince is rather connoted by *inaction*. As I have already suggested, Bethlen tends to watch the

---

[60] See *Zapolya*, Sequel, 1.1.226–30 and *Cymbeline*, 3.5.133–45.
[61] *Cymbeline*, 3.6.18.

events rather than determine them, surrendering to his royal fate rather than accomplishing it; the intertextual tension between the texts thus underscores Coleridge's concept of moral government, which should be in the hands of a divinely inspired absolute genius who doesn't need to—or rather, shouldn't—assert his own individual self.

At first sight, the less significant Shakespearean source for *Zapolya* is *Twelfth Night*. Coleridge's only allusion to Shakespeare's play lies in the geographical setting of *Zapolya*: Illyria. This would seem a superficial reference, merely indulging the early nineteenth-century taste for the exotic; in fact, Coleridge's *Remorse* is also set in a remote time and place (sixteenth-century Spain, during the religious persecution of the *moriscos*), which would seem to indicate that Coleridge yields to public taste, contradicting his theatrical theory. The allusion may seem even blander if we consider that the place would probably suggest a connection with contemporary Napoleonic history to the audience, since under Bonaparte's rule several provinces located north and east of the Adriatic Sea were renamed "Illyrian provinces."[62] In fact, considering the obvious references to Napoleon in *Zapolya*, such connection may be supposed to lie behind Coleridge's choice.

However, it seems unlikely that an attentive and enthusiastic Shakespearean scholar such as Coleridge wouldn't also keep *Twelfth Night* in mind. Thanks to the double reference implied by the setting, and to the "double nature" of the place, in *Zapolya* Illyria turns out to be an imaginary and a real place at once, in line with Coleridge's aesthetic ideal: real, because it is drawn in the contingent world by the references to Napoleonic events, and imaginary because the Shakespearean setting it alludes to doesn't correspond to a real locality but rather to a region beyond time and place. Setting the play in such a dual environment allows Coleridge to deal with events that *may* happen in actual history, but just potentially; a fusion of the particular with the universal is thus reached, which places the play on an ideal and symbolical ground:

> The ideal consists in the happy balance of the generic with the individual. The former makes the character representative and symbolical, therefore instructive; because, *mutatis mutandis*, it is applicable to whole classes of men. The latter gives it its *living* interest; for nothing *lives* or is *real*, but as definite and individual. ... "*Forma formans per formam formatam translucens*," is the definition and perfection of *ideal* art.[63]

The hypothetical presence of a "potential history" in *Zapolya* is confirmed by Coleridge's choice of evocative names. Although no consistent or accurate choice

---

[62] See Frank J. Bundy, *The Administration of the Illyrian Provinces of the French Empire, 1809–1813* (New York: Garland, 1987).

[63] BL, 2:214–15. See Coleridge's significant definition of symbol, as given in SM, 30: "a Symbol ... is characterized by a translucence of the Special in the Individual or of the General in the Especial or of the Universal in the General. Above all by the translucence of the Eternal through and in the Temporal."

has apparently been made, actual names recurring in past or present chronicles are here employed. Fragments of history are thus introduced into the play to connect it to a human sphere; at the same time, however, the lack of accuracy doesn't allow for any precise recognizability in the events described and therefore the plot doesn't make strict historical allusions. In other terms, universal forces showing themselves in worldly phenomena are represented; but avoiding strict reference to real human events, Coleridge prevents the action of the play from becoming "accidental." For instance, many names in the play are inspired by members of ancient and noble Hungarian houses,[64] whose history is characterized by dynastic conflicts; however, the action of the play doesn't refer to any specific episode. Moreover, some names and the vocabulary employed allude to Napoleonic history,[65] but the plot doesn't reproduce the development of contemporary French events with any exactness.

This technique, in which an imaginary world and reality continually interlace and refer to each other, seems to find its most significant instance in the allusion to *Twelfth Night*, which contains both poles. The very fact of employing Shakespeare as a source seems to imply that merging human history with an ideal world is here the aim. Coleridge in fact believes Shakespeare to be one of the highest instances—if not the highest—of the poetic ability to effectively combine the universal with the particular in the representation of individual characters and events:

> It was S[hakespeare]'s prerogative to have the *universal* which is potentially in each *particular*, opened out to him—the *homme generale* not as an abstraction of observation <from a variety of men;> but as the Substance capable of endless modifications of which his own personal Exhistence was but one—& to use *this one* as the eye that beheld the other, and as the Tongue that could convey the discovery.[66]

---

[64] The source of most of them is probably Karoly Ferencz Palma's *Notitia Rerum Hungaricarum* (1785), a text Coleridge widely discusses in a 1799 letter to Josiah Wedgwood. See *The Collected Letters of Samuel Taylor Coleridge*, ed. Earl Leslie Griggs, 6 vols. (Oxford: Clarendon Press, 1956–1971), 1:466–7n. Griggs remarks that nine out of twelve characters in Zapolya can be found in Hungarian history and that Coleridge's spellings are quite similar to Palma's.

[65] More precisely, there is a specific reference to a character, Barzoni, who only has a very minor role in the text (he never appears on stage). Although Mays doesn't identify a source for the name (CCW, *Plays*, 2:1334), at the turn of the eighteenth century an Italian polemicist served the British government for some time: Vittorio Barzoni, who repeatedly attacked Bonaparte (he was called the "anti-Napoleon"). Given the reputation of *Zapolya* as a celebration of the emperor's defeat at Waterloo, the mention of Barzoni in the text doesn't seem accidental, even though he is presented as Emerick's ally (Emerick being Bonaparte's alter ego), not as his opponent. Evidence that Coleridge knew of Barzoni and possessed at least one of his works can be found in the poet's library (now held at the University of Toronto), which contains both a copy in Italian of Barzoni's *Rivoluzioni della Repubblica Veneta*, given by the author, and an English translation of the same work.

[66] "Lecture on European literature," 1818, Lectures, 2:148.

In order for the combination of history and imagination, the "translucence" of eternity in time, to be revealed in *Zapolya*, Coleridge activates another intertextual relationship. Once connected to "eternal history" by the references to *Cymbeline*, once placed in an *intermundium* between the universal and the particular by the allusion to *Twelfth Night* and the scattered references to Napoleon and his empire, the piece must find a more consistent assonance with actual history in order to fulfil its educational intent. This is presumably why there are many allusions to texts that are much more concerned with present issues: Schiller's *Wallenstein* trilogy, especially *The Piccolomini* and *Wallenstein's Death*. Not only was the German dramatist very well known to contemporary audiences (thanks to the 1792 translation of *The Robbers*, which greatly influenced contemporary dramatic productions), but, given the close connections between the plot of the trilogy and the events of the French Revolution, Schiller's work is useful for linking the universal aspects of *Zapolya* with well-known human events. The explanation for Coleridge choosing Schiller, among the various options available, presumably lies in his admiration for his trilogy, and most of all in the possibility of connecting him to Shakespeare, although indirectly.[67] In the preface to his edition of *Wallenstein's Death* (a play he translated together with *The Piccolomini* between 1799 and 1800), Coleridge mentions the connection although he qualifies it: "Few, I trust, would be rash or ignorant enough to compare Schiller with Shakespeare; yet, merely as illustration, I would say that we should proceed to the perusal of Wallenstein, not from Lear or Othello, but from Richard the Second, or the three parts of Henry the Sixth."[68] Although the trilogy is not comparable to Shakespeare's plays, it is valuable enough to be read through a Shakespearean lens.

As in *Zapolya*, the plot of the German trilogy deals with a high-ranking noble's rebellion (Wallenstein's) against traditional power, embodied by the legitimate anointed sovereign (the Emperor of the Sacred Roman Empire). Here too the legitimate sovereign doesn't himself organize the fight against his opponent, leaving the whole procedure to his deputy, Octavio Piccolomini, who defends traditional law, just as Coleridge's Kiuprili does.[69] Moreover, a third Schillerian character seems to bear a striking resemblance to one of Coleridge's: Max Piccolomini, who, like Casimir, is the son of the man who aims at preserving the "divine" rule against its opponents, and a character who finds himself trapped between his father and the aristocrat opposing him.

The Wallenstein-Octavio-Max triangle is many ways similar to that composed of Emerick, Kiuprili, and Casimir. Initially persuaded by Wallenstein's arguments and convinced of his virtue, Max supports the nobleman, which causes a quarrel with his father, Octavio. Just as Kiuprili, Octavio represents the legitimate sovereign,

---

[67] On Coleridge's opinion of Schiller, see Carlson, "Command Performances," and Angela Esterhammer, "Cognitive Process, Commanding Genius, and Comparative Literature," *Coleridge Bulletin: The Journal of the Friends of Coleridge* 16 (2000): 56–62.

[68] CCW, *Plays*, 1:620.

[69] On Coleridge's and Schiller's different attitudes regarding traditional law see Carlson, "Command Performances," 126–7.

and fights against the seditious aristocrat in every possible way. Similarly to what happens in *Zapolya*, Max eventually breaks allegiance with Wallenstein when he realizes how his trust in him was founded on a mistaken evaluation. At this stage, Max goes back to his father's side, as Casimir does, and fights against his former ally. The similarity in the plot of the two plays is strengthened by a number of minor allusions. The web of lies Emerick and his associates weave is analogous to the deceits Wallenstein's supporters enact to reinforce their leader's position and to offer him an opportunity effectively to oppose the emperor. Moreover, small elements link the two plays more or less explicitly, such as the references to astrology by both Emerick and Schiller's protagonists, and the killer Pestalutz in *Zapolya*, who bears the same name of an assassin mentioned in *Wallenstein's Death*.

The similarities between the plays, as before, involve only part of the texts. While the German trilogy maintains a problematizing perspective, full of ambiguous nuances, Coleridge's view of the events depicted in *Zapolya* is almost Manichean. There is no interior struggle in his characters: their attitudes and points of view are clear-cut throughout the plot. This is apparent if we compare the critical positions in which Casimir and Max are placed, when they have to choose between keeping faith to their leader and being loyal to their fathers. At first sight, *Zapolya* seems to mirror the trilogy in this instance. Just as Max Piccolomini is divided between his friend Wallenstein and his father Octavio, Casimir has to choose between Emerick and his parent, Raab Kiuprili. There is a difference, however, between the two situations. Max suffers from a deep interior suffering, a "split" to which only his death puts an end. Wallenstein gains his trust not only by a political allegiance, or through a bond of affection (the youth's secret engagement to the leader's daughter, Thekla); his high ideal stature, however collapsing during the trilogy, also fascinates Octavio's son. The final result is a tragedy within the tragedy—that is, Max's interior laceration that will never be mended. In Raab Kiuprili's son, on the other hand, no such trauma can be noticed. In the single instance in which he seems to be troubled—an episode that, by the way, covers no more than four lines and a very brief stage direction (*Exit Casimir in agitation*)[70]—his behavior is not due to any doubt he may have regarding his choice, but to the fear for his father's fate. Eventually, he simply changes sides. The character we observe in the Prelude is completely different from that we see in the Sequel, but he is similarly unambiguous and unfaltering, so much so that while at the beginning he decisively supports the usurper, in the end he kills him with no uneasiness whatsoever. In the father/son/usurper triangle (or father/son/general triangle in Schiller's case), the other characters too show some relevant differences: while Wallenstein is a complex character showing both superior moral features and evil connotations, there can be no doubt about Emerick's fiendish and low personality; while Octavio Piccolomini's morality seems uncertain, Raab Kiuprili's probity is unquestionable.

Such diversity is due to the different conception of power maintained by each author, which is underscored by the very intertextual relationship here established. Writing in the light of the revolutionary events of the late eighteenth century,

---

[70] *Zapolya*, Prelude, 1.1.408, 421–3, 426 s.d.

Schiller underscores the need for change but also the impossibility of achieving it; once they rise up and try to take action, the protagonists of the new political course also get contaminated by corruption and treachery just like the traditional regime.[71] The trilogy supports the idea that in history no moral action can take place, because there is no superior ruling ethical principle to guide humanity.[72] The laceration determined by the tension between the desire for change and the impossibility of achieving it is interiorised by the characters, to the point that it kills those who are most affected by it (Max Piccolomini, Thekla); and death is also the fate for those who, like Wallenstein, deceive themselves about the possibility of acting morally in history and end up tainting their ideal vision with low actions caused by miserly material necessity. Coleridge's vision of history is considerably different. He believes in a superior mind that rules human events, which makes moral action possible: such is human action when the individual chooses to follow the divine plan instead of giving in to the temptation of following a purely human logic, which is necessarily destructive and devilish. In fact, the main contention of *The Statesman's Manual*—a basic work to keep in mind in order to understand *Zapolya*—is that the rule of the state is moral when it follows divine law. In wider terms, unlike Schiller, Coleridge believes moral action to be possible, provided such guide is followed. Whoever disobeys it, besides being immoral, is also fated to failure, because the whole history of humanity is already written in the Bible:

> Its contents present to us the stream of time continuous as Life and a symbol of Eternity, inasmuch as the Past and the Future are virtually contained in the Present. According therefore to our relative position on its banks the Sacred History becomes prophetic, the Sacred Prophecies historical, while the power and substance of both inhere in it Laws, its Promises, and its Comminations. In the Scriptures therefore both Facts and Persons must of necessity have a two-fold significance, a past and a future, a temporary and a perpetual, a particular and a universal application.[73]

When Coleridge establishes an intertextual relationship with the *Wallenstein* trilogy, his aim is to challenge the German dramatist's thesis. Keeping real history in the background but changing its framework from the French Revolution—to which Schiller alludes—to Napoleon's career, and employing multiple Shakespearean references to imbue his work with a "divine" atmosphere, Coleridge aims at creating a play that shows that—contrary to Schiller—a just, universal, divine design is the driving force of human history.

---

[71] Allusions to the emperor's iniquity and acts of corruption can be found in the entire trilogy, but especially in *Wallenstein's Camp*, which is centered on the discussion among army members about the sovereign's unwillingness to fulfill his promises.

[72] In this regard, see Roberta M. Glassey, "The Concept of Freedom in Schiller's Wallenstein," *Journal of European Studies* 4 (1980): 256–66 and John Neubauer, "The Idea of History in Schiller's Wallenstein," *Neophilologus* 4 (1972): 451–63.

[73] SM, 29–30.

## Chapter 8
# Contextual Hauntings: Shakespearean Ghosts on the Gothic Stage

Francesca Saggini

> But that I am forbid
> To tell the secrets of my prison-house,
> I could a tale unfold whose lightest word
> Would harrow up thy soul, freeze thy young blood
> Make thy two eyes like stars start from their spheres,
> Thy knotted and combined locks to part,
> And each particular hair to stand an end
> Like quills upon the fretful porpentine:
> But this eternal blazon must not be
> To ears of flesh and blood. List, list, O, list!
> If thou didst ever thy dear father love—
> —*Hamlet*

> Some of the shattered masses give most clear echoes: we stood before one, which repeated every syllable of several passages from the most sonorous languages, with an exactness of tone that was truly astonishing. It seemed as if a living spirit was in the rock, so near, so loud, and so exact! "Speak to it, Horatio!" I could have listened to it for hours.
> —Thomas Noon Talfourd, "Memoir of the Life and Writing of Mrs Radcliffe" (1826)

Drama critic and Shakespearean connoisseur James Boaden (1762–1839) is now a nearly forgotten literary figure, almost exclusively remembered as the author of five of the best known Romantic theatrical biographies.[1] Known for his skills as a translator (*The Voice of Nature, A Play in Three Acts*), Boaden was also the author of a handful of original plays, including *The Secret Tribunal* (1795), an oblique commentary on 1790s British politics that notably influenced both Ann Radcliffe's *The Italian* and Matthew Gregory Lewis's *The Monk*.[2] More importantly, during

---

[1] *Memoirs of the Life of John Philip Kemble, Esq.* (1825); *Memoirs of Mrs. Siddons* (1827); *The Life of Mrs Jordan* (1831); *Memoirs of Mrs. Inchbald* (1833); and *The Private Correspondence of David Garrick: with the Most Celebrated Persons of his Time* (1831). All of these biographies were published in London.

[2] David Warrall, "The Political Culture of Gothic Drama," in *A Companion to the Gothic*, ed. David Punter (Oxford-Malden: Blackwell, 2000), 95–7. For Boaden's biography and details of his literary works, see Steve Cohan, ed., *The Plays of James Boaden* (New York: Garland, 1980), v–lxv, and Temple Maynard, "James Boaden," in *Dictionary of Literary Biography*, ed. Paula Backscheider, vol. 89 (Detroit: Gale, 1989), 25–37.

the 1790s—the decade that saw the rise of the Gothic craze[3]—Boaden composed and staged dramatic adaptations of some of the most popular Gothic novels of the period. Two of these novels, Radcliffe's *The Romance of the Forest* and *The Italian*, were brought on stage respectively as *Fontainville Forest* (Covent Garden, 1794) and *The Italian Monk* (Haymarket, 1797). Later, Boaden's interest in Lewis's sensational novel—already implied by the hotchpotch title of *The Italian Monk*—led to another stage adaptation, *Aurelio and Miranda* (Drury Lane, 1798).

Boaden's midlife career as a dramatist may be attributed to his life-long involvement with the London Theatres Royal, in his triple role of stage-struck spectator, enthusiastic editor, and discriminating theater contributor (under the pseudonym of Thespis) to the daily newspaper *The Oracle, and Public Advertiser*. As well as bringing him in contact with the leading actors of the day, whose individual dramatic abilities he learned to discern and appreciate, Boaden's activity made him aware of the rapidly shifting tastes of late eighteenth-century audiences, who were more and more inclined to dramatic forms that privileged spectacularism and dramatic gigantism. As noted by his modern biographer, Temple Maynard, "Boaden was sensitive to the necessities of dramatic presentation, and his manipulation of stage effects certainly contributed to the enthusiastic reception of his plays."[4] Significantly, "effect" is one of the terms that frequently appear in Boaden's dramatic criticism. In his biography of John Philip Kemble, for instance, Boaden describes the vision that comes to Queen Katherine in *Henry VIII* as illustrated by Henry Fuseli: "Look at the *effect* of these circling and ascending spirits in Mr. Fuseli's picture of the scene."[5]

The term "effect" in Boaden's writing, I suggest, is all the more remarkable in the context of eighteenth-century dramatic criticism, particularly criticism of Shakespearean stage practice. Samuel Johnson, for instance, had praised the role of the Queen in *Henry VIII* as "among the greatest efforts of tragedy" and her scenes as the dramatic *loci* in which "the genius of Shakespeare comes in."[6] In particular, Johnson had singled out the same scene in *Henry VIII* that Boaden had found so effective:

> This scene is, above any other part of *Shakespeare*'s tragedies, and perhaps above any scene of any other poet, tender and pathetic, without gods, or furies, or poisons, or precipices, without the help of romantick circumstances, without improbable sallies of poetical lamentation, and without any throes of tumultuous misery.[7]

---

[3] Robert Miles, "The 1790s: The Effulgence of Gothic," in *The Cambridge Companion to Gothic Fiction*, ed. Jerrold Hogle (Cambridge: Cambridge University Press, 2002), 41–62.

[4] Maynard, "James Boaden," 27.

[5] James Boaden, *Memoirs of the Life of John Philip Kemble*, 2 vols. (London, 1825), 2:121, emphasis mine.

[6] Samuel Johnson, *Johnson on Shakespeare*, ed. Walter Raleigh (Oxford: Oxford University Press, 1908), 152.

[7] Ibid., 150–51.

Only a few years later, however, Johnson's laudatory views were no longer universally shared. One case in point is Thomas Davis, better remembered as one of David Garrick's biographers, who briskly rejected Shakespeare's presentation of the six white-clad spirits as a "little *pantomime* ... fitter to tempt an audience to mirth and ridicule than to serious attention."[8] Davis's words attest to the midcentury fears of the cultural and generic mixing that unlicensed shows were bringing to the London patent houses, especially to the sacred realm of Shakespearean drama. For instance, the 1762 adaptation of *Henry VIII* for Drury Lane was expanded by the insertion of an opulent pageant for the coronation of Ann Bullen, an effective, elaborate procession that "would make a sight to impress even one of 'judicious taste.'"[9]

It had become apparent, then, that sound and show—songs and lavish spectacle—might appeal to the audiences as much (and as lastingly) as masterful performances and stock repertory. Regarding the production of George Colman's *Bluebeard* at Drury Lane in 1798, for instance, Boaden remarked:

> The critic, who, in the preface to the Iron Chest, had made himself so merry with the ponderous machinery, the splendid processions, the elephants and the triumphal cars of Drury Lane Theatre, was induced to lend himself to the great work of corrupting the public taste, and succeeded beyond all competition in the dramatic romance of Blue Beard. ... It is dramatically drawn out by Mr. Colman, *with striking effect* and occasional pleasantry. The music, by Kelly, was remarkably well conceived, and the parts were all acted in the happiest manner imaginable.[10]

Boaden's activity as a writer of theatrical adaptations was limited to the 1790s; in his later life he became more interested in researching Shakespeareana and writing Shakespearean literary criticism, publishing works such as *A Letter to George Steevens, Esq. Containing a Critical Examination of the Papers of Shakespeare* (1796), *An Inquiry into the Authenticity of Various Pictures and Prints, Which ... Have Been Offered to the Public as Portraits of Shakespeare* (1824), and *On the Sonnets of Shakespeare* (1837). As an amateur Shakespearean philologist and critic, he was instrumental in shaming Samuel and William Henry Ireland's forgeries; a few years later his influential biographies of actors contributed to the formation of the Romantic dramatic canon. Despite these strong ties to the legitimate world of the metropolitan theaters, however, Boaden was fascinated by spectacle, visual shows, and similar forms of entertainment that had quickly risen

---

[8] Thomas Davies, *Dramatic Miscellanies* (1784). Cited in Martin Myrone, *Gothic Nightmares: Fuseli, Blake and the Gothic Imagination* (London: Tate, 2006), 152, emphasis mine.

[9] George C. Branam, *Eighteenth-Century Adaptations of Shakespearean Tragedy* (Berkeley: University of California Press, 1956), 156–7, 185.

[10] Boaden, *John Philip Kemble*, 2:208, emphasis mine.

to success in the London patented stage and which he deftly appropriated in his three Gothic adaptations.

This essay considers *Fontainville Forest*, the first of these plays, and shows how the presence of an onstage ghost offers a complex representation of the often implicit, yet far-reaching, Shakespearean influence on the arts in the 1790s.[11] In particular, my discussion of the transformation of Radcliffe's *The Romance of the Forest* into Boaden's *Fontainville Forest* brings into focus what is possibly the best known feature of Radcliffe's poetics: the representation of the "explained supernatural," one of Radcliffe's narrative trademarks. I contend that an analysis of the supernatural in *Fontainville Forest* benefits from a contextual and transmedial approach. By building on a reappraisal of Radcliffe's readings of the supernatural, the holistic analysis of Boaden's drama I present takes into consideration two complementary phenomena: the contemporary visual representations of Shakespearean ghosts and contemporary theatrical stagings of Shakespearean plays at Drury Lane.

\* \* \*

In 1794 Boaden adapted Radcliffe's *The Romance of the Forest* for Covent Garden, receiving both great public acclaim and critical abuse. The play was performed thirteen times as a mainpiece and once as an afterpiece in its first season (March 25, 1794, to June 18, 1794),[12] and was revived with good success in the following years. The choice of text must have been obvious for Boaden, since *The Romance of the Forest* was praised so widely at the time of its publication that it encouraged Radcliffe to acknowledge her authorship in the second edition of the novel, published in 1792.[13] Interestingly, although hardly surprisingly, *affect* and *effect*—the inner world of the emotions and the implied stage possibilities of their actualization and ostension—were the aesthetic coordinates Boaden valued most in Radcliffe's novel. "Mr. Boaden had read the Romance of the Forest with great pleasure, and thought that he saw there the ground-work of a drama of more

---

[11] See Jonathan Bate, *Shakespeare and the English Romantic Imagination* (Oxford: Clarendon Press, 1986).

[12] See the calendar of plays in John Genest, *Some Account of the English Stage from the Restoration in 1660 to 1830*, 10 vols. (Bath, UK: H. E. Carrington, 1832) and *The London Stage, 1660–1800: A Calendar of Plays, Entertainments & Afterpieces, Part 5: 1776–1800*, ed. Charles Beecher Hogan, 3 vols. (Carbondale: Southern Illinois University Press, 1968).

[13] For a critical biography of Radcliffe and discussion of her works, see Robert Miles, *Ann Radcliffe: The Great Enchantress* (Manchester: Manchester University Press, 1995) and Rictor Norton, *Mistress of Udolpho: The Life of Ann Radcliffe* (London: Leicester University Press, 1999).

than usual *effect*,"[14] he recalled in one of his biographical narratives, referring to himself in the third person.

By 1794 Radcliffe's novel had already reached its fourth edition, with raving critical reviews in the *Critical Review* and the *English Review*, among others.[15] Significantly, not only was *The Romance of the Forest* the first of Radcliffe's novels to be adapted for the stage (although published in 1789, *The Castles of Athlin and Dunbayne* was not dramatized until 1806, as George Manners's *Edgar, or Caledonian Feuds*); it was also a trendsetter among dramatic adaptations of Radcliffe's work.[16] As *The Mysteries of Udolpho* was awaiting publication, the successful production of *Fontainville Forest* was immediately followed in the same season by Henry Siddons's stage version of *A Sicilian Romance*, entitled *The Sicilian Romance, or The Apparition on the Cliffs* (Covent Garden, May 28, 1794). Six months later Miles Peter Andrews's opera, *Mysteries of the Castle* (Covent Garden, January 1, 1795), loosely based on *The Mysteries of Udolpho*, was staged.[17] Intertheatrical evidence thus shows that in the middle of the 1790s the generically popular Gothic dramas and entertainments put on at Covent Garden by the manager Thomas Harris were able to compete with the more culturally esteemed Shakespearean productions and the inexhaustible "treasures of our ancient authors"[18] presented at the new Drury Lane by John Philip Kemble.

Boaden may be considered the first and, arguably, the most sensitive of a long line of Gothic appropriators who realized the stage potential of Radcliffe's novels. Not only did he comprehend their stage viability and possible success, but also, more significantly, he managed to bring on stage—and thus physically actualized—the novelist's narrative technique. I contend that the reevaluation

---

[14] Boaden, *John Philip Kemble*, 2:96–7, emphasis mine.

[15] Deborah D. Rogers, ed., *The Critical Response to Ann Radcliffe* (Westport, CT: Greenwood Press, 1994), 5–7.

[16] Rogers, ed., *Critical Response*, xxvi.

[17] See W. Thorp, "The Stage Adventures of Some Gothic Novels," *PMLA* 43 (1928): 481–6.

[18] Boaden, *John Philip Kemble*, 2:97. The fact that the Covent Garden manager was more active in presenting new pieces may be partly explained by the fact that one of the proprietors of the Drury Lane was Richard Brinsley Sheridan, who promoted his own plays (*The School for Scandal*, *The Duenna*, and *The Critic* were among the twelve most frequently acted plays in the final quarter of the century). The Covent Garden company, on the other hand, did not include such heavyweight actors as the Kemble family (John Philip, Sarah Siddons, and Charles, who made his debut on April 22, 1794, with *Macbeth*). Moreover, the box receipts for *Fontainville Forest* were considerably less throughout the entirety of its run than those for *Macbeth*. Although the draw of *Fontainville Forest* was strengthened by coupling it with Thomas Didbin's successful pantomime *Harlequin and Faustus* as an afterpiece, the receipts remained considerably lower after the opening of *Macbeth*. It would thus appear that *The Sicilian Romance* was the Covent Garden's answer to the economic success of the Drury Lane's *Macbeth*. See Hogan, ed., *The London Stage*, clxxii–clxxiii.

of the intertextual dimension of *Fontainville Forest*—what we may define as its contextual framing—implies the rediscovery of the inescapable metatextual dimension implicit in textual dialogism.[19] The multiple languages present within the Gothic adaptation express a cultural negotiation that transforms the drama, cross-fertilizing the stage, the page, and the canvas at the same time—in my terms, the visual, spectacular, and theatrical ghosts that haunt the Gothic cultural products.

Despite the interest a dramatization of a popular novel must have had for the theatergoing public, the transmigration of *The Romance of the Forest* to the stage must have been far from easy given the novel's adaptation problems. The contemporary reviewers of the novel, for instance, noted that it solidified Radcliffe's reputation for poetical descriptions of landscapes. Praise for pictorialism was, however, accompanied by criticism: although original in their ability to blend poetry, narration, and landscape art, the many descriptive passages were often considered prolix, at times even tedious. More significantly, Boaden faced the problem of bringing on stage, and thus visualizing, the apparently marvelous occurrences that Radcliffe cleverly left to her readers'—as well as her heroine's—imaginations.

Boaden's controversial decision to include the presence of an onstage ghost must be considered daring and risky. Although Lewis's *The Castle Spectre* (Drury Lane, December 14, 1797) would soon mark the inclusion of ghosts in Gothic drama, in 1794 Boaden could only draw inspiration for the representation of ghosts from the Shakespearean tradition. As explained by Michael Gamer, "even the most spectacular of gothic dramas had avoided representing ghosts on stage, and exceptions to this unwritten rule were rare."[20] It does not come as a surprise, then, that many reviewers opposed Boaden's unorthodox ghosts. Among these was John Genest, one of the best known theater historians of the period, who chronicled with typical disparagement: "This is a moderate play by Boaden—the plot is professedly borrowed from the Romance of the Forest—the last scene of the third act is rendered contemptible by the introduction to a Phantom."[21] Similarly, Steve Cohan maintains that Thomas Harris himself was "so nervous about having

---

[19] My use of the terms "intertextual," "metatextual," "transtextuality," and "textuality in the second degree" is profoundly indebted to the theorization offered by Gérard Genette, *Palimpsestes: La littérature au second degré* (Paris: Seuil, 1982).

[20] Michael Gamer, *Romanticism and the Gothic: Genre, Reception, and Canon Formation* (Cambridge: Cambridge University Press, 2000), 131. One of the rare exceptions to this rule is Harriet Lee's *The Mysterious Marriage; or, The Heirship of Roselva* (1798), which John Franceschina defines as "the first play to employ the device of the ghost of the murdered heroine." See his edition of *Sisters of Gore: Seven Gothic Melodramas by British Women, 1790–1843* (New York: Garland, 1997), 68. In the advertisement to her play, Lee vindicates the originality of an otherworldly apparition by noting that her work preceded Lewis's ghost of Evelina by many years.

[21] Genest, *Some Account of the English Stage*, 7:163.

the ghost in the play that [he] persuaded Boaden to cut most of the lines to speed it along."[22]

In effect the inclusion of a supernatural figure would play a significant part in erasing the ever more flimsy dividing line separating legitimate drama from the drama of sensorial stimulation and spectacle. Michael Gamer has explained the Romantic dramatic ideology as the urge to define "tragedy as the most intellectual, imaginative, evocative, generically 'pure,' and innately British of dramatic forms ... dissociating it from contemporary trends toward spectacle and supernatural effect."[23] This cultural phenomenon helped create a widening rift between critical respectability and public popularity, dramatic theory and theatrical practice, contributing to the inexorable backsliding of contemporary theater from "words" towards striking gestures, lavish images, and special effects—normally the province of the popular entertainments thriving in the transpontine houses of the capital.

I argue that an analysis of the Gothic stage appropriations should investigate not only the generic context of Boaden's play, but also what the audience and the critics—both those knowing and those unfamiliar with the source text—actually saw and heard on stage as well as what they recognized. This contextual framing, I suggest, is crucial for an understanding of *Fontainville Forest*. How much did the familiarity with the novels bear upon the reception of their dramatic adaptations? And how much did the Gothic playwrights rely on this familiarity? What can intertheatricality and extraliterary intertextuality teach us about *Fontainville Forest*? And, finally, how did intertheatricality and extraliterary intertextuality inform the themes, form, and stage actualization of the drama? The influence on Boaden's stage practice of contemporary artistic illustrations of theatrical scenes (such as Henry Fuseli's) and competing Shakespearean performances (such as Kemble's) may help us focus on the closing gap between contemporary definitions of legitimacy and illegitimacy—and in so doing bring back to light the Gothic textual plurality.

\* \* \*

The plot of *Fontainville Forest* is very formulaic as it presents all the cultural icons of the Gothic tradition. In a forest outside Paris, Adeline, a beautiful orphan, is given by ruffians over to the Lamottes, a family in flight from Paris. They seek shelter in a crumbling abbey, the property of the Marquis Philippe de Montalt,

---

[22] Cohan, ed., *Plays of James Boaden*, xv.
[23] Gamer, *Romanticism and the Gothic*, 129. The dynamic relationship between licensed and unlicensed theater, popular and higher class dramatic forms in English Romanticism is illustrated, among others, by Jane Moody, *Illegitimate Theatre in London, 1770–1840* (Cambridge: Cambridge University Press, 2000) and Jeffrey Cox and Michael Gamer, eds., *The Broadview Anthology of Romantic Drama* (Peterborough, ON: Broadview, 2003).

who, unbeknownst to Adeline, is the girl's uncle as well as the murderer of her father, the rightful heir to the family fortune and title. Both Louis Lamotte and de Montalt fall in love with Adeline; de Montalt demands that Old Lamotte help him trick the girl into a mock marriage. He threatens to betray the family and give up Lamotte, who attacked him in the forest, if Lamotte refuses. Hence Lamotte's moral dilemma: whether to abandon Adeline to the lust of the Marquis, to whom he is under obligation, or to withstand the nobleman, thus jeopardizing his own and his family's safety.

Aware of the fact that the three-decker format offered a novelist a much broader canvas as it allowed her to "explore" in detail her subject, Boaden preferred to focus on the first part of the novel—in his words, so as simply to leave everything "touched rather than explored."[24] Therefore he relied on the extraliterary impact that could be achieved through the spectacular collaboration of stagecraft, scenery, music, and acting:

> The dramatic author has only at most five short acts to display all the peculiarities of his characters, however diversified in what our fathers called their humours. Here he has great aid, it is true, in the admirable skills of his actors, who, from the possession they take of a part, or allow a part to take of them, in the first word they utter convey "a whole history," and by their dress and action place the living being absolutely before you. The fable, however, neither abruptly nor languidly, must be completely developed and concluded in the short compass of eighty or a hundred pages.[25]

One of the major alterations devised by Boaden may be illuminating. In *Fontainville Forest* the suitably Gothic abbey is emphasized at the expense of the heroine's long wanderings through scenic parts of France and Switzerland, a journey that covers ten out of twenty-six chapters in the novel.[26] As well as being sensitive to the unity of place, Boaden's choice is coherent with Radcliffe's novels, which always make use of the house symbol. The ruinous condition of the abbey visually embodies the idea of a crumbling, constricting past that still tries to project its influence on the present and the future. At the same time, the single, claustrophobic location highlights Adeline's loneliness. Its forlornness duplicates the girl's solitude, actualizing and ostending the multiple threats—sexual, societal, and familial—experienced by Radcliffe's Adeline.

I suggest that Boaden's use of evocative local scenery is particularly respectful of the poetics of Radcliffe, who expressed her theory of "corresponding scenery" and "attendant circumstances" in the fragment "On the Supernatural in Poetry" (published posthumously with *Gaston de Blondeville* in 1826), illustrating it with examples drawn from four Shakespearean dramas: *Cymbeline, Macbeth, Julius*

---

[24] Boaden, *John Philip Kemble*, 2:144.
[25] Boaden, *Memoirs of Mrs. Siddons*, 161–2.
[26] Ann Radcliffe, *The Romance of the Forest*, ed. Chloe Chard (Oxford: Oxford University Press, 1999).

*Caesar*, and *Hamlet*. In this essay Radcliffe explains that corresponding scenery has the effect of heightening the readers' ideas of dramatic character so as to "prepare and interest them for his fate."[27] In this sense, Boaden's choice of a single location illustrates his indirect response to Radcliffe's poetic criteria. Not only does the playwright maintain the unity of emotion of the novel, I would argue; he even manages to enhance it, avoiding some of the common pitfalls lamented by the contemporary reviewers:

> The unity of the fable in this romance [*The Italian*] is well preserved; here we have no unmeaning episode, which might be entirely neglected without injury to the narrative, nothing like the history of the *la Luc* family in the Romance of the Forest, which destroys the simplicity of the story, and introduces new and independent objects of consideration, of a nature totally different from the principal subject.[28]

In light of Radcliffe's theory of creative evocation, the introduction of a ghost in *Fontainville Forest* may thus explain the aesthetics of Boaden's "Romantic" adaptation.

The dramatic relevance of the "unity of emotion" in Boaden's adaptation is convincingly illustrated by his staging of the supernatural. Whereas in *The Romance of the Forest* Radcliffe explains away her heroine's fears as the effects of her overstrained sensibility and wild imagination, in *Fontainville Forest* Boaden insists on embodying Adeline's anxiety through an onstage ghost who directly addresses her in the central part of the play:

> ADELINE.
> At last I am alone! And now may venture
> To look at the contents of this old manuscript.
> A general horror creeps through my limbs,
> And almost stifles curiosity.
>     (*Reads*)
> .....
> "They seiz'd me as I reached the neighbour wood,
> .....
> Yet, O my brother, I had never wrong'd you."
> His brother! What, yon Marquis?
>
> PHANTOM.
> Even he
>     (*heard within the chamber*)

---

[27] Ann Radcliffe, "On the Supernatural in Poetry," in *Gothic Readings: The First Wave, 1764–1840*, ed. Rictor Norton (New York: Leicester University Press, 2006), 312.

[28] Review in the *Monthly Mirror* 3 (March, 1797), 155–8, quoted in Rogers, ed., *Critical Response*, 53.

ADELINE.
Hark! Sure I heard a voice! No, 'tis the thunder
That rolls its murmurs thro' this yawning pile.
..........

PHANTOM.
O Adeline!

ADELINE.
Ha! sure I am call'd! No, all are now at rest.
How powerful is fancy![29]

On the surface, the structure of the dramatic heroine's experience would appear to follow the same narrative formula of the "explained supernatural": Adeline repeatedly invokes sensory evidence in order to refute her fears and condemn them as unjustified. Every time she turns to scientific and philosophic skepticism, however, the Phantom challenges her enlightened notions and her avowals of empiricism. Once her feelings have been stirred by the emotional and highly participative reading of the sorrowful tale of her father, both Adeline's sense and her sensibility are ready to acknowledge the reality of the supernatural sounds she is hearing. In a truly cathartic moment, terror overwhelms Adeline as pity moves her. This moment coincides with the apparition of her father's ghost:

ADELINE.
My sense does not deceive me! awful sounds!
'Twas here he fell!

[*The phantom here glides across the dark part of the Chamber, Adeline shrieks, and falls back. The Scene closes upon her.*] (40)

Although the lofty appearance majestically "floated along like a shadow"[30] in front of the footlights only for a few moments, the sudden shock experienced by the breathless public must have been artfully amplified by the falling of the curtain. This dramatic convention recodified for the stage Radcliffe's narrative suspense, making it all the more shocking through its proximity with the violently catastrophic opening of the following act.

SCENE – The Hall (dark)

Violent Thunder and Light'ning, the Abbey Rocks, and through the distant Windows one of the Turrets is seen to fall, struck by the Light'ning.

Enter the MARQUIS, wild and dishevell'd. (40)

---

[29] Boaden, *Plays of James Boaden*, ed. Cohan, 38–9. All references to the play are from this edition unless otherwise noted.
[30] Boaden, *John Philip Kemble*, 2:119.

In an adaptation of the ghost scene in *Hamlet*, explicitly evoked in the play's epilogue by Adeline, de Montalt's phantom has come back from the dead to demand a vengeance that his daughter duly promises to give him:

ADELINE.
Nay, let no thought of me withhold your purpose;
My boding spirit tell me that a great,
A mighty vengeance works to punish guilt?
Shall my weak fears prevent or thwart its aim?
No! For against all artifice I am steel'd
By horror and aversion; and the force
That violates my honour quenches life;
They can never be sundered ... (69–70)

As well as offering evidence of important points of contact with visual culture (for instance, the role played by late eighteenth-century pictorial supernaturalism),[31] Boaden's choice to stage the phantom undermines the idea of the Gothic playwrights as closet dramatists, while highlighting a crucial feature of his adaptational practice. The playwright realized that in Radcliffe's novels the character's consciousness offered a filter between the narrated events and the reader, who shared in the protagonists' uncertainties. This mechanism could not work in a play, a less mediated form that compels the artist to choose to admit or banish the supernatural. "Perhaps, when the attention is once secured and the reason yielded, the passion for the marvellous had better remain unchecked," the playwright later commented.[32]

Boaden firmly believed that the audience would appreciate the spectacle as a work of art, an artistic illusion composed by a playwright and acted by players in front of an audience that momentarily chose to be deceived: "the pen of the dramatic poet must turn everything into shape, and bestow on these 'airy nothings a local habitation and a name'."[33] Thus, reliance on dramatic illusion and the

---

[31] For pictorial supernaturalism see Myrone, *Gothic Nightmares*. A discussion of Hamlet's ghost, illuminating for an understanding of Boaden's poetics of the supernatural, is proposed in Boaden, *John Philip Kemble*, 1:103–9. Boaden's ghost is analyzed in Cohan, ed., *Plays of James Boaden*, "Introduction"; Robert Reno, "James Boaden's *Fontainville Forest* and Matthew G. Lewis' *The Castle Spectre*: Challenges of the Supernatural Ghost on the Late Eighteenth-Century Stage," *Eighteenth-Century Life* 9 (1984): 94–106; Gamer, *Romanticism and the Gothic*, 131–4; and Penny Gay, "Northanger Abbey: Catherine's Adventures in the Gothic Theatre," in *Jane Austen and the Theatre* (Cambridge: Cambridge University Press, 2002), 52–72. I have discussed Boaden's adaptation in Francesca Saggini, "Radcliffe's Novels and Boaden's Dramas: Bringing the Configurations of the Gothic on Stage," in *Rites of Passage: Rational/Irrational Natural/Supernatural Local/Global*, ed. Carmela Nocera, Gemma Persico, and Rosario Portale (Soveria Mannelli, Italy: Rubbettino, 2003), 193–203.

[32] Boaden, *John Philip Kemble*, 2:97.

[33] Ibid.

suspension of disbelief permitted him to deflate and reject any accusation of irreligious or unenlightened inspiration. As he explains in his remarks on Robert Jephson's *The Count of Narbonne* (Covent Garden, 1781), the Gothic adaptation that had already brought preternatural events on the stage, Walpole's novel remained superior to a drama in which "the supernatural was rather hinted than shewn."[34] Jephson, Boaden contends, "was not the man to describe the magic circle." He failed "in one great spring of tragic emotion—*terror*, he was not gifted in any striking degree with the other—*pity.*"[35] A self-styled "venturous bard,"[36] Boaden rose up to the challenge and attempted to "ascertain whether the failure of others had not proceeded from defective preparation as to supernatural incident, or from its imperfect or vulgar exhibition."[37]

On the metacritical level we might contend that Boaden appropriated for the stage the expectations of future horrors and dreadful anticipations experienced by Radcliffe's heroines and, vicariously, by her readers. His ghost transubstantiates both Adeline's and the reading audience's curiosity, of which it offers not only the stage actualization, but also the aesthetic fulfillment. In this way *Fontainville Forest* may be considered Boaden's critical and cultural response to the Radcliffean poetics, which was often criticized for exploiting the readers' highstrung expectations, turning them into bathos. As the reviewer for the *Critical Review* remarked in 1794, in the Gothic novel curiosity is raised so high that it can never find adequate gratification. This sense of frustration was clearly perceived by Boaden, who wrote:

> Even in romance it may be doubtful, whether there be not something *ungenerous* in thus playing upon poor timid human nature, and agonising it with false terrors. The disappointment is, I know, always resented, and the laboured explanation commonly deemed the flattest and most uninteresting part of the production.[38]

On the level of intertheatricality we may also notice that *Fontainville Forest* was produced a few weeks after the inauguration of the new Drury Lane (March 12, 1794). Haunted by his personal version of the "ghost of the Bard," to whose memory he dedicated the renovated theater, the actor-manager John Philip Kemble had chosen to open the season with a grandiose staging of *Macbeth* in which Banquo's ghost did not appear on stage.[39] This decision, which ran counter to a dramatic tradition that had been established for over a decade, took notice of those critics who had recently started to attack the presence of supernatural beings in Shakespearean plays. Concerning *Macbeth* in particular, Robert Lloyd had been one of the earliest commentators to recommend that the ghost be omitted: "The

---

[34] Ibid., 1:277.
[35] Ibid., 1:278.
[36] Boaden, epilogue to *Fontainville Forest*, in *Plays*, 69.
[37] Boaden, *John Philip Kemble*, 2:98.
[38] Boaden, *John Philip Kemble*, 2:97.
[39] Hogan, ed., *London Stage*, 1638.

King alone should form the Phantom there, / And talk and tremble at the vacant Chair."[40] Kemble must have taken heed of this as well as of similar suggestions. A memorandum published for the opening of the new Drury Lane, for instance, records that "great attention has evidently bestowed to the notes of the several commentators; among the boldest alterations is that of *laying* BANQUO's Ghost, and making the troubled spirit only visible to the 'mind's eye' of the guilty and distracted tyrant."[41] The *European Magazine* (May 1794) similarly notes:

> Some alterations were made with great judgment, particularly the omission of the visible appearance of the Ghost of Banquo, which some of the best judges of the drama had long since recommended the exclusion of. … We think ourselves warranted to give our opinion in favour of the alteration.[42]

Apparently, however, his decision did not gain the complete favor of all spectators. Although the audiences seemed to welcome this alteration, they remained astounded by the large-scale sensorial stimulation devised by Kemble, who significantly increased the number of spectacular effects originally introduced by William Davenant in 1664 and later David Garrick. The novelties included a crowd of over fifty singing witches dancing to the potent music of a full orchestra (at first introduced on a much smaller scale in Davenant's operatic version), Hecate and other devilish spirits flying backwards and ascending in a chair (a practice discontinued by Garrick), and, more importantly, the ethereal procession of Banquo's shadowy descendants who crossed the stage as deafening thunderclaps "rolled through the whole play."[43]

Other commentators did not quite reconcile themselves to the omission of the ghost of Banquo. According to an anecdote recorded in *Memoirs of Mrs. Siddons*, one of Boaden's friends, the history painter John Opie, strongly criticized those who censured the presence of "the visionary devil" in Sir Joshua Reynolds's portrait of Cardinal Beaufort by comparing it with Kemble's ghostless *Macbeth*:

> "This was the point on which rested the whole moral effect of the piece. …"
> He then, in a forcible manner, ridicules the objectors to this mode of treating the subject, and proceeds thus:—"Of the same class were those who of late endeavoured to rob the play of *Macbeth* of the resurrection of Banquo's ghost to fill the chair of the murderer. Happily, however, for the true lovers of

---

[40] Robert Lloyd, *The Actor* (1760), quoted in Joseph Donohue, "Kemble's Production of Macbeth (1794)," *Theatre Notebook* 21 (1967): 68.

[41] "The Opening of the New Drury Lane Theatre, 1794," in *Romantic and Revolutionary Theatre*, ed. Donald Roy (Cambridge: Cambridge University Press, 2003), 90. The emphasis is in the text.

[42] Hogan, ed., *London Stage*, 1638. Other reviews were published in April 1794 in the *London Packet*, the *Morning Chronicle*, the *World*, and the *Oracle and Public Advertiser*. See Donohue, "Kemble's Production," 69–70.

[43] Hogan, ed., *London Stage*, 1569.

Shakespeare, the genuine feelings of the public have decided against this most barbarous mutilation."[44]

Obviously, we cannot know whether Opie's comment represents the truth or, rather, is a deft strategy devised in his later life by Boaden himself, who had by then become actively engaged in the construction of the national dramatic canon. From the above remarks, however, we may argue that in choosing the ghost in *Hamlet* as his model, the playwright implicitly tried to equate his dramatic powers not only with those of Shakespeare, but also with Kemble's, one of the Bard's putative successors of whom Boaden had written a celebrative biography. Although the star actor had been actively engaged in "marketing himself" as the repository of the cultural memory of the Bard and "the true heir to the legacies of Shakespeare and the English stage,"[45] it was evident that he himself was significantly "reimagining" this tradition through the introduction of visual effects, musical accompaniment, and other forms of spectacular overcoding (vestimentary, cosmetic, pictorial).[46] In particular, the need to provide a balance between the novel demands of the stage on the one hand and fidelity to Shakespeare on the other must have been a strong concern among stage practitioners in the latter part of the century. Garrick's early spectacular innovations and, more strikingly, Kemble's selective approach to dramatic purity betray a similar awkwardness in giving substantial form to airy nothings. In this changing dramatic context, Boaden's justification of his practices by comparing himself to the "*great* masters"[47] seemed reasonable, and his dramatic ambitions appeared justified. The epilogue to *Fontainville Forest* is conclusive is this respect:

> Know you not, Shakespeare's petrifying pow'r
> Commands alone the horror-giving hour?
> .....

---

[44] Boaden, *Memoirs of Mrs Siddons*, 412–13. See also Boaden, *John Philip Kemble*, 2:120–21. For a negative critique of Reynolds' painting, see the *Times*, May 8, 1789: "But we rather apprehend that some Fiend had been laying siege to Sir Joshua's taste, when he determined to literalise the idea. The license of Poetry is very different from that of Painting; but the present subject is complete in itself, and wants not the aid of machinery from Heaven or from Hell." Quoted in Albert S. Roe, "The Demon Behind the Pillow: A Note on Erasmus Darwin and Reynolds," *Burlington Magazine* 113 (1971): 464.

[45] Gamer, *Romanticism and the Gothic*, 235n26. For instance, regarding Macbeth, see Kemble's pamphlet, *Macbeth Reconsidered* (1786), which he wrote as an answer to Thomas Whately's 1785 essay, *Remarks of Some Characters of Shakespeare*. Joseph Donohue suggests that the "pamphlet reveals beyond doubt the unusual scholarly interests of this actor and also reflects the great extent to which he had already studied the role." "Kemble and Mrs. Siddons in Macbeth: The Romantic Approach to Tragic Character," *Theatre Notebook* 21 (1967): 74.

[46] Jean Marsden, *The Re-Imagined Text. Shakespeare, Adaptation, & Eighteenth-Century Literary Theory* (Lexington: University Press of Kentucky, 1995).

[47] Boaden, preface to *Cambro-Britons*, 1798, in *Plays*, iii–iv.

> You mean to sanction then your own pale sprite,
> By his "that did usurp this time of night:"
> "I do, he answer'd, and beg you'll spare
> "My injured phantom ev'ry *red*-sea pray'r:
> "Why should your terror *lay* my proudest boast,
> "Madam I die, if I give up the ghost." (69)

Once again, Boaden's dramatic principles significantly intersect with Radcliffe's poetic theory, particularly her observations on the performance of an "*improved*" *Macbeth*, interestingly reminiscent of Kemble's version. In this play the witches, now "reduced to mere human beings" arrayed in Scottish attire, have lost "all that strange and supernatural air which had made them so affecting to the imagination":

> The wild attire, the look *not of this earth*, are essential traits of the supernatural agents, working evil in the darkness of mystery. Whenever the poet's witch condescends, according to the vulgar notion, to mingle mere ordinary mischief with her malignity, and to become familiar, she is ludicrous, and loses her power over the imagination; the illusion vanishes.[48]

The comparison between *Fontainville Forest* and *Hamlet* is made again in Boaden's biography of Kemble. Here Boaden goes to great lengths to explain the failure of the representation of the supernatural in Shakespeare's tragedy:

> The great author has written with his highest power; he has displayed unbounded knowledge of effect ... and yet, as far as the royal shade himself is concerned, all this charm is dispelled by the heavy, bulky, creaking substantiality of the spirit. Whereas the whole of this "gracious figure" should look as if it was collected from the surrounding air, and ready, when its impression should be made, to melt into thin air again.[49]

In Boaden's opinion, only Henry Fuseli had managed to give an appropriate representation of the sublime insubstantiality of Shakespeare's ghost:

> Perhaps the sublimest effort of painting is the figure of the Royal Dane, as he appeared in the large composition of Mr. Fuseli for the Shakespeare Gallery. It has what *seems* person, invested in what *seems* to be armour ... How is all this produced? ... By the artifice of the pallet; by keeping down all too positive indications of substance; by the choice of a cold slaty prevalent colour, touched

---

[48] Ann Radcliffe, "On the Supernatural in Poetry," 313. All emphases are in the text. For a contemporary representation of the Weird Sisters, see the several versions of Henry Fuseli's picture, *The Weird Sisters or The Three Witches* (originally exhibited at the Royal Academy in 1783) in Myrone, *Gothic Nightmares*, 130.

[49] Boaden, *John Philip Kemble*, 2:98.

slightly with the pale silvery tone of moonlight; by a step gigantic in extent, and action of the most venerable dignity and command.[50]

In the passage above Boaden touches on two specific visual components of Fuseli's painting: the grand posture of the ghost and the lighting effects that illuminate it with eerie hues. In so doing, we may argue, he suggests a *dramatic* reading of the picture—a theatrical interpretation that firmly places it in the context of contemporary scenography, acting techniques, and, quite symptomatically, late eighteenth-century Shakespearean criticism. Interestingly, a similar creative vision of the Ghost is also foreshadowed in Ann Radcliffe's journal entry on the terrace of Windsor Castle, as quoted by Talfourd:

> The massy tower at the end of the east terrace, stood up in high shade; but *immediately from behind it the moonlight spread*, and showed the flat line of the wall at the end of the terrace, with the figure of the sentinel moving against the light. ... Above this high dark line the stars appeared with a very sublime effect. ... It was on this terrace, surely, that Shakespeare received the first hint of the time for the apparition of his ghost.[51]

A similar description was later incorporated in the introduction to Radcliffe's final novel, *Gaston de Blondeville*: "You were talking a little while ago of Hamlet and towers; now, if you want towers that would do honour to Hamlet, go to Warwick Castle ... *If the moon is up*, you will see them to perfection, and, as you are so fond of ghosts, you can hardly fail to make an assignation with one there."[52] This is precisely the contextual framing and the striking visual effect Boaden strove to recall in *Fontainville Forest*.

During the first night rehearsal of *Fontainville Forest* "good, honest, jolly Thompson" went on stage in the "clumsy" armor of the contemporary Shakespearean tradition.[53] However, the result was far from satisfying for either Boaden or Thomas Harris. The playwright thus decided to make the actor appear as a representation of the pictorial sublime: "The great contrivance was, that the spectre should appear through a blueish-grey gauze, so as to remove the too corporeal effect of a 'live actor,' and convert the moving substance into a gliding

---

[50] Ibid., emphasis mine.

[51] Talfourd, "A Memoir of the Author," 97–8, emphasis mine.

[52] Introduction, *Gaston de Blondeville*, 6–7. The introduction to the novel, arguably Radcliffe's most overt tribute to "Shakespeare's wand" (71), bears testimony to Shakespeare's influence on the Romantics, and thus deserves critical attention. See Rictor Norton, "Ann Radcliffe, 'The Shakespeare of Romance Writers,'" in *Shakespearean Gothic*, ed. Christy Desmet and Anne Williams (Cardiff: University of Wales Press, 2009). For a reconstruction of Radcliffe's attendance at the 1781 performance of *Hamlet* at the Theatre Royal, Bristol, with Sarah Siddons in the leading role, see F. W. Price, "Ann Radcliffe, Mrs. Siddons and the Character of Hamlet," *Notes and Queries* (1976): 164–7.

[53] Boaden, *John Philip Kemble*, 2:117–18.

Fig. 8.1   Robert Thew after Henri Fuseli. The Platform Before the Palace of Elsinore—Hamlet, Horatio, Marcellus, and the Ghost (Hamlet I.iv). John & Josiah Boydell (London) 1796. The Metropolitan Museum of Art (New York) © Foto Scala Firenze.

essence."[54] The uncanny atmosphere of Fuseli's painting might be reproduced through special effects and a costume made of "dark blue grey stuff, made in the shape of armour."[55] Boaden's urgency in giving visual expression to the otherworldly presence must be considered as a response to contemporary scenic practice. Intriguingly, Kemble himself had recourse to transparencies for the procession of the eight kings followed by the ghost of Banquo, who passed behind a transparent screen of black crepe, possibly surrounded by a smoke effect.[56]

---

[54] Ibid., 2:117. As visual perception shifted from iconographism to emotionalism, transparencies (fabric screens of different colors), gauze curtains (placed in front of a character to create the effect of fog or an aerial atmosphere), and silk screens placed before lights were imported from the pantomimic shows onto the stage. Characteristically, Boaden explains that "when Follet was thus dressed," he was "faintly visible behind the gauze or crape spread before the scene."

[55] Boaden, *John Philip Kemble*, 2:119.

[56] See Sir Walter Scott's review, *Quarterly Review* (1826), 227–8, quoted in Donohue, "Kemble's Production," 70.

Once the dramaturge moves from the visual to the aural dimension, however, the problem of translating the imagined into the actual remains. In Boaden's adaptations, de Montalt's ghost was to be played by John Follet, "the clown so royally celebrated for the eating of *carrots* in the pantomimes."[57] As an actor of speechless shows, his strident voice was universally deemed inappropriate to achieve "the great desideratum." The mixing of words and gesture, however, seemed to offer a viable solution:

> We therefore settled it, that, in imitation of the ancients, he should be only the MIME, to make the action on the stage, and that poor Thompson, disencumbered from the pilch of the majesty of Denmark, should yet *at the wing*, with hollow voice, pronounce the two important words; to which the extended arm of Follet might give the consentaneous action.[58]

As Boaden's detailed narrative makes clear, *Fontainville Forest*'s ghost appropriates Radcliffe's novel in a twofold way. The verbal hesitation of the fantastic is appropriated and transmodalized into the dramatic language of visual uncertainty—a code that aims to place the apparition beyond the "heavy, bulky, creaking substantiality"[59] of the actor's body. Thus, the ghost's insubstantial representation translates to the stage Radcliffe's "modal formulae"[60]—the language of verbal hesitation (Boaden calls it "the doubtful of the narrative")[61] that syntactically and semantically marks the expression of the supernatural, as in this example:

> The wind was high, and as it whistled through the desolate apartment and shook the feeble doors, [Adeline] often started, and *sometimes even thought* she heard sighs between the pauses of the gust; but *she checked these illusions*, which the hour of the night and her melancholy *imagination* conspired to raise. ... She stepped forward, and having unclosed [the door], proceeded with faltering steps along a suite of apartments, resembling the first in style and condition, and terminating in one exactly like that where her dream had represented the dying person; the remembrance struck so forcibly upon her *imagination*, that she was in danger of fainting; and looking round the room, *almost* expected to see the phantom of her dream.[62]

It is likewise worthy of note the fact that Boaden sought—and apparently found—inspiration in the work of Henry Fuseli, a painter who was at the time

---

[57] Boaden, *John Philip Kemble*, 2:118.
[58] Ibid., emphasis mine.
[59] Ibid., 2:98.
[60] Tzvetan Todorov, *The Fantastic: A Structural Approach to a Literary Genre*, trans. R. Howard (Cleveland, OH: Press of Case Western Reserve University, 1973).
[61] Boaden, *John Philip Kemble*, 2:97.
[62] Radcliffe, *Romance of the Forest*, 114–15, emphasis mine.

creating a "distinctly visual idiom"[63] through which to express his idiosyncratic Shakespearean readings. Although Fuseli had established his fame as "the painter of Shakespeare," his visionary style set him apart from the more conventional iconographic tradition represented by such masters as Sir Joshua Reynolds, then the president of the Royal Academy. Fuseli, we may say, was approaching the cultural establishment and the contemporary aesthetic codes—in particular, albeit not exclusively, as regards his Shakespearian illustrations—with a destabilizing spirit and a highly distinctive vocabulary for the representation of the fantastic, which Boaden may have felt (or wished to feel) cognate to his own.

Fuseli's *The Death of Dido* and *The Vision of Queen Katherine* showed that he was capable of taking morally elevating subjects from well-known classical or quite well-known literary texts, and at the same time of drawing attention to himself by being more extreme and "poetical" in his treatment of them than the pillars of the artistic establishment, especially Reynolds and Benjamin West.[64] After all, Fuseli was the artist who had upturned the visual lexicon of the 1780s with his controversial *The Nightmare*, the visionary narrative of a dream or a hallucinatory state—itself a transcendent illustration of Edmund Burke's category of the sublime—he had put on display at the 1782 Royal Academy exhibition. As the Swiss painter wrote in the *Analytical Review* for October 1792, "Terror, as the chief ingredient of the Sublime, composes in all instances, and in the utmost extent of the word, fit material for both [the painter and the poet]."[65]

The Gothic narrated situations were few and limited, and the spectators' pleasure would be increased by a pattern of repetition.[66] Boaden's terrifying and unexpected apparition would strain against dramatic conventions, thus highlighting Adeline's essential contact with the ghost that is crucially set in the central part of the play. In this respect, the Phantom may also represent the heroine's encounter with her story, her way of coming to terms with her past and, finally, her passage into adulthood. In my reading, the ghost integrates narration into action, and brings past events concerning Boaden's Philip, Marquis de Montalt—the primordial crime—to the same temporal level of his daughter's present story. Accordingly, the preternatural apparition is endowed with an interaxial function. From a dramatic point of view, it reinstates the unity of action and, partly, the unity of time.

It is significant that as the ostension of what I have defined *Fontainville Forest*'s unity of emotion, the ghost also actualizes and at the same time imaginatively negotiates the culturally prestigious, specifically Shakespearean, dramatic tradition that Boaden would have defended from attack. At the same time, the Phantom—a character that is not part of Radcliffe's narrative economy—metaphorically brings back from the dead and actualizes the intersection of the visual, the verbal, and the

---

[63] Cristopher Frayling, "Fuseli's The Nightmare: Somewhere between the Sublime and the Ridiculous," in Myrone, *Gothic Nightmares*, 10.

[64] Ibid., 10.

[65] Quoted in ibid., 13.

[66] Paul Ranger, *"Terror and Pity Reign in Every Breast": Gothic Drama in the London Patent Theatres, 1750-1820* (London: Society for Theatre Research, 1991), 10–14.

dramatic—as well as the negotiations between higher- and lower-class genres—that I see as characteristic of Romantic drama. On the level I have tried to suggest here, not only does Boaden's *Hamlet*-like ghost appropriate the plurality of the Gothic; it is precisely the product of that appropriation.

In my reading, Boaden's ghost is also endowed with a precise transtextual function. Radcliffe's poetical descriptions connect with numerous inset texts, which metatextually link up to a forming literary canon based on the role of imagination, the study of the passions, and the appreciation of sublime poetry. Their function is to provide authorial commentary on the narrated events along with an illustration of the characters' emotions and inner life. As it has been noted, amongst its multiple metanarrative functions the author's "literary bandistry"[67] implies intellectual authentication, thus helping to canonically reposition and aggrandize her version of the Gothic novel. In similar fashion, in a staged production the metatextual link is purposely visual and dramatic, as shown most clearly by Boaden's deliberate revisioning of Fuseli's ghost scene on the one hand and, on the other, by his direct engagement with the production of Kemble's *Macbeth*. I argue that extraliterary intertextuality and intertheatricality thus contribute to the canonical repositioning and cultural aggrandizement of Boaden's Gothic drama. Consequently, the presence of de Montalt's ghost affects the cultural standing of *Fontainville Forest*. In its dealings with the aesthetic codes of the time it transforms debased spectacular terror into thrilling awe—a sublime aesthetic experience distanced and safely contained within the stage-frame.

I further suggest that in *Fontainville Forest* Boaden must have been only marginally concerned with the Enlightenment debate about the existence of ghosts.[68] In my reading, Boaden's phantom is a *fiction*—what we may be tempted to call the stage actualization of the author's cultural "family romance"[69]—an artificial *cultural effect* tailor-made for a public that valued Boydell's volumes, flocked to Shakespeare's Gallery, hailed Radcliffe as "the Shakspeare [*sic*] of Romance writers,"[70] and idolized the figure of the Bard. Responding to a precise ideological function that places *Fontainville Forest* in the context of the forming national dramatic canon, not only does the supernatural transvaluate the heroine's

---

[67] Emma Clery, *Women's Gothic: From Clara Reeve to Mary Shelley* (Hordon, UK: Northcote House, 2000), 54.

[68] On supernaturalism in the later eighteenth century see Jack Voller, *The Supernatural Sublime: The Metaphysics of Terror in Anglo-American Romanticism* (DeKalb: Northern Illinois University Press, 1994); Terry Castle, *The Female Thermometer: Eighteenth-Century Culture and the Invention of the Uncanny* (Oxford: Oxford University Press, 1995); and Emma J. Clery, *The Rise of Supernatural Fiction, 1762–1800* (Cambridge: Cambridge University Press, 1995).

[69] For an interesting reading of *The Romance of the Forest* in Freudian terms, see Elizabeth Bronfen, "Hysteria, Phantasy and the Family Romance: Ann Radcliffe's Romance of the Forest," *Women's Writing* 1, no. 2 (1994): 171–80.

[70] Nathan Drake, *Literary Hours* (London, 1798), quoted in Rogers, ed., *Critical Response*.

imaginative experience "from low superstition to aesthetic resource,"[71] as Emma Clery maintains. In the case of *Fontainville Forest*, it also operates the generic transvaluation of the drama itself. This is achieved through the strikingly modern (though clearly typical of the time) reconciliation of late eighteenth-century aesthetic norms with the increasing mass-market commercialization of the visual, through the grafting of dramatic theory (specifically as regarded Shakespeare) on to dramatic practice.[72]

\* \* \*

We might contend that *Fontainville Forest*'s ghost thus gives a local habitation and a name to the otherworldly existences banished by Radcliffe. These are brought on stage as the plastic manifestation of the imagination of Boaden in his double role of reader/author. Arguably, in his earliest adaptation of the work of Radcliffe—the writer who shared with Shakespeare the "golden keys ... of Horror ... and thrilling fears"[73]—Boaden set out to present himself not only as the intensely participative, deeply responsive, and highly creative Ideal Reader of the Gothic but also, in Roland Barthes's terminology, as its *writer* or active (re)creator, "no longer a consumer, but a producer of the text."[74] Not incidentally, Boaden's response mirrors the creative passions animating the typical Gothic (nationalistic) heroine, who is sensitive to landscape, moved by music and inspired by poetry, particularly Shakespeare's sublime lines:

> Adeline found that no species of writing had power so effectually to withdraw her mind from the contemplation of its own misery as the higher kinds of poetry, and in these her taste soon taught her to distinguish the superiority of the English from that of the French. ... She frequently took a volume of Shakespear [*sic*] or Milton, and, having gained some wild eminence, would seat herself beneath the pines, whose low murmurs soothed her heart, and conspired with the visions of the poet to lull her to forgetfulness of grief.[75]

Emma Clery has pointedly remarked that the powers of creativity associated with Gothic maidens constructs Adeline as a "heroine-poet alter ego of Radcliffe."[76] As a result, a further cultural transvaluation seems to emerge. Boaden identifies with the imaginative Gothic protagonist, who acts as one of Radcliffe's textual *personae*. This claim is borne out by a quick look at the critical apparatus of Chloe

---

[71] Clery, *Women's Gothic*, 8.

[72] Gillen D'Arcy Wood, *The Shock of the Real: Romanticism and Visual Culture, 1760–1860* (New York: Palgrave, 2001).

[73] Gray, *Progress of Poetry*, quoted in Myrone, *Gothic Readings*, 289.

[74] Roland Barthes, *S/Z*, trans. Richard Miller (London: Jonathan Cape, 1975), 4.

[75] Radcliffe, *Romance of the Forest*, 261.

[76] Clery, *Women's Gothic*, 80.

Chard's edition of *The Romance of the Forest*. Fourteen of the forty-one literary insertions (at times slightly adjusted) identified by the editor are taken from Shakespearean plays (*Macbeth, King Lear, As You Like It, Othello, 2 Henry IV, Julius Caesar, A Midsummer's Night Dream, King John*) and are used as epigraphs to various chapters as well as to the novel itself. The relevance of this paratextual positioning is evident at both the metatextual and the architextual level. Besides offering textual commentary, the Shakespearean references increase the cultural standing of the author/producer (Radcliffe) and provide the generic ennoblement of the cultural product (the Gothic romance). In similar fashion, Boaden's creative citation of *Hamlet*'s ghosts—both the stage and the canvas versions—reveals his literary pretensions through the implicit adoption of the same transtextual strategy enacted by Radcliffe, the most popular novelist of the time.

For all the above reasons I see *Fontainville Forest*'s Phantom as the embodiment of Boaden's own poetics and his "Romantic" stage appropriation of Shakespeare. In its links with spectacle and late eighteenth-century on-stage supernaturalism, the Ghost actualizes a traffic with the unpatented stage, while adherence to the Aristotelian unities and the Shakespearean tradition reveals the playwright's dramatic ambitions—his attempt to affiliate his work with the high cultural tradition of the Bard and such contemporary cultural heirs as John Philip Kemble and Henry Fuseli. Contextually, Boaden's Shakespearean Phantom appears not so much as a stage illusion, then, as the imaginative embodiment of his precise "Romantic" *creative* agenda.

*Fontainville Forest*'s ghost may thus be read as the cultural construction and public representation of James Boaden the play*wright*, the creative maker of material plays. As Jane Moody has convincingly argued in a different context, "play-wright" is a "linguistic back formation [that] should evoke neither the authority of writing, nor the permanence of print":

> "Wrighting", in the context of these medieval trades, took the form of making goods, perhaps from materials made or prepared by others, which would then be sold, assembled, or incorporated into larger objects, the identity of the craftsmen silently disappearing, without written trace, into history. The linguistic archaeology of playwrighting, then, suggests a delightful insouciance about authorship, property, and authority.[77]

With a powerful dramatic cue that deliberately recalls and revises one of Shakespeare's monumental "imaginative tragedies,"[78] Boaden's Phantom creatively actualizes the ghostly presence and highlights the ghostly product of the Gothic appropriator. As an apt metaphor of Boaden's ideal stage, it imbues *Fontainville Forest* with an ennobled cultural tradition—both visual and poetic—and it testifies to a dramatic vision that went beyond both the earthly and the mundane.

---

[77] Jane Moody, "Illusion of Authorship," in *Women and Playwriting in Nineteenth-Century Britain*, ed. Tracy C. Davis and Ellen Donkin (Cambridge: Cambridge University Press, 1999), 101–2.

[78] Bate, *Shakespeare*, 56.

## Chapter 9
# Shakespeare Reception in France: The Case of Ambroise Thomas's *Hamlet*

### Suddhaseel Sen

The reception of Shakespeare in Europe is intimately tied up with translations, adaptations, and criticism of his play *Hamlet*, whose eponymous protagonist, by the mid-nineteenth century, "had begun his ascent to the pantheon of cultural icons ... like Don Quixote and Faust."[1] What were the channels through which Shakespeare's play reached other countries in Europe, and in what forms did it reach these countries? How did his play alter, or how was it altered by, theatrical traditions in European countries in which it was performed for the first time, centuries after its first performances in England? While German commentators produced a valuable body of translations and criticism of Shakespeare in general, and of *Hamlet* in particular, it was a French version that provided the basis for subsequent first translations of *Hamlet* into at least three European languages—Italian, Spanish, and Dutch.[2] This was the *Hamlet* (1770) by Jean-François Ducis (1733–1816). The word "version" needs to be used with caution here, for Ducis, in an attempt to make *Hamlet* performable at the Comédie Française, made radical changes to Shakespeare's plot and language, such that his version conformed to the strict neoclassical rules of the Académie Française. Till the time of his death, Ducis continued to revise his adaptation, often at the behest of his leading actor Talma, who gradually brought the play somewhat closer to Shakespeare's original. Ducis's version was last performed by the Comédie Française in 1851.

Although Ducis's *Hamlet* is not performed anymore, it generated a number of French translations (some of them much closer to Shakespeare) as well as adaptations. Of particular importance is the *Hamlet* (1847) by Alexandre Dumas *père* (1802–1870) and Paul Meurice (1818–1905), which, like the version by Ducis, also underwent continual revision, and was last performed in 1932.[3] Both the Ducis and Dumas-Meurice versions provided the basis for the operatic *Hamlet* (first performed in 1868) by the composer Ambroise Thomas (1811–1896) and his librettists Jules Barbier (1825–1901) and Michel Carré (1822–1872). It remains

---

[1] Robert Hapgood, ed. *Hamlet, Prince of Denmark: Shakespeare in Production* (Cambridge: Cambridge University Press, 1999), 22.
[2] Romy Heylen, *Six French Hamlets: Translations, Poetics, and the Stage* (London: Routledge, 1993), 28–9.
[3] Ibid., 60.

the only operatic adaptation of *Hamlet* to have survived on the operatic stage, even if its own performance history has had its ups and downs.[4]

The various interpretive communities that translated, adapted, and produced critical commentaries on Shakespeare in Europe from the second half of the eighteenth century onwards can be broadly divided into two categories. The first attempted to adapt Shakespeare such that his works conformed to French neoclassical aesthetics, while the other used Shakespeare as a means to move away from the very same aesthetics. The second group, in which we could place opera composers like Hector Berlioz and Giuseppe Verdi, have proven to be more influential in the long run, but in their day, they and their counterparts in the other arts (such as Victor Hugo, Alessandro Manzoni, and Eugène Delacroix) defined the exception rather than the norm: their readiness to celebrate Shakespeare's mixing of different generic elements was by no means shared by all of nineteenth-century Europe. Thomas's *Hamlet* is one of those Shakespeare adaptations that attempted to combine the neoclassical tenets popular in France with a more Romantic conception of the play, and its significance lies in the fact that the opera reflects the tendency of the composer and his librettists to work within the limits imposed by contemporary generic, aesthetic, and critical paradigms. In this regard, Thomas's *Hamlet* is closer to Gioachino Rossini's *Otello*, another work based on a Ducis version of Shakespeare in which neoclassical dramatic conventions coexist with elements of musical Romanticism. We should, however, remember that although the Shakespeare operas of Thomas and Rossini do not overtly break away from convention, they are by no means run-of-the-mill either, as the successful revival of these works in recent years indicates. Indeed, I argue that Thomas's *Hamlet* is an important adaptation of Shakespeare's play—perhaps the only one from the nineteenth century that in some ways anticipated some of the twentieth-century readings of the play, while having its own performance tradition that continues to the present day.

In this essay, I shall first examine the critical and performance traditions of Shakespeare's *Hamlet* in France, focusing on the adaptations by Ducis and Dumas-Meurice. In particular, I will show how these adapters use Shakespeare's play as the basis for making reforms in French drama. Second, I shall examine how the process of intermedial adaptation, from spoken drama to sung drama, affects the structure and content of Thomas's *Hamlet*. Here, I shall focus on Ophélie's mad scene from the opera—specifically, its gendering of madness, a subject that Elaine Showalter

---

[4] Two vocal excerpts, however, always retained some popularity—the mad scene for Ophélie in Act 4 (a perennial favorite with sopranos) and, occasionally, Hamlet's drinking song from Act 2. During its post–World War I slump in popularity, the opera was kept alive, if only on the fringes of the repertory, by exponents of the title role: French baritones such as Victor Maurel, Jean Lassalle, and Maurice Renaud, as well as the Italians Titta Ruffo and Mattia Battistini. Its present-day relative popularity too has to do with the championing of the work by a number of distinguished baritones, such as Sherrill Milnes, Thomas Hampson, and Thomas Allen, as well as the increasing production of operas outside the traditional canon, the implications of which I discuss later in this essay.

discusses in her study of representations of Ophelia. I will argue that the medium of opera "envoices"[5] Ophélie in a way that makes the opera an important landmark in what Showalter calls Ophelia's own history, the history of her representation.[6] Given the radical changes made by Ducis (which subsequently found their way into other versions of *Hamlet* based on it), I shall also discuss whether these versions should be regarded as adaptations or appropriations of Shakespeare's play. Finally, I shall examine how, in the late 1980s, changing approaches towards adaptations, coupled with a spate of adaptations of Shakespeare on film as well as increasing performances and recordings of operas outside the traditional canon, paved the way for the revival of Thomas's *Hamlet*.

## *Hamlet* in Performance

"Since adaptations engage the discursive energies of their time, they become a barometer of the ideological trends circulating during the moment of production," writes Robert Stam with respect to film adaptations,[7] but the comment holds true of adaptations more generally, including those by Shakespeare himself. The story of Hamlet itself changed as it passed through several hands, from the *Historiae Danicae* of Saxo Grammaticus through François de Belleforest's *Histoires Tragiques* (first published in 1570) to Shakespeare, whose *Hamlet* transformed the genre of the revenge tragedy, a genre exemplified by works like Thomas Kyd's *A Spanish Tragedy* (c. 1587). The presence of several texts of Shakespeare's *Hamlet*—the First and Second Quartos (Q1, 1603; Q2, 1604–1605), and the First Folio (F, 1623)—and the textual differences between them, have problematized the very notion of a stable source text, making adaptational "fidelity" to Shakespeare well-nigh impossible. Hence, performances of *Hamlet* have varied according to the time and place where it was performed.

Although *Hamlet* in performance did not undergo much textual *modification* from the Restoration to the end of the nineteenth century, it nevertheless underwent considerable textual *abridgement*. Many scenes and characters were regularly omitted. For example, in the nineteenth century, even in England, Fortinbras was almost always left out altogether, and when Sir Johnston Forbes-Robertson reinstated Shakespeare's original ending at the urging of Bernard Shaw, it was a major theatrical innovation. Several speeches, some of them belonging to Hamlet,

---

[5] The term is taken from Carolyn Abbate, "Opera; or the Envoicing of Women," in *Musicology and Difference: Gender and Sexuality in Music Scholarship*, ed. Ruth A. Solie (Berkeley: University of California Press, 1993), 225.

[6] Elaine Showalter, "Representing Ophelia: Women, Madness and the Responsibilities of Feminist Criticism," in *Shakespeare and the Question of Theory*, ed. Patricia Parker and Geoffrey Hartman (London: Methuen, 1985), 79.

[7] Robert Stam, "The Theory and Practice of Adaptation," in *Literature and Film: A Guide to the Theory and Practice of Film Adaptation*, ed. Robert Stam and Alessandra Raengo (Malden, MA: Blackwell, 2005), 45.

were also regularly omitted.[8] Some of the changes can be linked to changing performing practices: for example, the Restoration saw both female actors tackling the parts of Gertrude and Ophelia, as well as the bowdlerization, as it were, of parts of *Hamlet*.[9] More importantly, as women rather than boys started performing Shakespeare's female roles, they "created new meanings and subversive tensions in these roles ... perhaps most importantly with Ophelia."[10]

Changes in performance conditions also helped shape critical responses. The apron stage of the Elizabethans was replaced in the Restoration and the eighteenth century by the proscenium arch; consequently, scene changes interrupted the flow of the action, and individual speeches and scenes became more prominent, leading Restoration and eighteenth-century theatrical commentators to be "primarily concerned with how the leading actor rendered particular speeches and scenes rather than with his overarching interpretative approach."[11] Literary critics, however, engaged with the play somewhat differently, attaching utmost importance to a character's consistency of behavior in the course of the entire play; indeed, in the latter part of the eighteenth century, they would engage increasingly in "character analysis," the emphasis being on the "careful differentiation of what is individual about Shakespeare's characters and appraising the consistency with which this individuality is rendered."[12] The proscenium stage was, therefore, instrumental in effecting a growing gap between a literary analysis of Shakespeare, on the one hand, and a performance-based approach, on the other—a cleavage that led Goethe in his essay "Shakespeare und kein Ende" (1815) to declare that Shakespeare "belongs by necessity in the annals of poetry" and that "in the annals of the theater he appears only by accident."[13] With respect to English critics, Jonathan Bate neatly sums up the situation:

> When Coleridge said that watching Edmund Kean act was "like reading Shakespeare by flashes of lightning," he meant that Kean could only illuminate certain striking moments in a play—an understanding of the overall *idea* of it was dependent on the insights of the critic in his study or lecture room.[14]

Because of the valorization of the verbal (logophilia) and the prejudice against visual representation (iconophobia) in Western culture,[15] textual criticism would often inform reviews of performances of Shakespeare in the nineteenth century. The reservations about Shakespeare as drama would be compounded in the case

---

[8] Hapgood, *Hamlet*, 7.
[9] Ibid., 11.
[10] Showalter, "Representing Ophelia," 80.
[11] Hapgood, *Hamlet*, 18.
[12] Ibid., 18–19.
[13] Jonathan Bate, ed., *The Romantics on Shakespeare* (London: Penguin, 1992), 76.
[14] Russell Jackson and Jonathan Bate, eds., *Shakespeare: An Illustrated Stage History* (New York: Oxford University Press, 1996), 93.
[15] Stam, "Theory and Practice," 5–7.

of opera in a foreign tongue (as in Thomas's *Hamlet*), where textual simplification and abridgement of a translated text were put to the service of a highly artificial mode of performance, with its own conventions of representation. Although opera and theater have different dramaturgies, there are also convergences between them that enable creators of operatic adaptations to draw upon contemporary theatrical performance traditions. Thomas's *Hamlet* is a case in point. To examine how the team of Thomas, Barbier, and Carré came to make their own operatic adaptation of *Hamlet*, we need to consider the reception history of Shakespeare in France, through translations, performances, and the critical responses his plays generated in France.

## *Hamlet* in France

A cross-cultural adaptation of a drama by Shakespeare arises from the transculturation of his work in the new (receiving) culture. To understand the process of transculturation, it is important to first study the critical context in which Shakespeare's works were first received and translated, since translation precedes adaptation. Translation, according to Romy Heylen, is a teleological activity. Even before beginning work on a translation, the translator has to keep in mind the objectives behind the translation. Heylen, therefore, classifies translation into three categories: those in which the translator adheres to the cultural codes informing the *source* culture, thereby avoiding the attempt to acculturate the original work; those that negotiate and introduce a cultural compromise between the source and receiving cultures; and finally, those in which the translator adheres to the cultural codes informing the *receiving* culture, in which case the "translated original may or may not attain a canonized position or stay on the periphery of the receiving culture." An awareness, then, of the cultural and sociohistorical conditions behind a translator's activity "offers a clearer insight into the mechanisms that allow translations to function in the receiving culture."[16] The adapter, like the translator, also has to pitch the adaptation keeping in mind audiences as well as the representational conventions of the medium of the adapted product.[17] As we shall see, in the case of French translations of Shakespeare's *Hamlet*, an awareness of the cultural and sociohistorical conditions shows how intricately the various translations of *Hamlet*—and, by extension, theatrical and operatic adaptations based on these translations—mirror the different stages of Shakespeare reception by the French artistic and critical establishment.

There was little knowledge of Shakespeare in France before the eighteenth century,[18] and it was principally Voltaire who—with his adaptation of *Julius*

---

[16] Heylen, *Six French Hamlets*, 24–5.

[17] Linda Hutcheon, *A Theory of Adaptation* (New York: Routledge, 2006), 142.

[18] For an overview of the reception history of Shakespeare in France in the eighteenth century, see Marion Monaco, *Shakespeare on the French Stage in the Eighteenth Century* (Paris: Didier, 1974).

*Caesar*, translations of excerpts of Shakespeare plays, and critical writings on Shakespeare—was first responsible for popularizing Shakespeare in France. However, when Pierre Le Tourneur (1736–1788), an influential translator of Shakespeare, suggested the English playwright as a model for real tragedy, Voltaire saw him as a real threat to French dramatic traditions. Nevertheless, as a result of the translations by Le Tourneur and Pierre-Antoine de La Place (1707–1793), and David Garrick's extremely influential visits to Paris (1751, 1763, and 1765), staged adaptations of the tragedies gradually came to be produced.[19]

The first of these was Ducis's *Hamlet*. Ducis, who knew no English, adapted Shakespeare's play so that it conformed completely to the conventions of the receiving culture—the world of French theater.[20] In a letter to Garrick, Ducis acknowledged that his aim was not so much to translate Shakespeare's tragedy as to "create an interesting role for the queen who kills a king, her husband; and especially, to portray in Hamlet's pure and melancholy soul a model of filial love."[21] (Such *tendresse filiale* is a popular sentiment in the genre of bourgeois drama that was developing around this time.) In fact, as Romy Heylen has suggested, Ducis's 1770 adaptation of *Hamlet* has, effectively, a different plot,[22] as well as altered relationships between the principal protagonists, while observing neoclassical considerations such as the unities of time and place.[23]

In Ducis's version, Claudius, a nobleman wronged by Hamlet's father, plots with Gertrude to kill the king. A willful accomplice in King Hamlet's murder, she had, nevertheless, repented at the last moment and tried to warn Hamlet's father of the impending danger to his life; after his murder, she acts as regent till the time Hamlet recovers from his mysterious madness. She has agency enough to defy Claudius, but her singular thought is to make up for her crime and devote the rest of her life to Hamlet. By the end of the play, however, she is killed, as is Claudius, and Hamlet is crowned king. Such an ending was meant to "please an audience who expected tragedy to uphold virtue and draw a moral lesson."[24] Gertrude's adultery and role in the murder, as well as Hamlet's accusation of Claudius, lack the ambiguity of Shakespeare's play, because French drama of the time required clarity of motive behind the protagonists' actions. Two of Ducis's changes made way into Thomas's opera—a tender scene between Hamlet and Ophelia at the end of Act 1 in Ducis's version, and a denouement that lets Hamlet live.

---

[19] Both Hector Berlioz's symphony *Roméo et Juliette* (1847) and Charles-François Gounod's opera of the same name (1867) are based on Garrick's version of the play (1750).

[20] Helen Phelps Bailey, *Hamlet in France: From Voltaire to Laforgue* (Geneva: Librairie Droz, 1964), 14.

[21] Letter of April 14, 1769, quoted in ibid., 14.

[22] This makes it open to question whether Ducis's version should be regarded as an adaptation at all, a question I address later in this essay.

[23] Heylen, *Six French Hamlets*, 30.

[24] Bailey, *Hamlet in France*, 15.

If the Ducis, Dumas-Meurice, and Thomas versions of *Hamlet* share a common interest in spectacle,[25] there is another aspect of Hamlet that is common to the versions by Ducis and Thomas. In neither version is Hamlet quite mad: he does not put up an "antic disposition" (1.5.173).[26] Rather, he is somber and lachrymose for the most part, as is the case with heroes of bourgeois dramas and Romantic heroes such as Chateaubriand's René, whom he anticipates. Heylen has argued that Ducis used his version of *Hamlet* in order to introduce elements of a new French theatrical model, the bourgeois drama, into the precincts of the more conservative and elite Comédie Française, by cloaking his *Hamlet* in neoclassical garb.[27] Ducis, then, used Shakespeare as a means of effecting a change in French theater.

Le Tourneur's prose translations (1776–1783) stay much closer to the Shakespearean texts—his *Hamlet* (1779) restores, among others, the gravediggers (who were left out in Ducis) and the original ending. Le Tourneur, who knew English well, left out only those passages where he felt the words were too vulgar for French tastes, or where the wordplay was too complicated; such passages were explained in his notes. Significantly, Le Tourneur's translations were meant for a *reading* public. It appears from the translations and adaptations of Shakespeare's *Hamlet* in France that, even when it was possible for translators such as Le Tourneur to negotiate a cultural compromise between the source and receiving cultures, it was more difficult for adapters for the theater or the opera to make a similar compromise. Because of the higher financial risks of mounting productions, as well as the well-entrenched conventions of genre and performance, adaptations *for performance* by Dumas and Thomas, like the adaptation by Ducis, were required to adhere more to the cultural codes informing the *receiving* (French) culture rather than those of the source culture. Therefore, when Dumas and Meurice made their version of *Hamlet*, they incorporated elements from the Ducis translation, even though Dumas knew Le Tourneur's translation almost by heart.[28]

In general, a greater degree of transculturation is to be found in those media where a number of semiotic codes are simultaneously in operation, such as theatrical or musico-dramatic performances, where verbal, visual, and musical codes come together. Each of these semiotic codes is used in culture-specific ways, and it is risky for an adapter to defamiliarize audiences from the conventions they are at home with, especially because art forms involving multiple media such as theater, film, or opera involve high production costs, compared to, say, printed translations

---

[25] Unlike Victor Hugo, who responded, among other things, to the language of Shakespeare's plays, Dumas was more responsive to some of the "external effects" of Shakespeare, a point noted by Bailey, *Hamlet in France*, 69, and Peter Raby, *"Fair Ophelia": A Life of Harriet Smithson Berlioz* (Cambridge: Cambridge University Press, 1982), 188–9.

[26] All references to Shakespeare's *Hamlet* are from William Shakespeare, *Hamlet*, ed. Philip Edwards (Cambridge: Cambridge University Press, 2003).

[27] Ibid., 28.

[28] Bailey, *Hamlet in France*, 69.

meant for readers. This kind of transculturation through performance—a process I term "performative transculturation"[29]—is a good indicator of the ways in which texts change as they travel across cultures.

This is not to assume that the conditions of reception, or theatrical or operatic conventions, are themselves ahistorical and therefore immutable. If Garrick's visits to France facilitated the reception of Shakespeare's tragedies, Charles Kemble's Paris debut in 1827, with an English troupe, stunned French audiences, which included Dumas, Berlioz, and Hugo; thus Shakespeare proved a major source of inspiration to the French Romantics. Dumas remarked, "It was the first time I saw in the theater real passions, giving life to men and women of flesh and blood,"[30] while Berlioz found in French neoclassicism "the pitiable narrowness of our old poetics, decreed by pedagogues and obscurantist monks."[31] The Romantic response to Shakespeare is reflected not only in Berlioz's Shakespeare-inspired works, but also in the paintings of Eugène Delacroix[32] and plays such as Alfred de Musset's *Lorenzaccio* (1834) and Alfred de Vigny's *Chatterton* (1835). Delacroix painted many of the play's scenes that had offended the neoclassicists, such as the Ghost scene, the play scene, the gravedigger scene, and Ophelia's madness and death. These scenes were also to feature prominently in the Dumas-Meurice adaptation as well as in Thomas's opera. In fact, if French neoclassical audiences found Ophélie an unnecessary diversion,[33] Dumas and Meurice brought her back into focus, thanks to the impact of the Kemble performances of 1827, with Harriet Smithson as Ophelia. In the Thomas opera, in fact, Hamlet and Ophelia would come to occupy center stage.

However, by the time the English actor Charles Macready toured Paris in 1844, the enthusiasm for Shakespeare had waned with the decline of the Romantic movement in France. As a result, when Dumas wanted to mount *Hamlet*, he found that no theater was willing to risk the enterprise. Consequently, Dumas established a *Théâtre Historique* in 1847, which he inaugurated with his adaptation of *Hamlet*. Given the conditions in which he opened his theater, it is reasonable to assume that Dumas deemed financial success essential. His adaptation had to be consonant

---

[29] Needless to say, I use the term "performative" in a very different sense from the one made famous by J. L. Austin in his book *How to Do Things with Words* (Oxford: Clarendon Press, 1962), and subsequently used by other theorists like Judith Butler.

[30] Quoted in Showalter, "Representing Ophelia," 82.

[31] Quoted in Jacques Barzun, *Berlioz and His Century: An Introduction to the Age of Romanticism* (New York: Meridian Books, 1956), 67. For the impact of Berlioz's wife, Harriet Smithson, on French audiences, see Raby, *"Fair Ophelia"*, esp. 176–93; Showalter, "Representing Ophelia," 119–20; and Bailey, *Hamlet in France*, 68.

[32] Raby is right to point out that both Berlioz and Delacroix expressed their admiration for Shakespeare through "forms freed from the restriction of words, or in forms to which words could be the adjunct and accompaniment." *"Fair Ophelia"*, 190. This partly explains why their works escape censure based on fidelity discourse, so often applied to *operatic* adaptations of Shakespeare, in which words play a more important role.

[33] Heylen, *Six French Hamlets*, 30.

with the cultural codes informing the *receiving* culture since, unlike in the 1820s, audiences were not likely to be responsive to something radically different from theatrical conventions with which they were familiar. Hence, Dumas and Meurice chose to produce a Shakespeare adaptation that would capitalize on theatrical spectacle, as did Ducis earlier, drawing especially on scenes that were made famous by the Romantics, such as by Delacroix through his paintings, rather than emphasizing the psychological complexities of Shakespeare's play. The conditions of production of theatrical adaptations explain, more than any other factor, why the "history of *Hamlet* in France during the rise and decline of the Romantic movement, shows greater progress towards faithful interpretations in the study than on the stage."[34]

For a number of reasons, the Dumas-Meurice adaptation of *Hamlet* became the basis for Thomas's operatic adaptation. For one, the Dumas-Meurice version was still regularly performed in France at the time the opera was composed in the 1860s, making it the most well-known version of *Hamlet* to French theatergoers. Second, this version, with its five-act structure (common to French *grands opéras* as well) and its emphasis on visual splendor rather than verbal richness, facilitated the task of adaptation from spoken play to opera (especially since it takes more time to sing words than to utter them, as a result of which opera librettos are almost always shorter than texts of spoken dramas). However, Hamlet's monologue, "Être ou ne pas être" (Act 3, scene 1), while considerably abridged in the opera, stays close to Hamlet's "To be, or not to be" monologue (3.1.56–90), while Dumas and Meurice virtually rewrite that monologue in their theatrical version. Indeed, the ways in which Thomas and his librettists achieve a balance between Shakespeare's *Hamlet* and the versions by which they were known in the eighteenth- and nineteenth-century French theater demand closer critical examination.

## *Hamlet* by Thomas, Barbier, and Carré

Jules Barbier and Michel Carré, the librettists of the Thomas opera, based their text on the 1847 Dumas-Meurice version of *Hamlet*.[35] The libretto cuts and simplifies the Dumas-Meurice text. In addition, it reduces the cast from more than thirty in Shakespeare (and nineteen-plus in the Dumas-Meurice version) to fifteen in the opera (including the four actors in the play); Rosencrantz, Guildenstern, and Fortinbras are left out. The opera also leaves out parts of Ophelia's songs deemed vulgar. Among the additions and alterations is the opening, which begins with the coronation scene discussed earlier. Moreover, in Shakespeare's play, Hamlet names Claudius as the murderer only in the final scene; in the opera, Hamlet does so in a public accusation in Act 2. In the opera, Hamlet also discovers that Polonius is a co-conspirator with Claudius (Act 3), and uses Polonius's involvement

---

[34] Bailey, *Hamlet in France*, 77.
[35] Bailey, *Hamlet in France*, 97.

to "justify" his spurning of Ophélie in the scene that follows. This appears to contradict Hamlet's line of reasoning in Act 5, where, speaking of Laertes, he says in an aside, "Le crime du père / Ne doit pas retomber sur le fils innocent."[36] It could be argued that this is the observation of a more mature Hamlet, but whether he has undergone this process of maturation is not clear from the opera. What is certain is that his rejection of Ophélie on the basis of her father's guilt paves the way for her death. On the other hand, Claudius is characterized more subtly in the opera—the closet scene is followed by a magnificent prayer for Claudius that shows him as a deeply repentant figure. Similarly, the opera's repentant Gertrude, though in some ways reminiscent of Ducis's Gertrude, is *not* killed in the end.

The ending of the Thomas *Hamlet* is especially interesting in that while Hamlet lives in the French version, after having killed Claudius at the instruction of his father's Ghost (who appears like a *deus ex machina* at the end), the composer and his librettists specially prepared a version for Covent Garden in which he dies after killing Claudius, hoping to join Ophelia in death (the Ghost does not turn up in this version). This was no doubt an attempt to make their adaptation acceptable to English audiences.[37] Curiously, this ending has never been performed on stage, not even at the Covent Garden premiere in 1869. For a performance in Sydney in 1982, the Australian conductor Richard Bonynge created a third alternative ending in which Hamlet dies of the wound inflicted on him by Laertes.

To modern audiences, the opera appears to depart significantly from the plot of Shakespeare's *Hamlet*. However, comparing the opera with the Shakespearean text and the two principal French theatrical versions reveals that, despite the problems posed by the translation from play to opera, Thomas's operatic *Hamlet* is actually remarkably successful in incorporating influences from different performance traditions. Such traditions include the Parisian *grand opéra*, the French spoken theater (in particular, the influential versions of *Hamlet* by Ducis and the Dumas-Meurice team), and theater performance traditions in England, with which comparisons would be inevitable in an age when fidelity in adaptation was held in high regard.

One of the problems of operatic adaptations is that, like film adaptations and unlike theatrical ones, they are very difficult to modify, excepting the staging details. Music plays the single most important role in determining the pacing of the action of an opera, as well as the tone of the singer (who enjoys far less freedom than the actor in the theater to change the tone of utterance of a sentence).[38] The style of the music itself is an indicator of the period in which the adaptation was made. Since

---

[36] "The crime of the father / Must not be visited upon the innocent son." Jules Barbier and Michel Carré, "Hamlet," libretto, 110, trans. Avril Bardoni, in Ambroise Thomas, *Hamlet*, Antonio de Almeida, London Philharmonic Orchestra, EMI CDS 7 54820 2. All references to the libretto are from this source unless otherwise noted.

[37] Elizabeth Forbes, liner notes, 26, in Thomas, *Hamlet*, EMI CDS 7 54820 2.

[38] See Christoph Clausen, *Macbeth Multiplied: Negotiating Historical and Medial Difference between Shakespeare and Verdi* (Amsterdam: Rodopi, 2005), 23.

words, melodic lines, and musical structure are all thoroughly imbricated in each other, it is very difficult to alter words without affecting the music. Thus, while old nineteenth-century French adaptations of Shakespeare could be improved upon, updated, or replaced by new ones, Thomas's opera either has to be performed as it stands, or ignored altogether, save for the textual alternatives suggested by the composer, or a limited number of other minor cuts (usually established by performance practice) that do not significantly alter the musical structure. Thus, among the various intermedial adaptations of Shakespeare available to a modern audience, Thomas's operatic *Hamlet* bears the strongest traces of nineteenth-century performance practice.

**The Music for Thomas's *Hamlet***

French music at the beginning of the nineteenth century was an arena of struggle over the influence of Italian and German styles, the former employing clear-cut melodies and putting primacy on the human voice, the latter making greater use of thematic development and transformations, making the orchestra an expressive instrument.[39] However, it is reductive to see this interaction between different operatic styles only in terms of conflict. In the earlier part of the nineteenth century, for example, when composing his opera *Macbeth*, Giuseppe Verdi capitalized on the enthusiasm of Florentine audiences for what was termed in Italy the *genere fantastico*, associated with supernatural elements in the works of German opera composers such as Carl Maria von Weber (especially his opera *Der Freischütz*) and Giacomo Meyerbeer (*Robert le diable*), although it is in the subject matter, rather than the music, where the German influence on *Macbeth* is most pronounced. While Verdi, in his *Macbeth*, took up only the subject matter of the *genere fantastico*, Thomas responded to the genre both in thematic and musical terms when he composed his *Hamlet*, and there were precedents in French performing traditions that enabled Thomas to do so. Berlioz, among the greatest nineteenth-century French composers as well as an ardent Shakespearean adapter, prepared the first "authentic" (and successful) French performance of *Der Freischütz* at the Paris Opéra,[40] while Meyerbeer's *Robert le diable* merged the fantastic genre with *grand opera*. There were dramatic precedents too. In the early nineteenth century, one of the popular theatrical genres was the *mélodrame*, and many of these adapted Shakespeare's tragedies only because of their potential for effects. Shakespeare's *Hamlet* was transformed into a magic-show-cum-pantomime mixed with dancing and an infernal *denouement*, and Jean-Baptiste-Augustin Hapdé produced a three-

---

[39] Hervé Lacombe, *The Keys to French Opera in the Nineteenth Century*, trans. Edward Schneider (Berkeley: University of California Press, 2001), 298.

[40] Since the Opéra did not permit spoken dialogue on its stage, Berlioz, otherwise a textual purist, had to compose recitatives to replace the spoken dialogue in Weber's original score. Berlioz also had to add music for the customary ballet, for which he orchestrated Weber's famous concert waltz for piano, *Invitation to the Dance*.

act *mélodrame, Les visions de Macbeth, ou les sorcières d'Ecosse*, which focused on spectacular visual effects.[41] In highlighting the "fantastic" element in *Hamlet*, Thomas was capitalizing on this performance tradition, while at the same time aligning his work with the more highbrow performance traditions in which the Ducis translation and the Dumas-Meurice adaptation held sway. And, in their own ways, Ducis and Dumas, by using Shakespeare in order to bring elements of the "lower" genre of the bourgeois drama into high tragedy, were attempting something similar in the field of spoken drama.

Contemporary reviewers, therefore, were quick to recognize Thomas's gift for creating a supernatural atmosphere by means of effective orchestration right from the opening prelude, and praised him for "a feeling for the fantastic that has rarely been encountered since the death of Weber."[42] Thomas's response lay not so much in imitation as in his ability to effectively use orchestral color for dramatic purposes, especially in an opera based on the principle of contrast between successive musical numbers. Indeed, as Elizabeth Rogeboz-Malfroy says, "The musical discourse is essentially based on the play of contrasts in orchestration and nuances."[43]

The opera begins with a dark prelude (while the curtains are still down), the musical material of which recurs (and is elaborated) in the so-called esplanade scene in which Hamlet meets the Ghost of his father: string tremolos in their lower registers predominate, underpinned by a rising-and-falling chromatic figure in the cellos and basses.[44] The curtain then rises, for a festive scene in which the new monarch and his queen, Gertrude, are greeted by the people: the brighter tones of brass fanfares here provide a strong contrast in timbre.[45] Thus, while departing from the Shakespeare play, Thomas establishes, by means of a symbolic contrast between the different sets of orchestral timbres, the binary between the murky inner world of Elsinore and its celebratory façade. This festive scene is followed by one featuring a pensive Hamlet professing his love to Ophélie; in the duet "Doute de la lumière," he tells her that what he wants to flee is not her but rather human inconstancy.[46]

---

[41] Ibid., 296–7.

[42] Nestor Roqueplan, *Le Ménestrel*, March 22, 1868, quoted in Lacombe, *Keys to French Opera*, 165.

[43] Elizabeth Rogeboz-Malfroy, *Ambroise Thomas, ou la tentation du lyrique* (Besançon: Cêtre, 1994), 232–3.

[44] Ambroise Thomas, *Hamlet*, vocal score, ed. M. Vauthrot (Paris: Heugel, c. 1868), 1.1–8. Since the Heugel vocal score does not provide bar numbers, I have used the following convention: page number. bar number (counting the first bar on each page as 1).

[45] Thomas, *Hamlet*, 4.1–8 to 5.1–6.

[46] Barbier and Carré, "Hamlet," 48–9. As has been pointed earlier, this scene also occurs in the Dumas-Meurice adaptation, with the words spoken by Hamlet taken from his love message to Ophelia, read out by Polonius to the King in the original Shakespeare (2.2.115–18). This scene is placed at the end of Act 1 in Ducis's version. Gary Schmidgall is right when he says in that this makes Hamlet more a romantic lover like Romeo, than the

The contrast between the multitude of choral voices heard in the festive scene and the duet between Hamlet and Ophélie show the protagonists, on their first appearance onstage, as figures isolated from the outer, public sphere of Elsinore. The festive scene thus sets up a contrast with both the prelude and the scene between Hamlet and Ophélie that follows, and, by itself, provides the opportunity for large-scale musical development and for display of splendor suited to the stage of the Paris Opéra. Gautier showed his understanding of the different dramaturgical requirements of the operatic stage when he wrote of the coronation scene: "This portrayal on stage of an earlier event, which Hamlet often recalls with such bitter sadness, has the advantage of being clearer and of providing the musical opportunity for songs, choruses, and marches of dazzling color, serving as a good contrast with the dark heart of the action."[47]

The intensification of mood or atmosphere by means of musical color is one of the principal strengths of Thomas's opera. But, as Clausen has noted, if operas intensify emotionally charged moments or the atmosphere or the musical profiles of some of the protagonists, they also, almost invariably, do so by reducing, simplifying, or omitting other elements of the original play.[48] This also holds true of the operatic *Hamlet*, and it shows especially in the way the composer and his librettists handle the chorus, whose banal words provide no new perspective on the action, although they are often musically impressive. Thomas's incorporation of Scandinavian tunes in Ophélie's mad scene or a cheerful Danish march (Act 2, scene 2)[49] into the score does little more than add the occasional touch of "local color." In fact, the focus is mostly on Hamlet and Ophelia, making the opera, in effect, a love story.

The opera's treatment of *Hamlet* as a domestic tragedy echoes, strangely enough, "the Anglo-American *Hamlet* [which] has often been read through Freud as primarily a domestic drama, with some productions to this day omitting Fortinbras and much of the play's politics,"[50] though in a very different way. However, in general, Clausen's thesis holds true: in the opera's limited discursive context (as

---

ironist or satirist he is in Shakespeare. See his *Shakespeare and Opera* (New York: Oxford University Press, 1990), 318. But, what appears a striking change to modern audiences was not so to nineteenth-century French audiences, who saw the play staged only in the Ducis or Dumas-Meurice versions. Moreover, as Clausen points out, "The particular suitability of music for the expression of love is a standard critical topos" (*Macbeth*, 245); this accounts for the focus on love (rather than, say, political or class or economic issues) in the majority of nineteenth-century Romantic operas based on Shakespeare, such as those by Berlioz, Gounod, Verdi, and Otto Nicolai.

[47] Théophile Gautier, *Le Moniteur universel*, March 16, 1868, quoted in Lacombe, *Keys to French Opera*, 107.

[48] Clausen, *Macbeth*, 239.

[49] Shakespeare also asks for a Danish March before the beginning of the play-within-the-play (3.2.81).

[50] Ann Thompson and Neil Taylor, eds., *Hamlet* (London: Thomson Learning, 2006), 29.

well as those of the versions by Ducis and Dumas-Meurice), many of the other crucial themes of the play, especially those of a sociopolitical nature, cease to exist. For example, it is impossible to read Thomas's *Hamlet* as "primarily a political play enacting the possibility of dissent from various forms of totalitarianism," as has been the case with Shakespeare's play.[51] Graham Holderness's argument that Hamlet himself seems to straddle the idealistic, medieval world of chivalric heroism of his father, on the one hand, and the more modern, Machiavellian world of Claudius, on the other,[52] cannot be applied to the opera, for Claudius's diplomatic skills are not within its purview at all. Again, Hamlet's attitude towards revenge differs in the play and the opera. John Kerrigan,[53] for example, argues that Shakespeare's Hamlet knows that evil cannot be undone; hence, exacting revenge is pointless. The sexuality that Hamlet denounces, Kerrigan argues, is that of Ophelia as well as that of his mother, Gertrude. Kerrigan further points out that in the last act of Shakespeare's play, Hamlet's father is simply not mentioned, even as, in striking contrast, Laertes remembers *his* father, Polonius, in his dying moments. Kiernan Ryan goes one step further and argues that in *Hamlet*, Shakespeare "sabotages the revenge-play formula and thereby strikes at the social order whose validity the formula presupposes, and whose axioms it would otherwise smuggle through unchallenged."[54]

In contrast, the operatic Hamlet has no qualms either about obeying the Ghost— he never doubts that the Ghost is that of his father—or about the ethics of revenge. Indeed, when the Ghost appears in Act 5 of the opera, like the *commendatore* of Mozart's *Don Giovanni*, a very decisive Hamlet obeys his father's commands and dutifully kills Claudius. And though Hamlet's own acute sense of the loss of his beloved is underlined in the words and music of his last utterance in the opera, the opera closes on a note of jubilation, with Hamlet crowned king (in the popular Paris version). Regicide has been avenged, and order restored. Hence, the eeriness of mood suggested by the music of the opera's prelude and of the esplanade scene is finally dispelled by jubilant trumpet fanfares at the close of the opera in conjunction with the onstage action.

On the other hand, the opera's departure from Shakespeare also leads to interesting rereadings of some of the principal characters and relationships. Gertrude is much more sympathetically portrayed in the opera: here, she is more of an independent character than she is in Shakespeare's play, and even the Ghost specifically instructs Hamlet to spare her. As has been stated before, the operatic Hamlet does not reject Ophélie's sexuality, as the words of their Act 1 love duet testify; it is only after learning of Polonius's conspiring that Hamlet rejects her. Such a reading of Hamlet is in refreshing contrast to the suggestions of misogyny often found in Shakespeare's play and echoed by critics such as Ernest Jones and

---

[51] Ibid.

[52] Graham Holderness, "Are Shakespeare's Tragic Heroes 'Fatally Flawed'? Discuss." *Critical Survey* 1 (1989): 53–62.

[53] John Kerrigan, *Revenge Tragedy* (Oxford: Clarendon Press, 1996), 184–91.

[54] Kiernan Ryan, *Shakespeare*, 3rd ed. (Basingstoke: Palgrave, 2002), 70.

T. S. Eliot.[55] In one respect, the opera elaborates on an aspect of Shakespeare's *Hamlet* that was eagerly picked up by nineteenth-century Romantics, in a way that strikingly anticipates the twentieth century: the representation of Ophelia.

**The Operatic Ophélie**

In one respect, though, the conventions of Thomas's opera elaborate on an aspect of Shakespeare's *Hamlet* that was eagerly picked up by nineteenth-century Romantics. Carol Thomas Neely has pointed out that Laertes' words describing the mad Ophelia—"Thought and affliction, passion, hell itself / She turns to favor and to prettiness" (4.5.183–4)—as well as Gertrude's narration of Ophelia's death "foreshadow later representations of it and representations of female hysterics as sexually frustrated and theatrically alluring," a standard that "implicitly introduces conventions for reading madness as gender-inflected."[56] Romantic theatrical representations of Ophelia took off in France, thanks to the productions of Charles Kemble in 1827, with Harriet Smithson as Ophelia.[57] Harriet Smithson became identified with Ophelia in French minds,[58] and in other important respects she played a considerable role in the reception of Shakespeare in France. As Jules Janin declared, as a result of Smithson's success, the French realized that "the poet Shakespeare was in fact the inspired poet of the great tragic actresses."[59] This implies, first, that tragedy was no more an exclusively male preserve and that female actresses could also play important roles in them; and, second, thanks to Smithson, Ophelia came to occupy a more central position in performances of *Hamlet*. Delacroix not only used female models for his paintings of Hamlet,[60] but also made a lithograph in 1843 showing a scene that is found in Thomas's opera but is only mentioned by Gertrude in Shakespeare's play: a portrait of Ophelia drowning.[61]

Thomas's opera, naturally, is influenced by these Romantic readings in its representation of Ophelia, though there are significant differences that arise from issues of translation and intermedial adaptation. Shakespeare's primary mode of representing Ophelia's madness is verbal: Neely notes that, through Ophelia's "alienated speech," Shakespeare "represents distinctions between female hysteria and feigned male melancholy in *Hamlet*." Furthermore, Ophelia mourns her father's

---

[55] See Jacqueline Rose, "Sexuality in the Reading of Shakespeare: *Hamlet* and *Measure for Measure*," in *Alternative Shakespeares*, ed. John Drakakis (London: Methuen, 1985), 95–118; Thompson and Taylor, eds., *Hamlet*, 30.

[56] Carol Thomas Neely, "'Documents in Madness': Reading Madness and Gender in Shakespeare's Tragedies and Early Modern Culture," *Shakespeare Quarterly* 42 (1991): 325.

[57] Showalter, "Representing Ophelia," 82.

[58] Raby, *"Fair Ophelia"*, 177. Berlioz, many of whose major musical compositions are based on Shakespeare, married Smithson in 1833.

[59] Rachel et la tragédie, 67; quoted in Raby, *"Fair Ophelia"*, 178.

[60] Bailey, *Hamlet in France*, 63n54.

[61] Raby, *"Fair Ophelia"*, 181.

death through a song into which her other losses are absorbed.⁶² Since, in the opera, Polonius does not die, Ophélie's mad scene dispenses with the theme of paternal loss.⁶³ The focus, instead, is entirely on the bitter outcome of her love for Hamlet: as in Shakespeare, where her distribution of flowers has been symbolically read as a ritual symbolizing her lost love, deflowering, and death,⁶⁴ Ophélie distributes flowers to village girls surrounding her (this scene is set in a village):

> Partagez-vous mes fleurs! *(à une jeune fille)*
> A toi cette humble branche
> De romarin sauvage.
> Ah!... Ah!... *(à une autre)*
> A toi cette pervenche.
> Ah!... Ah!...
> Et maintenant écoutez ma chanson!⁶⁵

She goes on to sing a song about the Wilis, who, in Slavonic mythology, are young brides-to-be who die before their wedding day. They rise from their graves at night, and make young men who come across them dance till they fall dead. Ophélie imagines herself to be one, exclaiming in her delirious state to Hamlet (who, she thinks, is present), "Ah! cruel! Je t'aime!/ ... Ah! cruel, tu vois mes pleurs! Ah!/ Pour toi je meurs!"⁶⁶ Finally, in an act of supreme irony, just before she is drowned, she recalls the words and music of their Act 1 love duet ("Doute de la lumière"), in which Hamlet had promised her his undying love.⁶⁷

---

⁶² Neely, "Documents in Madness," 323–4.

⁶³ The directions in the libretto read: "Ophélie enters, dressed in a long white robe and bizarrely covered with flowers and vines intertwined in her dishevelled hair," quoted in Morton Jay Achter, "Félicien David, Ambroise Thomas, and French *Opéra Lyrique*" (PhD diss., University of Michigan, 1972), 299n107. This is, curiously, close to the "sharply defined" conventions of representations of insanity on the Elizabethan stage, in which "Ophelia dresses in white, [and] decks herself with 'fantastical garlands' of white flowers." See Showalter, "Representing Ophelia," 117. Moreover, in the opera, Ophélie's mad scene is in rhymed verse throughout, and there is no contrast with Hamlet, who does not feign madness at all.

⁶⁴ Neely, "Documents in Madness," 324–5; Showalter, "Representing Ophelia," 117.

⁶⁵ "Let me share my flowers with you! *(To a young girl)* / For you a humble sprig of wild rosemary, /Ah! ... Ah! ... *(To another)*/ Here's periwinkle for you, / Ah! ... Ah! ... / And now listen to my song!" (Barbier and Carré, "Hamlet," 103).

⁶⁶ "Ah, cruel one, I love you! / ... Ah, cruel one, see, I weep! Ah! / I die for you!" (Barbier and Carré, "Hamlet," 105). Thus, Valerie Traub's observation about Shakespeare's Ophelia holds true for Thomas' Ophélie as well: "Ophelia's death is as much an outcome of Hamlet's rage as it is an expression of her grief, madness, or self-destruction." See Valerie Traub, "Desire and Anxiety: Circulations of Sexuality in Shakespearean Drama**,**" in *William Shakespeare's "Hamlet": A Sourcebook*, ed. Sean McEvoy (London: Routledge, 2006), 64.

⁶⁷ Since in this final section of the mad scene, the offstage chorus *hums* the "Scandinavian" tune sung earlier in the scene by Ophélie, an innovative production can suggest that the music comes from Ophélie's hallucinatory mind. In the 2003 Théâtre de

Critics have generally found this reference to the Wilis to be dramatically unnecessary. Winton Dean finds the inclusion of Scandinavian motifs and the "almost Griegian ballade in the mad scene, and the expansion of Ophélie's part beyond the requirements of the drama" to be signs that "Thomas's courage, or his artistic integrity, seems to have failed."[68] A more sympathetic Hervé Lacombe writes that it is "devoid of dramatic import, but is nicely set to music and furnishes a poetic moment."[69] Given the plot changes and the way the allusion to the Wilis is incorporated in the mad scene, it does seem to have some dramatic validity.[70]

In many ways, Ophélie's mad scene is typical—like other operatic mad figures, she is unable to recognize those around her, and she dwells on her memories in a state of hallucination, thinking that Hamlet is present. Two motifs from the love duet, therefore, figure prominently.[71] The accompanying dance rhythms, like that of other mad scenes, capitalize on a representational tradition that links madness to dancing, and both to a loss of sexual inhibition.[72] This has led critics to read the dance rhythms and coloratura in Ophélie's mad scene in terms of an implicitly sexualized hysterical syndrome.[73] But whether the opera prepares the audience for

---

Genève (London) and the Gran Teatre del Liceu productions of the opera, Natalie Dessay, playing Ophélie, had blood trickling down her dress, indicating that she was killing herself; the latter production is available on DVD.

[68] Winton Dean, "Shakespeare and Opera," in *Shakespeare in Music*, ed. Phyllis Hartnoll, (London: Macmillan, 1964), 167. The Scandinavian provenance of the tune has been questioned by Achter, "Felicién David," 301n18.

[69] Lacombe, *Keys to French Opera*, 108.

[70] Thomas wanted to avoid the ballet (omitted in modern productions) that precedes Ophélie's death scene in Act 4, but was forced to provide the music by Emile Perrin, director of the Opéra. See Rogeboz-Malfroy, *Ambroise Thomas*, 234. By replacing the "vulgar" songs of Ophelia with a reference to the Wilis and accompanying it by music of a dance-like character, Thomas and his librettists could have intended to evoke Adolphe Adam's famous ballet *Giselle* as an intertext, one that was already present in the libretto and that neatly dovetailed at both dramatic and musical levels into their operatic *Hamlet*. Like Thomas's *Hamlet*, some of the music for Adam's *Giselle* also evokes a mysterious, supernatural world, and Adam himself spelt the parallel between opera and ballet when he likened the Act 1 finale of *Giselle* to an operatic finale—possibly that of Donizetti's *Lucia di Lammermoor* (the famous mad scene). This intertextual strategy is lost on twentieth-century audiences because of the gradual separation of ballet (or, more precisely, the *ballet-pantomime*) from opera by the twentieth century, but that was certainly not the case with nineteenth-century Parisian audiences at the Opéra. See Marian Smith, *Ballet and Opera in the Age of Giselle* (Princeton, NJ: Princeton University Press, 2000), xi–xvii and 167–200.

[71] The first (Thomas, 26.7 ff to vs 28.9), recurs at 285.3 ff, and the second, the melody of "Doute de la lumière," appears, transformed, in the final section of the mad scene (Thomas, 308.6 ff).

[72] Clausen, *Macbeth*, 133.

[73] Christoph Clausen, "Shakespeare in Opera," in *Sh@kespeare in the Media: From the Globe to the WorldWide Web*, ed. Stefani Brusberg-Kiermeier and Jörg Helbig (Frankfurt am Main: Peter Lang, 2004), 108n4.

the mad scene by showing her as someone having a "prior hysteric disposition"[74] remains open to question, as the fragmentary, asymmetrical, rhythmically nervous musical idiom associated with Ophélie in the mad scene is not typical of the way she is characterized in the rest of the opera, as Clausen seems to suggest.[75] Another reason why it is difficult to read Ophélie as a docile, virtuous girl or one with a prior hysterical disposition is because opera *as a medium* enables the audience to engage in a different relationship with the performer than does the theater:

> What happens when we watch and hear a female performer? We are observing her, yet we are doing something for which there's no word: the aural vision of staring. ... Seeing a female figure may well more or less automatically invoke our culture's opposition of male (active subject) and female (passive object) ... But listening to the female singing voice is a more complicated phenomenon. Visually, the character singing is the passive object of our gaze. But aurally, she is resonant; her musical speech drowns out everything in range, and we sit as passive objects, battered by that voice. As a voice she slips into the "male/active/subject" position in other ways as well, since a singer, more than any other musical performer, enters into that Jacobin uprising inherent in the phenomenology of live performance and stands before us having wrested the composing voice away from the librettist and composer who wrote the score.[76]

Abbate's argument may seem to valorize music over drama, but it does make an important point. From the very first performance, Christine Nilsson, the Swedish soprano who became the first Ophélie, "electrified the entire house," so much so that it was feared that her mad scene would make everything else in the opera pale.[77] And indeed, when the opera did drop out of the regular operatic repertoire, it was the mad scene (along with Hamlet's drinking song) that continued to be regularly performed. Ralph P. Locke's counterargument, that Abbate "risks turning the female voice into a disembodied instrument (and thereby turning opera into a string of vocal concertos)"[78] needs to be tested against the realities of performance practice and audience response. For good or ill, audiences do respond to the concerto-like potential of Ophélie's mad scene; in a theatrical performance of the complete opera, the singer performing the role still has the potential to

---

[74] Given that Jean-Martin Charcot's photographic records of hysteria come from the 1870s, it is tempting to assume that the cultural climate was conducive to such a reading of Ophelia. As has been noted, images of one of his patients, Augustine, frequently resemble the reproductions of Ophelia then available in wide circulation. See Showalter, "Representing Ophelia," 85.

[75] Clausen, "Shakespeare," 109. At the other extreme, it has been argued that "Ophelia's character is limited by her symmetrical, short phrases over a static bass." See David Charlton, "Opera: 1850–1890. (b) France," in *The Oxford History of Music*, ed. Gerald Abraham (London: Oxford University Press, 1990), 9:366.

[76] Abbate, "Opera," 254.

[77] Paul Bernard, quoted in Schmidgall, *Shakespeare and Opera*, 319.

[78] Quoted in Clausen, *Macbeth*, 256.

assert her artistry despite the fact that her character is crushed by uncontrollable forces. The reworking of gender dynamics that, according to Showalter, "comes as much from the actress's freedom as from the critic's interpretation" of the role of Ophelia,[79] happens to an even greater extent in this opera. By representing Ophélie's madness as the result of Hamlet's treatment rather than her sexuality, as well as by "envoicing" her through the nature of the operatic medium itself, Thomas's opera offers a reading of Ophelia that strikingly departs from typical nineteenth-century readings of Ophelia, anticipating twentieth-century readings of the character.

### *Hamlet* by Ducis, Dumas, and Thomas: Adaptations or Appropriations?

As Linda Hutcheon has noted, most theories of adaptation assume that "the story is the common denominator, the core of what is transposed across different media and genres, each of which deals with the story in formally different ways and ... different modes of engagement."[80] Each medium highlights different aspects of the story. But in the course of retelling, plots of stories sometimes also undergo radical modification, rather than just a shift of emphasis, whether or not a different medium or language is involved in the retelling. Both radical modification of the plot as well as a shift of emphasis can be likened to a theme-and-variation pattern, for sure, but the difference (in degree) between plot modification on the one hand, and a shift of emphasis on the other, is significant and needs to be explored further. Compared to Shakespeare's play, there is a change of content in Ducis's *Hamlet* (because there are changes to the plot) that is not caused by the necessities of intermedial transfer or change of language; rather, the change in plot is necessitated because of *the different conditions of reception in the receiving culture* (in this case, the strict rules and conventions of the eighteenth-century neoclassical French theater). This is even truer of twentieth-century reworkings of Shakespeare, many of which are inflected by the theoretical concerns of psychoanalysis, postcolonialism, feminism, queer theory, or a combination of these.[81] In such cases, the plots of Shakespeare's plays are enriching intertexts to those audiences or readers who know both the original text and its reworkings. Yet, irrespective of whether issues of translation or intermedial transfer are involved, the process of rewriting a story with a difference has generated works that define their relationship to Shakespeare's plays in a wide variety of ways, whether it be one of homage (Verdi's opera *Otello*), indirect allusion (Bernstein-Sondheim musical *West Side Story*), or one of contestation (Aimé Césaire's *Une Tempête*).

Julie Sanders makes an interesting distinction between *adaptation* and *appropriation* by suggesting that while an adaptation "signals a relationship with an informing sourcetext or original," an appropriation

---

[79] Showalter, "Representing Ophelia," 80.
[80] Hutcheon, *A Theory of Adaptation*, 10.
[81] Julie Sanders, *Adaptation and Appropriation* (London: Routledge, 2006), 46.

frequently affects a more decisive journey away from the informing source into a wholly new cultural product and domain. This may or may not involve a generic shift, and it may still require the intellectual juxtaposition of (at least) one text against another that we have suggested is central to the reading and spectating experience of adaptations. But the appropriated text or texts are not always as clearly signalled or acknowledged as in the adaptive process.[82]

Sanders's distinction is useful, especially in the case of works like Tom Stoppard's *Rosencrantz & Guildenstern are Dead* or Césaire's *Une Tempête*, where, in the process of retelling, something more than a change of language, place or time ("transculturation," to use Hutcheon's term) takes place. Shakespeare's *Hamlet*, for example, does retain an intertextual connection with *Rosencrantz*, but the degree of plot divergence in Stoppard is considerably greater than in other retellings, such as, say, the Grigori Kozintsev film adaptation of *Hamlet*. Indeed, in *Rosencrantz* and *Une Tempête*, there is more than just a change of emphasis resulting from a different point of view or setting. However, Sanders's distinction also implies that an appropriation of a source text involves a lack of a clear acknowledgement of a relationship with prior texts. This need not always be the case: a "decisive journey away from the informing source" need not always go hand-in-hand with a lack of acknowledgement of the appropriated text, or vice versa.

For example, Kurosawa's film *Kumonosu-jō* (lit., "Spider Web Castle," 1957), known in the West as *Throne of Blood*, does not clearly acknowledge its relationship with Shakespeare's *Macbeth* in either its Japanese or English titles. However, despite the changes of language, place, time, names of protagonists, and medium, the film adheres to Shakespeare's plot closely enough for audiences familiar with Shakespeare's play to recognize the film as an adaptation. By keeping its intertextual link with Shakespeare unannounced, *Throne of Blood* foregoes making use of Shakespeare's cultural capital, while at the same time avoiding the possibility of it being regarded as a derivative work.

On the other hand, both *Rosencrantz* and *Une Tempête* take the "decisive journey away from the informing source," yet their titles announce their relationships with the Shakespeare plays from which they both draw and depart. In fact, they draw their power as revisionary readings of Shakespeare precisely by announcing their departure, by making radical changes to perspective and plot while alluding to Shakespeare through their titles. Hence I would suggest that only Kurosawa's *Throne of Blood*, which stays very close to Shakespeare in terms of plot, is a true adaptation. The other two works, whose plots depart considerably from Shakespeare, are better regarded as appropriations. In Hutcheon's continuum model,[83] at one end are forms such as translations or musical transcriptions, which seek to achieve complete fidelity, even if only as a theoretical ideal, while at the other end lie spin-offs, prequels, and sequels. In this model, adaptations stay closer

---

[82] Ibid., 26.
[83] Hutcheon, *A Theory of Adaptation*, 170–72.

to the fidelity end of the scale than appropriations, parodies, and spin-offs, which appear further and further away from the fidelity end.

Conversely, the ascription of the name *Hamlet* to any work "based" on the Shakespeare play does not necessarily make it an adaptation, for both adaptations and appropriations can have an extended and announced relationship with a prior text. The plays of Dumas-Meurice and Ducis, as well as Thomas's opera, because of their significant alterations to the plot of the Shakespeare play, are therefore probably better regarded as appropriations. If these French versions did not "write back" to Shakespeare, as many twentieth-century postcolonial and feminist reworkings of Shakespeare do, they nonetheless carry the burden of their authors' own agendas. As I have discussed previously, Ducis's version strove to infuse French neoclassical tragedy with elements of the bourgeois drama, while the Dumas-Meurice version strove to make *Hamlet* compatible with theatrical genres popular in Dumas's time and representative of Dumas's own dramatic works.[84]

**The Afterlife of Thomas's *Hamlet***

As stated earlier, Thomas's opera fell into obscurity by the end of the First World War, for a few possible reasons. Like Verdi's *Macbeth* (and unlike *Otello* and *Falstaff*), Thomas's opera is built on what has been called a "dramaturgy of contrasts,"[85] in which the "characters function not so much as personalities, self-sufficient psychological entities, but rather as events, actor-agents in situations."[86] It is the situations, not the characters, that determine the oppositions fundamental to the "dramaturgy of contrasts." However, the choice of the situations and their musical treatment in Thomas's *Hamlet* is done with remarkable skill and finesse, so that the "dramaturgy of contrasts" on which this opera is built is not incompatible with a musical characterization of the psychological dimension of the protagonists, especially Hamlet and Ophélie, albeit in a limited way. Nevertheless, the development of the through-composed operas of Richard Wagner, and Verdi's own variety of through-composition, especially in *Otello* and *Falstaff*, opened up newer and more effective means of musical depiction of the inner psychology of operatic characters in a way that made operas like Thomas's *Hamlet* seem outmoded by comparison to twentieth century audiences. Moreover, Thomas's opera, like Gounod's *Roméo et Juliette* and many of Verdi's earlier operas, bear transparent signs of the adapters' attempt to make a compromise with the cultural codes of the *receiving* culture, an approach that appears to subject the composer's individual artistic ideals to convention. As Richard Taruskin has pointed out, such an approach was incompatible with notions of musical modernism for a trend-

---

[84] Heylen, *Six French Hamlets*, 48.
[85] Lacombe, *Keys to French Opera*, 107.
[86] Harold Powers, "Making 'Macbeth' *Musicabile*," in *Macbeth. ENO Opera Guide 41*, ed. Nicholas John (London: John Calder, 1990), 16.

setting composer like Wagner.[87] It was only when other composers, Verdi included, articulated fidelity to personal artistic ideals over audience expectations as their artistic credo, that it became possible for them to be considered modern, and their works of art to gain serious critical attention from musicologists.

On the other hand, three factors can be said to have helped the revival of Thomas's *Hamlet*. First, as mentioned earlier, is the championing of the work by baritones of international repute. Second, as David Littlejohn has observed, "the 'standard repertoire' of opera has never been larger or more diverse" than in the present day,[88] ranging from Monteverdi to newly composed operas. With operas from different periods and different styles available on CD and DVD, critics and audiences are better prepared to accept a wide diversity of singing styles, subject matter, and forms. Such conditions, then, open up the possibility for interested audiences to place operas in their proper historical contexts and, therefore, be aware of the conventions of a less frequently performed part of the operatic repertory, such as nineteenth-century French *grand opéra*,[89] in which Thomas's *Hamlet* is placed. Finally, with the rise of critical interest in adaptations and adaptation theory, unfavorable views of adaptations, based on a discourse of fidelity, have been increasingly challenged.[90] The revival of Thomas's *Hamlet* took place at a propitious time, the late 1980s, when there was also an increase in the number of Shakespeare adaptations on film.

While as readers and audiences of Shakespeare we should not, of course, ignore the "potentialities of meaning" that pertain only to Shakespeare's plays,[91] given the fact that Shakespeare has been, and is being, adapted the world over in different cultures and languages, we cannot dismiss adaptations of Shakespeare as secondary works. Nor can we ignore the complex ways in which adaptations (or appropriations) have themselves been crucial to the dissemination of Shakespeare. Since Shakespeare himself was a master adapter of stories by others, we can regard the adaptations discussed here as "form[s] of collaboration across time ... culture and language,"[92] collaborations that not only helped Shakespeare's plays spread across Europe but also proved influential centuries later to the development of European drama and opera.

---

[87] Richard Taruskin, *The Oxford History of Western Music*, 5 vols. (New York: Oxford University Press, 2005), 3:599.

[88] David Littlejohn, *The Ultimate Art: Articles around and about Opera* (Berkeley: University of California Press, 1992), 27.

[89] Achter, however, argues that Thomas's *Hamlet* should be considered "lyric, not grand, opera." See Achter, "Felicién David," 311.

[90] Hutcheon, *A Theory of Adaptation*, 8–9; Sanders, *Adaptation*, 13–14; Stam, "Theory and Practice," 7–8.

[91] Clausen, *Macbeth*, 14.

[92] Sanders, *Adaptation*, 47.

# PART IV
# Harnessing the Renaissance: Markets, Religion, Politics

# Chapter 10
# Reconstructing the Boydell Shakspeare Gallery

## Ann R. Hawkins

In early November 1803, after sixty years as a print-dealer, publisher, and entrepreneur, John Boydell declared bankruptcy.[1] His lucrative continental markets had collapsed in the Napoleonic wars, what Boydell called a "vandalick revolution ... convulsing all Europe."[2] To save his company, Boydell gained parliamentary approval to lottery off the contents of his Shakspeare Gallery—a collection of sculpture and paintings illustrating the works of Shakespeare—which he had hoped ultimately to give to the nation.[3] The disposition of this London landmark garnered strong public attention. Between April and November 1804, 20,000 tickets sold at three guineas apiece, and as soon as the last ticket sold, local papers carried advertisements offering as much as 25 guineas for a ticket.[4] After the January 28, 1805 lottery, the winner, William Tassie, indicated he would "dispos[e] of" the Gallery either at "public auction or by private contract," and he opened the Gallery for "the last time that the pictures can ever be seen as an entire collection" to promote the auction.[5] Public interest did not even wane after the

---

[1] I am indebted to the Folger Shakespeare Library for a short-term fellowship in 2001 to further my research on Romantic commodifications of Shakespeare, particularly Boydell's, and for the opportunity of guest curating an exhibition on Boydell's Gallery in 2007–08 with Georgianna Zeigler. The expertise and graciousness of the Folger curators (particularly Erin Blake and Heather Wolfe), reading room staff (particularly Elizabeth Walsh, LuEllen DeHaven, Rosalind Larry, and Harold Batie), and fellowship coordinator, Carol Brobeck, is exceptional. My debts to them are too many to be fully detailed here.

Boydell's house stopped payment on its debts on or shortly before November 9, 1803. Joseph Farington, *Diary*, ed. Kenneth Garlick and Angus Macintyre, 6 vols. (New Haven, CT: Yale University Press, 1979), 6:2159.

[2] John Boydell to Sir John N. Anderson, February 4, 1804. Folger Shakespeare Library.

[3] Ibid. For the progress of the lottery request through Parliament, see Sven H. A. Bruntjen, *John Boydell, 1719–1804: A Study of Art Patronage and Publishing in Georgian London* (New York: Garland, 1985): 116, 148n100, 151n102.

[4] Farington, *Diary*, 6:2437. Winifred Friedman, *Boydell's Shakespeare Gallery* (New York: Garland, 1976), 89.

[5] *London Times*, April 5, 1805, 3D; *The Exhibition of the Shakspeare gallery, Pall-Mall, being the last time the pictures can ever be seen as an entire collection* (London: W. Bulmer and Co., 1805). This catalogue's preface refers to Tassie as the "present proprietor of the Gallery."

Christie's auction on May 17–20, 1805, for interested parties could buy a printed catalogue documenting the sale, purchasers, and purchase prices.[6]

The closing of the Gallery offers such a dramatic climax to Boydell's story that all critical discussion to date has focused on the Gallery as it appeared together for the last time. The Gallery at its end neatly offers critics a *finished* product, and from this perspective critics have tackled a range of topics:

- Boydell as entrepreneur: his career; his influence on engraving and painting; his nationalistic aims; his intentions for English art
- The painters and/or engravers: the place of Shakspeare Gallery works in artistic careers; relationships with Boydell as a patron
- The paintings themselves: the contributions of a particular artist; the place of the Boydell images in the context of contemporary artistic movements
- The literary context: the illustrations of a particular Shakespeare play as a group; the individual picture's "interpretation" of a particular act, scene, or play
- The dramatic context: the influence of contemporary stagings or actors on the composition of an image
- Broader artistic concerns: the rise of the Royal Academy, the conflict between portraiture and history painting, the rise of commercial patronage, the shift from line engraving to etching
- Cultural questions: the rhetoric of an "English art"; the importance of cultural tourism[7]

---

[6] *A Catalogue of that Magnificent and Truly Valuable collection of Pictures, (with the Prices they sold for, and Names of the Purchasers,) ... known as the collection of the Shakspeare Gallery ...* (London: T. Beckett, [1805]).

[7] Most of the articles and books that have referred to Boydell or his gallery in recent years simply recount the accepted scholarship in a handful of sources. Most often cited are Bruntjen, *John Boydell*, a biography of Boydell and his career; Friedman, *Boydell's Shakespeare Gallery*, a book-length study of the origins of the Gallery and the painters and engravers involved; Winifred Friedman, "Some Commercial Aspects of the Boydell Shakespeare Gallery," *Journal of the Warburg and Courtauld Institutes* 36 (1973): 396–401; and Frederick Burwick and Thomas Pape, eds., *The Boydell Shakespeare Gallery* (Bottrop, Germany: Peter Pomp, 1996). For my purposes, these and the following offer the most useful discussions of the Boydell Gallery: W. Moelwin Merchant, *Shakespeare and the Artist* (London: Oxford University Press, 1959); Richard Altick, *Paintings from Books* (Columbus: Ohio State University Press, 1985); Jonathan Bate, *Shakespearean Constitutions: Politics, Theatre, Criticism 1730–1830* (Oxford: Clarendon, 1989) and "Shakespearean Allusion in English Caricature in the Age of Gillray," *Journal of the Warburg and Courtauld Institutes* 49 (1968): 196–210; A. E. Santaniello, *The Boydell Shakespeare Prints* (New York: Arno, 1979); Morris Eaves, *The Counter-Arts Conspiracy: Art and Industry in the Age of Blake* (Ithaca, NY: Cornell University Press, 1992) and his related essay, "The Sister Arts in British Romanticism," in *Cambridge Companion to British Romanticism*, ed. Stuart Curran (Cambridge: Cambridge University Press, 1993), 236–70. Individual paintings in Boydell's Gallery have received attention from critics, usually limited to passing acknowledgments of

This perspective on Boydell's Gallery is so engrained that some studies have referred to the paintings by the exhibition numbers assigned in the 1864 retrospective—numbers that do not represent the order in which the paintings were described in the exhibition catalogues from 1789 to 1797, though they are close to the order in the final Boydell exhibition catalogue, the one for 1802.[8] Alternatively, studies list engravings according to their appearance in Boydell's nine-volume illustrated "National Edition" of Shakespeare, a collection that includes pictures never exhibited in the physical gallery.[9]

These representations of the Gallery and the concerns they generate have also patterned the ways scholars have approached the Gallery's products: the two-volume collection of the atlas folio prints, the nine-volume "National Edition," and the one-volume *Boydell's Graphic Illustrations of the Dramatic Works of Shakespeare*. The contents of these books *combined* have constituted the "Shakspeare Gallery."[10] But, to speak in bibliographic terms, this "Shakspeare Gallery" is an eclectic edition, one created from a variety of exemplars to represent a lost original. In their original forms, this combining would be fraught with complications. As engravings of different sizes, the large and small plates could not form one whole except in an unbound portfolio or on the walls of a long-dismantled physical exhibition space. Further, the pictures—produced for different ends—are compositionally dissimilar: the large plates offer monumental history painting, the small plates concise book illustration. The "Shakspeare Gallery," as created by critical discussion, is a manufactured text, but because its sophistication is not readily apparent to the user, it obscures the lost original. In this way the "text" of the Shakspeare Gallery participates in the same sorts of problems that scholars have long identified with the texts of *Lear* or *Hamlet*.

Certainly, those writing on the Shakspeare Gallery might object, claiming that this eclectic edition *re-creates* the contents of that long-dismantled space. I would argue, however, that this moment of stasis offers an inaccurate or, at best, incomplete vision of the Gallery. It provides the only moment in the Gallery's 15 years of existence when the Gallery appeared to contain a fixed content. And

---

Boydell's importance as an art patron or identifications (sometimes incorrect) of a particular image as originating in his collection. The best of this type of study is Alan R. Young, *Hamlet and the Visual Arts, 1709–1900* (Newark: University of Delaware Press, 2002). Stuart Sillars, *Painting Shakespeare* (Cambridge: Cambridge University Press, 2006) and Christopher Rovee, *Imagining the Gallery: The Social Body of British Romanticism* (Stanford, CA: Stanford University Press, 2006) have both devoted chapters to Boydell. The present essay assumes that the reader will have access to the collections of images available either in Santaniello or Burwick and Pape.

[8] *The Shakespeare Gallery: A Reproduction in Commemoration of the Tercentenary Anniversary of the Poet's Death* (London: L. Booth, 1864).

[9] See for example Santaniello, *Boydell Shakespeare Prints* or Burwick and Pape, *Boydell Shakespeare Gallery*.

[10] In speaking of Boydell's enterprise, I use the spelling Boydell's documents prefer— Shakspeare—rather than the spelling preferred by recent scholarship.

this perspective has elided from view the fact that the Gallery all along offered an experience of Shakespeare in fragments: the 19 installments of the atlas folio prints, the 18 installments of the National Edition, and the 15 years of changing exhibitions. Even when a painting was exhibited continuously in the Gallery, newspaper reports record paintings being "retouched, and considerably improved" between exhibitions.[11] This experience of a fragmentary Shakespeare continued after the closing of the Gallery with Josiah Boydell's publication in 12 installments of the small plates in the *Graphic Illustrations*.[12] In this way, the Boydell Gallery participates in the larger Romantic tension we see in poetry between the fragment and the epic, between the coherence of individual installments and the reshaping of those installments in a bound collection. In this way, too, the Boydell Gallery draws our attention to issues important in the nineteenth-century book trade, such as periodical and serial publication.

Having considered Boydell's Gallery as a completed artifact, we should turn our attention to the growth of the Gallery over its 15 years of exhibitions. I argue for a new perspective on the Boydell enterprise, one that examines the Gallery not as a completed and coherent object, but as a series of "galleries," of distinct moments in a complicated cycle of Shakespearean representation and consumption in the Romantic era. This chronological presentation will examine the various Shakespeares that the Gallery presents over its years of exhibitions, the kinds of Shakespeare Boydell marketed, and the nature of Romantic appetites for Shakespeare. Specifically, we should examine how the Gallery's growth indicates a market for Shakespeare, how the Gallery responded to that market, and in turn how the Gallery perpetuated that market. These marketing issues can indicate to us what British Romantic culture thought about Shakespeare at a significant juncture in his reception, when Shakespeare was still being canonized as the British National Poet.

**The Exhibition Catalogues: A General Description**

To examine the Boydell Gallery's growth from 34 to 174 (or more) images, I draw on the extant yearly exhibition catalogues and the 1803 stock list.[13] Annual exhibition catalogues are extant for the years 1789–1797 and for 1802; whether catalogues were published for the years 1798 to 1801 is unknown. When I refer to the catalogues collectively, I refer to the extant catalogues only. Past criticism has

---

[11] "The Shakespeare Gallery," *London Times*, March 29, 1792, 3B.

[12] Advertisement for "New and Splendid Works, Published by Messrs. Boydell and Co. No. 90, Cheapside," 1813, John Johnson Collection of Ephemera, Bodleian Library, Oxford University.

[13] Scholars have had difficulty fixing the number of paintings in the gallery, proposing most frequently 167 (Friedman, *Boydell's Shakespeare Gallery*, 83; Bruntjen, *John Boydell*, 100; Altick, *Paintings from Books*, 43) or 170 (Jonathan Bate, ed., *The Romantics on Shakespeare* [New York: Penguin, 1991], 47). In my figure of 174, I count only illustrations of scenes from Shakespeare's plays.

treated these catalogues as reference books answering factual questions: For what purpose did Boydell start the Gallery? In raw numbers, how many pictures were exhibited in a particular year? Who painted what? How many pictures illustrate a particular play? The information provided in these catalogues has received uncritical acceptance: no catalogue has been considered more authoritative than another, though the 1802 catalogue—which groups illustrations by play—has received some preference for its numbering. Yet all these printed sources are bibliographically inconsistent and sometimes internally contradictory (even when providing information about a painting previously exhibited).

To reexamine the Boydell Shakspeare Gallery, we must reconsider these catalogues as material objects.[14] To do so, I examined all the extant catalogues in the Folger Shakespeare Library, the British Library, the Bodleian Library, and the Cambridge University Library as well as the electronic texts now available in the Eighteenth Century Collections Online database and an electronic version of the 1797 catalogue held by Princeton University.[15] As material objects, Boydell's exhibition catalogues presented so similar an appearance from year to year that without careful analysis it is difficult to tell if the catalogue was reprinted or if newly printed pages were appended to leftover catalogue stock. But bibliographic examination indicates most catalogues were reset from the previous year's iteration. Generally, catalogues show signs of being hastily or cheaply printed (or both), as one finds poor registration, errors in pagination, skipped or repeated entries, and reordered pages or signatures. Printing errors are typically corrected in the next year's catalogue, indicating at least some editorial oversight.

---

[14] Subscribers received free admission to the Gallery each year, but it's unclear whether they also received a gratis copy of each year's catalogue. The exhibition catalogues aren't listed for sale in Boydell's stock list nor do any of the copies I have examined carry a price. However, in 1790 at least, the *Critical Review* records that the catalogues were sold "at the place of exhibition" for 1s. 6d. Review of *A Catalogue of the Pictures, &c. in the Shakspeare Gallery*, in *Critical Review* 70 (1790): 581. The *Critical*'s review suggests that the price of the catalogues was separate from that of admission, but what the admission fee was remains unclear. Boydell did waive the admission fee for some groups in addition to subscribers: apprentice engravers placed an advertisement in the *London Times* thanking Boydell for free admission to the Gallery.

[15] In considering the bibliographic nature of the catalogues, my article redresses somewhat the lack Roland Frye identifies in his review of Friedman's work. See Roland Frye, "A Study of the Boydell Gallery," *Shakespeare Quarterly* 28, no. 3 (1977): 377–8. *Eighteenth Century Collections Online* (*ECCO*), published by Gale/Cengage, often removes blank pages from its scans and reorders "facing" pages to elide their absence, making *ECCO* texts unsuitable for collation formulas. But *ECCO* texts do allow other sorts of bibliographic analysis, such as comparing the relative locations of particular pieces of type, the relative length of bar and headings, etc. In this way, these texts allow scholars to compare copies from different holding libraries side by side. Thanks to Lorraine Madway, curator of rare books at Wichita State Library, for describing a fragile 1796 catalogue; and to Stephen Ferguson, curator of rare books at Princeton University, for his gracious and speedy provision of the 1797 catalogue in PDF format.

In terms of content, the catalogues provided the same types of information from year to year. The catalogues—quartos sized between 19 x 12.2 cm and 23 x 12.2 cm, depending on trimming—offered relatively consistent design elements, such as title-page layout, headings to entries, and layout of excerpts. However, those elements often exhibit differences in printing, such as slightly different fonts and thicker (or longer) rules. The contents also followed a consistent order: title-page; Boydell's 1789 preface; the 1790 advertisement; entries for individual pictures, numbered consecutively; and back matter, usually advertisements for other Boydell projects. Inside this broader overall organization, the entries for specific pictures provided information in the following order: item number, play title, act and scene numbers, a short description of the scene, the name of the painter, the name of the engraver (in 1802 only), and an excerpt of play text ranging from a few lines to several pages. In general the length of the excerpts decreased over the years, suggesting a desire to maintain a consistent catalogue length, despite the addition of four to twenty-eight paintings each year.

Each year up to 1802, additions to the Gallery appear following a header indicating the year of exhibition; these yearly subdivisions are appended to the end of the previous year's pictures, and the new entries are numbered consecutively with the old. This organizational strategy offered several advantages. From a production standpoint, adding the pictures in groups to the end of the catalogue meant that the catalogue did not require significant oversight between exhibitions. Printers could be given a copy of the old catalogue, perhaps with corrections marked, and told to place the new material at the end. Since press figures suggest the printing was divided between as many as six pressmen, Boydell's strategy helped ensure quality control; bibliographic problems typically appear in the later pages, particularly where old materials joined with new.

From a viewer's standpoint, Boydell's strategy allowed quick identification of new additions. Subscribers, for example, who received free admission, might wish only to look at the *new* paintings in a given year. However, a viewer interested in a single play couldn't locate all of those entries quickly: for example, in the 1797 catalogue entries for *Merry Wives of Windsor* appear on pages 17, 19, 82, 121, 139, 183, and 184. Thus the order of pictures in the catalogue was likely a less important guide than the number on the picture frame.

In 1795, a change in organization might have posed problems for users. Before the back matter, Boydell added a new section, "A catalogue of small pictures, painted for the Shakspeare Gallery Pall-Mall." This addition separated the catalogue into two parts: one catalogue for large pictures and one for small. How new pictures were added to the catalogue depended on size: large pictures continued to be listed at the end of the previous year's exhibition, while small pictures were integrated by play into the "small pictures" catalogue. Adding a further layer of difficulty, the "small pictures" catalogue renumbered its entries from one, thus duplicating numbers one to seventy-eight with the "large pictures" catalog. For example, pictures of *Merry Wives of Windsor* appear as entries 2, 3, 39, 66, and 57 in the large pictures and as entries 1, 2, and 3 in the small. The duplication here—2 and 3 indicating both large *and* small pictures—required a user to check both sections for the explanation of a particular painting. Further, since pictures were now separated by format, viewers would have to know a picture's size (large or small) to know where to find its entry. This might seem an easy task, but Boydell's large paintings were of "Various Sizes, chiefly as large as Life."[16] Unfortunately, "large as Life" differed from picture to picture: Benjamin West's *Hamlet* at 276.9 x 387.4 cm (9.1' x 12.7', or 116 square feet) was nearly twice as large by area as Henry Fuseli's *Titania and Bottom* at 217.2 x 275.6 cm (7.2' x 9', or 65 square feet). Further, a particular painting's status as large or small could change between exhibitions: the two images of Puck (by Fuseli and by Joshua Reynolds) exhibited as "large" pictures since 1791 became "small" pictures in 1802.

These catalogues, with their clear indications of each year's additions, offer us the best representation of what the Gallery looked like over time. They offer us a diachronic record of Boydell's enterprise, revealing trends in the growth of the Gallery as Boydell responded to his perceptions of popular appetites for Shakespeare. This diachronic view highlights the contrast between Boydell's earliest intentions for the Gallery and its actual growth.

## Growing the Gallery: Original Intentions, 1786–1793

The 1786 prospectus for subscribers outlined Boydell's plan for the Shakspeare Gallery: a set of 72 paintings from which large *and* small engravings would be made, the large to be bound together, the small integrated into the "National Edition," the paintings themselves to be hung in a purpose-built gallery. If evenly allocated, 72 pictures would provide two pictures per Shakespeare play. But Boydell planned to allocate pictures not by play, but by the level of interest a particular play demonstrated:

> As, however, some of them [Shakespeare's plays] exhibit more interesting Subjects than others, the Plates will be given without Regard to any certain Number for each Drama.—For Instance; HAMLET, KING LEAR, ROMEO and JULIET, MACBETH, OTHELLO, and the two Parts of HENRY IV. may furnish three apiece, while the MIDSUMMER NIGHT'S DREAM, the COMEDY OF ERRORS, the TWO GENTLEMEN of VERONA, LOVE'S LABOUR'S LOST, ALL'S WELL THAT ENDS WELL, TROILUS and CRESSIDA, and TITUS ANDRONICUS, may each contribute only one.[17]

Boydell's 14 examples are instructive. The seven "more interesting" plays included five tragedies and two histories; the seven least interesting plays included five comedies and two histories. Thus, Boydell predicted that tragedy (and some history) would be more interesting than comedy (and some history), and the plays would receive illustrations accordingly. By this plan, in the completed gallery,

---

[16] *Shakspeare. Mr. Alderman Boydell, Josiah Boydell, and George Nicol, propose to publish by Subscription a most Magnificent and accurate edition of the Plays of Shakspeare, in Eight volumes ...* (London, 1786), 2. Cited hereafter as 1786 Call for Subscribers.

[17] 1786 Call for Subscribers, [1].

tragedy would be most illustrated overall, followed by history, then comedy (which for Boydell included what are now called romances).

In reality, however, the contents of the Gallery ran counter to these expectations. In the brief sections that follow, I overview the growth of the Gallery year-by-year as well as examine the bibliographic aspects of the catalogues. Below I offer two tables indicating how the Gallery grew over time in each genre. Table 10.1 provides the raw numbers of pictures added to the Gallery, divided among the categories of comedy, history, and tragedy for each year. Table 10.2 indicates how each genre grew cumulatively over time.

Table 10.1   Paintings added each year to the Boydell Gallery by genre

|  | 1789 | 1790 | 1791 | 1792 | 1793 | 1794 | 1795 | 1796 | 1802 | Totals |
|---|---|---|---|---|---|---|---|---|---|---|
| Comedy | 18 | 12 | 6 | 1 | 0 | 0 | 9 | 21 | 6 | 73 |
| History | 8 | 6 | 2 | 7 | 2 | 4 | 12 | 2 | 5 | 48 |
| Tragedy | 8 | 7 | 1 | 5 | 3 | 0 | 6 | 5 | 18 | 53 |
| Annual Totals | 34 | 25 | 9 | 13 | 5 | 4 | 27 | 28 | 29 | 174 |

Table 10.2   Cumulative growth of the Boydell Gallery by genre

|  | 1789 | 1790 | 1791 | 1792 | 1793 | 1794 | 1795 | 1796 | 1802 |
|---|---|---|---|---|---|---|---|---|---|
| Comedy | 18 | 30 | 36 | 37 | 37 | 37 | 46 | 67 | 73 |
| History | 8 | 14 | 16 | 23 | 25 | 29 | 41 | 43 | 48 |
| Tragedy | 8 | 15 | 16 | 21 | 24 | 24 | 30 | 35 | 53 |
| Cumulative Totals | 34 | 59 | 68 | 81 | 86 | 90 | 117 | 145 | 174 |

These tables include *only* pictures exhibited in the Gallery. It does *not* include those pictures included in the atlas folios or in the National Edition but not exhibited at the Gallery; nor does it include pictures exhibited at the Shakspeare Gallery, but not illustrating scenes from Shakespeare's plays, such as George Romney's *Infant Shakespeare Attended by Nature and the Passions*. The subsequent sections explain more fully the changes the Gallery underwent during each of these years.

**1789.** The exhibition catalogue for 1789 exhibited the highest production values of any year.[18] Each entry began on its own page, offered roughly three

---

[18] *A Catalogue of the Pictures in the Shakespeare Gallery, Pall-Mall* (London, 1789). Since the title pages for the catalogues are identical, with the exception of changing publication dates, I provide only this one citation and leave my bibliographic descriptions in the body of the essay to identify the differences between years and printings.

pages of excerpted text, and left any space at the end of the final page unfilled. In this first exhibition visitors viewed 34 pictures illustrating 21 Shakespeare plays. Generically, 18 scenes came from 10 comedies, eight scenes from six history plays, and eight scenes from five tragedies. Of course these generic divisions are complicated by the fact that in contemporary acting versions both *Romeo and Juliet* and *King Lear* ended happily. Whether Gallery visitors would have counted the five illustrations for *Romeo and Juliet* and *Lear* as scenes from tragedies or comedies is uncertain. However, the composition of the Gallery in its opening exhibition valued comedy over both history and tragedy.

Most importantly, in this first year, eight plays received their full complement of anticipated illustrations. Of the 10 comedies, five plays received multiple images: two pictures each for *Merry Wives* and *Midsummer Night's Dream*; three pictures each for *Much Ado*, *As You Like It*, and *Winter's Tale*. Of the five tragedies, two received multiple illustrations: *Lear*, with three pictures, and *Romeo and Juliet*, with two. Of the seven history plays, only *Richard III* (with two illustrations) received more than one image.[19] The multiple illustrations provided for some plays is especially significant since 15 Shakespeare plays remained without a single illustration in the Gallery.

**1790**. In 1790, the Gallery holdings almost doubled, adding 25 scenes from 18 plays, for a total of 59 pictures, including the basso-relievos. The increased number of entries influenced both the length and detail of the descriptions. Entries were trimmed to just over two pages each, and that trimming perhaps led to the other editorial changes: 11 of the 34 1789 taglines were altered to demonstrate a tighter relationship between the pictures and the catalogue's description of it. Further, paper was conserved throughout: rather than leaving white space at the end of entries, entries followed one another immediately. These typographical changes, combined with the doubling of the Gallery contents, placed stress on the production process. Four versions of the 1790 catalogue appear to be extant: two of the 1790 catalogue, and two slightly differing versions of a combined 1790/91 catalogue (which I discuss under 1791). For the most part the two 1790-only catalogues offer a good product. The Folger copy appears to be an earlier state than the British Library's, with blank pages intervening between sections. Removal of the blank pages, and the subsequent shifting of the contents forward, accounts for the duplication of page 80 as page 81 in the British Library copy. Though the entry for the model of Thomas Banks's alto-relievo had concluded the 1789 catalogue, that entry was replaced by the entries for the three basso-relievos by Anne Damer.

Of the 18 plays represented by the 1790 additions, 11 were new to the Gallery, indicating Boydell's interest in providing at least one illustration for each of the

---

[19] The remaining plays in the 1789 exhibition received only one illustration: *The Comedy of Errors*; *Love's Labour's Lost*; *Measure for Measure*; *The Taming of the Shrew*; *The Tempest*; *1 Henry IV*; *Henry VI Parts 1, 2, and 3*; *King John*; *Titus Andronicus*; *Hamlet*; and *Macbeth*.

plays. Two plays —*Twelfth Night* and *Henry VIII*—entered the Gallery with two illustrations.[20] Scenes from comedies continued to predominate, making up 12 of the 25 new illustrations, or around 48 percent of the pictures added. Of the eight comedies represented in the new pictures, only four illustrated previously unrepresented plays: *Two Gentlemen of Verona*, *The Merchant of Venice*, and *All's Well* received one picture each; *Twelfth Night* received two. History plays were the next best represented, with six scenes from five plays. *Henry VIII* entered the collection with two pictures; and *3 Henry VI* received three additional pictures, for a total of four. Tragedies received seven pictures from five plays, four of these new to the Gallery: *Antony and Cleopatra*, *Timon of Athens*, *Troilus and Cressida*, and *Coriolanus*.[21] *Romeo and Juliet* received a third illustration, complementing the two from 1789.

The 1790 exhibition for the most part remedied the gaps in illustration. At this point, all of the comedies were represented by at least one illustration, and only four plays remained without representation: *Cymbeline*, *Othello*, *Richard II*, and *Julius Caesar*. The 1790 additions brought the overall total for the Gallery to 30 scenes from 14 comedies; 14 scenes from 10 histories; and 15 scenes from 12 tragedies.

**1791.** The Gallery's huge growth in 1789 and 1790 was not without growing pains, as evidenced by the three extant states of the 1791 catalogue: two versions of a combined 1790 and 1791 catalogue (referred to as 1790/91) and a catalogue with a 1791 publication date, which shows signs of redesign. The 1790/91 catalogue offers evidence of a breakdown in communication during production. Most conspicuously, the title page transposed the CX for XC in the publication date, indicating MDMCCCX (1810) rather than MDMCCXC (1790). The 1790/91 catalogue reinforces the impression that the press set new catalogues using the previous year's catalogue as a guide. But the strategy failed in this catalogue: when new material needed to be added, a number of later pages had apparently already been printed (these include one gathering of Shakspeare Gallery entries and the back-matter catalogue for other paintings also hung in the Gallery). The press then needed both to add material in the midst of already printed pages and to keep the pagination consistent between the added pages and those already printed.

---

[20] This could indicate that one or both of these images were originally commissioned for inclusion in the 1789 exhibition. My essay focuses on the perspective of a visitor to the Gallery and what that visitor would have seen on its walls from year to year. Even if it were possible to know when all the Gallery's paintings were commissioned and when each picture was expected to be delivered for exhibition, this information would not have been available to all visitors.

[21] I use the word "pictures" intentionally, since Boydell himself uses it in the catalogues; it also accommodates Ann Damer's three basso-relievo sculptures, added this year, which provide one image from *Antony and Cleopatra* and two from *Coriolanus*.

Unfortunately, the new gatherings were paginated to be added before gathering R, when they should have been paginated to follow it. [22]

The 1791 catalogue corrected these errors from the 1790/91 catalogue and shows signs of extra care in production. It provided a table of contents, headed by the year of exhibition (a feature of the Folger 1790 catalogue). It also reinstituted the entry for the alto-relievo but moved that entry to the front following the advertisement. The 1791 edition also made small changes throughout to the entry headers, adding R. A. for painters recently elected to the Royal Academy, and so on. The length of the entries now became standardized at only slightly more than two pages, on average.

After the sizeable additions to the Gallery in 1789 and 1790 (59 pictures from 32 plays), the Gallery grew only slightly in 1791, adding nine images from eight plays. Though the 1790 exhibition ended with four plays yet unrepresented—*Cymbeline, Othello, Richard II,* and *Julius Caesar*—the 1791 exhibition did not remedy the situation. Instead, all the pictures added in 1791 increased the presence of plays already represented. Six comedies received one additional picture each, bringing the totals for *Taming* and *Merchant* to two illustrations each; for *Merry Wives, The Winter's Tale,* and *As You Like It* to four each; and *A Midsummer Night's Dream* to five. Two history plays were represented in the additions: *Coriolanus* increased by one for a total of three illustrations; and *2 Henry VI*—the only play to receive more than one image in 1791—boasted four illustrations total.

At this point, after three years of exhibitions, 18 plays already had at least two pictures. Of those, 11 plays had three or more pictures. Both history and tragedy were represented by 16 pictures from nine plays. But comedy predominated, with 36 pictures from 14 plays, or more than double the holdings of history and tragedy combined.

**1792.** In the 1792 exhibition, Boydell rectified the heavy predisposition to comedy and provided illustrations for plays not yet represented. Of the 13 new pictures added to the Gallery, only one—a picture from *Merry Wives*—illustrated a comedy. The remaining pictures were devoted to history (seven illustrations from six plays) and tragedy (five illustrations from three plays). Three history plays received an additional picture: *2 Henry IV* (now with three pictures), *1 Henry VI* (with two pictures), and *Richard III* (now with four pictures). *Henry VIII* received an additional two pictures, increasing its representation to four. Most notably, however, *Othello* and *Cymbeline* garnered two pictures each and *Richard*

---

[22] Given their content, the gatherings should have appeared as Q, R, R*, S*, T*, S, T, rather than the order the pagination suggests. The clearest indication that these * gatherings were intended to integrate into the existing pagination is the extra-large spacing for entries provided at the end of added gathering T* in an attempt to match up with the beginning of gathering S. In addition, though the end pages of T* were spaced to connect with the advertisements, they do not account for a full page of information, and as a result, a separate leaf was wrapped around the final gatherings (appearing between T* and S) to provide the missing content.

*II* garnered one: this marked the first time in the Gallery's four-year history that these three plays were pictured.

Despite this year's attempt for greater balance, comedies still comprised the majority of the overall collection, with 37 scenes illustrated. *Merry Wives* and *Midsummer Night's Dream* were the most illustrated comedies with five pictures each. Histories were illustrated by 23 pictures: three plays—*3 Henry VI, Richard III,* and *Henry VIII*—were represented by four pictures each. Further, with the 1792 addition of a scene from *Richard II*, all the history plays had at least one illustration. Tragedies were represented by 21 pictures, and of those, *Lear* and *Romeo and Juliet* were most represented with three paintings each.[23] Most important, however, was the size of the exhibition: by 1792, the Gallery had grown to include 81 paintings, nine more illustrations than Boydell had initially indicated the Gallery would hold when complete.

**1793.** As in 1791, the 1793 catalogue exists in three different states: a catalogue dated 1792 but also containing pictures for 1793 (which I call 1792/3 and discuss here); a catalogue dated 1793; and a catalogue dated 1793, but containing 1794 pictures (which I discuss under 1794). Pagination evidence suggests that the 1792/3 catalogue is a composite of remaining stock from 1792 with the section for the 1793 pictures added to the back. At the end of the catalogue, one sees evidence of the accommodations made for adding the new material—the Infant Shakespeare entry is split from those of the basso-relievos with which it typically formed a closing unit—but otherwise the catalogue is unremarkable for errors or accuracy. The fact that Boydell had 1792 catalogue stock remaining in 1793 makes it tempting to speculate about attendance at the Gallery. The remaining stock might indicate that attendance had dropped in 1792, but it might just as likely indicate that Boydell had more visitors than he anticipated and had to reprint in midseason, leaving him with stock at the end of the year.

With the 1792 exhibition, Boydell surpassed his projected 72 pictures, so the 1793 exhibition added only five pictures to the Gallery: two history pictures (one each for *1 Henry IV*, and *1 Henry VI*) and three tragedies (one each for *Cymbeline, Hamlet,* and *Macbeth*). All five pictures offered additional illustrations for plays already represented. These five pictures narrowed comedy's lead somewhat, but not by any significant margin; and tragedy remained with only one less illustration than history.

**Growing the Gallery: Expansion and Revision, 1794–1802**

**1794.** By 1794, only five years from the opening of the Gallery, Boydell had more than fulfilled his projected number of illustrations. Exhibiting 90 paintings, the Shakspeare Gallery offered at least one illustration for each of Shakespeare's

---

[23] If viewers counted the pictures from *Lear* and *Romeo and Juliet* as comedies, tragedy's portion of the gallery would fall to 15 pictures, and comedy's portion would increase to 45.

plays, with the sole exception of *Julius Caesar*, still unrepresented after five years. Of the 34 Shakespeare plays, 27 boasted at least two pictures, and 10 of the plays (five comedies and five histories) already merited four pictures, or double the number originally projected on average for the plays.

Unsurprisingly, then, the Gallery grew the least in 1794, adding only four pictures, all from the history plays. Two scenes from *1 Henry IV* raised its total to four pictures; one scene for *2 Henry IV* increased its representation to four pictures; and one picture for *Richard II* brought that play's representation to two pictures. For a year with so few additions to the physical gallery, however, the catalogue (dated 1793, but including the 1794 pictures) is rife with errors: entry No. XXV and XXIV (a combined entry for two scenes from *Richard III* by James Northcote) dropped the paragraph for XXIV, but didn't renumber the subsequent item entries; item XLIX, Fuseli's picture of *Henry V*, was dropped from the catalogue, again without renumbering the subsequent item entries; 1792 pictures LXXIV (James Barry's *Cymbeline*, Act 2, scene 2) and LXXV (Thomas Stothard's *Othello*, Act 2, scene 1) were also skipped, but the error was caught before the production process was complete. As a result, the two were added in a new gathering at the end of the pictures for 1794. These errors plagued subsequent catalogues.

The early surfeit of paintings in the Shakspeare Gallery likely encouraged Boydell to revise his plans, making the subjects of the large and small engravings different from one another for each play. Boydell explained his rationale for this change in his update on the progress of the work, published in January 1794:

> The prints to be bound up with the book [the National Edition] were originally intended to be engraved from the same designs as the large prints; but at the solicitation of the subscribers, and to give the work a greater variety, original pictures, from scenes different from the large, are painted by the first masters for the smaller plates.[24]

Boydell claimed that the decision to change to different scenes for the small plates was one intended to give greater variety to the design. However, it might have been also a choice dependent on medium. As Sven Bruntjen notes, paintings for the large prints differ from the smaller ones compositionally: "In the former a few predominant figures are placed in a foreground set against stage-like backdrops," a quality drawing perhaps from theatrical print conventions.[25] Further, experienced book illustrators—William Hamilton, Robert Smirke, and Richard Westall—produced the majority of the small pictures.[26] Of the 78 small pictures, Hamilton and Smirke painted 17 each, and Westall 18, for an aggregate of two thirds of the total small pictures.

---

[24] *The substance of the original proposals for publishing, by subscription, a collection of large and capital prints, engraved after pictures painted by the most celebrated Artists, which are now exhibited in the Shakspeare Gallery, Pall-Mall*, London, 1794. Bodleian Library, Oxford, MS Gough Lond. 34 (13).

[25] Bruntjen, *John Boydell*, 107.

[26] Ibid.

Increasing the number of illustrations from two paintings per play on average to two paintings per play *per format* would be costly, but Boydell assured subscribers that their costs would not rise: "This improvement on the plan which will cost the proprietors some thousand pounds, was not adopted till the two first numbers were published; but the subscribers, in the course of the work, will receive duplicate plates for these two numbers *Gratis*."[27] Eight years later, in the 1802 catalogue, Boydell reiterated his reasons for this "improvement, on the original Plan": "It occurred to the Proprietors, that new designs for the small plates, by different Painters, would both give beauty and variety to the Work."[28] He also reminded visitors of his own patronage of the project: "although this improvement, has cost some thousands of pounds, they [the Proprietors] have added nothing to the price of the Work."[29] This narrative of improvement also appeared in Boydell's 1803 stock list: the "alteration was made ... to make the Work more interesting by varying the subjects."[30] Boydell's decision doubled his investment, requiring not 72 images overall, but 144.

**1795.** With the expansion of the projected number of illustrations to 144, Boydell shifted from commissioning "large as life" paintings to more modestly sized canvases. The 1795 exhibition added 27 pictures in small format to the collection. Nine pictures came from five comedies: one picture each to *Twelfth Night* and *Two Gentlemen of Verona*; two pictures each to *Love's Labour's Lost* and *Taming* and three pictures for *Winter's Tale*. Twelve pictures represent six histories: one picture for *3 Henry VI*; two pictures each for *1 & 2 Henry IV* and *1 & 2 Henry VI*; and three scenes from *Henry VIII*. Six pictures illustrated three tragedies: one picture for *Troilus and Cressida*, two for *Titus Andronicus*, and three for *Lear*. In changing his plan, Boydell lost the most ground with plays for which he already had more than two images in the large pictures. In 1795 and subsequent years, we see an attempt to make that ground up quickly.

This effort to provide pictures for the small format engravings apparently took attention away from the exhibition catalogue. The catalogue containing the 1795 pictures is an amalgam, dated 1794. The most significant change is the division of the catalogue into two parts: the catalogue for the large pictures at the front of the

---

[27] *The substance of the original proposals*, 13. Since subscribers could subscribe only to the large prints, or the small, or to the National Edition, Boydell's offer of "gratis" copies may have extended only to the subscribers for the full project (the large prints and the National Edition). Otherwise Knight, who had subscribed only to the small prints, would have had no reason to cancel his subscription.

[28] Boydell, 1802 catalogue, 149.

[29] Ibid.

[30] *An alphabetical catalogue of plates, engraved by the most esteemed artists, after the finest pictures and drawings of the Italian, Flemish, German, French, English, and other schools, which compose the stock of John and Josiah Boydell, engravers and printsellers, No. 90, Cheapside, and at the Shakespeare Gallery, Pall Mall; preceded by an account of various works, sets of prints, galleries, &c forming a great part of the same stock* (London, 1803), xxviii–xxix.

catalogue, followed by a separate catalogue for the "small pictures," with entries internally paginated and numbered. The errors of the 1793/94 catalogue continued in the large pictures catalogue: item XXVI and item XLIX remained missing (without renumbering to remove their places); renumbering later in the catalogue left no room for *Cymbeline* and *Othello* to return to their original places in the 1792 section, so these two entries remained in the 1794 section. An explanatory note at the end of the catalogue might clarify the problem with *Cymbeline* and *Othello*, indicating that *Othello* was "now for the first time exhibited." This may suggest that the picture of *Othello* was meant to be cut from the 1793/4 catalogue's listing of 1792 pictures, but when *Othello* was cut, *Cymbeline* was deleted as well.[31] Angelica Kaufmann's *Two Gentlemen of Verona*, exhibited since 1790 as Act 5, scene 3, was now identified as Act 5, scene 4: this change may indicate shifting scene numbers in the National Edition rather than a printer's error. However, these continued errors suggest that Boydell and Co. were focused strongly on the pictures themselves, on engraving them, and producing the National Edition, not on correcting the copy of an ephemeral document like an exhibition catalogue.

**1796 & 1797**. The 1796 exhibition added 28 pictures, illustrating 12 plays—all added to the small pictures catalogue. Comedies led once more with 21 images from eight plays. One third of those pictures came from the addition of Smirke's *Seven Ages* from Jaques's speech in *As You Like It*, offering one picture for each age. *Comedy of Errors* only garnered one picture; but five comedies received two pictures (*Twelfth Night*, *All's Well*, *Measure*, *Merchant*, and *Taming*), and one (*Merry Wives*) received three pictures. After a strong showing for history plays in the 1795 exhibition, 1796 added only two pictures, one each for *3 Henry VI* and for *King John*. Of the tragedies, only *Romeo and Juliet*, with two new illustrations, received additional representation. In the 1797 exhibition, no additional small pictures were added.

Given that Boydell changed the number of pictures anticipated to represent each play, in the early years of the Gallery it is difficult to determine which plays offered the most interest to viewers. By 1796, however, the number of illustrations per play offered some strong indicators of public preferences. *As You Like It*'s 13 pictures made it the most illustrated play so far. *Merry Wives* with eight images stood second for comedy: in many of these images Falstaff was the clear focus, indicating a popular preference for that character. By 1797, *The Winter's Tale* was represented by seven pictures, making it the third most illustrated comedy. Though the three most illustrated comedies matched or outnumbered the histories, more history plays at this point had received heavy illustration. Seven pictures illustrated *Henry VIII*; six pictures each illustrated *1 & 2 Henry IV*; and *3 Henry VI*; and five pictures represented *1 Henry VI*. Not so for the tragedies: only *Cymbeline* and *Lear* had six pictures, and *Romeo and Juliet* had garnered five.

The 1797 catalogue showed signs of editorial oversight, as errors in the previous year's catalogue were corrected, particularly those involving dropped or

---

[31] Boydell, 1791 Catalogue, 212.

skipped entries. Skipped paintings, however, were not reinstated in the catalogue; instead, pictures from the end of the catalogue were moved up to fill the open numbers. For example, No. XXVI, previously the small Northcote *Richard III*, was replaced with Northcote's *Richard II*, Act 5, scene 2, up from its previous position as No. LXXXVI. Wheatley's picture from *Midsummer Night's Dream*, Act 4, scene 1 and Downman's picture from *As You Like It*, Act 1, scene 2 were replaced by Barry's *Cymbeline* and Stothard's *Othello* (now placed at No. XI and XII). Westall's picture from *1 Henry IV*, Act 3, scene 1, was moved to No. XLIX space vacated by Fuseli's *Henry V*. Since all of these shifts moved pictures exhibited in 1792 or 1794 pictures into the 1789 or 1790 groupings, the headings designating the year of exhibition were removed. Whereas with past exhibitions, visitors could turn directly to a particular year's grouping of pictures, the removal of headings by year required visitors to rely solely on the picture frame numbers (and their correspondence with the exhibition catalogue) to find information on a particular picture. An index keyed to the "number[s] on the Frames" at the back of the catalogue reiterated this strategy.[32]

At the same time, the 1796 and 1797 catalogues clarified or corrected some information: the scene of James Durno's 1789 *Merry Wives* was changed from Act 4, scene 1 to Act 4, scene 2; Fuseli's 1792 *1 Henry IV* was changed from Act 2, scene 4 to Act 5, scene 4; and Hamilton's 1792 *Cymbeline* Act 1, scene 2 was changed to Act 1, scene 1.[33] It is unclear whether these were longstanding errors finally corrected or whether the changed scene numbers (especially in the case of the Durno and Hamilton) reflected alterations in the texts of the National Edition being prepared at this time. Finally, some changes brought the Shakspeare Gallery exhibitions closer to the project's printed texts: Damer's basso-relievo of *Coriolanus*, Act 4, scene 5, not chosen as one of the two National Edition title-page vignettes, was removed from the catalogue. At the same time, errors persisted in the 1797 catalogue, which dropped Smirke's *Seven Ages*.

In 1797, the small pictures catalogue was paginated consecutively with the large pictures and introduced only by a header, rather than a full title page. The length of large picture entries, stable since the early years of the Gallery, remained at slightly longer than two pages; the small picture catalogue entries, however, averaged only half a page each, with far shorter excerpts.

**1802.** Since catalogues are not extant for the years between 1798 and 1801, the 1802 catalogue offers the only evidence of the 29 pictures added between 1798 and 1802. Of these 29, six were comedies: one scene from *Comedy of Errors*, two scenes from *As You Like It*, and three scenes from *Winter's Tale*. Five scenes illustrated histories: one picture each for *Henry V*, *John*, and *Richard III*; and two scenes from *Richard II*. The remaining pictures, 18 in all, illustrated tragedies: two of these were in large format (Westall's *Macbeth*, Act 1, scene 5 and *Julius Caesar*, Act 4, scene 3), and the remainder were all small pictures, one for *Troilus*;

---

[32] Boydell, 1797 Catalogue, 211.

[33] The year provided here is the year of exhibition, not necessarily the year of painting.

two each for *Coriolanus, Timon of Athens, Antony and Cleopatra, Hamlet, Julius Caesar,* and *Othello*; and three small pictures for *Macbeth*. Interestingly, two pictures—the images of Puck by Fuseli and Reynolds—changed format in 1802, moving from the large pictures to the small pictures section.

With the 1802 catalogue, Boydell reorganized the large pictures catalogue following the strategy of the small. Before in the large print catalogue, pictures from a particular play were discussed according to their year of first exhibition in several different locations; the 1802 catalogue grouped all large pictures from a particular play together. Further, the entries that always concluded the catalogue were reorganized and integrated into that catalogue's numbering of items: the basso-relievos preceded, rather than followed, the Infant Shakespeare (which for the first time received its own item number), and the entry for the alto-relievo, appearing after the advertisement since 1791, moved to the end of the large pictures catalogue and concluded it.

Since 1802 was the last exhibition catalogue under Boydell's supervision, I will analyze its contents in my discussion of cumulative trends following the 1803 stock list.

**1803**. The stock list for 1803 indicates how the pictures in the physical gallery translated into the contents of Boydell's two print projects. In it, an 11-page section details the contents of the atlas-folio print volumes (100 large engravings based on the large pictures) and the National Edition (95 small engravings based on the small pictures) in the order in which those illustrations appear in the print volumes. The order of the pictures in the 1803 stock list follows the same order as in the 1802 catalogue: this suggests first that the 1803 stock list was likely based on the 1802 catalogue, and second, that the reordering of the pictures in 1802 may have been done to reflect the order in which the illustrations appeared in the printed collections. The stock list also reflected changes to act and scene numberings appearing on the print engravings, perhaps made to correspond more closely to divisions provided in the National Edition.

Most importantly, however, the 1803 stock list reveals that Boydell's print collections did not include *only* pictures exhibited as part of the "Shakspeare Gallery" collection. Three pictures "not engraved from the large pictures" but worthy of being "added" to atlas-folio volumes were included in volume two: Romney's *Shakspeare Nursed by Tragedy and Comedy*; Westall's *Cymbeline*, Act 3, scene 6 (Imogen in Boy's Clothes) and Josiah Boydell's *Othello*, Act 5, scene 2 (Desdemona Asleep).[34] Further, Smirke's *1 Henry IV*, Act 2, scene 3, was added to the National Edition illustrations, though it had never been included in the exhibition catalogues.

---

[34] Romney's *The Infant Shakespeare attended by Nature and the Passions* was added to the Shakespeare Gallery exhibitions in 1791 and appeared in all catalogues from that point; Romney's *Shakespeare Nursed by Tragedy and Comedy*, however, was included only in the print editions. It is important to note, however, that these pictures may have been hung in the rooms of the Gallery devoted to Boydell's other pictures, but they were never identified as part of the "Shakspeare" exhibitions.

Because of their inclusion in the stock list and in the printed title pages based on it, these four pictures—not included in the exhibition catalogues—became more closely associated with the "Shakspeare Gallery" than four paintings included in the yearly exhibitions but not in the print versions. I discuss these "lost" pictures below.

**The "Lost" Paintings**

As early as 1796 Boydell decided not to engrave four pictures hung in the yearly exhibitions. Though these pictures had no part in the printed versions of the Gallery Boydell was advertising, they still were part of the public experience of Shakespeare in exhibition that the Pall Mall gallery offered. I overview below when those pictures disappeared from the exhibition catalogues, and when possible, account for why they might have done so.

One painting never intended for the engravings was one of Northcote's two scenes from *Richard III*, identified as "Prince of Wales, Duke of York his brother, Dukes of Gloster and Buckingham, Cardinal Bourchier, Lord Hastings, Lord-Mayor, and his train," exhibited from 1789 to 1793. Introduced in the catalogues under a single header—"Nos. XXV and XXVI"—and illustrated by a single quotation, the two pictures of this scene in different sizes hung as pendants to one another. In each catalogue, a note in small italics described XXVI as "[t]he same scene painted by NORTHCOTE of a smaller size, before this work [the Shakspeare Gallery] was begun and not intended to appear in it." Boydell may have hung the small picture to indicate to subscribers that his engraving was based on a different *large* painting of the same scene. His point had apparently been made by 1794, when the entries for XXV and XXVI are split, and No. XXVI and its accompanying note disappear from the catalogue (No. XXVI is simply missing in 1794 and 1795); in 1796, the rest of the catalogue is renumbered to remove the lacunae. At issue was the small size of the picture, not its having been painted before the "work was begun": for in every year of exhibition, the catalogue entry for Northcote's *Richard III*, Act 4, scene 3, included the following explanatory note: "This picture was painted before the present work was undertaken; but has been deemed by the best judges highly deserving of a place in it."

In other cases, Boydell replaced one version of a scene with another or chose between two pictures hung in the Gallery. For example, art historians have noted that Robert Hodges provided a scene from the *The Winter's Tale*, depicting Antigonus and the Bear, but most have evaded the question of when the painting was removed. Some accounts suggest Boydell never hung the painting, but rejected it for its rough handling; others, that he commissioned the same scene from Joseph Wright of Derby in replacement.[35] However, according to Judy Egerton, Boydell

---

[35] Negative responses to Hodges's scene appeared as early as Humphrey Repton's *The Bee; or a Companion to the Shakespeare Gallery* (London: T. Cadell, [1789]) which claimed the picture "limps behind" its "companion" scene from *As You Like It* (32). Isabel Stuebe's *Life and Works of William Hodges* (New York: Garland, 1979) indicates

did not commission Wright's picture, but purchased it anonymously during the 1791 Society of Artists exhibition since he and Wright had a long-standing disagreement over fees.[36] Evidence from the catalogues reveals that the exhibition history of the two pictures was more complicated than criticism suggests. Though Wright's picture was engraved for the printed versions of the Gallery, Hodges's painting remained on exhibition in the Gallery as late as 1797. In that exhibition catalogue, Hodges's painting was clearly a pendant to Wright's: both received the single number XVII, with Hodges indicated as XVII*, and both shared the same excerpt from the play.[37]

Similarly, between 1790 and 1795, both Fuseli and Francis Wheatley exhibited scenes from *Midsummer Night's Dream*, Act 4, scene 1. However, Fuseli's depiction appears to have been more popular than Wheatley's rendition. Wheatley's painting—described in the catalogues as "A Wood. Theseus, Egeus, Hippolita, and Train, Demetrius, Lysander, Hermia, and Helena"—was not engraved for inclusion in the large or small engravings, nor was it exhibited at the Gallery after 1795.[38] Finally, of Ann Damer's three basso-relievos, two were picked to serve as vignettes for the title pages of the two-volume folio prints; with no need for a third vignette, her scene from *Coriolanus*, Act 4, scene 5, was dropped from exhibition.

The greatest puzzle remains Barry's *Cymbeline*, often victim of the catalogues' printing problems: the entry for this picture first appeared in 1793 as entry LXXIII; moved to entry LXXXIV in 1794 when entry LXXIII was skipped in the printing process and the entry was added in at the end of the catalogue; dropped entirely in 1795 (though another picture appeared as entry LXXXIV); added back in as entry XI in 1796 and 1797; and removed entirely from the 1802 catalogue, the 1803 stock list, and the 1805 auction catalogue.[39]

**Assessing the Gallery: Public Appetites for Shakespeare**

There is much we do not know about Boydell's Shakspeare Gallery. For example, other than a handful of receipts and letters detailing payments, deliveries, or delays, little information is extant for when Boydell commissioned particular paintings or

---

only the 1789–1790 and 1796 exhibitions (344). Geoff Quilley and John Bonehill, eds., *William Hodges, 1744–1797: The Art of Exploration* (New Haven, CT: Yale University Press, 2004), offer full entries on Hodges's other Boydell paintings in their version of the exhibition catalog, but mention the Antigonus only in passing. Rovee seems to suggest that the painting was "rejected" by Boydell prior to hanging in the exhibition. Rovee, *Imagining the Gallery*, 99.

[36] *Wright of Derby*, exhibition catalogue, ed. Judy Egerton (New York: Metropolitan Museum of Art, 1990), 253.

[37] Boydell, 1797 Catalogue, 45.

[38] Mary Webster notes that Boydell engraved 12 of Wheatley's 13 contributions but does not account for this picture's removal from the gallery. *Francis Wheatley* (London: Routledge, 1970), 87–9.

[39] Thanks to William Pressly for pointing out the omission of the Barry *Cymbeline* from Tassie's 1805 auction.

engravings. More extant information about how Boydell intended for his gallery to grow would supplement the narrative I provide, but it would not change how visitors experienced the shape of the gallery over time. Furthermore, though visitors might have asked for images from a particular play not yet represented (as did Edward Jerningham in his laudatory long poem on the Gallery), their queries could only influence how many images from a particular play Boydell commissioned, not when (after having been commissioned, painted, and engraved) they were hung in the Gallery.

However, we do know enough to suggest some interesting things about public taste for Shakespeare in the Romantic age. Because an average of four paintings per play was the gallery's goal, plays with more than four illustrations suggest greater popularity. Eighteen plays garnered more than four illustrations each, comprising 112 of the Gallery's 174 paintings. Of these 18 plays, seven comedies predominated, with 50 illustrations; following that, six history plays were illustrated 35 times. Only five tragedies garnered more than four illustrations each, with a total of 27 images (11 of these illustrated *Romeo and Juliet* or *Lear*).

Considered by genre, the most popular plays over the 14-year history of the Gallery offer some surprises. In tragedy, the greatest number of illustrations for a play was six, with *Cymbeline* and *Lear* receiving equal honors. *Romeo and Juliet* was well illustrated with five pictures, but, perhaps unexpectedly, so was *Coriolanus*. Further, *Romeo and Juliet* received an additional picture when John Opie—after his canvas had been engraved—painted over and reworked portions of the scene, requiring a "variant" engraving to correspond with the "new" painting. *Troilus and Cressida* received four illustrations, the same as *Hamlet* and *Othello*. But the popularity of tragedies is complicated by the number of illustrations the histories received, because tragedies received 52 illustrations overall and history plays 48. When taking into consideration that there are only 10 history plays, but 12 tragedies, we have to consider that the histories might well have been more popular than the tragedies (by a very slight margin). Of the histories, *Henry VIII* garnered seven illustrations, more scenes than the most illustrated tragedy. At the same time, *1 & 2 Henry IV* and *3 Henry VI* were equally as popular as *Cymbeline* and *Lear*, with six illustrations. *1 Henry VI* and *Richard III* were equally as popular as *Romeo and Juliet*, *Macbeth*, and *Coriolanus* with five illustrations each.

But the number of illustrations that the comedies received remains rather surprising, particularly given Boydell's expectation that comedy would offer the least interest. Of the five most frequently illustrated plays, four were comedies. The most illustrated comedy was *As You Like It* with 13 illustrations; *Merry Wives of Windsor* took second with eight illustrations, and *Winter's Tale* and *Tempest* tied for third with *Henry VIII*, at seven illustrations each. While four comedies earned more than six illustrations, no tragedy did so—as a result, the 67 illustrations devoted to the comedies is striking. The example of *As You Like It* reveals Boydell creatively responding to the play's phenomenal popularity. With three paintings exhibited in the very first exhibit, *As You Like It* needed only one more painting (added in 1791) to be fully illustrated by the 1795 revised plan. But the popularity of the play was such that Boydell commissioned scenes for each of the "Seven Ages" (*As You Like It*, Act 5, scene 7) and engraved those scenes in both large and small formats.[40] If the large and small engravings count as different pictures, then the number of *As You Like It*'s pictures rises to 20 (I do not add duplicate images for the "Seven Ages" or the variant *Romeo and Juliet* into final totals).

The rule-of-four also indicates plays and illustrations that failed to catch the popular imagination. The least illustrated (and by extension the least liked) plays were *Two Gentlemen of Verona* and *Henry V*, with two illustrations each, and *Julius Caesar* with three illustrations. *Two Gentleman of Verona* apparently didn't garner the expected popular interest. Boydell commissioned a scene from *Two Gentlemen* in the initial years of the Gallery and had it engraved by 1792. His decision to do so was likely a response to the play's staging "for the first time in twenty years" at the Drury Lane theater in January and June of 1790. Though its three 1790 performances earned moderate box office returns, it was not staged again until after 1800. Perhaps the 1792 engraving didn't sell well, for Boydell did not hang another scene from the play until the shift to small pictures in the 1795 exhibition. *Henry V* offers further evidence that Boydell delayed adding pictures for unpopular plays. In 1790, *Henry V* received its first illustration, a scene by Fuseli from Act 2, scene 2, depicting the King, Scroop, Cambridge, and Grey in Southhampton; but in 1794, this picture was dropped from the exhibition catalogues and never reinstated, though it was eventually engraved for the printed editions. Only in 1802 did *Henry V* receive its second picture, as part of the small pictures. Though *Julius Caesar* received three illustrations in the Gallery, its history in the gallery suggests it was the least liked play of all. Not represented in the Gallery before 1797, *Caesar* received two illustrations after 1797, and those illustrations were not engraved for sale until December 1801—when Boydell needed two illustrations for the printed projects.

Had Boydell's gallery closed with a total of 144 pictures, its growth over time would indicate how long it took to complete a sizeable project. But by the Gallery's closing, Boydell had commissioned 174 illustrations from Shakespeare for the Gallery. Only 10 of Shakespeare's 37 plays received just the four images Boydell projected; 18 plays received five or more illustrations, and eight received three illustrations or fewer. At these points—where plays received more or less pictures, according to their "interest"—we see Boydell responding to public appetites for Shakespeare.

Given the preponderance of comedies in the Boydell Gallery's inception, growth, and final form, we can perhaps see why comedic versions of Shakespeare's

---

[40] The 1803 stock list shows the large plate engravings at 21 x 17.5. In the 1801 publication announcement—*This Day are published, price £5. 5s. By J. and J. Boydell, No. 90, Cheapside, and at the Shakespeare Gallery, Pall Mall, Seven prints from the celebrated Seven Ages of Shakespeare, painted by R. Smirke, Esq. R. A. and engraved by Messrs. Thew, Simon, Ogborne, Tomkins, and Leney* (London: W. Bulmer, 1801)— the smaller size is recorded as 15 3/8 x 19 7/8.

tragedies, such as those by Colley Cibber, were in such demand and retained such popularity during the period. Although the Romantic preoccupation with comedic versions of tragedies tends to be denigrated today, understanding the cultural significance of Shakespeare during the Romantic period requires that we reassess the motives behind such revisions, and the information provided by the revisions themselves will, perhaps, provide some insight into the Romantic frame of mind. The evidence from the Boydell Shakspeare Gallery suggests strongly that a Romantic Shakespeare was a more comedic one than we might have thought.

**Rereading the Shakspeare Gallery**

The evidence from the Shakspeare Gallery catalogues then offers some correctives to current approaches to Boydell's enterprise and suggests new avenues for research into Romantic appetites for Shakespeare. Knowing how the Gallery grew can help scholars be more precise in using Boydell Gallery materials. The pictures are not parts of a static whole, but representations of moments through which we can learn more about Shakespeare in the Romantic period; we can now see the Boydell Shakspeare Gallery not as synchronic, which artificially focuses our attention on the Gallery's closing, but as diachronic. A picture (or scene from Shakespeare) included in the Gallery from its beginning to end, consistently reimaged, reproduced, and popular, is more significant for our understanding of Romantic Shakespeare and his audience than a picture included in one or two exhibitions in the middle, then dropped for lack of interest, or one added at the very end to fulfill Boydell's promise to have a scene or two from every play. In examining the Gallery, we must consider not just the fact of a picture's existence, but how it entered the Gallery and what its tenure there was like. We must balance any discussion of a particular image against the frequency and regularity of a particular play's inclusion. Good examples of this would be *As You Like It* and *Julius Caesar*, one filling its complement of pictures early but receiving additional pictures across the life of the Gallery, the other receiving its allotment only late in the game.

We also come to understand the value of the Gallery itself not as a once-on, once-off failure, but as a dynamic, growing collection more successful than any other of its kind. Much of the rhetoric surrounding Boydell's lottery seems more emotional than practical; most scholars describe Boydell's Gallery as an episode of overreaching, hubris, and inevitable failure, placing Boydell's Shakspeare Gallery on the level of other failed galleries, such as Woodmason's Irish Shakespeare Gallery, Fuseli's Milton Gallery, Macklin's Poet's Gallery, or Bowyer's Historic Gallery which closed by lottery the year after Boydell. Yet Boydell's Gallery was far more successful and long lived than any of its competitor galleries, most of which went out of business within only two to three years. Boydell's Gallery was viable for 15. Boydell, having met his obligations to subscribers very early on, could have focused on engraving the pictures he already had in hand and moved on to another project. But he didn't. His expansion of the original plan—the shift first to different images for the large and small engravings and the subsequent shift to double the number of images to be provided—suggests that the Gallery was for many years a successful business venture. Understanding how the Gallery grew brings the narrative of its demise more in line with Boydell's own explanation in his petition to Parliament: that the unanticipated collapse of multiple markets across Europe placed his ventures at risk. And in this period of general and widespread economic distress, it was his most ambitious project—the Shakspeare Gallery—that was successfully liquidated to repair the Boydell family fortunes. Though Boydell was not able to continue the Shakspeare Gallery as an enterprise in itself, and though he had invested large sums in it, the lottery successfully saved his company, and that company continued until the death of his nephew and partner Josiah in 1818, at which time Hurst, Robinson, and Co. took over as Boydell's successors. Looking at the Gallery as a dynamic organism, rather than static object, helps bring Boydell's accomplishment into a more appropriate light.

## Chapter 11
# *Pericles* and the Spiritual Wisdom of Joanna Baillie's Sacred Dramas *The Martyr* and *The Bride*

### Marjean D. Purinton and Marliss C. Desens

In *An Enquiry Concerning Human Understanding* (1748), David Hume defines a miracle as a violation of the laws of nature, "a transgression of a law of nature by a particular volition of the Deity, or by the interposition of some invisible agent."[1] Hume's devotion of an entire section to miracles in his famous treatise exposes the interest expressed in eighteenth- and nineteenth-century Great Britain with phenomena beyond natural causes. Joanna Baillie's sacred dramas *The Martyr* (1812) and *The Bride* (1826) translate the secular miracles of William Shakespeare's *Pericles* (c. 1608) into religious reflection. While both Baillie's and Shakespeare's plays resonate with the wondrous, the miraculous of medieval mystery cycle plays, their deployment of divine Providence suggests that *Pericles* has spiritual affinities to Baillie's drama. Shakespeare and Baillie complicate the miraculous with their romantically engaged women who both challenge and emphasize notions of secular and spiritual love as sacred acts. *Pericles*, *The Martyr*, and *The Bride* dramatize the sacred as what Catherine Clément and Julia Kristeva have theorized as "the celebration of a mystery," a register of experience associated with the language of the feminine body.[2] Baillie admired in Shakespeare the quality that Keats called "negative capability"—the ability to be "in uncertainties, Mysteries, doubts, without any irritable reaching after fact & reason"[3]—or what Hume calls miraculous and what Clément and Kristeva identify as sacred.

Although editors debated the inclusion of *Pericles* in Shakespeare's collected works, and some eighteenth-century editors omitted it, *Pericles* was available in the widely used editions of Malone (1790) and Steevens (4th edition, 1793).[4] Thus, in the Romantic period, anyone familiar with Shakespeare's complete

---

[1] David Hume, "Of Miracles," in *An Enquiry Concerning Human Understanding: A Letter from a Gentleman to his Friend in Edinburgh*, ed. Eric Steinberg (Indianapolis: Hackett, 1977), 77.

[2] Catherine Clément and Julie Kristeva, *The Feminine and the Sacred*, trans. Jane Marie Todd (New York: Columbia University Press, 2001), 13.

[3] John Keats, *Letters of John Keats: A Selection*, ed. Robert Gittings (Oxford: Oxford University Press, 1970), 43.

[4] William Shakespeare, *Pericles*, ed. Suzanne Gossett (London: Thomson, 2004), 422.

works would have known it as an unstaged play that, with its inclusion of such dark subject matter as incest, murder, and brothels, would have had a forbidden appeal for readers, much as the Gothic novels did. However, the play also presents readers with a succession of fantastic adventures that portray the vicissitudes of life, before concluding in a final divine reconciliation that reunites the family. *Pericles* is the earliest of Shakespeare's late romances, a genre in which the painful events of worldly existence are ultimately situated within an encompassing cycle of rebirth and renewal. Beginning with *Pericles*, Shakespearean romance becomes a form in which an initial move to exclude the feminine is subsumed by a countermovement, so that such a division is rejected and the importance of the feminine is reaffirmed. Ultimately what matters is not whether the gods intervene but whether, by acknowledging the feminine, the characters develop the humanity necessary for dealing with the tumult of their world.

The association of Shakespeare's late romances with some form of religious revelation is not, of course, new. Romance is a form, as T. G. Bishop has suggested, whose roots lie in the medieval miracle plays, intimately related to the experience of wonder.[5] Howard Felperin and the editors of the New Cambridge edition have also called attention to *Pericles* as a play of the miraculous and transformative, and they have argued persuasively for it not as a torn and damaged text but as a sophisticated inquiry into the miraculous and its role in the theater and in human life.[6] Two further lines of inquiry may have bearing on Joanna Baillie's two spiritual plays, written over two hundred years after *Pericles*. First, historical religious concerns shared by Baillie and Shakespeare may have led to their decisions to set *The Bride*, *The Martyr*, and *Pericles* in exotic locales and, in the case of the latter two, in the distant historical past. The removal from a familiar context encourages audiences to ponder the issues raised without triggering the defenses that might immediately be associated with seeing those issues in a contemporary context. Second, all three plays focus on what happens when the feminine is disregarded or damaged, thereby leaving humanity incomplete.

As recent scholarship has asserted, Baillie's dramas appear to be expressions of distinctly religious, Christian ideas, but they can also be read as manifestly "sacred" in their representation of female sexuality and eroticism not associated with organized or institutionalized religion.[7] *The Martyr* is set during the reign of Nero in Rome, and its conflict centers on Portia, who comes to accept that

---

[5] T. G. Bishop, *Shakespeare and the Theatre of Wonder* (Cambridge: Cambridge University Press, 1996), 93–124.

[6] See Howard Felperin, *Shakespearean Romance* (Princeton, NJ: Princeton University Press, 1972), 143–76. See also Doreen Delvecchio and Antony Hammond, eds., *Pericles* (Cambridge: Cambridge University Press, 1998), 1–78.

[7] See for example, Christine Colòn's assertion that Baillie emphasizes Christian principles on the stage for their transformative power and pedagogical potential. "Christianity and Colonial Discourses in Joanna Baillie's *The Bride*," in *Renascence: Essays on Values in Literature* 54, no. 3 (Spring 2002): 163–4.

her beloved Maro, an officer of the imperial guards who has been converted to Christianity, must forsake her for a higher spiritual love in the cause of the persecuted Nazarenes. In Baillie's dramatic account, no intervention of divine providence or Christian miracle can save him from his fate at the end. Set in Ceylon, *The Bride* challenges religious sanctions for the secular practice of polygamy through the providential intercession of Juan de Creda, a Spanish physician and a Christian who changes perceptions of marital arrangement and who helps to mediate fraternal strife between Rasinga and Samarkoon, his brother-in-law. *Pericles* appears to be the first play in which Shakespeare began to explore, outside a Christian context, values that unite people across sectarian lines, while simultaneously invoking a providence that rarely intervenes, in spite of the presence of both inevitable suffering and human evil in the world. While both of Baillie's plays undoubtedly reflect the Christian tenets of early nineteenth-century Britain as well as her own upbringing, they nonetheless resonate with the Shakespearean treatment of "sacredness" dramatized in *Pericles*, in which the world is righted in the end by the *deus ex machina*. All three plays emphasize doing the moral, ethical, "sacred" in the face of personal challenges—Maro's willingness to die for his belief system in *The Martyr* and the familial dysfunction in *The Bride*. All three plays assert the significance of spiritual, sacred self-determination, as well as an approach to religious values that transcends the doctrinal distinctions of both Renaissance and Romantic culture.

Renaissance plays, of course, did not deal directly with religious issues other than what was in the general cultural context. Shakespeare and his contemporaries, however, had lived through a time of extraordinary religious upheaval that had raised questions that would never again be resolved into a single belief system. It was not just a matter of the relationship between Church of England and Catholicism; there were Protestant sects that agreed with neither, nor with each other. Yet the need for the context provided by religion in dealing with the timeless issues of human life was constant: Why is there suffering? Why do good people suffer at the hands of evil? What is the ultimate truth? New Historicism finds *Pericles* particularly irritating, in that the play does not appear to have a direct political and social correlation with Renaissance society.[8] According to Steven Mullaney, *Pericles* "represents not so much a turning point in Shakespeare's career as a concerted turning away from the cultural contexts and associations that had shaped his dramaturgy in the past."[9] *Pericles*, however, does not turn inward on itself but is actually radical in its subtle transformation of the particulars of a contemporary historical context into a universal, spiritual one. The need for the drama to reflect the questions of its society does not go away simply because a

---

[8] For a summary of the views of New Historicist critics on the play, see Amelia Zurcher, "Untimely Monuments: Stoicism, History, and the Problem of Utility in The Winter's Tale and Pericles" *ELH* 70 (2003): 917–18.

[9] Steven Mullaney, *The Place of the Stage: License, Play, and Power in Renaissance England* (Chicago: University of Chicago Press, 1988), 147.

variety of religious views exist, or because it cannot or will not deal with them directly. The setting of *Pericles* in classical antiquity aids the attempt to address these issues in a way that transcends a single religious faith by focusing on the essentiality of humanness. F. Elizabeth Hart has pointed out that Ephesus, the city in which the play concludes, is one that some critics have "linked to images of religious division," while other have stressed its diversity as a place where, in "Paul's day, Christians, Jews, and pagan Greeks lived and worked together—not always harmoniously but at least together." In *Pericles*, this transcendence of division is framed by the feminine, as the frequent invocations of Diana—a goddess associated with Ephesus and who is "herself a hybrid of mainland Greek traditions"[10]—and her final intervention make clear. It is the feminine, then, in *Pericles*, *The Martyr*, and *The Bride* that disrupts correlations between religion of any kind and the sacred.

By the early nineteenth century, the spiritualist movement's challenging of religious and scientific accounts of supernatural phenomena were widespread knowledge, but would have been of particular interest to Baillie, whose background had been shaped by a father (professor of Divinity at the University of Glasgow) and uncles and a brother (leading anatomists of the day), and whose familiarity with animal magnetism and materialism Marjean Purinton has demonstrated elsewhere. According to Margaret Carhart, Baillie enthusiastically studied Shakespeare's plays and drew on them in her own dramas,[11] but there has been no study linking Baillie's sacred drama with Shakespeare's earliest romance, *Pericles*. While Baillie's theological journey from Scottish Presbyterian to Unitarianism has been charted by Judith Bailey Slagle,[12] no study has posited the possibility of Baillie's interest in Romantic pantheism, including the Greek Mystery cults that celebrated the sacredness of life and sexuality. As Margot K. Louis has pointed out, early nineteenth-century Britain experienced a revival of paganism in its fascination with the Mystery cults of the chthonian deities Persephone, Dionysus, and Adonis as an alternative to the rationalism and dogma of Christianity.[13] By the time a mature Baillie writes her sacred dramas, she brings together multiple systems of thought that she invites her plays' characters and readers and audiences to reflect upon.

The opening scene of *Pericles*, with its depiction of father-daughter incest, foregrounds a basic taboo of human society. The death of Antiochus's queen has removed the feminine from his realm. He sexually violates and effectively silences

---

[10] F. Elizabeth Hart, "'Great is Diana' of Shakespeare's Ephesus," *Studies in English Literature 1500–1900* 43, no. 2 (2003): 347, 348.

[11] Margaret Carhart, *The Life and Work of Joanna Baillie* (New Haven, CT: Yale University Press, 1923), 73.

[12] Judith Bailey Slagle, *Joanna Baillie: A Literary Life* (Madison, NJ: Farleigh Dickinson University Press, 2002), 231–34.

[13] Margot K. Louis, "Gods and Mysteries: The Revival of Paganism and the Remaking of Mythography through the Nineteenth Century," *Victorian Studies* 47 (2005): 329–30.

his unnamed daughter. Antiochus's control over his daughter's language is shown by her silence; she speaks only two cryptic lines to Pericles before he is presented with the riddle (lines that suggest she sees him as a hope of escape): "Of all 'say'd yet, may'st thou prove prosperous! / Of all 'say'd yet, I wish thee happiness!"[14] Antiochus's control over his daughter's body is shown by his death threat, directed at Pericles, by what he interprets as a move toward physical contact: "Prince Pericles, touch not" (1.1.87). It is unlikely that Pericles actually moves toward Antiochus's daughter, since he had just told her, probably in an aside, that by interpreting the riddle he rejects her; it is more likely that the desperate daughter reaches toward him. Her isolation is the more complete in that she is likely the only female appearing in the scene. No god or goddess intercedes to protect or rescue her, just as none interceded to save the princely suitors who seek her as their bride. When the gods do, later, choose to punish Antiochus, his daughter dies as well, but her death is reported almost as incidental:

> Antiochus of incest lived not free;
> For which the most high gods not minding longer
> To withhold the vengeance that they had in store
> .......
> When he was seated in a chariot
> Of an inestimable value, *and his daughter with him*,
> A fire from heaven came and shrivell'd up
> Those bodies, even to loathing. (2.4.2–10, emphasis ours)

The play puts the blame primarily on Antiochus; he is the one who "her to incest did provoke." She is a "bad child" but he a "worse father, to entice his own" (Prologue, 26–7). The "most high gods" punish the guilty but do not protect the innocent.[15] Similarly, Baillie's Prefaces to *The Martyr* and *The Bride* might suggest that the sacred dramas' intent is to save the heathen children of Ceylon from corrupt religion, when in fact we see a powerful reclamation of feminine sacred in her work for all spirituality, including bad daughters, worse fathers, and misdirected lovers, identified here in Shakespeare's prologue to *Pericles*.

Pericles is the one suitor who escapes death at Antiochus's hands. The others die because they cannot explicate Antiochus's riddle—a riddle that reveals the incest between Antiochus and his daughter. Therefore, a suitor can openly solve the riddle only by acknowledging that such a horror can exist. They fail because

---

[14] William Shakespeare, *Pericles*, ed. Hallet Smith, in *The Riverside Shakespeare*, 2nd ed., ed. G. Blakemore Evans (Boston: Houghton Mifflin, 1997), 1.1.59–60. All references to the play are from this edition.

[15] Our reading differs from that of Zurcher, who focuses on incest as a metaphor that ultimately shows that "in a world in which they move forward into marriage and procreation is intricately implicated in political and sexual corruption, incest as retreat toward origins, and the oblivion that precedes them, looks more attractive than the example of Antiochus and his Daughter would at first suggest." Zurcher, "Untimely Monuments," 919.

they lack a vision of evil. Pericles' horror of this knowledge leads to depression and a loss of trust that will only be repaired at the court of Simonides, a widower king with a marriageable daughter in whose honor suitors compete in a birthday tournament—a contest Pericles wins. Simonides' court includes the presence of women, as the dancing at the end of 2.3 clearly shows. His daughter Thaisa is also a woman who speaks her mind, making it clear that she will marry only Pericles, and he is delighted with her assertiveness: "how absolute she's in't, / Not minding whether I dislike or no!" (2.5.19–20). Simonides initially takes the role of the objecting father, thus permitting his daughter to demonstrate her readiness for marriage in choosing her future husband over him. His respect for, and nurturance of, feminine independence contrasts sharply with Antiochus's destruction of it. Pericles' experiences at Simonides' court restore for him the possibility of pure, unselfish love for others, a love that is possible only because here the feminine is embraced.

In her preface to *The Martyr*, Baillie describes the period in which the play is set as one in which Christianity existed in a "pure, uncorrupted state," when it was "unencumbered with many perplexing and contradictory doctrines."[16] Baillie denies the stageability of the play because of its sacred subject, but writes that she was impelled by a strong desire to show the "noblest of all human emotions" in dramatic form (Preface, 511). These prefatory comments suggest that while the manifest content of the play is situated in the early Christian era, its latent and most powerful messages address the sacredness of the human condition. Both the Roman soldier Maro and the persecuted Nazarenes are cast as pure in heart, noble in spirit. A fellow soldier confirms that Maro's character "in Nero's court / May pass for curious and unnatural" (1.1, 512–13), and that the Nazarenes' willingness to adhere to their faith betrays some kind of strong power or sorcery. Another officer describes the rites practiced by the Nazarenes as "hateful orgies" accompanied by "enchantments wooing" and with the "intercourse of demons" (1.2, 514). The Nazarenes are depicted as being possessed and mad in clinging to their faith, and as Cordenius Maro describes, the sacred ones exercise some incomprehensible power "surpassing nature" and "mocking all thought" (1.4, 515).

In this opening conversation among Roman soldiers, we discover a clue about how to decipher the latent, sacred content of *The Martyr*. Maro queries Sylvius as to whether the learned and enlightened can become victims of delusion, and can see unreal things and hear sounds that are not: "My unsettled thoughts were busy / With things mysterious; with those magic powers / That work the mind to darkness and destruction" (1.4, 515–16). He has come to believe that in the lives of those professing the Christian faith, "a generous, powerful, noble faith" (2.1, 518) serves as an example for all humankind. *The Martyr* suggests here that its message

---

[16] Joanna Baillie, *The Martyr: A Drama*, in *The Dramatic and Poetical Works of Joanna Baillie* (London: Longman, Brown, Green, and Longman, 1851), preface, 511. All further references to Baillie's plays are from this edition and will appear in the text. Citations include act, scene, and page number.

is not so much about the Christian faith exclusively, but about a belief in the sacred that might take diverse forms. The Roman soldiers "other" the Christian faith as demonic and indicative of sorcery in ways that ironically replicate the "othering" of Greek deities and Mystery cults, creating a religion divorced from the sacred. It is the appropriation and exploitation of the miraculous by religions to which David Hume vehemently objects: "A religionist may be an enthusiast, and imagine he sees what has no reality: He may know his narrative to be false, and yet persevere in it, with the best intensions in the world, for the sake of promoting so holy a cause."[17] The window dressing of a faith is not, Baillie's drama implies, the same as the sacred and noble character it engenders from its believers.

In an oppositional scene to that of the Roman soldiers, the play turns to the Mystery cults of Greece when Sulpicius, a Roman Senator, and his daughter Portia pay homage to Flora in the garden in the early morning. Portia insists that on occasion she has sensed the radiant forms of Venus or Diana near her and wished that she could look upon the deities. Like the Roman soldiers, however, Sulpicius is suspicious of belief systems that challenge his, and he accuses Maro of becoming enchanted by the Christians: "If it were possible, / I could believe thee touch'd with sorcery, / The cursed art of those vile Nazarenes" (2.2, 521). When Maro is unable to swear an oath of hatred to the Nazarenes, Sulpicius warns him, "Demoniac power / Will drag thee to thy ruin. Cast it off; / Defy it. Say thou wilt forbear all intercourse / With this detested sect" (2.2, 521). We learn that one of Nero's major concerns about the potential conversion of the Romans to Christianity is the utter disrespect that Christians demonstrate for any other belief system than their own—their determination to make the object of their faith the only one worthy of homage and worship while they hold the temples of Roman gods in contempt. Nero admits that Rome formerly accommodated diverse powers amongst its gods, "the foreign deities / Of friendly nations" (3.2, 353). It is this undeniable self-righteousness that fans the fires of the Roman executions of the Christian Nazarenes.

When Maro is willing to take the place of the condemned Ethocles for preaching Christian theology, Nero is amazed that one of Rome's brave soldiers has been by "wizard sorcery so charmed" (3.2, 523). Nero accuses Maro of having lost his rationality in embracing the ecstasy of Christianity. For Nero, Maro has become deluded by the power of strong and dire enchantment and has been reduced to a maniac who speaks in raving words. Nero is willing to pardon Maro if he will proclaim that he is a Roman in heart and faith, but he refuses, even when Portia begs. Maro is spared the infamy of a Christian execution, however, as Orceres kills him with bow and arrow as he is marched to the den of lions. The ambivalent ending of *The Martyr* embraces the potential of nobility for both systems of the sacred, Greco-Roman and Christian, if only they could seek a way to cohabitate. In refusing to seek such a compromise, Maro denies the sacredness embodied in Portia—her love for the goddesses of beauty and home, the sacred that comes from

---

[17] David Hume, "Of Miracles," 79.

daily living rather than grandiose sacrifice. Baillie's sacred drama suggests that Maro's passion is destructive in its extreme. Truly a faith that can admit no space for another is a weak one in its sacred foundations. While Judith Slagle maintains that *The Martyr* is Baillie's only religiously dogmatic play,[18] we assert that the drama is undogmatic in its paradoxical demonstration of the folly of self-sacrifice to the extent of denying the sacredness of life and love. Here is no miracle, no *deus ex machina* that might lighten the play's tragic ending.[19]

*Pericles* clearly shows that just as there can be a destructive masculine nature, so too is there a destructive feminine nature. Believing his wife dead, Pericles arranges to leave his infant daughter, along with her nurse, in the care of Cleon and Dionyza. His decision is partly practical: he will not risk the health of the motherless infant on a long sea voyage, and a woman must be found to nurse her. However, Pericles also makes a vow that, until his daughter be married, "by Bright Diana, whom we honor, all / [Unscissor'd] shall this hair of mine remain" (3.3.28–9). He invokes Diana, the goddess of militant chastity, in his vow. Does Pericles separate himself from his daughter in order to protect her, because, unable to comprehend how Antiochus could have committed incest, he seeks another barrier against it? If so, what he has done instead is to remove his ability to protect his daughter. Dionyza, jealous that Marina overshadows her own daughter, orders her death, and only the arrival of the pirates who seize Marina saves her life. Cleon, although horrified at his wife's crime, ultimately participates in covering it up, a crime for which his people "him and his they in his palace burn; / The gods for murder seemed so content / To punish, although not done, but meant" (5.3.98–100). Embracing a destructive feminine leads to the annihilation of the family line.

Marina moves from threat of death to threat of sexual violation, but she does not react passively. The pirates sell her to a brothel where women are mere commodities, and the owners plan to auction her maidenhead to the highest bidder. Marina invokes Diana, not necessarily to save her life, but to aid her in preserving her virginity by whatever means necessary:

> If fires be hot, knives sharp, or water's deep,
> Untied, I still my virgin knot will keep.
> Diana aid my purpose! (4.2.146–7)

---

[18] Slagle, *Joanna Baillie*, 260.

[19] Sean Carney maintains that Baillie's typically tragic pattern posits a protagonist hampered by a volatile passion, an interior mob mentality that eventually isolates and destroys the character: "Central characters are overwhelmed by an inner audience, and, while they resist this force, they finally succumb to a ruinous interior mob rule, providing a cautionary tale for the watching audience." "The Passion of Joanna Baillie: Playwright as Martyr," *Theatre Journal* 52 (2000): 234. We would note, however, that the irony of *The Martyr* is that Maro resists the external mob voice and succumbs to his own sacrificial intent.

Marina, however, does not need to resort to suicide, for she possesses the power of intellect. She converts all the men seeking sexual relations with her to chastity, by the power of her language, rhetoric, and arguments.[20] As the Bawd laments: "When she should do for clients her fitment, and do me the kindness of our profession, she has me her quirks, her reasons, her master reasons, her prayers, her knees, that she would make a puritan of the devil, if he should cheapen a kiss of her" (4.6.5–10). When Lysimachus the governor arrives, expecting to enjoy discreet sex, she challenges him to live up to the character and morality that should accompany his public position. He says in surprise, "I did not think / Thou couldst have spoke so well, ne'er dreamt thou couldst" (4.6.102–3). When Boult later threatens to rape her, in order to make her compliant, she both appeals to his self-image—"Do any thing but thou doest" (4.6.174)—and indicates that she can make a higher profit by being allowed to open a school for young women where she will teach the feminine arts: "I can sing, weave, sew, and dance, / With other virtues, which I'll keep from boast" (4.6.183). Marina is thus saved not by Diana's grace but by her own artistic and linguistic skills as well as by her assertion of militant femininity and chastity. To use a phrase of Clément and Kristeva's, she exercises the sacred feminine "at the crossroads of sexuality and thought, body and meaning, which women feel intensely."[21]

Throughout the play, Pericles, in spite of the traumatic events he endures—initial disillusion with love and marriage, shipwreck, apparent death of his wife—remains engaged with life. In speaking of the loss of Thaisa, he does not question why she died but, holding his infant daughter, accepts that it must be so:

> We cannot but obey
> The powers above us. Could I rage and roar
> As does the sea she lies in, yet the end
> Must be as 'tis. (3.3.9–12)

This acceptance of the flow of life, the mysteries of birth and death, is an embracing of the feminine in life and the world. However, when he is told that his daughter is dead, he "puts on sackcloth, and in a mighty passion departs" (4.4.22 s.d.). When his ship arrives at Mytilene, Pericles has isolated himself from the other men on board, not only physically but also linguistically by refusing to speak to, or acknowledge the presence of, anyone else. In his grief, he has turned inward, thereby refusing to be a part of the flow of the world. The men consider Marina, who arrives with a companion maid (thereby preventing her from being the lone female on stage) as the last hope of reaching him, but he is unresponsive to her

---

[20] Although Zurcher argues that Marina converts Lysimachus "to virtue by her own absolute and preternatural virtue" ("Untimely Monuments," 919), Bishop points out the importance of her linguistic skills: "She relentlessly insists that Lysimachus put names to his desires precisely where he wishes to mask in expedient pseudonyms" (*Theatre of Wonder*, 111).

[21] Clément and Kristeva, *Feminine and the Sacred*, 1.

song, neither seeming to hear it nor to see her. When she insists on speaking to him, he pushes her back. Marina's power, however, is the power of words, and slowly her words move him from his catatonic state to the recognition of the miracle that not only does his daughter live, but that she stands before him and gives him life: "Thou that beget'st him that did thee beget" (5.1.195). Pericles is healed not by the gods but by the effort and skill of his daughter and by his own willingness to be open to the feminine power she embodies.

Indeed, except for the punishment of Antiochus, and the punishment of Cleon and Dionyza (mentioned in the play's epilogue), the gods in *Pericles* do not intervene, nor are they expected to do so by the play's characters. The one exception is Diana's appearance to Pericles in a vision, after his reconciliation with his daughter, and her direction that he travel to her temple in Ephesus and there reveal before the assembled worshipers the story of his life. However, Diana makes clear that the choice to do so is Pericles' own: "Or perform my bidding, or thou livest in woe; / Do't, and happy, by my silver bow" (5.1.247–8). Again, Pericles demonstrates his willingness to embrace the feminine by doing Diana's bidding. Ultimately, *Pericles* is less a play about divine intervention and more a play about how humans respond to the moral and ethical decisions that they face. When those decisions are made by sundering the masculine and the feminine, they produce death, but when they are made from a balancing of the masculine and the feminine, they produce life. In the end, it is we humans who must choose. Divine providence, or the gods, are silent, but the sacred feminine speaks powerfully for the human spirit.

In her preface to *The Bride*, Baillie situates her drama within the context of the missionary enterprise, for the drama was commissioned by Sir Alexander Johnston, President of His Majesty's Council in Ceylon after her play *The Martyr* had been translated into the Cingalese language. The British East India Company seized control of Ceylon in 1796, and by 1802, it was a British Colony.[22] While the manifest content of *The Bride*, like that of *The Martyr*, may point to its utility in the civilizing and Christianizing projects associated with British colonialism, Baillie's prefatory comments give us hints to a more inclusive and tolerant sense of the sacred. She writes of her hopes of a time "when the different races of the East will consider every human creature as a brother; while Englishmen, under whose rule or protection they may live, will contemn that policy which founds its security upon ignorance" (preface, 665). Christine Colòn maintains that *The Bride* complicates imperialist narratives, including its Christian contexts, by marginalizing faulty Western interpretations of biblical scriptures.[23] The ambiguity here impels us to ponder whose "ignorance" is brought into the question: the un-Westernized views of Cingalese or the narrow perspectives of the English? *The Bride* interrogates ironically Hume's presumption that all supernatural and miraculous relations

---

[22] Slagle, *Joanna Baillie*, 270.
[23] Colòn, "Christianity," 165–6.

abound chiefly among the ignorant or barbarous, or are imposed upon civilized nations by ignorant and barbarous peoples.[24]

*The Bride*, however, demonstrates the "ignorance" of both Eastern and Western theologies that ignore the sacredness of women. By the laws and mores of Ceylon, Artina must respect and welcome her husband's polygamy, and his desire to bring yet another young, beautiful woman into her household. Having seen the face of this virgin while rescuing her from robbers, Rasigna lusts for her. The entire robbery scenario was orchestrated by Samarkoon as a way to make the young woman feel beholden to him for her life. Rasinga stumbled onto his brother-in-law's setup and determined to save the virgin himself. Because two rival chiefs have looked upon her face, one must become her husband. The bride is thus objectified as the prize of conquest by Rasigna, who deigns to possess the young female, and by his brother-in-law Samarkoon, who desires to marry her. Agitated, Artina fears her children will experience reductions of love from Rasinga whose children yet to be born of this bride will demand his favor. In desperation, she sends for the Spanish physician Juan de Creda, whose magic had cured a malady Rasinga had suffered at an earlier time. She hopes that from the miracles of the West she can find the "magic" to cure her current marital ills. Both Artina and the nameless bride lack the autonomy and power to design their own destinies because their sacredness has been erased by cultures that see them as possessions for men. Samarkoon woos the virgin as booty: "And now, dear maid, thou pearl and gem of beauty, / The prize for which this bloody fray was fought" (2.2, 673), and inquires as to whether he is not a worthy choice for marriage. She vehemently responds: "My choice! a modest virgin hath no choice" (2.2, 673). The rival chiefs barter to possess her. Samarkoon dangles the promise of an egalitarian marriage if she chooses him. An attendant reminds her that as Rasinga's younger wife she will be favored and Artina will be expected to withdraw herself. It is in the context of this battle that Samarkoon is implicated in the young virgin's robbery, captured, and imprisoned. Juan De Creda, who appears as the play's *deus ex machina*, persuades Rasinga to suspend judgment on his brother for two days and implores him to pardon rather than punish his brother-in-law, an act that for Rasinga seems "unnatural duty" (2.5, 676) to the vengeance required of his cultural theology.

In readings of the play that promote a European theological interpretation of the conflict, what is overlooked is the fact that it is not only De Creda who intercedes with Christian forgiveness but Montebesa, Rasigna's mother, who also begs her son to spare Samarkoon. In the face of cultural prescriptions of manhood that would require revenge, Montebesa asserts a value of feminine sacredness that assures Rasinga that there is no dishonor in forgiveness. Montebesa reflects on her son's behavior:

> I fear the fierceness of his untamed spirit
> Will never yield until it be too late;

---

[24] Hume, "Of Miracles," 79–80.

> And then he will, in brooking, vain repentance,
> The more relentless be to future criminals;
> As though the death of one he should have spared
> Made it injustice e'er to spare another.
> I know his dangerous nature all too well. (2.7, 677)

Rasigna's spirit is untamed because it is unschooled in the feminine sacred. His nature is dangerous because he fails to respect those attributes of humankind typically associated with femininity. His manhood is shaped by a patriarchal "fierceness" that demands retribution rather than respect. Artina, likewise, pleads for her brother's life, but Rasigna rejects their sacredness as the same kind of hypocrisy that drives Christians to "speak like holy saints, and act like fiends" (2.7, 677).

When words of compassion fail to move Rasigna, Artina determines to act, to exercise her feminine sacredness in her struggle for life. Artina attempts to assist Samarkoon's escape by way of a secret passage when, alerted by a spy, Rasigna interrupts their efforts. Rasigna chastises Artina for her rebellion against "female honour, matronly allegiance" (2.8, 678). Artina responds with a plea to heed the feminine sacred:

> Matronly allegiance,
> E'en in a favour'd and beloved wife,
> O'errules not every duty; and to her,
> Who is despised, abandon'd, and disgraced,
> Can it be more imperious? No, Rasigna;
> I were unmeet to wear a woman's form,
> If, with the means to save my brother's life,
> Not implicating thine, I had, from fear
> Of thy displeasure, grievous as it is,
> Forborne to use them. (2.8, 678)

Angered at this female audacity, Rasigna threatens Artina with the punishment that law provides for faithless and disobedient wives. Laws that suppress female participation in political and familial matters are not found exclusively in Ceylon. Judith Slagle has pointed out that the sacred drama exposes masculine control of women in multiple patriarchal societies.[25] Samarkoon declares Rasigna the fellest, fiercest, meanest tyrant that ever joined human form to demon spirit. As Rasigna has Artina imprisoned along with Samarkoon, he cries: "I came not here to hold a wordy war / With criminals and women" (2.8, 678).

Montebesa and Artina force Rasigna to contemplate his behavior, and in his private chamber, Rasigna wrestles with his conscience as he tries to justify his actions to himself. He rationalizes that the meanest chief is allowed to take a younger wife when his earlier wife begins to fade, and yet for this rightful action, he is "deem'd a slave, / A tamed—a woman bound—a simple fool" (3.1, 679).

---

[25] Slagle, *Joanna Baillie*, 269.

He argues that he did not seek to create his current situation, for it was fate that unveiled the captivating face of the beautiful virgin for whom he then lusted. He confesses that his mind is troubled by his wife's role in the matter, but his mental machinations reveal his disregard for the sacred feminine:

> It needs must be: I'm driven to the brink.
> What is a woman's life, or any life
> That poisons his response for whom it flourish'd?
> I would have cherish'd, honour'd her, yet she,
> Rejecting all, has e'en to this extremity—. (3.1, 679)

His explanation for Artina's noncompliant behavior blames Samarkoon, whom he rationalizes must have urged her to be deviant so as to satisfy his sexual desires and to cause Rasinga dishonor. The important function of Montebesa and Artina is to set up Rasinga for De Credo's intervention. The feminine sacred softens Rasinga's resolve for revenge and for selfish actions.

De Credo visits Rasinga and provides an alternative perspective to his mental debate that would justify killing his wife and brother-in-law. De Credo begs Rasinga not to wreck his happiness to save his honor, and he urges Rasinga to exercise pardon rather than revenge. Rasinga retorts that the Christian scriptures from which De Credo preaches

> hath bred more discord
> Than all other firebrands of the earth,
> With church opposed to church, and sect to sect,
> In fierce contention; ay, fell bloody strife. (3.1, 680)

Here we find a similar argument against organized religion and institutionalized theology that we saw expressed in *The Martyr*, an intolerance for difference that the churches of the West had come to embrace in their interpretative and dogmatic doctrines of faith. The sacred had somehow gotten lost in the struggle for the "right" interpretation of scripture and the "just" application of sacred words. Rasinga sticks to his theology and orders the executions of the prisoners.

As Samarkoon and Artina are brought to a large courtyard for public execution, Artina laments that she is the cursed cause of this human wreck. Artina's young son Samar wishes to die with her, and moved by his boy's courage, Rasinga pardons Artina's crime. Seizing the moment when Rasinga seems vulnerable to forgiveness, Artina pleads that he spare Samarkoon as well. Rasinga complies with her wishes, and Artina capitulates to her husband's desire to take a younger wife. It is the feminine sacred, not institutionalized theology, that compels both Rasinga and Artina to compromise their earlier steadfast positions. In a reversal of attitude that defies probability—a miracle created by Rasinga's embracing of the feminine sacred—Rasinga resigns the bride to Samarkoon and orders a feast of celebration. Proclaiming that Ceylon has weathered a dark storm of familial strife, Rasinga invites De Credo to join their supper and to bring his sacred book. Recent readings of the play interpret the ending as an expression of Christian conversion, but Baillie is not so clear or explicit.[26] There is, however, one virgin martyr at the end of the play, the bride, who has absolutely no choice in her being "given" to Samarkoon by the "generous" Rasinga. She remains the conquest of the rival chiefs, the property to be bartered or bestowed, the passive object about which the two chiefs fight and cause familial and political unrest. Here, the bride does not sacrifice her sexuality for a deity, but for a man privileged by cultural and theological laws. According to Karen A. Winstead, virgin legends do not necessarily propagate Christian values but raise critiques about issues of authority and tradition.[27] The bride becomes the erotic element which Clément and Kristeva identify as the sacrificial incompleteness explored in metaphorical and actual ceremonies.[28] Bailie's integration of the virgin martyr in *The Bride* suggests concern about feminine conduct, sexuality, and sacredness in Western and Cingalese cultures alike. Pagan magic and Christian miracles disguise misogyny equally well. Like the dénouement of *The Martyr*, the ending of *The Bride* is ambivalent about the cultural awakening to Christianity read into it by critics. We experience at the end of both plays a conversion of the human heart, moved to forgiveness, tolerance, and equity by a number of forces, not the least of which is the privilege of the feminine sacred.

Of all Shakespeare's romances, only *Pericles* takes an approach that might have helped lay the foundations for Baillie's sacred dramas by pointing toward the feminine as an essential component of the spiritual life and wisdom. Admittedly, the influence of one writer upon another can be difficult to discern. Sometimes we can trace similarities in plot, character, or writing style, but the influence of modes of thought is subtle. We know that Baillie read Shakespeare enthusiastically, and so it is likely that she read all of Shakespeare's plays. In Shakespeare's work, she would have found female characters beset by dilemmas in a patriarchal world that would have been similar to dilemmas in her own. In Shakespeare's romances, she would have been able to note less of the broad religious context that informed his earlier plays, and in *Pericles* she would have seen a play that stands apart from the other late plays in that there is very little indication of divine providence—only an emphasis on the moral choices that face human beings and what they make of such choices. She also would likely have noted an emphasis on honoring the feminine as an essential part of life both in *Pericles* and *The Winter's Tale*. Baillie would have seen in Shakespeare's late romances how a repression or neglect of the feminine could lead to destructive, excessive passions in any culture. Her sacred dramas *The Martyr* and *The Bride* perceive and transform the miraculous potential of *Pericles* into spiritual wisdom for all humanity, a wisdom derived from the reverence and respect given to the feminine in its multiple and mysterious aspects.

---

[26] On this point, see Colòn, "Christianity," 173–4; Slagle, *Joanna Baillie*, 268–71; and Carhart, *Life and Work*, 54–8.

[27] Karen Winstead, *Virgin Martyrs: Legends of Sainthood in Late Medieval England* (Ithaca, NY: Cornell University Press, 1997), 5.

[28] Clément and Kristeva, *Feminine and the Sacred*, 26–7.

## Chapter 12
# A Written Warning:
## Lady Caroline Lamb, Noblesse Oblige, and the Works of John Ford

### Leigh Wetherall-Dickson

Lady Caroline Lamb is better known for her tempestuous relationship with Lord Byron than she is for her literary endeavors, with the possible exception of *Glenarvon* (1816), a roman à clef that has at its core a representation of that notorious affair. Lamb's fictional portraits of Byron, particularly in *Glenarvon*, have been read as an expression of her spleen towards her erstwhile lover. However, Lamb portrays her relationship with Byron as a microcosm of a morally bankrupt section of society to which they both belong, that of the Whig aristocracy. It is towards this section of society that Lamb orientates her writing, and it is her extended use of the works of John Ford that exemplifies her view that the Whig aristocracy had lost sight of the fact that with privilege comes grave responsibility. From Lamb's perspective, if the Whigs wished to return to power (having been in opposition for the duration of her lifetime) on the platform of parliamentary reform, then they crucially needed to initiate an internal reform of both individual behavior and community standards. Ford is significant here for Lamb as a covertly political writer who exemplifies not only the effectiveness but also the legitimacy of the aristocracy and their intermediary position between the monarchy and the people.

Very little is known about Ford as an individual, but Lisa Hopkins has traced an affiliation among Ford's dedicatees that reveals a network of familial, religious, and political sympathies: a tightly defined group of people with whom Ford obviously had very close links.[1] Hopkins discovers that of the 19 dedicatees, the majority of them are related by blood or marriage and form a core of aristocratic opposition to Charles I.[2] Among the dedicatees was William Cavendish, Earl of Newcastle, to whom Ford's play *Perkin Warbeck* was dedicated in 1634—a play that Lamb draws heavily upon. Cavendish's father was the younger son resulting from Bess of Hardwick's second marriage to Sir William Cavendish, making the Earl of Newcastle cousin to the first Duke of Devonshire. Lamb's beloved aunt, Georgiana, was the first wife of the fifth Duke of Devonshire, and the cousin to

---

[1] Lisa Hopkins, *John Ford's Political Theatre* (Manchester, UK: Manchester University Press, 1994), 29.
[2] Ibid., 4.

whom Lamb was closest became the sixth Duke. So despite Ford's resurgent popularity during the Romantic period—his works being discussed by the likes of Charles Lamb, William Gifford (who acted as a reader and advisor to Lamb on *Ada Reis*, her third novel, on behalf of John Murray), and William Hazlitt, and a new edition of his works being published by Henry Weber in 1811—Lamb may already have been familiar with Ford because of her family connections with him. Both Ford and Lamb wrote for an audience that would recognize themselves in relation to the message of aristocratic reform embedded in the text. Ford registers a voice oppositional to an autocratic monarch, Charles I, who needs a lesson in kingship and needs reminding not only how to be a nobleman, but how to treat the nobility to whom he owes his throne and to whom Ford dedicated his work. While the general reader of Lamb's novels may not have had the necessary information to decode the covert remonstrance directed at contemporary political figures (or to identify the actual persons represented by characters in a play like *Glenarvon*), the persons actually represented in her works would certainly have recognized themselves, just as they were intended to.

## *The Broken Heart* and *Glenarvon*: Annihilation of the Self and the Aristocratic Ideal

There are distinct parallels between *The Broken Heart*, *Glenarvon*, and, to an extent, Lamb's own life. In all three instances, a woman was originally intended to be married in a dynastic rather than a love match: Princess Calantha to Nearchus the Prince of Argos in *The Broken Heart*; Lady Calantha to her cousin William Buchanan in *Glenarvon*; and Lamb herself, it was commonly supposed within the family, to her cousin "Hart," the Marquis of Hartington, heir to the title of Duke of Devonshire.[3] Ford illustrates the undesirability of the dynastic marriage: Penthea is forced by her brother into a socially desirable but personally disastrous match to the insanely jealous, older Bassanes. She is kept prisoner, loses her mind, and eventually starves herself to death in order to escape the tyranny of Bassanes. Ford's Calantha, Lamb's Calantha, and Lamb herself were allowed to make their own choices to marry Ithocles, Lord Avondale, and William Lamb, respectively. In *Glenarvon* Lamb draws attention to the similarities between Lady Calantha and her literary predecessor:

> The heiress of Delaval [Lady Calantha], decked in splendid jewels ... was the reigning favourite of the moment: everyone observed it, and smiled upon her

---

[3] Hart was apparently so devastated by Lamb's acceptance of William Lamb's proposal that doctors were summoned to deal with his ensuing hysteria. Paul Douglass suggests that his decision to remain a bachelor until his death was due to his attachment to Lamb, to whom he remained loyal throughout the scandal caused by Lamb's association with Byron. Paul Douglass, *Lady Caroline Lamb: A Biography* (New York: Palgrave Macmillan, 2004), 46.

more on that account. To be the favourite of the favoured was too much ... but alas a deeper interest employed her thoughts, and Glenarvon's attention was her sole object. ... Lord Glenarvon had conversed with her with his customary ease but something had wounded her; ... possibly her heart reproached her [but] she danced on with energy and perseverance, which excited the warmest approbation in all. ... She herself only sighed. "Have you ever read a tragedy of Ford's?" whispered Lady Augusta as soon as she had ceased to exhibit—"a tragedy entitled *The Broken Heart*. ... At this moment you put me vastly in mind of it. You look most woefully. Come, tell me truly, is not your heart in torture? And, like your namesake Calantha, while lightly dancing the gayest in the ring, has not the shaft already been struck, and shall you not die ere you attain your goal."[4]

This is a reenactment of Princess Calantha's final scene in which she continues a public dance of celebration and hears of the successive deaths of her father, her friend Penthea, and Ithocles. Princess Calantha's Spartan stoicism allows her to attend to her duty as queen first and foremost: she bequeaths her crown to her cousin and dispenses justice for the murderer of Ithocles, before giving into her emotions on the deaths of her loved ones. Thus, public duty comes before displays of private grief. Lamb's Lady Calantha is similar in repressing her emotions, but she attempts to mask an emotion not quite as noble—that of guilt for her obsession with Glenarvon and for her lapse of duty towards her husband and her family. The goal that Lamb's Lady Augusta is referring to is, for both Calanthas, to be united with their chosen lovers, Ithocles and Glenarvon. Lady Augusta's prediction does come true: Lamb's Lady Calantha will die before she attains her goal, not realizing until too late that she was already married to her choice of lover in the form of Lord Avondale, and that her temporary infatuation with Glenarvon was a dereliction of her responsibilities to herself, her husband, and her family, having been allowed the freedom of choice to begin with.

Frances Wilson identifies Lamb's adoption of Edmund Burke's psychological sublime as a model for this fatal passion, in which "the mind is so entirely filled with its object, that it cannot entertain any other."[5] The Burkean sublime passion is exhilarating to contemplate, dreadful and daunting in the threat of annihilation to the self—a truthful, ruling emotion that neither Lady Calantha nor indeed Lamb were able to resist and that was destructive in its intensity. Interestingly, considering Lamb's historical reputation as a woman whose monomaniacal desire for Byron shattered her mental equilibrium and destroyed her life, Lamb does not allow Lady Calantha to die after Glenarvon extricates himself from her in the same abrupt manner in which Byron did from Lamb. Glenarvon severs his relationship with Lady Calantha with a version of the letter that Byron had sent

---

[4] Lady Caroline Lamb, *Glenarvon*, 1816, in *The Works of Lady Caroline Lamb*, ed. Leigh Wetherall Dickson and Paul Douglass, vol. 1 (London: Pickering and Chatto, 2009), 152. All references to *Glenarvon* will be to this edition unless otherwise stated.

[5] Lady Caroline Lamb, *Glenarvon*, ed. Frances Wilson (London: Everyman, 1995), xxi.

to Lamb declaring that he was no longer her lover. Lady Calantha feels herself annihilated by Glenarvon's rejection, but this feeling is a state of mind that is only temporary. In *The Broken Heart*, Princess Calantha's self is annihilated after being denied Ithocles, and Penthea, starved of love from both her true love Orgilus and her husband Bassanes, literally starves to death, but not before losing all reason—an extremely resonant image when considering Lamb's own description of herself in a letter to Byron in 1814 that denigrates herself as "ugly & thin & mad."[6] In *Glenarvon* Alice MacAllain follows a similar path as Penthea, descending into skeletal madness after having been abandoned by Glenarvon, returning to the narrative after disappearing to give birth to his child as an "emaciated form" with a "wild and haggard eye" (218). Alice is unable to speak of her trauma and has written down the story of her annihilation in a letter to her father. Lady Calantha, like her namesake, is nearly destroyed by her all-consuming love for Glenarvon, but in this case only to discover that her emotional investment is not reciprocated. On receiving the fateful letter from Glenarvon informing her that he is "no longer [her] lover," under the seal of his new lover Lady Mandeville, Calantha was instantaneously "overpowered, annihilated, she called for mercy and release. She felt that mortal passion domineered over reason; and, after one desperate struggle for mastery, had conquered and destroyed her" (273). However, on recovery from the initial shock, Lady Calantha recalls the appearance and actions of her literary forebear:

> When the very soul is annihilated by some sudden and unexpected evil, the outward frame is calm—no appearance of emotion, of tears, of repining, gives notice of the approaching evil. Calantha, motionless, re-perused Glenarvon's letter, and spoke with gentleness to those who addressed her. Oh! did the aunt that loved her, as she read that barbarous letter, exhibit equal marks of fortitude? No: in tears, in reproaches, she vented her indignation: but still Calantha moved not. (274)

Michel Foucault identifies a link between madness and passion, where love that is disappointed or abandoned has no other recourse but to "pursue itself into the void of delirium."[7] However, he goes on to state that passion is, in fact, a temporary form of madness and a form of blindness:

> Blindness: one of the words which comes closest to the essence of classical madness. It refers to that night of quasi-sleep which surrounds the images of madness, giving them, in their solitude, an invisible sovereignty; but it also refers to ill-founded beliefs, mistaken judgements, to the whole background of errors inseparable from madness.[8]

---

[6] Douglass, *Lady Caroline Lamb*, 158.

[7] Michel Foucault, *Madness and Civilization: A History of Insanity in the Age of Reason* (New York: Vintage Press, 1988), 30.

[8] Ibid., 105.

Unreason, to use Foucault's phrase, that is associated with dream-like error and delirium is not, he explains, reason lost, alienated, or diseased; it must be understood as reason dazzled, effecting a temporary blindness in which moral errors and misjudgments are made, and this is what both Lady Calantha and Lamb come to realize. Like Ford's Princess Calantha, Lamb's Lady Calantha does eventually die of grief after being denied the fulfillment of her true love. On her deathbed she cries "Oh, is it too late?" (298), signaling an awareness that the object of her true passion was, and always had been, Lord Avondale, and that Glenarvon was only a form of temporary madness. Lamb, acknowledging her source, writes of Lady Calantha's death rattle as "a piercing shriek [that] had escaped from a broken heart" (298), as she clings to what Ford would have referred to as her contracted lord.

## *Glenarvon* and *The Chronicle History of Perkin Warbeck*: Assumed Identity and Innate Nobility

Lady Calantha is not the only person in the novel to be dazzled by Glenarvon's presence. The Irish rebels whose cause Glenarvon adopts on his mysterious arrival into Ireland are similarly blinded by his charismatic leadership. As part of the novel's insistent concern with concealed and manipulated identity and its inquiries into the performative and charismatic elements of leadership, *Glenarvon* invokes the story of Perkin Warbeck, a young man who claimed to be Richard, Duke of York, the younger of the princes in the Tower, previously thought to have died in captivity along with his brother, Edward. As such, he tormented Henry VII for eight years with uncertainty and a possible legitimate claim to Henry's crown.[9] Warbeck was not the first pretender to Henry's throne; Lambert Simnel was paraded as the Earl of Warwick, a potential threat to Henry's position as he had been (for a short time at least) named as Richard III's heir. Henry VII had the real Earl of Warwick in the Tower, so Simnel's role as pretender was short lived. However, Warbeck was the one who unnerved and unsettled the king and threatened the status quo of the country that was now enjoying a hard-won peace after the prolonged War of the Roses. What impresses about Warbeck from the outset is not so much the actual evidence that supports his claim, but the inherent nobility of his bearing that lends legitimacy to his claim.

The physical and temporal setting of *Glenarvon* is revolutionary Ireland, 1798. This was a rebellion that was inspired by the successes of America and France and that sent the clear message that home rule was a distinct possibility for the indigenous population hoping to rid themselves of their oppressive overlords. With the promised aid of the French, the Society of United Irishmen set aside their religious differences to, as Robert Kee puts it, "eradicate the baneful English

---

[9] Ian Arthurson, *The Perkin Warbeck Conspiracy 1491–1499* (Stroud, UK: Sutton, 1997), 42–53.

influence and destroy the aristocratic tyrants of the land."[10] The landscape of Lamb's Ireland has been criticized as being unknown and unknowable, an appropriation of a literary myth of the country as "sublimely wild and desolate; ominously castellated; infested by banditti variously known as rapparees ... who reflected a historical muddle of Jacobite or Jacobin conspiracies of rebellion."[11] The view that the novel reflects suspicion of the Irish from the landholding elite is echoed by Malcolm Kelsall, who argues that there is no account of the oppression that provoked the rebellion, and that there exists a naivety in a landscape of the "picturesque imagination."[12] Lamb's depiction of Ireland was likely informed by her picturesque imagination because it is a place that she had limited experience of, only having visited it during the few months in 1812 when her family removed her from Byron's immediate vicinity. But the conspiracy of rebellion in *Glenarvon* is no fiction of the imagination, although it is fictionalized. Lamb does indeed write from the position of her inherent Englishness, but she was also well placed to write with authority upon the disintegration of Anglo-Irish relations.

The Duke of Devonshire, Lamb's uncle, was Lord High Treasurer of Ireland, the governor of County Cork, and the owner of Lismore Castle in County Waterford. The earls of Bessborough, of which Lamb's father was the third, traced their descent and acquisition of Irish lands to Sir John Ponsonby, an English colonel in a horse regiment in Cromwell's army. He was granted lands at Kildaton in County Kilkenny, under the Act of Settlement, which he later renamed Bessborough in honor of his second wife. His great-grandsons, William, the second Earl of Bessborough, and his brother John Ponsonby, both married daughters of the third Duke of Devonshire, thereby creating an alliance between two families that were equally powerful in Irish and English politics. William Lamb was also heir to the Irish viscountcy of Melbourne, seated at Kilmore in County Cavan.[13] Due to the interconnecting nature of family estates, Lamb was conscious that the families of the English aristocracy and Irish Protestant Ascendancy, which owned the majority of Irish lands, had stronger familial and material connections with England than Ireland; as such, the portrait she paints of the aristocracy is not a flattering one. In *Glenarvon* the Duke of Altamonte has retired from social and political life, having overrated his own superiority and having failed to realize his ambitions. He has retreated "sullen and reserved" to Ireland, and as a representative of the landholding elite he is ineffective as the Irish rebellion gathers momentum around him; his own tenants are "mutinous and discontented" because he "refused to attend to the grievances and burthens of which the nation generally complained"

---

[10] Robert Kee, *The Green Flag*, 3 vols. (London: Penguin, 1989), 1:50.

[11] Joseph Garver, "Gothic Ireland: Lady Caroline Lamb's *Glenarvon*," *Irish University Review: A Journal of Irish Studies* 10 (1980): 216.

[12] Malcolm Kelsall, "The Byronic Hero and Revolution in Ireland: The Politics of *Glenarvon*," *Byron Journal* 9 (1981): 6.

[13] T. Barnard, *A New Anatomy of Ireland: The Irish Protestants 1649–1770* (New Haven, CT: Yale University Press, 2003), 21–41.

(132). Lamb sums up the state of Irish dissatisfaction with the occupation by the Anglo-Irish: "Numerous absentees had drawn great part of the money out of the country; oppressive taxes were continued; land was let and sub-let to bankers and stewards of estates, to the utter ruin of the tenants; and all this caused the greatest discontent" (132).

Ireland represents the endemic neglect of aristocratic responsibility by Lamb's familial connections and therefore a betrayal of trust between the rulers and the ruled. Ireland is also the site of a very personal sense of betrayal. Joseph Garver points out the connection between Lamb, Byron, and Ireland by also reminding us that it was in Ireland that she received the vituperative letter informing her that Byron was no longer her lover, thereby revealing his duplicity, as he had been up until that moment writing to assure her of his affections.[14]

The combination of Byron's duplicity being revealed to her in Ireland, Lamb's association with Anglo-Irish politics, and the conscious choice of the 1798 rebellion as the temporal setting for the novel elevates this portrayal of Byron above and beyond a simple retelling of their disastrous relationship. Lamb makes illustrative use of Byron as Glenarvon; he becomes a microcosm of Whig society, whose opposition to tyranny (as demonstrated by their support for the French and American revolutions and for Catholic emancipation) could be criticized as self-serving, strategic posturing rather than a republican commitment.[15] Glenarvon has a dual identity that demonstrates his opportunistic appropriation of the United Irishmen's cause for his own ends. He plots to bring down the house of Delaval by whatever means necessary; first by insinuating himself into the favors of Lady Margaret and pretending to kidnap and murder the newborn heir of the Duke of Altamonte on her instructions, and second by adopting the cause of the United Irishmen, the timing of which could not be more fortuitous for Glenarvon's purpose. The personal vendetta of Glenarvon becomes enmeshed with the political clash between the Protestant Ascendancy landholding elite, represented by Castle Delaval, and the indigenous population, represented by Belfont Abbey, the ruined estates of the Earls of Glenarvon.

Ford's dramatization of the historical account, *The Chronicle History of Perkin Warbeck*, was entered in the Stationers' Register in January 1634, and it explores the theme of inherent nobility. Ford does not allow Perkin's claim to falter, and the suppression of the historical Perkin's confession that he was an imposter allows Perkin's aristocratic bearing to stand as testimony to his claim. Other characters comment upon their responses to his presence. James IV of Scotland's acknowledgment of the veracity of Perkin's claim is based upon his "instinct of

---

[14] Garver, "Gothic Ireland," 224.

[15] Barbara Judson, "Roman á Clef and the Dynamics of Betrayal: The Case of *Glenarvon*," *Genre* 33 (2000): 160.

sovereignty"[16] and he urges the Earl of Huntly, soon to be Perkin's reluctant father-in-law, to be assured of this judgment:

> Peace, old frenzy. –
> How like a king 'a looks! Lords, but observe
> The confidence of his aspect! Dross cannot
> Cleave to so pure a metal; royal youth!
> Plantagenet undoubted![17]

James's perception of Perkin's innate nobility is preceded by that of the Countess of Crawford and Lady Katherine Gordon, the daughter of the Earl of Huntly and soon to be Perkin's wife:

> COUNTESS.
> I have not seen a gentleman
> Of a more brave aspect or goodlier carriage;
> His fortunes move not him. – Madame, y'are passionate.
>
> KATHERINE.
> Beshrew me, but his words have touched me home,
> As if his cause concerned me. I should pity him
> If 'a should prove another than he seems.[18]

Glenarvon's caution to his followers that "I am not what I seem" is a direct echo of Katherine's concern for Perkin's safety should he prove to be an imposter, and of the theme of charismatic leadership and uncertain identity.

Glenarvon and Perkin Warbeck both make their debut as legitimate leaders in Ireland, laying claim to titles to which some observers believe they have a spurious claim. When Lady Calantha's cousin refers to Glenarvon by his title, she is rebuked by her mother:

> "I wish Frances," said Mrs Seymour, "you would call people by their right names. The young man you call Lord Glenarvon has no claim to that title; his grandfather was a traitor; his father was a poor miserable exile, who was obliged to enter the Navy by way of gaining a livelihood; his mother was a woman of very doubtful character ...; and this young man, educated nobody knows how, having passed his time in a foreign country, nobody knows where ... is now unfortunately arrived here to pervert and mislead others .... Oh he is a dishonour to his sex; and it makes me mad to see how you all run after him, and forget both dignity and modesty, to catch a glimpse of him." (101)

---

[16] John Ford, *The Chronicle History of Perkin Warbeck: A Strange Truth*, in *'Tis Pity She's a Whore and Other Plays*, ed. Marion Lomax (Oxford: Oxford University Press, 1995), 2.3.42. All references to the play are from this edition.

[17] *Perkin Warbeck*, 2.3.72–5.

[18] *Perkin Warbeck*, 2.1.115–20.

Mrs. Seymour refers to not only the doubtful legitimacy of the claim to the title but also to the fact that Glenarvon himself is not fit to uphold the rank; the nobility of his bearing, as well as his lineage, is also called into question, although there is apparently no doubt of his abilities of persuasion. Much is made in both stories of the contrast between the new arrivals and the indigenous population of Ireland. Lamb's portrayal of Glenarvon as appearing "amidst the grotesque and ferocious rabble, like some God from a higher world" (250) is evocative of Perkin's appearance in Ireland in an attempt to initiate Yorkist support for his claim. According to earlier sources examined by Ann Wroe, Perkin appeared in Ireland dressed in gorgeous silks that nobody below the rank of knight could wear, amongst people whose loyalty to Henry was bought with "lengths of green and blood-red woollen cloth."[19] Wroe identifies discrepancies in the various versions as to whether the silks actually belonged to Perkin, but the point is that they marked him out as being of an higher order. As Hopkins wryly observes, Perkin, having been apprenticed to a silk merchant, arrives in Ireland, "dressed in some of his master's ware, and is immediately hailed as so good-looking that he must be the long-lost Plantagenet prince."[20] Ford touches upon this only briefly, writing within a condensed time frame and concentrating upon the disparate natures between the English and Scottish courts of Henry VII and James IV, but Henry's brief summation of Perkin's career to date includes a derisory commentary upon the dramatic effect of his appearance:

> We know all, Clifford, fully, since this meteor
> This airy apparition, first discradled
> From Tournai into Portugal, and thence
> Advanced his fiery blaze for adoration
> To th'superstitious Irish[21]

Ford's description of Perkin as a meteor places him above the human sphere of activity, but in Henry's mouth it becomes a derisory description of what he perceives as the flashy transience of the perceived threat that blinds the population with his garish wardrobe. Though Lamb may not have been aware of these earlier, more detailed accounts, one of which is the official Tudor version of events in the form of the historical confession, it is the legitimizing of Perkin through external signifiers that is repeated in *Glenarvon*.

Glenarvon adopts the anthems, ballads, and insignia of Ireland to his cause and uses the secrecy of the rebellion as a powerfully cohesive force for ensuring loyalty and solidarity via codes, secret hideouts, and oaths of allegiance, all of which are external signifiers for what is assumed to be an internal conviction of the cause of liberating the oppressed population. But despite his apparent egalitarianism Glenarvon is not a democrat and insists that he alone still be referred to by his

---

[19] Ann Wroe, *Perkin: A Story of Deception* (London: Jonathan Cape, 2003), 48.
[20] Hopkins, *John Ford's Political Theatre*, 39.
[21] *Perkin Warbeck*, 1.3.35–9.

title (to which he has a very dubious claim) when all others have renounced theirs. His title and the ancestral lands that he claims back in the name of Glenarvon, St Alvin Priory and Belfont Abbey, fulfill the same legitimizing functions as the trappings of achievement of the existing rulers; they mark Glenarvon out as a figure of distinction and authority, with a tradition of leadership in his genealogy. The corridors of Belfont Abbey are lined with ancestral portraits, which are shown to the visitors from the neighboring Castle Delaval. The title and estates legitimize Glenarvon on three fronts: to himself; to the Delavals, for whom the visual signifiers of lineage represent a legitimate member of the aristocracy whom they must visit out of courtesy; and to the indigenous population, for whom these symbols of noble bearing imply an education, political experience, and leadership. That he betrays both the governors and the governed underlines Lamb's concern with the deceptive and persuasive nature of social signifiers and rhetoric, and makes clear that the present state of unrest, because of the neglect of "senatorial duties" by the ruling elite, allows for the possibility of rebellion.

## *The Fancies, Chaste and Noble* and *The Witch of Edmonton*: Misrepresentation and Misunderstanding in *Graham Hamilton* and *Ada Reis*

The theme of true identity is found in other works by Ford that Lamb draws upon in *Graham Hamilton* (1822) and *Ada Reis* (1823), in which identity is misrepresented and misconstrued. Published in 1638, Ford's *The Fancies, Chaste and Noble* features a glut of characters pretending to be something other than they are, rather than somebody else as in the case of Perkin Warbeck. The title is representative of the contradictory characters within the play: the "Fancies" are three young women who are perceived by the other characters and the audience to be of dubious morality, kept in what is thought to be a type of harem by an old man, the Duke Octavio, for dubious motives. By the end of the play the Fancies are revealed to be of "chaste and noble" character—the nieces of Octavio, who is providing them with education and protection. Castamela, a young woman who is taken to live with the Fancies, learns the truth about the Duke and his nieces but perpetuates the misconception by acting like a concubine in order to teach her brother a lesson. In the subplot of the play, Spadone pretends to be a eunuch, Flavia adopts an "antique carriage"[22] to fend off advances from her husband's servants, and Morosa is wrongly portrayed as an adulteress and procurer of young girls for the bower of Fancies. As Dominick J. Hart observes, the misunderstandings that pervade the play are also heralded by the title in that "fancy" can mean a groundless supposition as well as an amorous inclination.[23]

Lamb fully understood the weighty impact of social judgment; before her own experience in the Byron affair she was well acquainted with the precarious

---

[22] John Ford, *The Fancies, Chaste and Noble*, ed. Dominick J. Hart (New York: Garland, 1985), 2.1.126. All references to this play are from this edition.

[23] Ibid., 34.

nature of female social position. On the fringes or outside of Lamb's society, there were women whose actions had removed them from the sphere of acceptable company, such as the divorced Ladies Wellesley and Holland; the latter having married again, to her co-respondent in her divorce, and with whom Lamb kept company with at the risk of her own reputation. Lady Melbourne once wrote to Lamb that "when one braves the opinion of the World, sooner or later they will feel the consequences of it,"[24] an observation and a warning that was given before Lamb's involvement with Byron but that proved no less true in her case than it did for Lady Wellesley and Lady Holland. The theme of social judgment is one that is also explored in *Graham Hamilton*, in the relationship between Lady Orville and Graham Hamilton that remains ambiguous and can be interpreted in one of two ways: Lady Orville has ensnared the young and inexperienced Graham Hamilton with her physical charms, seeing him as a possible cash cow with which to solve her financial problems (as when Sir Malcolm warns Hamilton "she's only making much o'ye to get at my money"),[25] or that Graham Hamilton is the one true friend that Lady Orville can confide in where they are thin on the ground.

The ambiguous nature of the relationship between Graham Hamilton and Lady Orville encourages Lamb's reader and the other characters in the novel to think the worst of the situation. Juliet Sutton observes a similar device in *The Fancies, Chaste and Noble*. Sutton points out that both the main plot and subplots are based upon the "groundless suspicion" interpretation of "fancy," and that the act of misunderstanding extends to the audience as well as the other characters.[26] The opening of the very first scene sets the precedent in which Troylo, the nephew of the Duke Octavio, and Livio, the brother of Castamela, are brought on stage during the heated conversation in which Troylo is trying to convince Livio to send Castamela to his uncle's bower of "fancies." Troylo never actually says that the bower is a harem but Livio, and the audience, think the worst. Lamb's use of a Jonathan Swift poem as an epigram is deployed to reprimand the readership and flags the censorious nature of an acquisitive and competitive culture, echoing Castamela's accusation to her brother that he has "forgot the noblenesse of truth / and fixt on scandal":[27]

> Bare innocence is no support,
> When you are tried in Scandal's court.
> Stand high in honour, wealth or wit;
> All others who inferior sit,
> Conceive themselves in conscience bound

---

[24] Quoted in Douglass, *Lady Caroline Lamb*, 91.

[25] Lady Caroline Lamb, *Graham Hamilton* (1822), in *The Works of Lady Caroline Lamb*, ed. Leigh Wetherall Dickson and Paul Douglass, vol. 2 (London: Pickering and Chatto, 2009), 48. All references to the novel are from this edition.

[26] Juliet Sutton, "Platonic Love in Ford's *The Fancies, Chaste and Noble*," *Studies in English Literature 1500–1900* 7, no. 2 (1967): 301.

[27] *The Fancies*, 1.3.36–8.

> To join and drag you to the ground.
> Your altitude offends the eyes
> Of those, who want the power to rise.
> The World, a willing stander-by,
> Inclines to aid a specious lie;
> Alas! they would not do you wrong;
> But all appearances are strong![28]

In Lamb's novels, Scandal's court is "the world," the habitus of the social elite that is described by Lamb as "censorius, officious, intermeddling ... ever greedy of scandal, ever ready to adopt the worst construction, and hasty to condemn."[29] Gossip about the nature of Hamilton's relationship with Lady Orville gathers momentum because of a series of misinterpreted scenarios. At a ball held by Lady Orville, Graham Hamilton is witnessed being called to say goodnight to her children and is seen later, at the same ball, supporting Lady Orville and leading her from the ballroom in obvious distress after being confronted by a man she has reduced to destitution and criminality by her refusal to acknowledge her debts to him. A servant of Lord Orville's also witnesses Hamilton leaving Lady Orville's extremely late after being closeted away in her boudoir for hours. It is only the readers, rather than the novel's characters, who discover that, in the latter scenario, Hamilton and Lady Orville were discussing her future prospects for retirement to the country in a bid to save her morally and financially. It appears to the other characters that they are indeed having an affair because the concept of platonic friendship is distinctly lacking.

In *Ada Reis* it is Fiormonda, as a literary descendent of Castamela, who further connects Lamb's work to Ford's. Fiormonda is the daughter of Ada Reis and Bianca Castamela, an amalgamation of Castamela and Bianca from another of Ford's works, *Love's Sacrifice*, published in 1633. Ford's Bianca is misrepresented to her husband, the Duke of Pavia, as being unfaithful by the Duke's sister, Fiormonda, who is jealous of the attention that Bianca receives from the Duke's friend Fernando. While it is true that Bianca and Fernando have fallen in love, they have not consummated the relationship. However, the Duke believes the worst of them and so stabs Bianca. Lamb's Bianca Castamela is similarly murdered; she becomes the lover of Ada Reis and when she discovers she is pregnant, they plan to run away together. Bianca, frightened by a storm, refuses to sail, and Ada Reis promises to return to fetch her, which he does but only after three years have elapsed, by which time she is married to another man. In a similar fit of jealousy Ada Reis first strangles then stabs her, taking their child, Fiormonda, with him. It is in this child, a literary descendant of Ford's Castamela, that Lamb invests the theme of misrepresentation of character. But whereas Ford's Castamela does so for comic effect and to teach a salutary lesson, Lamb's Fiormonda does so to satisfy her pride—with disastrous results.

---

[28] *Graham Hamilton*, 60.

[29] *Graham Hamilton*, 63.

Lamb's Fiormonda has been brought up in isolation by her father, Ada Reis, in anticipation of the fulfillment of the prophecy that she will wear an imperial crown. This does come to pass but, in the manner of all Faustian pacts, not quite in the way anticipated; the crown Fiormonda wears is that of the queen of the underworld. Her only companion, as she reaches maturity, is Condulmar, whom she and her father save after he has apparently been shipwrecked. Unbeknown to Fiormonda and her father, Condulmar's father is the Spirit of Darkness who has sent Condulmar to arrange events that will ensure that Fiormonda and her father condemn themselves into his eternal care by playing on their pride and greed. Having managed to get her youthful temper and passions under control, Fiormonda's only weakness is Condulmar, even when she knows that he boasts of his conquest of her virtue and that he abuses her character in public. Fiormonda is not only misrepresented as Condulmar's mistress but is also wrongly held responsible for the death of an attached suitor. Alphonso, the Duke of Montevallos, is believed to have killed himself because of what is perceived as Fiormonda's coldness towards him. The Duke was actually murdered by Condulmar, from whom the Duke wished to rescue Fiormonda. Alphonso, being the only person who recognizes Condulmar's claims about Fiormonda's virtue as fraudulent but does not understand his nature, echoes Glenarvon's assertion that he is not who he appears to be by crying out to Condulmar during their fatal combat, "What are you?"[30] Condulmar's cruelty in misrepresenting Fiormonda as his mistress, his making a mockery of the death of Alphonso, and the mortification that Fiormonda suffered at the hands of women with "high rank but little morality" (100) spur her to avenge herself in the only way that this fickle and shallow society will recognize. Fiormonda sets out to ensure that "their names will be forgotten when mine is celebrated," at the pinnacle of the society that Condulmar dominates and making sure that those that passed "with such insolence of contempt, shall do [her] homage" (122). The ghost of Alphonso warns Fiormonda to renounce all earthly pride in rank and beauty in favor of humility, charity, and faith, but her determination to conquer the social world proves to be her undoing. Up to this point in the narrative Fiormonda has been a pawn in the ambitions of her father; she is held out as matrimonial bait to the highest bidder when Ada Reis deems the prophecy is taking too long to reach fulfillment, and up to this point she is safe from the damnation that is promised to her father, who is urged by the agents of darkness to continue his course of murderous ambition. However, Fiormonda, sick of being misrepresented and misjudged by those she considers beneath her, decides to match those who "have only thought of the world" in terms of social ambition and greedy revenge, thereby supplanting her true nature of compassion and devotion with one that is driven by the worthless opinion of the "sneer[ing] multitude" (113). Fiormonda dares to risk her "fair name" in this

---

[30] Lady Caroline Lamb, *Ada Reis* (1823), in *The Works of Lady Caroline Lamb*, ed. Leigh Wetherall Dickson and Paul Douglass, vol. 3 (London: Pickering and Chatto, 2009), 114. All references to *Ada Reis* are from this edition.

highly judgmental milieu that takes superficial appearances at face value, but she is warned that she is sadly mistaken if she thinks she can "outlive the world's contempt" as it is "too powerful to be ... opposed; too precious its good report to be despised" (113). At the climax of the novel, Fiormonda is condemned to an exclusively aristocratic underworld because of her pride and arrogance, and she finds herself alongside those in positions of power who had perpetrated crimes against their people through greed and selfish neglect. However, there are others who have committed no actual crime. Ada Reis observes a woman whom he did not expect to meet in the infernal regions and asks his guide what sin she is being punished for:

> "You are very much mistaken," said Kabkarra, "if you suppose that that lady has any actual misconduct to answer for:—she has to account for falling under the suspicion of errors that she did not commit, and having lost her character without any reason." "Is that her fault?" said Ada Reis. "That is owing to the censoriousness of the world, the general love of scandal, the envy of rivals, the malice of enemies. ... But, after all, is it a crime?" "One of the greatest that can be committed: it has all the effects of actual guilt; it sets a bad example, and it injures the individual ... because in your world, no one can injure himself without injuring all with whom he is connected, and more particularly those with whom he is the most nearly connected, and whom it is his particular duty to benefit and assist." (178)

It is not only this sense of duty to self and others neglected by this condemned soul that Lamb is concerned with, but also the criteria by which the society that has tried, judged, and condemned her. Although innocent of any wrongdoing, the shade is misrepresented as guilty by a society that is inclined to believe the worst and construct its own reading of her character in light of its own low standards. Lamb's fury at the weight of social judgment and her determination to uncover the endemic inconsistencies and hypocrisies of high Regency culture would have found full expression in a final planned use of a Fordian model.

In July 1823, Lamb wrote a letter to her cousin, the sixth Duke of Devonshire, saying that she was working on a new novel entitled *The Witch of Edmonton*.[31] Although this manuscript can now only be traced through references in her correspondence, it is significant that Lamb planned to make use of another of Ford's plays, which he co-authored with Thomas Dekker and William Rowley. In the preface written for the second edition of *Glenarvon*, also published in 1816, Lamb wrote:

> This work is not the offspring of calm tranquillity, and cool deliberation, it does not bear the marks of such a temper, or of such a situation. It was written under the pressure of affliction, with the feelings of resentment which are excited by

---

[31] Quoted in Susan Normington, *Lady Caroline Lamb: This Infernal Woman* (London: House of Stratus, 2001), 225.

misrepresentation, and in the bitterness of a wounded spirit, which is naturally accompanied by a corresponding bitterness both of thought and expression.[32]

This motive for writing *Glenarvon* explains the close affiliation between Ford's work and Lamb's, and it demonstrates Lamb's empathy for his misunderstood characters, whose course of behavior is dictated by misrepresentation. In *The Witch of Edmonton*, the "witch," Mother Sawyer, lives beyond the physical boundaries of Edmonton and the metaphorical boundaries of acceptable, ordinary society—banished by, and made a scapegoat for, the community:

> MOTHER.
> And why on me? Why should the envious world
> Throw all their scandalous malice upon me?
> 'Cause I am poor, deform'd and ignorant,
> And like a bow buckl'd and bent together
> By some more strong in mischiefs than myself?
> Must I for that be made a common sink
> For all the filth and rubbish of men's tongues
> To fall and run into? Some call me witch,
> And being ignorant of myself, they go
> About to teach me how to be one; urging
> That my bad tongue, by their bad usage made so,
> Forespeaks their cattle, doth bewitch their corn,
> Themselves, their servants, and their babes at nurse.
> This they enforce upon me, and in part
> Make me credit it.[33]

Mother Sawyer seeks the aid of the devil, in the guise of a talking dog, and "becomes" a witch only after she has been misrepresented as such for so long. When questioned directly by the magistrate as to whether she is a witch, Mother Sawyer laughs in his face and replies "Who is not?"[34] alluding to others in Edmonton more deserving of condemnation than herself. Sir Arthur Clarington, the local landowner, has impregnated his servant girl, Winnifride. Clarington dismisses Winnifride from her position and tricks Frank Thorney into thinking the child is his, then urges Frank to marry her. Later, Frank conceals his marriage to Winnifride and enters into a bigamous marriage with Susan Carter, the daughter of a wealthy yeoman, for her money to repair the fortunes of his father. Frank eventually murders Susan as a way out of bigamy and shifts the blame onto previous suitors of Susan, Warbeck and Sommerton. Like Mother Sawyer,

---

[32] Lady Caroline Lamb, *Glenarvon*, 2nd ed., 3 vols. (London: Henry Colburn, 1816), 1:iv.

[33] Thomas Dekker, John Ford, and William Rowley, *The Witch of Edmonton* (London: Methuen, 1983), 2.1.1–15. All references to *The Witch of Edmonton* will be from this edition.

[34] Ibid., 4.1.104.

Lamb was surrounded by those whose own transgressions went unreported to the wider world, and she perhaps recognized the act of scapegoating. To an unnamed correspondent, possibly as early as 1810 and before the scandal with Byron, Lamb wrote: "What is the meaning of right and wrong—all is but appearance—who that looks innocent can be thought guilty—what is guilt—there is no such thing as a conscience ... who shall dare say that I am not good."[35]

Again, in the same year, she wrote to her cousin Hart that she was "pitted all over" with sin, but "many a fair outside covers a blacker heart" and to Lady Holland over the row that erupted over Lamb's brief flirtation with Lady Holland's son by her first marriage, Sir Godfrey Webster:

> [A]s to the gnats [and] mites that dare to peck at me let them look to themselves—I will turn upon them before long with the vengeance which one baited [and] pursued at length is taught to feel [and] level them to the dust from which they sprung—what are these things that dare to speak of me—at best only my equals [and] by what I can find many of them inferior to me in the satiric powers they would stab me with.[36]

Lamb's anger at being vilified by Lady Holland and others whose presence could not be tolerated in "decent" society echoes the fury of Mother Sawyer at having been made a scapegoat for a hypocritical society. In all of Ford's plays it appears that where both men and women are guilty of social and moral transgression, the women are the primary sufferers when deviancy is suspected or discovered: Bianca is murdered, Penthea destroyed by the jealousy of her husband, Mother Sawyer is vilified, scapegoated, and hanged. Likewise, Lamb bore the full brunt of social animosity whereas the misdemeanors of others were treated as a matter of course as long as they remained hidden.

**Contemporary Recognition of Ford: Byron and Mary Shelley**

Whether some of Lamb's intended, or indeed wider, readership recognized her extensive use of Ford is past knowing, but there are two people connected to Lamb that would have done so instantly: Byron and Mary Shelley.[37] Although Lamb did not know Shelley personally, she was connected with Shelley through Byron, through her friendship with Shelley's father, William Godwin, and through her admiration for the works of Shelley's mother, Mary Wollstonecraft. Like Lamb, both Byron and Shelley had familial links with Ford and drew upon Fordian themes in their work. Having led lives marked by sexual scandal and social disjunction, it is perhaps of little wonder that Lamb, Byron, and Shelley were drawn to the most

---

[35] Quoted in Douglass, *Lady Caroline Lamb*, 82.
[36] Quoted in ibid., 97.
[37] I would like to thank Christine Kenyon Jones for sharing her knowledge of Byron's references to Ford.

sexually daring of dramatists, in whose work the difficulty of reconciling sexual and social impulses is most strongly figured. Ford does demonstrate sympathy for lovers who go against the grain of public opinion, whatever the consequences. As Hopkins suggests in her brief discussion of Lamb's use of Ford, the attraction of his works may lie in his "sensitive treatment of those cast outside their social group because of their sexual sins."[38] Significantly, though *'Tis Pity She's a Whore*, a play that examines the incestuous relationship between brother and sister, is possibly Ford's most famous play, Lamb avoids any overt reference to it. It would be reasonable to suggest that this was primarily due to Lamb's close proximity to Byron and Annabella, Byron's wife and Lamb's cousin by marriage, and because of the scandal of Byron's presumed relationship with his half-sister, Augusta. Instead, Lamb refers to Ford's play obliquely: the Fordian phrase "ties of blood" refers to the extended and somewhat incestuous familial and social network of Lady Calantha and Lamb (93). In addition, Lady Calantha has a daughter named Annabella, and, more tellingly, there is a clear hint of incest in the description of Glenarvon's feelings for Calantha being described as "the attachment of a brother to the sister whom he loved" (167).

Byron recognized Ford's innovative exploration of the difficult theme of incest in relation to his own work, *The Bride of Abydos* (1813). In a letter of December 11, 1813 to his friend and fellow writer John Galt, Byron alludes to Ford and *'Tis Pity She's a Whore*:

> I meant to have gone on with the story [of making Selim and Zuleika brother and sister], but on second thoughts, I thought myself two centuries at least too late for the subject; which, though admitting of very powerful feeling and description, yet is not adapted for this age, at least this country, though the finest works of the Greeks, one of Schiller's and Alfieri's in modern times, besides several of our old (and best) dramatists have been grounded on incidents of a similar cast.[39]

A couple of days later, Byron wrote to Professor Edward Daniel Clarke on the subject of the close relationship intended for Zuleika and Selim, this time making a direct reference to Ford:

> It was with this notion that I felt compelled to make my hero and heroine relatives—as you well know that none else could there obtain that degree of intercourse leading to genuine affection—I had nearly made them rather too much akin to each other—& thought the wild passions of the East—& some great examples in Alfieri—Ford—& Schiller (to stop short of Antiquity) might have pleased in favour of a copyist—yet the times and the North ... induced me to alter their consanguinity & confine them to cousinship.[40]

---

[38] Lisa Hopkins, "Mary Shelley, Caroline Lamb and John Ford," unpublished paper.

[39] Lord Byron, *Byron's Letters and Journals*, ed. Leslie Marchand, 12 vols. (London: John Murray, 1974–1982), 3:196.

[40] Ibid., 3:199.

Presumably "the North" refers to Annabella, with whom Byron was corresponding at the time and whose parental home was located at Seaham, on the northeast coast of County Durham. Byron's defense of incest and the almost celebratory recognition of the unflinching attitude of previous ages may be interpreted as an attempt to justify to himself his own relationship with his half-sister Augusta—a relationship that was not yet common knowledge. Augusta gave birth to the baby generally believed to be his, Elizabeth Medora, on April 15, 1814, so the deed would have been committed sometime in the beginning of August 1813, and *The Bride of Abydos* was written in November of the same year. Interestingly, the one woman who did appear to know of the relationship between Byron and Augusta at the time it occurred was Lamb's mother-in-law and Byron's confidante, Lady Melbourne.

Byron refers to Ford once more in his letters, this time in Murray's defense of *Don Juan* in 1819:

> If the poem has poetry—it would stand—if not—fall ... As to the Cant of the day—I despise it—as I have ever done all its other finical fashions,—which become you as paint became the Ancient Britons. If you admit this prudery— you must omit half Aristoso—La Fontaine—Shakespeare—Beaumont— Fletcher—Massinger—Ford—all the Charles the second [sic] writers—in short, Something of most who have written before Pope.[41]

It would appear that Byron, like Lamb, also appreciated Ford's sympathetic position on sexual relationships that were socially taboo and his much more direct approach when discussing them. There is also the possibility that Byron appreciated Ford's interpretation of Robert Burton's heroical love, in that, like Giovanni in *'Tis Pity*, he could interpret his passion for his own sister as a physical condition that he could do not do anything about—a parallel that is suggested in his borrowing of Ford's phrase "the leprosy of lust" in *Marino Faliero* (1821).[42] This image of contagion appears in two of Ford's plays: in *'Tis Pity She's a Whore*, the Friar urges Giovanni to "beg Heaven to cleanse the leprosy of lust / That rots thy soul,"[43] and in *The Fancies, Chaste & Noble*, Livio accuses Castamela as being infected with "a whorish itch ... a leprosie / of raging lust."[44] As leprosy was historically believed to be contagious and sexually transmitted, this image of sexuality that rages like a bodily disease, coupled with the social ostracism experienced by sufferers of the condition, is an apt metaphor for the social ostracism that attended Byron and Augusta, who clearly felt unable to deny their attraction to one another.

---

[41] Ibid., 6:95.

[42] Lord Byron, *Marino Faliero*, in *Byron: Poetical Works*, ed. Frederick Page, rev. John Jump (Oxford: Oxford University Press, 1970), 2.1.315.

[43] John Ford, *'Tis Pity She's a Whore and Other Plays*, ed. Marion Lomax (Oxford: Oxford University Press, 1995), 1.1.74.

[44] *The Fancies*, 4.1.68–9.

Byron's interest in Ford can also be attributed to the fact that Byron's mother, Catherine Gordon of Gight, was descended from the historical heroine of *Perkin Warbeck*, Lady Katherine Gordon. Katherine was the daughter of the Earl of Huntly, and his first wife Annabella Stewart was the daughter of James I of Scotland. Hopkins observes that Byron is known to have had an interest in Richard III, having ordered a copy of Sir George Buc's defense of Richard and having begun a poem on Bosworth.[45] Patricia Brady suggests that this family connection would almost certainly have been known to Byron, who was "inordinately proud of his lineage," which may have been the "possible spark" for Mary Shelley's decision to write a novel based on Warbeck's story.[46] Another "possible spark" for Mary Shelley may have been Shelley's own connection with Ford, also traced by Hopkins: Ford's grandmother was a member of the important Welsh family Stradling of St. Donat's. Whilst Ford was growing up the head of the family would have been Sir Edward Stradling, who was succeeded by Sir John Stradling. Both Sir Edward and Sir John married members of the Gage family from Sussex, and Sir Edward's wife, Agnes, was the granddaughter of Sir John Shelley of Michelgrove.[47] As Brady points out, this kinship network would not have been lost on Mary Shelley, and neither would the subject matter of a play that concentrates upon a code of aristocratic behavior.[48]

Mary Shelley would also have been sensitive to Ford's dramatization of the theme of incest, having been a member of the "league of incest" that was, as William Keach put it, "supposedly flourishing in the summer of 1816 on the shores of Lake Geneva" between Shelley, Percy Shelley, Byron, and Shelley's step-sister and Byron's lover, Claire Clairmont.[49] Unlike Byron and Lamb, Shelley avoids all mention of such a scandalous period of her life in an attempt to secure financial stability for herself and her son. Mary Shelley's debt to Ford is immediately apparent in her novel, *The Fortunes of Perkin Warbeck*. While Shelley's choice of subject matter could be interpreted as ancestral flattery towards her father-in-law, her novel also takes up Ford's theme of innate nobility lacking in the behavior of the parsimonious Sir Timothy, who kept Shelley and her son in a ruthless stranglehold of financial dependence. In trying to make a new and respectable life for herself and her son, Shelley's choice of an historical theme could not be construed as cause for offense, but perhaps she chose this particular history because of its illustration of an ideal, not only of nobility but also a marriage. Shelley's retelling of *Perkin Warbeck* adheres to Ford's play in that a convincing

---

[45] Hopkins, "Mary Shelley, Caroline Lamb and John Ford."

[46] Patricia Brady, "Mary Shelley's *Perkin Warbeck* and Lord Byron," *The Ricardian* 9 (1991): 173.

[47] Hopkins, "Mary Shelley, Caroline Lamb and John Ford."

[48] Brady, "Mary Shelley's *Perkin Warbeck*," 173.

[49] William Keach, "Early Shelley: Vulgarisms, Politics, and Fractals," *Romantic Circles, Praxis Series*, ed. Orrin N. C. Wang (August 1997), http://www.rc.umd.edu/praxis/earlyshelley/keach/keach.html (accessed October 26, 2009).

confession of imposture is conspicuous by its absence, and she consistently refers to her protagonist as Richard rather than Perkin, thereby reinforcing his claims of legitimacy. When he apparently does publicly confess to Katherine, in front of a crowd, it is unconvincing as he is chained in an "instrument of disgrace"; his confession is clearly made under the duress of physical suffering.[50] Certainly, Katherine gives no credence to the confession and urges that he "recal the false words wrung from his agony."[51] Shelley takes Ford's cue in omitting the later life of Katherine, who not only married a further three times but also accepted a pension from her husband's executioner, Henry VII; Shelley merely presents Katherine as the perpetually grieving widow. Shelley's representation of Katherine's devotion to Richard after his death is emblematic of Shelley's devotion to the memory of Percy Shelley, again possibly for the benefit of Sir Timothy. The close bond between Katherine and those that were close to Richard, in particular his sister Elizabeth of York, Queen of England, is reminiscent of Shelley's attachment to those that knew her husband, in particular Jane Williams, whose husband drowned alongside Percy Shelley. Katherine, speaking of the Queen, talks of how "they wept together – how long and how bitterly – the loss of our loved one,"[52] two women united in grief for the same object in same way that Shelley and Jane were for the same tragic accident, although this relationship would eventually sour.[53]

In the conclusion of *The Fortunes of Perkin Warbeck* there is a suggestion of time moving on and of the inevitability of recovery—a suggestion that Shelley repeats in *Lodore* eight years later. Shelley's opening line in the last chapter of *The Fortunes of Perkin Warbeck* is imbued with the bitterness of what Hopkins calls the "grief of the survivor":[54]

> Time, we are told by all philosophers, is the sole medicine for grief. Yet there are immortal regrets which must endure while we exist. Those who have met one, with whose every feeling and thought their thoughts and feelings were entwined, who knew no divided past, nor could imagine a solitary futurity, to them what balm can time bring?[55]

This is a statement of suffering that speaks for both Shelley and Katherine and appears to be insurmountable. Shelley then gives Katherine a speech that confirms that while she does not cease to grieve she is also "human ... whose weakness it

---

[50] Mary Shelley, *The Fortunes of Perkin Warbeck*, in *The Novels and Selected Works of Mary Shelley*, ed. D. D. Fischer (London: Pickering Masters, 1996), 366–7.

[51] Ibid., 367.

[52] Ibid., 399.

[53] Miranda Seymour, *Mary Shelley* (London: John Murray, 2000), 323–4.

[54] Lisa Hopkins, "The Self and The Monstrous: *The Fortunes of Perkin Warbeck*," in *Iconoclastic Departures: Mary Shelley After "Frankenstein*," ed. Syndy Conger, Frederick Frank, and Gregory O'Dea (Madison, NJ: Fairleigh Dickinson University Press, 1997), 271.

[55] Shelley, *The Fortunes of Perkin Warbeck*, 395.

is, too eagerly, and too fondly, to seek objects on whom to expend [the heart's] yearnings."[56] Katherine then refers to her doting upon Elizabeth's children as Shelley doted on her own son, but there is also a suggestion here of Shelley's own humanity and thoughts of remarriage that finds expression in *Lodore*.

## Conclusion: Ford's Offer of a Safe Haven

The frontispiece of all three volumes of *Lodore* has an epigraph from Ford's *The Lover's Melancholy*:

> In the turmoil of our lives,
> Men are like politic states, or troubled seas,
> Tossed up and down with several storms and tempests,
> Change and variety of wrecks and fortunes;
> Till, labouring to the havens of our homes,
> We struggle for the calm that crowns our ends.[57]

It is this struggle for calmness after a turbulent voyage through life that is echoed at the end of the novel, again concluding with an epigraph from Ford's last play, *The Lady's Trial* (1638), by way of introducing the conclusion of the novel:

> None, I trust,
> Repines at these delights, they are free and harmless:
> After distress at sea, the dangers o'er,
> Safety and welcomes better taste ashore.[58]

Cornelia Lodore does indeed find a calm happiness in the reunion with her daughter and in her second marriage to Horatio Saville, after a lifetime of subservience to her domineering mother, her unsuccessful marriage to Lord Lodore, and what she believed to be an enforced separation from her only child. One cannot help but wonder if Shelley, after her own unconventional childhood; elopement; marriage; successive losses of mother, children, and husband; and the trials of Sir Timothy, also wished to find respite. Shelley, like Lamb, appreciates Ford's sensitivity towards human needs and desires, unconventional or otherwise, that are met with social ostracization. There is one final parallel between Shelley and Lamb that arises in this context, although not strictly relating to Ford. As Hopkins has already commented, in *The Fortunes of Perkin Warbeck* Shelley introduces a character who does not appear in Ford's version—that of Jane Shore, who is cast by Shelley as the antithetical fallen and repentant woman to Katherine Gordon's virtuous

---

[56] Ibid., 399.
[57] John Ford, *The Lover's Melancholy*, in *'Tis Pity*, ed. Lomax, 5.1.4–9.
[58] Mary Shelley, *Lodore*, in *The Novels and Selected Works of Mary Shelley*, ed. Nora Crook, Pamela Clemit, and Betty T. Bennett (London: Pickering Masters), 311.

wife.[59] Jane Shore was the historical mistress of Edward IV, whom she powerfully influenced with her beauty and wit. Richard III accused her of sorcery, imprisoned her and made her do public penance. Shelley's inclusion of Jane Shore possibly alludes to her own earlier status as mistress to a married man and to the fact she was humbled to the status of a penitent by Sir Timothy. Lamb's public penance is well known, and she writes of her position to Lady Morgan that she "might have died by a diamond" but will now do so "by a brickbat," but takes comfort in William being to her "what Shore was to Jane Shore,"[60] the implication being that not only was William complicit with Lamb's affair with Byron, but that he also stood by her side when all others had abandoned her to her fate.

Shelley, like Lamb, draws upon Ford for not only his covert criticism of aristocratic behavior but also for his expression of the ideal in matrimony. Lamb casts her husband William as the "contracted lord" to her Lady Calantha, who realizes only too late that he had stood by her throughout her adultery and was the ideal to begin with. Similarly, if Shelley appears in her retelling of *Perkin Warbeck* as Katherine, then Percy Shelley is represented as the idealistic Warbeck whose conviction in himself never falters, even though it places him at odds with his autocratic father. Ford's work also offered Lamb and Shelley a model for the sensitive treatment of unconventional love and the critique of social ostracism, particularly in the case of women. These were topics that both Lamb and Shelley had personal experience of as women and that they expressed by drawing upon Ford as writers.

---

[59] Hopkins, "Mary Shelley, Caroline Lamb and John Ford."

[60] Lady Sydney Morgan, *Lady Morgan's Memoirs: Autobiography, Diaries and Correspondence*, 3 vols. (Leipzig: Tauchnitz, 1863), 2:334.

# Bibliography

**Printed Primary Sources**

Aikin, Dr. John, *An Essay on the Application of Natural History to Poetry* (London: Warrington, 1777).
Allen, Charles, *A New and Improved History of England ... Designed for the Use of Schools* (London, 1793).
*An alphabetical catalogue of plates ... which compose the stock of John and Josiah Boydell, engravers and printsellers, No. 90, Cheapside, and at the Shakespeare Gallery, Pall Mall; preceded by an account of various works, sets of prints, galleries, &c forming a great part of the same stock* (London, 1803).
Ashburton, Charles Alfred, *A New and Complete History of England...* (London, 1795).
Austen, Jane, *Mansfield Park*, in *The Novels of Jane Austen*, ed. R. W. Chapman, vol. 3 (London: Oxford University Press, 1933).
Baillie, Joanna, *The Dramatic and Poetical Works of Joanna Baillie* (London: Longman, Brown, Green, and Longman, 1851).
Barbier, Jules, and Michel Carré, "Hamlet," libretto, trans. Avril Bardoni, in Ambroise Thomas, *Hamlet*, Antonio de Almeida, London Philharmonic Orchestra, EMI CDS 7 54820 2.
Boaden, James, *The Life of Mrs Jordan* (London, 1831).
———, *The Private Correspondence of David Garrick: with the Most Celebrated Persons of his Time* (1831).
———, *Memoirs of Mrs. Siddons* (Philadelphia: J. B. Lippincott Co., 1893 [1827]).
———, *Memoirs of the Life of John Philip Kemble* (2 vols, New York: Benjamin Blom, 1969 [1825]).
———, *The Plays of James Boaden*, ed. Steve Cohan (New York: Garland, 1980).
Boye, Caspar Johannes, *William Shakespeare* (Copenhagen, 1826).
Byron, Lord, *Byron: Poetical Works*, ed. Frederick Page, rev. John Jump (Oxford: Oxford University Press, 1970).
———, *Byron's Letters and Journals*, ed. Leslie Marchand (12 vols, London: John Murray, 1974–82).
Capell, Edward (ed.), *Mr William Shakespeare, his Comedies, Histories, and Tragedies* (10 vols, London, 1768).
*A Catalogue of that Magnificent and Truly Valuable collection of Pictures, (with the Prices they sold for, and Names of the Purchasers,) ... known as the collection of the Shakspeare Gallery ...* (London: T. Beckett, [1805]).
*A Catalogue of the Pictures in the Shakespeare Gallery, Pall-Mall* (London, 1789).
Chalmers, George, *Apology for the Believers in the Shakspeare-Papers, which were Exhibited in Norfolk-Street* (London, 1797).

Cole, John William, *The Life and Theatrical Times of Charles Kean, F.S.A.* (2 vols, London: Richard Bentley, 1859).
Coleridge, Samuel Taylor, *The Complete Works of Samuel Taylor Coleridge*, ed. W.G.T. Shedd (7 vols, New York: Harper & Brothers, 1853).
———, *The Table Talk and Omniana of Samuel Taylor Coleridge*, ed. T. Ashe (London: G. Bell and Sons, 1888).
———, *The Collected Letters of Samuel Taylor Coleridge*, ed. Earl Leslie Griggs (6 vols, Oxford: Clarendon Press, 1956–71).
———, *The Collected Works of Samuel Taylor Coleridge, Volume 4: The Friend*, ed. Barbara E. Rooke (2 vols, Princeton, NJ: Princeton University Press, 1969).
———, *The Collected Works of Samuel Taylor Coleridge, Volume 6: Lay Sermons*, ed. Reginald James White (Princeton, NJ: Princeton University Press, 1972).
———, *The Collected Works of Samuel Taylor Coleridge, Volume 7: Biographia Literaria*, ed. James Engell and W. Jackson Bate (2 vols, Princeton, NJ: Princeton University Press, 1983).
———, *Table Talk*, ed. Carl Woodring (2 vols, Princeton, NJ: Princeton University Press, 1990).
———, *The Collected Works of Samuel Taylor Coleridge, Volume 16: Poetical Works: Part 3, Plays*, ed. James C. C. Mays (2 vols, Princeton, NJ: Princeton University Press, 2001).
Craig, Edward Gordon, *On the Art of the Theatre* (London: W. Heinemann, 1912).
———, *Index to the Story of My Days: Some Memoirs of Edward Gordon Craig 1872–1907*, intro. Peter Holland (Cambridge: Cambridge University Press, 1981).
Davies, Thomas, *Memoirs of the Life of David Garrick* (2 vols, London, 1780).
———, *Dramatic Micellanies* [sic]: *consisting of critical observations on several plays of Shakespeare: with a review of his principal characters* (3 vols, London, 1783–84).
Dekker, Thomas, John Ford, and William Rowley, *The Witch of Edmonton* (London: Methuen, 1983).
De Quincey, Thomas, *The Works of Thomas De Quincey*, ed. Grevel Lindop et al. (21 vols, London: Pickering and Chatto, 2000–2003).
Dickinson, Emily. *The Poems of Emily Dickinson: Variorum Edition*, ed. Ralph W. Franklin (Cambridge, MA: Harvard University Press, 1983).
Dodd, William, *Beauties of Shakespeare* (New York: Augustus M. Kelley, 1971 [1752]).
Drake, Nathan, *Shakspeare and his Times* (2 vols, London, 1817).
Dryden, John, *Essays*, ed. W.P. Ker (2 vols, Oxford: Clarendon Press, 1900).
———, *The Poems and Fables of John Dryden*, ed. James Kinsley (London: Oxford University Press, 1962).
*The Exhibition of the Shakspeare gallery, Pall-Mall, being the last time the pictures can ever be seen as an entire collection* (London: W. Bulmer and Co., 1805).
Fane, Violet, *Collected Verses by Violet Fane* (London: Smith, Elder & Co., 1880).
Farington, Joseph, *Diary*, ed. Kenneth Garlick and Angus Macintyre (6 vols, New Haven, CT: Yale University Press, 1979).

Ford, John, *The Fancies, Chaste and Noble*, ed. Dominick J. Hart (New York: Garland, 1985).

———, *'Tis Pity She's a Whore and Other Plays*, ed. Marion Lomax, (Oxford: Oxford University Press, 1995).

Franceschina, John (ed.), *Sisters of Gore: Seven Gothic Melodramas by British Women, 1790–1843* (New York: Garland, 1997).

Genest, John, *Some Account of the English Stage from the Restoration in 1660 to 1830* (10 vols, Bath, UK: H. E. Carrington, 1832).

Gentleman, Francis (ed.), *Bell's Edition of Shakespeare's Plays*, 1773 (8 vols, London: Cornmarket, 1969).

Goethe, J.W. von, *Wilhelm Meister's Apprenticeship*, trans. E.A. Blackall (New York: Suhrkamp, 1989).

Goldsmith, Oliver, *An History of England, in a series of letters from a Nobleman to his Son*, vol. 1 (London, 1783).

*Hamlet ... arranged for representation at the Princess's Theatre with explanatory notes by Charles Kean ... ; as performed on Monday, January, 1859* (London: John K. Chapman and Co., 1859).

*Hamlet, Prince of Denmark ... Altered from Shakspeare, by J.P. Kemble* (London: C. Lowndes, 1796).

*Hamlet, Prince of Denmark: A Tragedy. As it is now acted at the Theatres Royal, in Drury-Lane, and Covent-Garden* (London: Hawes and Co., 1763).

Hazlitt, William, *The Collected Works of William Hazlitt*, ed. A.R. Waller and Arnold Glover (12 vols, London: J.M. Dent & Co., 1903).

———, *The Complete Works of William Hazlitt*, ed. P.P. Howe (21 vols, London: Dent, 1930–34).

———, *Characters of Shakespeare's Plays* (London: Oxford University Press, 1966 [1916]).

———, Preface to "Characters of Shakespear's Plays," in Jonathan Bate (ed.), *The Romantics on Shakespeare* (New York: Penguin Books, 1992 [1817]).

———, "On Siddons, Kemble, and Kean," in Jonathan Bate (ed.), *The Romantics on Shakespeare* (New York: Penguin Books, 1992 [1816–20]).

———, *The Selected Writings of William Hazlitt*, ed. Duncan Wu (9 vols, London: Pickering and Chatto, 1998).

Hegel, G.W.F., *Phenomenology of Spirit*, trans. A.V. Miller (Oxford: Oxford University Press, 1977).

Highfill Jr., Philip H., Kalman A. Burnim, and Edward A. Langhans (eds), *A Biographical Dictionary of Actors, Actresses, Musicians, Dancers, Managers and Other Stage Personnel in London, 1660–1800*, vol. 14 (Carbondale: Southern Illinois University Press, 1991).

Hume, David, "Of Miracles," in Eric Steinberg (ed.), *An Enquiry Concerning Human Understanding: A Letter from a Gentleman to his Friend in Edinburgh* (Indianapolis, IN: Hackett, 1977).

Ireland, Samuel, *Picturesque Views on the Upper, or Warwickshire Avon* (London, 1795).

J. T., "An Essay on the English Sonnet; illustrated by a Comparison between the Sonnets of Milton and those of Charlotte Smith," *Universal Magazine* 91 (1792): 408–14.

Johnson, Samuel, *Johnson on Shakespeare*, ed. Walter Ralegh (Oxford: Oxford University Press, 1908).

———, *Johnson on Shakespeare*, ed. R.W. Desai (Oxford: Oxford University Press, 1929).

———, Dedication to *Shakespear Illustrated* by Charlotte Lennox, in W. K. Wimsatt, Jr. (ed.), *Samuel Johnson on Shakespeare* (New York: Hill and Wang, 1965 [1753]).

———, "Notes on Shakespeare's Plays," in Arthur Sherbo (ed.), *Johnson on Shakespeare*, vol. 7 (New Haven, CT: Yale University Press, 1968).

———, "The Plays of William Shakespeare," in Donald Greene (ed.), *Samuel Johnson* (New York: Oxford University Press, 1984 [1765]).

———, *Samuel Johnson on Shakespeare*, ed. H.R. Woudhuysen (Harmondsworth, UK: Penguin, 1989).

Kant, Immanuel, *Critique of the Power of Judgment*, ed. Paul Guyer, trans. Paul Guyer and Eric Matthews (Cambridge: Cambridge University Press, 2000).

Keats, John, *The Letters of John Keats 1814–1821*, ed. Hyder E. Rollins (2 vols, Cambridge, MA: Harvard University Press, 1958).

———, *Letters of John Keats: A Selection*, ed. Robert Gittings (Oxford: Oxford University Press, 1970).

———, "Mr Kean," in Jonathan Bate (ed.), *The Romantics on Shakespeare* (New York: Penguin Books, 1992 [1817]).

Lamb, Charles, "On the Tragedies of Shakspeare, Considered with Reference to their Fitness for Stage Representation," in Jonathan Bate (ed.), *The Romantics on Shakespeare* (New York: Penguin Books, 1992 [1811]).

Lamb, Charles, and Mary Lamb, *The Works of Charles and Mary Lamb*, ed. E.V. Lucas (7 vols, London: Methuen, 1903).

Lamb, Lady Caroline, *Glenarvon,* 2nd ed. (3 vols, London: Henry Colburn, 1816).

———, *Glenarvon*, ed. Frances Wilson (London: Everyman, 1995).

———, *The Works of Lady Caroline Lamb*, ed. Leigh Wetherall Dickson and Paul Douglass (London: Pickering and Chatto, 2009).

Landor, Waltor Savage, *The Complete Works of Walter Savage Landor*, ed. T. Earle Welby and Stephen Wheeler (16 vols, London: Chapman and Hall, 1927–36).

Lennox, Charlotte, *Shakespear Illustrated: or the Novels and Histories, on which the Plays of Shakspear are Founded* (3 vols, London, 1753–54).

Malone, Edmond, ed., *The Plays and Poems of William Shakespeare* (10 vols, London, 1790).

Milton, John, *Complete Shorter Poems*, ed. John Carey, 2nd ed. (London: Longman, 1997).

———, *Paradise Lost*, ed. Alastair Fowler, 2nd ed. (London: Longman, 1998).

Morgan, Lady Sydney, *Lady Morgan's Memoirs: Autobiography, Diaries and Correspondence* (3 vols, Leipzig: Tauchnitz, 1863).

Polwhele, Richard, *The Unsex'd Females: A Poem*, 1798, ed. Gina Luria (New York: Garland, 1974).
Pope, Alexander, ed., *The Works of Shakespear* (6 vols, London, 1723–25).
Radcliffe, Ann, *The Romance of the Forest* (London: Hookman and Carpenter, 1792).
———, *The Romance of the Forest*, ed. Chloe Chard (Oxford: Oxford University Press, 1999).
———, "On the Supernatural in Poetry," in Rictor Norton (ed.), *Gothic Readings: The First Wave, 1764–1840* (New York: Leicester University Press, 2006).
Repton, Humphrey, *The Bee; or a Companion to the Shakespeare Gallery* (London: T. Cadell, [1789]).
Robinson, Mary, *The Poetical Works*, ed. Caroline Franklin (3 vols, London: Routledge, 1996 [1806]).
Rowe, Nicholas, ed., *The Works of Mr. William Shakespear* (6 vols, London, 1709).
Russell, William, *The Tragic Muse: A Poem Addressed to Mrs. Siddons* (London: G. Kearsley, 1783).
Schlegel, A. W. von, *Lectures on Dramatic Art and Literature* (1808–11), in Jonathan Bate (ed.), *The Romantics on Shakespeare* (London: Penguin, 1992[1801–11]).
Scott, Sir Walter, *The Miscellaneous Prose Works of Sir Walter Scott, Bart.*, vol. 1 (Edinburgh: Cadell, 1847).
———, *Kenilworth*, ed. J.H. Alexander (Edinburgh: Edinburgh University Press, 1993).
Shakespeare, William, *The Riverside Shakespeare*, ed. Gwynne Blakemore Evans (Boston: Houghton Mifflin, 1974).
———, *King Lear*, ed. R. A. Foakes (Walton-on-Thames, UK: Thomas Nelson and Sons, 1997).
———, *The Norton Shakespeare*, ed. Stephen Greenblatt et al. (New York: W.W. Norton, 1997).
———, *Hamlet*, ed. Philip Edwards (Cambridge: Cambridge University Press, 2003).
———, *Pericles*, ed. Suzanne Gossett (London: Thomson, 2004).
———, *Hamlet*, ed. Ann Thompson and Neil Taylor (London: Arden, 2006).
———, *Hamlet: The Texts of 1603 and 1623*, ed. Ann Thompson and Neil Taylor (London: Arden, 2007).
*The Shakespeare Gallery: A Reproduction in Commemoration of the Tercentenary Anniversary of the Poet's Death* (London: L. Booth, 1864).
*Shakspeare. Mr. Alderman Boydell, Josiah Boydell, and George Nicol, propose to publish by Subscription a most Magnificent and accurate edition of the Plays of Shakspeare, in Eight volumes ...* (London, 1786).
Shattuck, Charles H. (ed.), *John Philip Kemble Promptbooks* (11 vols, Charlottesville: University of Virginia Press, 1974).
Shelley, Mary, *The Novels and Selected Works of Mary Shelley*, ed. Nora Crook, Pamela Clemit, and Betty T. Bennett (London: Pickering Masters, 1996).

Siddons, Sarah, *The Reminiscences of Sarah Kemble Siddons 1773–1785*, ed. William van Lennep (Cambridge: Widener Library, 1942).
Smith, Charlotte, *Montalbert: A Novel* (London: Sampson Low, 1795).
———, *The Poems of Charlotte Smith*, ed. Stuart Curran (New York: Oxford University Press, 1993).
———, *The Collected Letters of Charlotte Smith*, ed. Judith Phillips Stanton (Bloomington: Indiana University Press, 2003).
Somerset, Charles A., *Shakspeare's Early Days* (London, n.d., ca. 1829).
Swinburne, Algernon Charles, *A Study of Shakespeare* (London, 1880).
Terry, Ellen, *The Story of My Life: Recollections and Reflections* (New York: McClure, 1908).
Theobald, Lewis, *Shakespeare restored ... ever yet publish'd* (London: R. Francklin et al., 1726).
*This Day are published, price £5. 5s. By J. and J. Boydell, No. 90, Cheapside, and at the Shakespeare Gallery, Pall Mall, Seven prints from the celebrated Seven Ages of Shakespeare, painted by R. Smirke, Esq. R. A. and engraved by Messrs. Thew, Simon, Ogborne, Tomkins, and Leney* (London: W. Bulmer, 1801).
Thomas, Ambroise, *Hamlet*, vocal score, ed. M. Vauthrot (Paris: Heugel, c. 1868)
*The Tragedy of Hamlet ... As it is now Acted at his Highness the Duke of York's Theatre* (London: Andrew Clark, 1676).
Wheler, R.B., "Shakspeare's Marriage License Bond," *Gentleman's Magazine*, 109 (1836): 266–8.
Williams, Helen Maria, *Letters Written in France, In the Summer of 1790, to a Friend in England, Containing Various Anecdotes Relative to the French Revolution*, ed. Neil Fraistat and Susan L. Lanser (Peterborough, ON: Broadview, 2001).
Wordsworth, William, *The Poetical Works of William Wordsworth*, vol. 4, ed. Ernest de Selincourt and Helen Darbishire (Oxford: Clarendon, 1947).
———, *The Prelude: The Four Texts (1798, 1799, 1805, 1850)*, ed. Jonathan Wordsworth (Harmondsworth, UK: Penguin, 1995).
———, *The Major Works*, ed. Stephen Gill, rev. ed. (Oxford: Oxford University Press, 2000).
*The Works of Shakspeare ... With a Biographical Memoir ... By W. Harvey, Esq.* (London, 1825).

## Secondary Sources

Abbate, Carolyn, "Opera; or the Envoicing of Women," in Ruth A. Solie (ed.), *Musicology and Difference: Gender and Sexuality in Music Scholarship* (Berkeley: University of California Press, 1993).
Abrams, M.H., *The Mirror and the Lamp: Romantic Theory and the Critical Tradition* (New York: Oxford University Press, 1953).
———, *Natural Supernaturalism* (New York: W. W. Norton, 1971).

Achter, Morton Jay, "Félicien David, Ambroise Thomas, and French *Opéra Lyrique*" (PhD diss., University of Michigan, 1972).
Alpers, Paul, *What Is Pastoral?* (Chicago: University of Chicago Press, 1996).
Altick, Richard, *Paintings from Books* (Columbus: Ohio State University Press, 1985).
Archer, William, "Masks or Faces?", in *The Paradox of Acting by Denis Diderot and Masks or Faces? by William Archer* (New York: Hill and Wang, 1957).
Arthurson, Ian, *The Perkin Warbeck Conspiracy 1491–1499* (Stroud, UK: Sutton, 1997).
Austin, J. L., *How to Do Things with Words* (Oxford: Clarendon Press, 1962).
Babcock, Robert Witbeck, *The Genesis of Shakespeare Idolatry 1766–1799* (Chapel Hill: University of North Carolina Press, 1931).
Bailey, Helen Phelps, *Hamlet in France: From Voltaire to Laforgue* (Geneva: Librairie Droz, 1964).
Bainbridge, Simon, *Napoleon and English Romanticism* (Cambridge: Cambridge University Press, 1995).
Barber, C. L., *Shakespeare's Festive Comedy* (Princeton, NJ: Princeton University Press, 1959).
Barnard, T., *A New Anatomy of Ireland: The Irish Protestants 1649–1770* (New Haven, CT: Yale University Press, 2003).
Barthes, Roland, *S/Z*, trans. Richard Miller (London: Jonathan Cape, 1975).
Bartholomeusz, Dennis, *"The Winter's Tale" in Performance in England and America 1611–1976* (Cambridge: Cambridge University Press, 1982).
Barton, Anne, "Byron and Shakespeare," in Drummond Bone (ed.), *The Cambridge Companion to Byron* (Cambridge: Cambridge University Press, 2004).
Barzun, Jacques, *Berlioz and His Century: An Introduction to the Age of Romanticism* (New York: Meridian Books, 1956).
Bate, Jonathan, "Shakespearean Allusion in English Caricature in the Age of Gillray," *Journal of the Warburg and Courtauld Institutes*, 49 (1968): 196–210.
———, *Shakespeare and the English Romantic Imagination* (Oxford: Clarendon, 1986).
———, *Shakespearean Constitutions: Politics, Theatre, Criticism 1730–1830* (Oxford: Oxford University Press, 1989).
———, "The Politics of Romantic Shakespearean Criticism: Germany, England, France," *European Romantic Review*, 1, no. 1 (1990): 1–26.
——— (ed.), *The Romantics on Shakespeare* (London: Penguin, 1992).
———, *The Genius of Shakespeare* (London: Picador, 1997).
———, Review of "A Man for All Ages," Books Section, *The Guardian*, April 14, 2007.
Battersby, Christine, *Gender and Genius: Towards a Feminist Aesthetics* (Bloomington: Indiana University Press, 1990).
Beer, John Bernard, "Coleridge's Originality as a Critic of Shakespeare," *Studies in the Literary Imagination*, 2 (1986): 51–69.

Bennett, Andrew, "Expressivity: The Romantic Theory of Authorship," in Patricia Waugh (ed.), *Literary Theory and Criticism: An Oxford Guide* (Oxford: Oxford University Press, 2006).

Bennett, Paula, "'The Orient is in the West': Emily Dickinson's Reading of *Antony and Cleopatra*," in Marianne Novy (ed.), *Women's Re-Visions of Shakespeare* (Urbana: University of Illinois Press, 1990).

Bennett, Susan, "Decomposing History (Why Are There So Few Women in Theater History?)," in W. B. Worthen and Peter Holland (eds), *Theorizing Practice: Redefining Theatre History* (New York: Palgrave Macmillan, 2003).

Berkoff, Steven, *I Am Hamlet* (London: Faber and Faber, 1989).

Bernstein, Jane A., "'Bewitched, Bothered and Bewildered': Lady Macbeth, Sleepwalking, and the Demonic in Verdi's Scottish Opera," *Cambridge Opera Journal*, 14 (2002): 31–46.

Bewell, Alan, *Wordsworth and the Enlightenment: Nature, Man, and Society in the Experimental Poetry* (New Haven, CT: Yale University Press, 1989).

Binns, J. W., "Some Lectures on Shakespeare in Eighteenth-Century Oxford: The *Praelectiones poeticae* of William Hawkins," in Bernhard Fabian and Kurt Tezeli von Rosador (eds), *Shakespeare: Text, Language, Criticism. Essays in Honour of Marvin Spevack* (New York: Olms-Weidmann, 1987)

Bishop, T.G., *Shakespeare and the Theatre of Wonder* (Cambridge: Cambridge University Press, 1996).

Bloom, Harold, *Shakespeare: The Invention of the Human* (New York: Riverhead, 1998).

Bossy, John, *The English Catholic Community, 1570–1850* (New York: Oxford University Press, 1976).

Bradley, A.C., *Shakespearean Tragedy*, 4th ed. (Basingstoke, UK: Palgrave, 2007).

Branam, George C., *Eighteenth-Century Adaptations of Shakespearean Tragedy* (Berkeley: University of California Press, 1956).

Bronfen, Elizabeth, "Hysteria, Phantasy and the Family Romance: Ann Radcliffe's *Romance of the Forest*," *Women's Writing*, 1, no. 2 (1994): 171–80.

Brooks, Douglas, *From Playhouse to Printing House: Drama and Authorship in Early Modern England* (Cambridge: Cambridge University Press, 2000).

Brown, Sarah Annes, "'There Is No End but Addition': The Later Reception of Shakespeare's Classicism," in Charles Martindale and A. B. Taylor (eds), *Shakespeare and the Classics* (Cambridge: Cambridge University Press, 2004).

Bruntjen, Sven H.A., *John Boydell, 1719–1804: A Study of Art Patronage and Publishing in Georgian London* (New York: Garland, 1985).

Bundy, Frank J., *The Administration of the Illyrian Provinces of the French Empire, 1809–1813* (New York: Garland, 1987).

Burton, Robert, *The Anatomy of Melancholy*, ed. Thomas C. Faulkner, Nicholas K. Kiessling, and Rhonda L. Blair (Oxford: Clarendon, 1989).

Burwick, Frederick, and Thomas Pape (eds), *The Boydell Shakespeare Gallery* (Bottrop, Germany: Peter Pomp, 1996).

Capps, Jack L., *Emily Dickinson's Reading: 1836–1886* (Cambridge, MA: Harvard University Press, 1966).

Carhart, Margaret, *The Life and Work of Joanna Baillie* (New Haven, CT: Yale University Press, 1923).
Carlson, Julie A., "An Active Imagination: Coleridge and the Politics of Dramatic Reform," *Modern Philology*, 1 (1988): 22–33.
———, "Command Performances: Burke, Coleridge, and Schiller's Dramatic Reflections on the Revolution in France," *The Wordsworth Circle*, 23 (1992): 117–34.
———, *In the Theatre of Romanticism: Cambridge, Nationalism, Women* (Cambridge: Cambridge University Press, 1994).
———, "Remaking Love: Remorse in the Theatre of Baillie and Inchbald," in Catherine Burroughs (ed.), *Women in British Romantic Theatre: Drama, Performance, and Society, 1790–1840* (Cambridge: Cambridge University Press, 2000).
Carlson, Marvin, "Elizabeth Inchbald: A Woman Critic in Her Theatrical Culture," in Catherine Burroughs (ed.), *Women in British Romantic Theatre: Drama, Performance, and Society, 1790–1840* (Cambridge: Cambridge University Press, 2000).
Carney, Sean, "The Passion of Joanna Baillie: Playwright as Martyr," *Theatre Journal*, 52 (2000): 227–52.
Carson, Julie A., *In the Theatre of Romanticism: Cambridge, Nationalism, Women* (Cambridge: Cambridge University Press, 1994).
———, "Remaking Love: Remorse in the Theatre of Baillie and Inchbald," in Catherine Burroughs (ed.), *Women in British Romantic Theatre: Drama, Performance, and Society, 1790–1840* (Cambridge: Cambridge University Press, 2000).
Castle, Terry, *The Female Thermometer: Eighteenth-Century Culture and the Invention of the Uncanny* (Oxford: Oxford University Press, 1995).
Chambers, E. K., *William Shakespeare: A Study of Facts and Problems*, vol. 2 (Oxford: Clarendon Press, 1930).
Chandler, David, "Lamb, *Falstaff's Letters*, and Landor's *Citation and Examination of William Shakspeare*," *Charles Lamb Bulletin*, n.s. 131 (2005): 76–85.
Charlton, David, "Opera: 1850–1890. (b) France," in *The Oxford History of Music*, ed. Gerald Abraham (London: Oxford University Press, 1990), 9:366.
Clausen, Christoph, "Shakespeare in Opera," in Stefani Brusberg-Kiermeier and Jörg Helbig (eds), *Sh@kespeare in the Media: From the Globe to the WorldWide Web* (Frankfurt am Main: Peter Lang, 2004).
———, *Macbeth Multiplied: Negotiating Historical and Medial Difference between Shakespeare and Verdi* (Amsterdam: Rodopi, 2005).
Clément, Catherine, and Julie Kristeva. *The Feminine and the Sacred*, trans. Jane Marie Todd (New York: Columbia University Press, 2001).
Clery, Emma, *The Rise of Supernatural Fiction, 1762–1800* (Cambridge: Cambridge University Press, 1995).
———, *Women's Gothic: From Clara Reeve to Mary Shelley* (Hordon, UK: Northcote House, 2000).

Coates, J.D., "Coleridge's Debt to Harrington: A Discussion of *Zapolya*," *Journal of the History of Ideas*, 3 (1977): 501–8.

Colòn, Christine, "Christianity and Colonial Discourses in Joanna Baillie's *The Bride*," in *Renascence: Essays on Values in Literature*, 54, no. 3 (2002): 163–76.

Comment, Kristin M., "Dickinson's Bawdy: Shakespeare and Sexual Symbolism in Emily Dickinson's Writing to Susan Dickinson," *Legacy*, 18, no. 2 (2001): 167–81.

Cox, Jeffrey N., "Baillie, Siddons, Larpent: Gender, Power, and Politics in the Theatre of Romanticism," in Catherine Burroughs (ed.), *Women in British Romantic Theatre: Drama, Performance, and Society, 1790–1840* (Cambridge: Cambridge University Press, 2000).

Cox, Jeffrey, and Michael Gamer (eds), *The Broadview Anthology of Romantic Drama* (Peterborough, ON: Broadview, 2003).

Curran, Stuart, *Poetic Form and British Romanticism* (New York: Oxford University Press, 1989).

———, "Charlotte Smith and British Romanticism," *South Central Review*, 11, no. 2 (1994): 66–78.

———, "Romantic Poetry: Why and Wherefore?", in Stuart Curren (ed.), *The Cambridge Companion to British Romanticism* (Cambridge: Cambridge University Press, 1996).

Dávidházi, Péter, *The Romantic Cult of Shakespeare: Literary Reception in Anthropological Perspective* (London: Macmillan, 1998).

Davis, Tracy C., "'Reading Shakespeare by Flashes of Lightning': Challenging the Foundations of Romantic Acting Theory," *ELH*, 62, no. 4 (1995): 933–54.

Dean, Winton, "Shakespeare and Opera," in Phyllis Hartnoll (ed), *Shakespeare in Music* (London: Macmillan, 1964).

de Grazia, Margreta, *Shakespeare Verbatim: The Reproduction of Authenticity and the 1790 Apparatus* (Oxford: Clarendon, 1991).

———, "*Hamlet* before Its Time," *Modern Language Quarterly*, 62 (2001): 355–75.

———, *"Hamlet" Without Hamlet* (Cambridge: Cambridge University Press, 2007).

Delvecchio, Doreen, and Antony Hammond (eds), *Pericles* (Cambridge: Cambridge University Press, 1998).

Diderot, Denis, "The Paradox of Acting," trans. Walter Herries Pollock, in *The Paradox of Acting by Denis Diderot and Masks or Faces? by William Archer* (New York: Hill and Wang, 1957).

Dobson, Michael, *The Making of the National Poet: Shakespeare, Adaptation and Authorship, 1660–1792* (Oxford: Clarendon, 1992).

Dolven, Jeff, "Shakespeare and the New Aestheticism," *Literary Imagination*, 5, no. 1 (2003): 95–109.

Donohue, Joseph, "Kemble's Production of Macbeth (1794)," *Theatre Notebook*, 21 (1967): 63–74.

———, "Kemble and Mrs. Siddons in *Macbeth*: The Romantic Approach to Tragic Character," *Theatre Notebook*, 22 (1968): 65–86.
Douglass, Paul, *Lady Caroline Lamb: A Biography* (New York: Palgrave Macmillan, 2004).
Eagleton, Terry, *William Shakespeare* (Oxford: Blackwell, 1986).
Eaves, Morris, *The Counter-Arts Conspiracy: Art and Industry in the Age of Blake* (Ithaca, NY: Cornell University Press, 1992).
———, "The Sister Arts in British Romanticism," in Stuart Curren, (ed.), *Cambridge Companion to British Romanticism* (Cambridge: Cambridge University Press, 1993).
Egerton, Judy (ed.), *Wright of Derby*, exhibition catalogue (New York: Metropolitan Museum of Art, 1990).
Elfenbein, Andrew, *Romantic Genius: The Prehistory of a Homosexual Role* (New York: Columbia University Press, 1999).
Eliot, T. S., *The Sacred Wood: Essays on Poetry and Criticism* (New York: Knopf, 1930).
Elwin, Malcolm, *Landor: A Replevin* (London: Macdonald, 1958).
Engell, James, *The Creative Imagination: Enlightenment to Romanticism* (Cambridge, MA: Harvard University Press, 1981).
———, "Coleridge, Johnson, and Shakespeare: A Critical Drama in Five Acts," *Romanticism: The Journal of Romantic Culture and Criticism*, 4, no. 1 (1998): 22–39.
Erne, Lukas, *Shakespeare as Literary Dramatist* (Cambridge: Cambridge University Press, 2003).
Esterhammer, Angela, "Cognitive Process, Commanding Genius, and Comparative Literature," *Coleridge Bulletin: The Journal of the Friends of Coleridge*, 16 (2000): 56–62.
Farley-Hills, David (ed.), *Critical Responses to Hamlet 1600–1900* (4 vols, New York: AMS Press, 1996).
Farr, Judith, "Emily Dickinson's 'Engulfing' Play: *Antony and Cleopatra*," *Tulsa Studies in Women's Literature*, 9, no. 2 (1990): 231–50.
Felperin, Howard, *Shakespearean Romance* (Princeton, NJ: Princeton University Press, 1972).
Festa, Thomas, "'All in All': The *Book of Common Prayer* and *Hamlet*, I.ii.186," *Notes and Queries*, 54, no. 3 (2007): 289–90.
Finnerty, Pàraic, *Emily Dickinson's Shakespeare* (Amherst: University of Massachusetts Press, 2006).
Fisher, Judith W., "The Stage on the Page: Sarah Siddons and Ann Radcliffe," *Eighteenth-Century Women*, 2 (2002): 243–63.
Fletcher, Loraine, *Charlotte Smith: A Critical Biography* (Basingstoke, UK: Palgrave, 2001).
Foakes, R. A. (ed.), *The Collected Works of Samuel Taylor Coleridge, Volume 5: Lectures 1808–1819: On Literature* (2 vols, Princeton, NJ: Princeton University Press, 1987).

Forster, John, *Walter Savage Landor: A Biography* (2 vols, London, 1869).
Foucault, Michel, *Madness and Civilization: A History of Insanity in the Age of Reason* (New York: Vintage Press, 1988).
Friedman, Winifred, "Some Commercial Aspects of the Boydell Shakespeare Gallery," *Journal of the Warburg and Courtauld Institutes*, 36 (1973): 396–401.
———, *Boydell's Shakespeare Gallery* (New York: Garland, 1976).
Fry, Carrol L., *Charlotte Smith* (New York: Twayne, 1996).
Frye, Roland, "A Study of the Boydell Gallery," *Shakespeare Quarterly*, 28, no. 3 (1977): 377–8.
Gamer, Michael, *Romanticism and the Gothic: Genre, Reception, and Canon Formation* (Cambridge: Cambridge University Press, 2000).
Garber, Marjorie, *Shakespeare After All* (New York, Pantheon, 2004).
Garver, Joseph, "Gothic Ireland: Lady Caroline Lamb's *Glenarvon*," *Irish University Review: A Journal of Irish Studies*, 10 (1980): 213–28.
Gay, Penny, *Jane Austen and the Theatre* (Cambridge: Cambridge University Press, 2002).
Genette, Gérard, *Palimpsestes: La litterature au second degré* (Paris: Seuil, 1982).
Gevirtz, Karen Bloom, "Ladies Reading and Writing: Eighteenth-Century Women Writers and the Gendering of Critical Discourse," *Modern Language Studies*, 33 (2003): 60–72.
Gilbert, Sandra M., and Susan Gubar, *The Madwoman in the Attic: The Woman Writer and the Nineteenth-Century Imagination* (New Haven, CT: Yale University Press, 1979).
Glassey, Roberta M., "The Concept of Freedom in Schiller's Wallenstein," *Journal of European Studies*, 4 (1980): 256–66.
Goring, Paul, *The Rhetoric of Sensibility in Eighteenth-Century Culture* (Cambridge: Cambridge University Press, 2005).
Gould, Timothy, "The Audience of Originality: Kant and Wordsworth on The Reception of Genius," in Ted Cohen and Paul Guyer (eds), *Essays in Kant's Aesthetics* (Chicago: University of Chicago Press, 1982).
Griffith, Elizabeth, *The Morality of Shakespeare's Drama Illustrated* (London: T. Cadell, 1775).
Habegger, Alfred, *My Wars Are Laid Away in Books: The Life of Emily Dickinson* (New York: Random House, 2001).
Halliwell, Stephen, *The Aesthetics of Mimesis: Ancient Texts and Modern Problems* (Princeton, NJ: Princeton University Press, 2002).
Hamilton, Paul, "Wordsworth and Romanticism," in Stephen Gill (ed.), *The Cambridge Companion to Wordsworth* (Cambridge: Cambridge University Press, 2003).
Hapgood, Robert, ed. *Hamlet, Prince of Denmark: Shakespeare in Production* (Cambridge: Cambridge University Press, 1999).
Hardy, Barbara, "'I Have a Smack of Hamlet': Coleridge and Shakespeare's Characters," *Essays in Criticism*, 8, no. 3 (1958): 238–55.

Hart, F. Elizabeth, "'Great is Diana' of Shakespeare's Ephesus," *Studies in English Literature 1500–1900*, 43, no. 2 (2003): 347–74.

Hartman, Geoffrey H., *Wordsworth's Poetry 1787–1814* (New Haven, CT: Yale University Press, 1964).

Hawley, Judith, "Charlotte Smith's *Elegiac Sonnets*: Losses and Gains," in Isobel Armstrong and Virginia Blain (eds), *Women's Poetry in the Enlightenment: The Making of the Canon, 1730–1820* (London: Macmillan, 1999).

Haynes, Kenneth, "Text, Theory, and Reception," in Charles Martindale and Richard F. Thomas (eds), *Classics and the Uses of Reception* (Oxford: Blackwell, 2006).

Haywood, Eliza, from *The Female Spectator*, Book 8 (1745), in Brian Vickers (ed.), *William Shakespeare: The Critical Heritage, Volume 3: 1733–1752* (Boston: Routledge & Kegan Paul, 1975).

Heffernan, James A.W., *Wordsworth's Theory of Poetry: The Transforming Imagination* (Ithaca, NY: Cornell University Press, 1969).

Heginbotham, Eleanor, "Dickinson's 'What If I Say I Shall Not Wait!'," *Explicator*, 54, no. 3 (1996): 154–60.

Helgerson, Richard, *Forms of Nationhood: The Elizabethan Writing of England* (Chicago: University of Chicago Press, 1992).

Heller, Janet Ruth, "Hazlitt's Appeal to Readers in His Dramatic Criticism," *Charles Lamb Bulletin*, 57 (1987): 7–9.

Heylen, Romy, *Six French Hamlets: Translations, Poetics, and the Stage* (London: Routledge, 1993).

Hilbish, Florence May Anna, *Charlotte Smith, Poet and Novelist* (Philadelphia: University of Pennsylvania Press, 1941).

Hill, R.F., "Shakespeare's Early Tragic Mode," *Shakespeare Quarterly*, 9 (1958): 455–69.

Hogan, Charles Beecher (ed.), *The London Stage 1660–1800, Part 5: 1776–1800* (3 vols, Carbondale: Southern Illinois University Press, 1968).

Holderness, Graham, "Are Shakespeare's Tragic Heroes 'Fatally Flawed'? Discuss." *Critical Survey*, 1 (1989): 53–62.

Holland, Peter, "A History of Histories: From Flecknoe to Nicoll," in W. B. Worthen and Peter Holland (eds), *Theorizing Practice: Redefining Theatre History* (New York: Palgrave Macmillan, 2003).

Hopkins, Lisa, *John Ford's Political Theatre* (Manchester, UK: Manchester University Press, 1994).

———, "The Self and The Monstrous: *The Fortunes of Perkin Warbeck*," in Syndy Conger, Frederick Frank, and Gregory O'Dea (eds), *Iconoclastic Departures: Mary Shelley After "Frankenstein"* (Madison, NJ: Fairleigh Dickinson University Press, 1997).

Howard, Tony, *Women As Hamlet: Performance and Interpretation in Theatre, Film and Fiction* (Cambridge: Cambridge University Press, 2007).

Hudson, Arthur Palmer, "Romantic Apologiae for Ophelia," *ELH*, 9 (1942): 59–70.

Hutcheon, Linda, *A Theory of Adaptation* (New York: Routledge, 2006).
Inchbald, Elizabeth, Preface to *Hamlet*, in *Remarks for "The British Theatre"* (Delmar, NY: Scholars' Facsimiles and Reprints, 1990 [1806–9]).
Jackson, Russell, and Jonathan Bate (eds), *Shakespeare: An Illustrated Stage History* (New York: Oxford University Press, 1996).
Jarvis, Simon, *Scholars and Gentlemen: Shakespearean Textual Criticism and Representations of Scholarly Labour, 1725–1765* (Oxford: Clarendon Press, 1995).
———, *Wordsworth's Philosophic Song* (Cambridge: Cambridge University Press, 2007).
Jenkins, Annibel, *I'll Tell You What: The Life of Elizabeth Inchbald* (Lexington: University Press of Kentucky, 2003).
Joughin, John J., "Shakespeare, Modernity and the Aesthetic: Art, Truth, and Judgement in *The Winter's Tale*," in Hugh Grady (ed.), *Shakespeare and Modernity: Early Modern to Millenium* (London: Routledge, 2000).
Judson, Barbara, "Roman á Clef and the Dynamics of Betrayal: The Case of *Glenarvon*," *Genre*, 33 (2000): 151–69.
Kastan, David Scott, *Shakespeare and the Book* (Cambridge: Cambridge University Press, 2001).
Keach, William, "Early Shelley: Vulgarisms, Politics, and Fractals," in Orrin N. C. Wang (ed.), *Romantic Circles, Praxis Series* (August 1997), http://www.rc.umd.edu/praxis/earlyshelley/keach/keach.html.
Kee, Robert, *The Green Flag* (3 vols, London: Penguin, 1989).
Kelsall, Malcolm, "The Byronic Hero and Revolution in Ireland: The Politics of *Glenarvon*," *Byron Journal*, 9 (1981): 4–19.
Kerrigan, John, *Revenge Tragedy* (Oxford: Clarendon Press, 1996).
Knapp, Jeffrey, *Shakespeare Only* (Chicago: University of Chicago Press, 2009).
Kramnick, Jonathan Brody, *Making the English Canon, Print-Capitalism and the Cultural Past, 1700–1770* (Cambridge: Cambridge University Press, 1998).
Labbe, Jacqueline M., "'Transplanted into More Congenial Soil': Footnoting the Self in the Poetry of Charlotte Smith," in Joe Bray, Miriam Handley, and Anne C. Henry (eds), *Ma(r)king the Text: The Presentation of Meaning on the Literary Page* (Aldershot, UK: Ashgate, 2000).
———, *Charlotte Smith: Romanticism, Poetry and the Culture of Gender* (Manchester, UK: Manchester University Press, 2003).
Lacombe, Hervé, *The Keys to French Opera in the Nineteenth Century*, trans. Edward Schneider (Berkeley: University of California Press, 2001).
Lamb, Susan, "Applauding Shakespeare's Ophelia in the Eighteenth Century: Sexual Desire, Politics, and the Good Woman," in Susan Shifrin (ed.), *Women as Sites of Culture: Women's Roles in Cultural Formation from the Renaissance to the Twentieth Century* (Aldershot, UK: Ashgate, 2002).
Larson, Victoria Tietze, *The Role of Description in Senecan Tragedy* (Frankfurt am Main: Peter Lang, 1994).
Lease, Benjamin, *Emily Dickinson's Readings of Men and Books: Sacred Soundings* (New York: St. Martin's Press, 1990).

Levine, Lawrence W., *Highbrow/Lowbrow: The Emergence of Cultural Hierarchy in America* (Cambridge, MA: Harvard University Press, 1988).
Littlejohn, David, *The Ultimate Art: Articles around and about Opera* (Berkeley: University of California Press, 1992).
Louis, Margot K., "Gods and Mysteries: The Revival of Paganism and the Remaking of Mythography through the Nineteenth Century," *Victorian Studies*, 47 (2005): 329–61.
Luxford, Dominic, "Sounding the Sublime: The 'Full Music' of Dickinson's Inspiration," *Emily Dickinson Journal*, 13, no. 1 (2004): 51–75.
Mander, Raymond, and Joe Mitchenson, *Hamlet Through the Ages: A Pictorial Record from 1709*, 2nd ed. (London: Rockliff, 1955).
Manheim, Daniel, "The Signifying Spinster: How Emily Dickinson Found Her Voice" *ESQ*, 51, no. 4 (2005): 213–49.
Manvell, Roger, *Sarah Siddons: Portrait of an Actress* (New York: G.P. Putnam's Sons, 1971).
Marcus, Leah, *Unediting the Renaissance: Shakespeare, Marlowe, Milton* (New York: Routledge, 1996).
Marsden, Jean, *The Re-Imagined Text. Shakespeare, Adaptation, and Eighteenth-Century Literary Theory* (Lexington: University Press of Kentucky, 1995).
Masten, Jeffrey, *Textual Intercourse: Collaboration, Authorship, and Sexualities in Renaissance Drama* (Cambridge: Cambridge University Press, 1997).
Maynard, Temple, "James Boaden," in Paula Backscheider (ed.), *Dictionary of Literary Biography*, vol. 89 (Detroit: Gale, 1989).
Mellor, Anne K., "A Criticism of Their Own: Romantic Women Literary Critics," in John Beer (ed.), *Questioning Romanticism* (Baltimore: Johns Hopkins University Press, 1995).
Merchant, W. Moelwin, *Shakespeare and the Artist* (London: Oxford University Press, 1959).
Miles, Robert, *Ann Radcliffe: The Great Enchantress* (Manchester, UK: Manchester University Press, 1995).
———, "The 1790s: The Effulgence of Gothic," in Jerrold Hogle (ed.), *The Cambridge Companion to Gothic Fiction* (Cambridge: Cambridge University Press, 2002).
Modiano, Raimonda, "Metaphysical Debate in Coleridge's Political Theory," *Studies in Romanticism*, 3 (1982): 465–74.
Monaco, Marion, *Shakespeare on the French Stage in the Eighteenth Century* (Paris: Didier, 1974).
Moody, Jane, "Illusion of Authorship," in Tracy C. Davis and Ellen Donkin (eds), *Women and Playwriting in Nineteenth-Century Britain* (Cambridge: Cambridge University Press, 1999).
———, *Illegitimate Theatre in London, 1770–1840* (Cambridge: Cambridge University Press, 2000).
Moore, John David, "Coleridge and the 'Modern Jacobinical Drama': *Osorio*, *Remorse*, and the Development of Coleridge's Critique of the Stage, 1797–1816," *Bulletin of Research in the Humanities*, 4 (1982): 443–64.

Moretti, Franco, *Modern Epic*, trans. Quintin Hoare (London: Verso, 1996).
Morrow, John, *Coleridge's Political Thought* (London: Macmillan, 1990).
Mullaney, Steven, *The Place of the Stage: License, Play, and Power in Renaissance England* (Chicago: University of Chicago Press, 1988).
Myrone, Martin, *Gothic Nightmares: Fuseli, Blake and the Gothic Imagination* (London: Tate, 2006).
Neely, Carol Thomas, "'Documents in Madness': Reading Madness and Gender in Shakespeare's Tragedies and Early Modern Culture," *Shakespeare Quarterly*, 42 (1991): 315–38.
———, *Distracted Subjects: Madness and Gender in Shakespeare and Early Modern Culture* (Ithaca, NY: Cornell University Press, 2004).
Neubauer, John, "The Idea of History in Schiller's Wallenstein," *Neophilologus*, 4 (1972): 451–63.
Newlyn, Lucy, *"Paradise Lost" and the Romantic Reader* (Oxford: Clarendon Press, 1993).
Normington, Susan, *Lady Caroline Lamb: This Infernal Woman* (London: House of Stratus, 2001).
Norton, Rictor, *Mistress of Udolpho: The Life of Ann Radcliffe* (London: Leicester University Press, 1999).
———, "Ann Radcliffe, 'The Shakespeare of Romance Writers,'" in Christy Desmet and Anne Williams (eds), *Shakespearean Gothic* (Cardiff: University of Wales Press, 2009).
Novy, Marianne, "Women's Re-Visions of Shakespeare 1664–1988," in Marianne Novy (ed.), *Women's Re-Visions of Shakespeare* (Urbana: University of Illinois Press, 1990).
Nuttall, A.D., *A New Mimesis: Shakespeare and the Representation of Reality* (London: Methuen, 1983).
Orgel, Stephen, *Imagining Shakespeare: A History of Texts and Visions* (New York: Palgrave, 2003).
Ortiz, Joseph M., *Broken Harmony: Shakespeare and the Politics of Music* (Ithaca, NY: Cornell University Press, 2011).
O'Sullivan, Maurice J., "Shakespeare's Other Lives," *Shakespeare Quarterly*, 38 (1987): 133–53.
Pascoe, Judith, "Female Botanists and the Poetry of Charlotte Smith," in Carol Shiner Wilson and Joel Haefner (eds), *Re-Visioning Romanticism: British Women Writers 1776–1837* (Philadelphia: University of Pennsylvania Press, 1994).
Pechter, Edward, *What Was Shakespeare?: Renaissance Plays and Changing Critical Practice* (Ithaca, NY: Cornell University Press, 1995).
Perkins, Pam, "Sixteenth-Century Queens in Eighteenth-Century Literature," *Eighteenth-Century Women*, 2 (2002): 109–35.
Petrino, Elizabeth, "Allusion, Echo, and Literary Influence in Emily Dickinson," *Emily Dickinson Journal*, 19, no. 1 (2010): 80–102.
Pinch, Adele, *Strange Fits of Passion: Epistemologies of Emotion, Hume to Austen* (Stanford, CA: Stanford University Press, 1996).

Pollak, Vivian R., "Emily Dickinson's Literary Allusions," *Essays in Literature*, 1 (1974): 54–68.
Postlewait, Thomas, "The Criteria for Evidence: Anecdotes in Shakespearean Biography, 1709–2000," in W. B. Worthen and Peter Holland (eds), *Theorizing Practice: Redefining Theatre History* (New York: Palgrave Macmillan, 2003).
Powers, Harold, "Making 'Macbeth' *Musicabile*," in Nicholas John (ed.), *Macbeth. ENO Opera Guide* 41 (London: John Calder, 1990).
Price, F.W., "Ann Radcliffe, Mrs. Siddons and the Character of Hamlet," *Notes and Queries*, (1976): 164–7.
Quilley, Geoff, and John Bonehill (eds), *William Hodges, 1744–1797: The Art of Exploration* (New Haven, CT: Yale University Press, 2004).
Raby, Peter, *"Fair Ophelia": A Life of Harriet Smithson Berlioz* (Cambridge: Cambridge University Press, 1982).
Ranger, Paul, *"Terror and Pity Reign in Every Breast": Gothic Drama in the London Patent Theatres, 1750-1820* (London: Society for Theatre Research, 1991).
Reno, Robert, "James Boaden's *Fontainville Forest* and Matthew G. Lewis' *The Castle Spectre*: Challenges of the Supernatural Ghost on the Late Eighteenth-Century Stage," *Eighteenth-Century Life*, 9 (1984): 94–106.
Ricks, Christopher, *Allusion to the Poets* (Oxford: Oxford University Press, 2002).
Roe, Albert S., "The Demon Behind the Pillow: A Note on Erasmus Darwin and Reynolds," *Burlington Magazine*, 113 (1971): 460, 462, 470.
Rogeboz-Malfroy, Elizabeth, *Ambroise Thomas, ou la tentation du lyrique* (Besançon: Cêtre, 1994).
Rogers, Deborah D. (ed.), *The Critical Response to Ann Radcliffe* (Westport, CT: Greenwood Press, 1994).
Rogers, Nicholas, "The Gordon Riots Revisited," *Historical Papers*, 16 (1988): 16–34.
Rose, Jacqueline, "Sexuality in the Reading of Shakespeare: *Hamlet* and *Measure for Measure*," in John Drakakis (ed.), *Alternative Shakespeares*, 2nd ed. (London: Routledge, 2002).
Rosenberg, Marvin, *The Masks of Hamlet* (Newark: University of Delaware Press, 1992).
Rovee, Christopher, *Imagining the Gallery: The Social Body of British Romanticism* (Stanford, CA: Stanford University Press, 2006).
Roy, Donald (ed.), *Romantic and Revolutionary Theatre* (Cambridge: Cambridge University Press, 2003).
Ryan, Kiernan, *Shakespeare*, 3rd ed. (Basingstoke: Palgrave, 2002).
Sabor, Peter, and Paul Yachnin (eds), *Shakespeare and the Eighteenth Century* (Aldershot, UK: Ashgate, 2008).
Saggini, Francesca, "Radcliffe's Novels and Boaden's Dramas: Bringing the Configurations of the Gothic on Stage," in Carmela Nocera, Gemma Persico, and Rosario Portale (eds), *Rites of Passage: Rational/Irrational Natural/Supernatural Local/Global* (Soveria Mannelli, Italy: Rubbettino, 2003).

———, "The Art of Fine Drama: Inchbald's *Remarks for The British Theatre* and the Aesthetic Experience of the Late Eighteenth-Century Theatre-Goer," *Textus*, 28 (2005): 133–52.
Sanders, Julie, *Adaptation and Appropriation* (London: Routledge, 2006).
Santaniello, A.E., *The Boydell Shakespeare Prints* (New York: Arno, 1979).
Schmidgall, Gary, *Shakespeare and Opera* (New York: Oxford University Press, 1990).
Schoenbaum, Samuel, *Shakespeare's Lives* (Oxford: Clarendon Press, 1970).
Senelick, Laurence, "The Craig-Stanislavsky *Hamlet* at the Moscow Art Theatre," *Theatre Quarterly*, 6, no. 22 (1976): 56–122.
Sewall, Richard B., *The Lyman Letters: New Light on Emily Dickinson and Her Family* (Amherst, MA: University of Massachusetts Press, 1965).
———, *The Life of Emily Dickinson* (New York: Farrar, Straus and Giroux, 1980).
Seymour, Miranda, *Mary Shelley* (London: John Murray, 2000).
Shapiro, James, *A Year in the Life of William Shakespeare, 1599* (New York: Harper, 2006).
Shiels, W. J., "Catholicism from the Reformation to the Relief Acts," in Sheridan Gilley and W. J. Shiels (eds), *A History of Religion in Britain: Practice and Belief from Pre-Roman Times to the Present* (Oxford: Blackwell, 1994).
Showalter, Elaine, "Representing Ophelia: Women, Madness, and the Responsibilities of Feminist Criticism," in Patricia Parker and Geoffrey Hartman (eds), *Shakespeare and the Question of Theory* (London: Methuen, 1985).
Sillars, Stuart, *Painting Shakespeare* (Cambridge: Cambridge University Press, 2006).
Slagle, Judith Bailey, *Joanna Baillie: A Literary Life* (Madison, NJ: Farleigh Dickinson University Press, 2002).
Smith, Marian, *Ballet and Opera in the Age of Giselle* (Princeton, NJ: Princeton University Press, 2000).
Stafford, William, *English Feminists and their Opponents in the 1790s: Unsex'd and Proper Females* (Manchester, UK: Manchester University Press, 2002).
Stam, Robert, "The Theory and Practice of Adaptation," in Robert Stam and Alessandra Raengo (eds), *Literature and Film: A Guide to the Theory and Practice of Film Adaptation* (Malden, MA: Blackwell, 2005).
Stanton, Judith Phillips, "Charlotte Smith's 'Literary Business': Income, Patronage, and Indigence," *The Age of Johnson*, 1 (1987): 375–401.
Starr, G. Gabrielle, *Lyric Generations: Poetry in the Novel in the Long Eighteenth Century* (Baltimore: John Hopkins University Press, 2004).
Stonum, Gary Lee, "Dickinson's Literary Background," in Gudrun Grabher et al. (eds), *The Emily Dickinson Handbook* (Amherst: University of Massachusetts Press, 1998).
Stuebe, Isabel, *Life and Works of William Hodges* (New York: Garland, 1979).
Super, R.H., *Walter Savage Landor: A Biography* (New York: New York University Press, 1954).

Sutton, Juliet, "Platonic Love in Ford's The Fancies, Chaste and Noble," *Studies in English Literature 1500–1900*, 7, no. 2 (1967): 299–309.
Taruskin, Richard, *The Oxford History of Western Music* (5 vols, New York: Oxford University Press, 2005).
Taylor, Gary, *Reinventing Shakespeare* (London: Hogarth Press, 1990).
Thorp, W., "The Stage Adventures of Some Gothic Novels," *PMLA*, 43 (1928): 476–86.
Todorov, Tzvetan, *The Fantastic: A Structural Approach to a Literary Genre*, trans. R. Howard (Cleveland, OH: Press of Case Western Reserve University, 1973).
Traub, Valerie, "Desire and Anxiety: Circulations of Sexuality in Shakespearean Drama," in Sean McEvoy (ed.), *William Shakespeare's "Hamlet": A Sourcebook* (London: Routledge, 2006).
Voller, Jack, *The Supernatural Sublime: The Metaphysics of Terror in Anglo-American Romanticism* (DeKalb: Northern Illinois University Press, 1994).
Warrall, David, "The Political Culture of Gothic Drama," in David Punter (ed.), *A Companion to the Gothic* (Oxford-Malden, UK: Blackwell, 2000).
Webster, Mary, *Francis Wheatley* (London: Routledge, 1970).
Welsh, Alexander, *Hamlet in His Modern Guises* (Princeton, NJ: Princeton University Press, 2001).
West, Shearer, "The Public and Private Roles of Sarah Siddons," in Robyn Asleson et al. (eds), *A Passion for Performance: Sarah Siddons and her Portraitists* (Los Angeles: J. Paul Getty Museum, 1999).
White, R.S., *Keats as a Reader of Shakespeare* (London: Athlone Press, 1987).
Winstead, Karen, *Virgin Martyrs: Legends of Sainthood in Late Medieval England* (Ithaca, NY: Cornell University Press, 1997).
Wolff, Cynthia Griffin, *Emily Dickinson* (Reading, MA: Perseus Books, 1988).
Wolfson, Susan, "Shakespeare and the Romantic Girl Reader," *Nineteenth-Century Contexts*, 21, no. 2 (1999): 191–234.
———, "Charlotte Smith's *Emigrants*: Forging Connections at the Borders of a Female Tradition," in Anne K. Mellor, Felicity Nussbaum, and Jonathan F.S. Post (eds), *Forging Connections: Women's Poetry from the Renaissance to Romanticism* (San Marino, CA: Huntington Library, 2002).
Wood, Gillen D'Arcy, *The Shock of the Real: Romanticism and Visual Culture, 1760–1860* (New York: Palgrave, 2001).
Wroe, Ann, *Perkin: A Story of Deception* (London: Jonathan Cape, 2003).
Yates, Frances A., *Shakespeare's Last Plays: A New Approach* (London: Routledge & Kegan Paul, 1975).
Young, Alan R., *Hamlet and the Visual Arts, 1709–1900* (Newark: University of Delaware Press, 2002).
Zimmerman, Sarah, "Charlotte Smith's Letters and the Practice of Self Presentation," *Princeton University Library Chronicle*, 53 (1991): 50–77.
Zurcher, Amelia, "Untimely Monuments: Stoicism, History, and the Problem of Utility in *The Winter's Tale* and *Pericles*," *ELH*, 70 (2003): 903–27.

# Index

Abbate, Carolyn 200
Abrams, M. H. 86
acting, *see* theater
actresses 8, 38, 53, 58–74, 197
    as singers 68
adaptation theory 201–3
Addison, Joseph 32–3
Aeschylus 150
aesthetics, debates over 67, 78–80, 97, 156, 164–5, 179, 181, 184
Aikin, John 111
Allen, Charles 45
*All's Well That Ends Well* 216, 221
allusion, theories of 78, 82–3, 86–7, 97, 102, 115, 125–6
Alpers, Paul 92
American Revolution 249, 251
*The Analytical Review* 179
Andrews, Miles Peter 165
anti-Semitism 43
*Antony and Cleopatra* 41, 43, 49, 96, 121–2, 124, 129, 135, 216, 223
Aristotle, theory of drama 142, 150–52, 182
Ashburton, Charles Alfred 45
*As You Like It* 19, 25, 37, 39, 41, 92–3, 95, 182, 215, 217, 221–2, 226–7
Austen, Jane 101

Baillie, Joanna 10, 231–44
    *The Bride* 231–5, 240–44
        as missionary project 240
    *The Martyr* 231–8, 240, 244
Banks, Thomas 215
Barber, C. L. 24–5
Barbier, Jules 183, 187, 191
Bardolatry 3, 7, 9, 13–14, 17, 20, 23, 30, 34, 36, 77–8, 180
Barnett, Ephraim 21
Barry, James 219, 222, 225
Barthes, Roland 181
Bate, Jonathan 3–5, 8, 52, 86, 108, 115, 186

Beaumont, Francis 89
Beerbohm, Max 73
Bell, Edward 72
Belleforest, François de 185
Bennett, Paula 124, 126
Bennett, Susan 49
Berkoff, Steven 53
Berlioz, Hector 70, 184, 190
Bernhardt, Sarah 73
Bernstein, Leonard 201
Bible 160
    Corinthians 86–7
birds 107, 110, 112
Bishop, T. G. 232
Blake, William 8
Boaden, James 9, 61, 66–7, 161–82
    *Fontainville Forest* 9, 162, 164–82
Bodleian Library 211
Bonynge, Richard 192
*Book of Common Prayer* 87
book trade 210
Bossy, John 46
Boswell, James 17, 21
Bowyer, Robert 228
Boydell Shakspeare Gallery 5, 10, 180, 207–29
    exhibition catalogues 210–25
Boydell, John 5, 10, 180, 207–8, 228–9; *see also* Boydell Shakspeare Gallery
Boydell, Josiah 210, 223, 229
Bradley, A. C. 52, 54
Brady, Patricia 263
British East India Company 240
British Library 211
Bronte, Charlotte 135–6
Brooks, Douglas A. 7
Brown, Ford Madox 25–6
Bruntjen, Sven 219
Bryant, William Cullen 126
Bullen, Ann 163

Burke, Edmund 179, 247
Burney, Fanny (Frances) 60, 100
Byron, Lord 13, 35, 66, 245, 250–51, 260–63

Cambridge University 92, 211
Campbell, Thomas 1
Capell, Edward 21, 23, 25
Capps, Jack 124
Carhart, Margaret 234
Carlson, Julie A. 63
Carlson, Marvin 42, 47
Carre, Michel 183, 187, 191
Catholicism 31, 45–7, 117, 233, 251
Cavendish, William 245
Césaire, Aimé 201–2
Chalmers, George 20
Chard, Chloe 181–2
Charke, Charlotte 39
Charles I 245–6
Chateaubriand, François-René de 189
Chaucer, Geoffrey 99, 102
Christianity 236–7, 244; *see also* Catholicism, Protestantism, religion
Cibber, Colley 34, 228
Clarke, Edward Daniel 261
classicism 25, 93, 100, 141–3, 150, 179, 234; *see also* Hellenism
Clausen, Christoph 195–6, 200
Clément, Catherine 10, 231, 244
Clery, Emma 181
Cohan, Steve 166
Coleridge, Hartley 14
Coleridge, Samuel Taylor 3–4, 8–9, 13–14, 30, 32, 34–5, 39, 42, 51–2, 60, 62, 70, 84–6, 139–60, 186
  ideas about genius 144–6
  lectures on Shakespeare 151
  theory of drama 139–43
  Satyrane Letter 142
  *Zapolya* 9, 139, 144–60
Collins, William 111
Colman, George 163
Colòn, Christine 240
colonialism 240–41
Comédie Française 9, 183, 189
*The Comedy of Errors* 38, 41, 221–2
Cooke, George Frederick 38–9
*Coriolanus* 14, 42–3, 216–17, 222–3, 225–6

costumes 71–3
Covent Garden 2, 38, 57–8, 67–8, 140, 165, 192
  size of 67–8
Cox, Jeffrey 35
Craig, Edward Gordon 52, 55
*The Critical Review* 103, 172
Cromwell, Oliver 250
Cumberland, Richard 68
Cushman, Charlotte 53
*Cymbeline* 3, 9, 37, 40, 45, 94, 106–7, 152, 154–5, 168, 216–19, 221–3, 225–6

Damer, Anne 215, 222, 225
Dana, Richard Henry 125
Darwin, Erasmus 100, 110
Davenant, William 173
Dávidházi, Péter 78
Davies, Thomas 57, 59–63, 65, 68, 70, 163
Davis, Tracy C. 60–61
Dean, Winton 199
Dekker, Thomas 258
Delacroix, Eugène 184, 190–91, 197
Denis, John 52
De Quincey, Thomas 13, 17, 30
Dickinson, Emily 9, 121–36
  "He Fumbles At Your Soul" (Poem 477) 9, 122–36
  letters to friends 121–2, 125, 135
Diderot, Denis 63, 70
Dobson, Michael 6, 78
Downman, John 222
Drake, Nathan 18, 21–2
drama, *see* theater
Drury Lane (theater) 1–2, 5, 38, 57, 59, 61, 67–8, 140, 163–6, 172–3, 227
  size of 67–8
Dryden, John 38, 81, 94, 99–100
Ducis, Jean-François 9, 183–5, 188–92
Dumas, Alexandre 183–4, 190–91
Durno, James 222

Eagleton, Terry 30
education, theories of 92
Edward IV 266
Egerton, Judy 224
Eighteenth Century Collections Online 211
Elfenbein, Andrew 73
Eliot, T. S. 197

Elizabeth I 28–9, 45–6
Ellison, Ralph 125
Elwin, Malcolm 15
Engell, James 32
Erne, Lukas 6
*The European Magazine* 173
exoticism 156, 232

fables 99
Fane, Violet 70–71
Farley-Hills, David 52
Felperin, Howard 232
female
    aesthetic judgment 62–3
    archetypes 10
    characters 43–4, 47, 53, 63–4
    critics, *see* Shakespeare, feminist views of
    equality with male writers 100, 102, 106, 110, 119
    experience 44
    hysteria 199–200
    quality 9
    relation to patriarchy 242
    Romanticism 48–9
    sexuality 232
    singers 200–201
the feminine 231–2, 234, 238–42; *see also* psychoanalysis
femininity 63–5, 67, 69, 72
festivity 24–6
feudalism 89–90; *see also* politics; social rank
Fielding, Henry 22
Finnerty, Parraic 123
First Folio 6, 55, 185
Fisher, Judith W. 65
flowers 112–13
Foakes, R. A. 32
Folger Shakespeare Library 211
folk stories, *see* Shakespeare, biographies of
Follet, John 178
Forbes-Robertson, Sir Johnston 185
Ford, John 10, 245–66
    *The Broken Heart* 246–9
    *The Fancies, Chaste and Noble* 254–5, 262
    *Perkin Warbeck* 245, 251–3, 263–4
    *'Tis Pity She's A Whore* 261–2
    *The Witch of Edmonton* 258–9
Foucault, Michel 248–9

France 9, 40, 94, 113–15
    emigrants from 117
    French Revolution 143, 158–9, 207, 249, 251
    musical traditions in 193–4
    reception of Shakespeare in 183–204
    Romanticism in 190–91
    theatrical conventions in 188–9, 192
Franklin, Ralph 122
Freud, Sigmund 195
Fulbroke 19
Fuseli, Henry 162, 167, 175–9, 182, 213, 219, 222–3, 225, 228

Gamer, Michael 166–7
Garrick, David 13, 34, 38–9, 57, 59, 78, 163, 173, 188
Garver, Joseph 251
Gates, Henry Louis 125
gender 44–5, 73–4, 101–2; *see also* femininity; masculinity
Genest, John 166
genius, *see* Shakespeare, and genius
Gentleman, Francis 117
Geoffrey of Monmouth 32, 154
George III 117
Gerard, John 112
ghosts 166–7, 169–78, 180; *see also* supernaturalism
Gifford, William 246
*The Globe* (periodical) 68
Godwin, William 260
Goethe, Johann Wolfgang von 80, 186
Golding, Arthur 100
Goldsmith, Oliver 46
Gordon Riots 46
Goring, Paul 60–61, 63
Gothicism 2, 9–10, 65–6, 162, 165–7, 171–2, 180–82, 232
Gough, Silas 21
Gounod, Charles 203
Gray, Thomas 111
de Grazia, Margreta 6, 18, 51–2
Greenblatt, Stephen 125
Griffith, Elizabeth 33, 47

Habegger, Alfred 124
Halliwell, Stephen 90
Hamilton, William 219, 222

*Hamlet* 4, 9, 32, 34–5, 41–2, 48, 51–74, 80–87, 95, 107, 123, 125–36, 169, 174–6, 180, 182, 183–204, 209, 213, 218, 223, 226
  French versions of 183–204
  ghost in 174–6, 180, 182, 196
  operatic version, *see* Ambroise Thomas
  Ophelia 4, 8–9, 53–74, 107, 184–6, 190–92, 194–201
  Player's Speech 123, 125–36
  quarto versions 55–6
  Restoration performances 186
Hanmer, Sir Thomas 33
Hapdé, Jean-Baptiste-Augustin 193
Harris, Thomas 165–6, 176
Hart, Dominick J. 254
Hart, F. Elizabeth 234
Hartman, Geoffrey 86
Harvey, William 17
Hathaway, Anne 22–3
Haywood, Eliza 34
Hazlitt, William 4–5, 7–8, 14, 32, 35, 38, 42, 48, 77, 79, 96, 246
Hegel, Georg Wilhelm Friedrich 51, 78
Helgerson, Richard 6
Hellenism 1–2, 5, 130, 234, 237
*1 Henry IV* 8, 40, 44, 47, 218–23, 226
*2 Henry IV* 40, 43, 96, 108, 114–15, 182, 217, 219–21, 226
*Henry V* 9, 40, 47, 49, 107–8, 113–14, 219, 222, 227
Henry V 49
*1 Henry VI* 158, 217–18, 220–21, 226
*2 Henry VI* 158, 217, 220–21
*3 Henry VI* 158, 216, 218, 220–21, 226
Henry VII 249, 253, 264
*Henry VIII* 44–5, 162–3, 216–17, 220–21, 226
Heylen, Romy 187–8
Higginson, Thomas Wentworth 128, 135
historicism 78–79
history 40, 80, 91, 94–5, 97, 113–14, 148, 156–7, 160, 204
  English 40, 45–7, 154–5, 249, 251–3
Hodges, Robert 224–5
Holderness, Graham 196
holidays, *see* festivity
Holinshed, Raphael 32, 100, 154–5
Holland, Peter 33
Hopkins, Lisa 245, 253, 261, 263–5

Howard, Tony 53, 55, 59, 73
Hudson, Arthur 35
Hugo, Victor 184, 190
Hume, David 45, 231, 240–41
Hunt, Leigh 35
Huntington Library 67
Hutcheon, Linda 201

idolatry, *see* Bardolatry
Inchbald, Elizabeth 8, 31–49, 66–7
interiority 51, 62, 69, 94, 123, 164
Ireland, resistance to England 249–54
Ireland, Samuel 163
Ireland, William Henry 163
Irving, Henry 71–2
Italian literature 37, 40

Jacobinism 143
James I (Scotland) 263
James II 45
James IV (Scotland) 251–3
Janin, Jules 197
Jarvis, Simon 78
Jenkins, Annibel 31, 38
Jephson, Robert 172
Jerningham, Edward 226
Johnson, Joseph 110
Johnson, Samuel 2, 8, 18, 32–3, 35, 41–2, 81, 162–3
Johnston, Sir Alexander 240
Jones, Ernest 196
Jonson, Ben 81, 89
*Julius Caesar* 168, 182, 187–8, 217, 219, 222–3, 227–8

Kant, Immanuel 79, 97, 133–5
Kastan, David Scott 6
Katherine of Aragon 45–6
Kaufmann, Angelica 221
Keach, William 263
Kean, Charles 57, 63, 68–70, 72
Kean, Edmund 60–61, 63–4, 186
Keats, John 8, 13, 30, 35, 94, 118, 231
Kee, Robert 249
Kelsall, Malcolm 250
Kemble, Charles 197
Kemble, John Philip 1–2, 35, 39, 57–9, 61, 64, 66–8, 162, 165, 167, 172–5, 180, 182, 190

Kerrigan, John 196
*King John* 39, 104–5, 107, 182, 221–2
*King Lear* 33–4, 38, 45, 87–8, 106, 116–17, 158, 182, 209, 215, 218, 221, 226
Kirkby, Joan 125
Knapp, Jeffrey 6
Kozintsev, Grigori 202
Kristeva, Julia 10, 231, 244
Kyd, Thomas 185

Labbe, Jacqueline 102, 105
Lacan, Jacques 53
Lacombe, Hervé 199
Lacy, Walter 71–2
La Fontaine, Jean de 99, 117
Lamb, Charles 14–15, 32, 34–5, 38–9, 42, 47–8, 246
Lamb, Lady Caroline 10, 245–66
  *Ada Reis* 246, 254, 256–8
  *Glenarvon* 10, 245–54, 258–9
  *Graham Hamilton* 254–5
Lamb, Mary 47
Lamb, Susan 58–9, 69
Lamb, William 246, 250, 266
Lambourne, Michael 29
Landor, Walter Savage 7, 13–18, 21–30
La Place, Pierre-Antoine de 188
Leeds University 51
Lennox, Charlotte 25, 33, 40, 44
Le Tourneur, Pierre 188–9
Lever, J. W. 112–13
Lewis, Matthey Gregory 161–2, 166
literary criticism, *see* Shakespeare, criticism of
Littlejohn, David 204
Lloyd, Robert 172–3
Locke, Ralph P. 200
Lockhart, J. G. 62
Longfellow, Henry Wadsworth 126
Longman (publisher) 31, 33
Louis XVI 113
Louis, Margot K. 234
*Love's Labour's Lost* 112–13, 220
Lucy, Sir Thomas 15, 19–23, 25, 27–8, 30
Luddism 143
Luxford, Dominic 128–9, 131
Lyceum Theater 71–2
Lyman, Joseph 121–2

*Macbeth* 25, 30, 33, 38, 40, 42, 48, 60, 63–7, 72, 111, 115–16, 118, 168, 172–3, 175, 177, 180, 182, 202, 218, 222–3, 226
Mackenzie, Henry 47
Macklin, Thomas 228
Macready, Charles 190
Macready, William 5
madness 53, 55, 61–3, 67, 69–70, 72, 184, 200, 248–9
Malone, Edmond 16–18, 21–2, 32–4, 40, 231
Manheim, Dan 125–6
Manichean philosophy 159
Manzoni, Alessandro 184
Marcus, Leah 6
Martyn, Thomas 113
masculinity 63, 65, 73
Masten, Jeffrey 6
Maynard, Temple 162
materialism 87
Meadowbank, Lord (Alexander Maconochie) 63
*Measure for Measure* 36–7, 39, 45, 221
medieval mystery plays 231–2
melancholy 72–3
Mellor, Anne 47–9
*The Merchant of Venice* 38, 43, 118–19, 216–17, 221
*The Merry Wives of Windsor* 10, 25, 39, 212, 215, 217–18, 221–2, 226
Meurice, Paul 183–4
Meyerbeer, Giacomo 193
*A Midsummer Night's Dream* 25, 29, 88–91, 96, 100, 182, 215, 217–18, 222, 225
Miller, Philip 113
Milton, John 81, 83–4, 86–7, 93, 99–100, 102, 106, 111, 113, 144, 228
  *Paradise Lost* 83, 86–7
minorities 43–4
miracles, *see* religion; supernaturalism
misogyny 54
modernity 51–2
Montagu, Elizabeth 44, 52
Montagu, Lady Mary Wortley 100
Monteverdi, Claudio 204
Moody, Jane 182
More, Hannah 47
Moscow Arts Theater 55

Mozart, Wolfgang Amadeus 196
*Much Ado About Nothing* 215
Mullaney, Steven 233
Munden, Joseph 67
Murray, John 246, 262
music 2, 4, 61, 68–9, 71, 83, 87, 112, 129, 131, 163, 168, 173–4, 181, 183–4, 191–7, 203–4; *see also* opera
Musset, Alfred de 190
mythology 25, 130, 198–9

Napoleon 145, 156–8, 160
natural history 100, 109–13
Neely, Carol Thomas 53, 197–8
neoclassicism 9, 68, 81, 183–4, 188–90, 201, 203
Nilsson, Christine 200
Nimrod 144
North, Thomas 100
Northcote, James 219, 222, 224
novels 49, 80, 100, 105, 162, 182, 245–66
  dramatic adaptations of 164–7, 171–2, 178

opera 68, 183–204
Opie, John 173–4
*The Oracle* (periodical) 67, 162
*Othello* 10, 42–3, 94–5, 117, 158, 182, 216–17, 219, 221–3, 226
Orgel, Stephen 6
O'Sullivan, Maurice J. 15
Otway, Thomas 34, 64
Ovid 100
Oxford University 28

paganism 234, 237–8, 244
painting, *see* Shakespeare, illustrations of
Paris Opéra 193, 195
Parliament, Acts of 46
pastoral 92–3, 112, 116
performance, *see* theater; Shakespeare, theatrical productions of
*Pericles* 10, 231–6, 238–40, 244
Petrarch 105, 107
philosophy 85, 88, 97
Plato 89
Plutarch 32, 100
poetic subjectivity 8
poetry, theories of 2, 80, 85, 90–91, 95, 97, 128, 157; *see also* aesthetics

politics 10, 24, 27, 45–6, 89–90, 100–103, 117, 146, 154, 156, 159–60, 161, 196
  conservatism 14, 27, 29–30, 117, 245–6, 249–55; *see also* Toryism
  critiques of 9, 113–15
Pope, Alexander 32, 81, 94, 100, 102
populism 25, 39
Postlewait, Thomas 34
Prévost, Abbé 103
Princeton University 211
Pritchard, Hannah 60–61, 63, 70
Protestantism 233, 251
psychoanalysis 10, 54, 231; *see also* Freud
psychology 43, 123, 136
*The Public Advertiser* 72, 103, 162
Purinton, Marjean 234
Puritanism 24

Raby, Peter 68–70
Radcliffe, Ann 9, 65–7, 100, 161–2, 164–6, 176
  *The Romance of the Forest* 9, 162, 164–6
realism 79–80
reception theory 78–9, 97; *see also* allusion
Reed, Isaac 34
religion 231–44; *see also* Catholicism; Protestantism
Rembrandt 79, 96
Reynolds, Sir Joshua 173, 179, 213, 223
*Richard II* 10, 42, 158, 216–19, 222
*Richard III* 22, 38–40, 215, 217–19, 222, 224, 226
Richard III 249, 266
Ricks, Christopher 86
Robinson, Mary 100
Rogeboz-Malfroy, Elizabeth 194
Rogers, Nicholas 46
romance 232
*Romeo and Juliet* 25, 34, 39, 95, 110–11, 215–16, 218, 221, 226
Romney, George 214, 223
Rosenberg, Marvin 53–4, 61
Rossini, Gioachino 184
Rousseau, Jean-Jacques 106
Rowe, Nicholas 16, 19, 64, 81
Rowley, William 258
The Royal Academy 179, 208
Russell, William 65
Ryan, Kiernan 196

Sabor, Peter 3
sacredness, *see* religion
Saggini, Francesca 31, 42, 47
Sanders, Julie 201–2
Saxo Grammaticus 185
Schiller, Friedrich 158–60
Schoenbaum, Samuel 15, 18, 21
Scott, Sir Walter 28–9, 35
sensibility 42, 47–8, 59, 61–3, 65, 72
    and gender 62–3
Sewall, Richard B. 124
Seward, Anna 103
Shakespeare, John 23
Shakespeare, Susanna 21–2
Shakespeare, William
    adaptations of 9, 34–6, 38, 40, 163, 183–204, 215
    and authorship 6–8, 78
    biographies of 14–30
    canonization of 6, 7, 13, 30, 39, 51–2, 101, 174, 210
    criticism of 4–6, 7–8, 10, 31–49, 51, 57–8, 77, 162–3, 172–3, 183, 186
    editing of 33–4, 47, 56–7, 185, 231–2
        National Edition 209–10, 213, 219, 221–3
    educational background 9, 25, 28, 89, 100
    eighteenth-century views 3, 31–4, 36, 41–4, 49, 51–3, 57, 62, 81, 94, 101, 176, 184, 186
    feminist views of 8, 31, 54, 59, 197
    film versions 185, 202
    forgeries of 15, 17, 163
    French productions of 67, 69, 72; *see also* Ambroise Thomas, *Hamlet*
    and genius 8, 14, 52–3, 59–62, 70, 73–4, 89, 92, 96, 162
    idealization of, *see* Bardolatry
    illustrations of 5, 9–10, 16, 25–6, 52, 72, 162, 164, 167, 173–9, 190, 197, 207–29
    and imagination 3, 79–81, 88–91, 94–7, 140–42
    knowledge of law 21
    market for 210, 225–9
    marriage 21–3
    and nature 19, 41, 80–83, 86–7, 93–4, 96, 111–13, 128
    reading vs. viewing 35–6, 39–41, 47–8, 54–5, 70, 85, 186–7, 189, 197
    reception in Europe, *see* France
    relationship to nature 2
    self-reflexivity in 107–8
    sexuality of 21
    sonnets 103, 126, 128
    theatrical productions of 1–2, 5, 9, 35–6, 38–40, 53, 55, 57–74, 141, 164–5, 172–6, 182, 185–6; *see also* Covent Garden; Drury Lane
    translations of 183–4, 187–90
    twentieth-century versions of 196–7, 201–2
Shaw, Bernard 185
Shelley, Mary 260, 263–6
Shelley, Percy Bysshe 35, 263–4, 266
Shiels, W. J. 46
Shore, Jane 64
Showalter, Elaine 53–4, 59, 67, 72, 184–5, 201
Siddons, Henry 165
Siddons, Sarah 1, 8, 38–9, 53–4, 58–69
Simnel, Lambert 249
Slagle, Judith Bailey 234, 238, 242
sleep 108–9
Smirke, Robert 219, 222–3
Smith, Charlotte 8–9, 47, 99–119
    generic mixing in 100–101, 105, 107, 109, 118–19
    and nature 105–6, 109–10
Smithson, Harriet 59, 61, 67, 69–70, 72, 190, 197
social anthropology 78
social rank 27–8, 251–3, 263, 266; *see also* politics
Socrates 89
Somerset, Charles A. 15, 20–22
Sondheim, Stephen 201
songs, *see* music
sound 9, 61, 112, 122–3, 128–9, 131–3, 163; *see also* music
Southerne, Thomas 67
Southey, Robert 35
Spain 156
Spenser, Edmund 93
Stam, Robert 185
Star Chamber 24
Starr, G. Gabrielle 100, 105
Steevens, George 32, 102, 231
Sterne, Laurence 22
Stoppard, Tom 202

Stothard, Thomas 219, 222
Stratford 16, 78
subjectivity 48, 74, 79, 91, 97
the sublime 1, 4–5, 9, 36, 42, 48, 66, 81, 83, 87, 90, 94, 96, 123, 128–9, 131, 133–5, 151, 175–6, 179–80, 247–8
Suckling, John 52
Super, R. H. 15
supernaturalism 164, 166–75, 178, 180–82, 194, 232
Sutton, Juliet 255
Swift, Jonathan 255
Swinburne, Algernon Charles 14
sympathy 85–7, 94, 97; see also sensibility

*The Taming of the Shrew* 217, 221
Taruskin, Richard 203–4
Tate, Nahum 33–4
Taylor, Gary 77
Taylor, Neil 56
Taylor, William 90
*The Tempest* 25, 38, 41, 140, 226
Tennyson, Lord Alfred 84
Terry, Ellen 52, 71–3
theater
    acting styles 64–5, 67–8
    audience tastes 162–3, 166–7, 173, 179
    debates over 2, 4, 36–7, 39, 60–61, 66, 69–70, 139–43, 151, 167–8, 172, 175, 179, 184, 203
    dramatic criticism 31, 162, 181
    eighteenth-century stage practices 186
    European traditions 183
    Greek drama 142; see also classicism; Hellenism
    nineteenth-century stage practices 31, 142–3, 167, 176–7, 192
    patent theaters 140, 163–4; see also Covent Garden, Drury Lane
    as visual spectacle 163–4, 168, 171–4, 176, 180
Theobald, Lewis 34, 40
theology, *see* religion
Thomas, Ambroise 9
    *Hamlet* (opera) 183–204
Thompson, Ann 56
*Timon of Athens* 216, 223
*Titus Andronicus* 220
Toryism 8, 14, 30
translation theory 187, 189–90

Tree, Ellen 68
*Troilus and Cressida* 94, 216, 220, 223, 226
Trojan War, *see Hamlet*
translation 37
*Twelfth Night* 152, 156–8, 216, 220–21
*Two Gentleman of Verona* 216, 220–21, 227

universalism 123, 140, 143, 156–8, 233–4

Vallon, Annette 94
Van Dyck, Anthony 52
Verdi, Giuseppe 184, 193, 201, 203–4
Vigny, Alfred de 190
Voltaire 52, 187–8

Wagner, Richard 203–4
Walpole, Horace 172
war, critiques of 116–17
Warbeck, Perkin 249, 254; *see also* John Ford
Wars of the Roses 27, 249
Warwickshire 13, 20
Weber, Carl Maria von 193–4
Weber, Henry 246
Webster, Sir Godfrey 260
West, Benjamin 179, 213
West, Shearer 59, 68
Westall, Richard 219, 222–3
Wheatley, Francis 222, 225
Whigs 10, 245, 251
White, Gilbert 113
White, James 15
Williams, Helen Maria 100
Wilson, Frances 247
Winstead, Karen A. 244
*The Winter's Tale* 1–3, 5, 9, 41, 95, 97, 151–4, 215, 217, 220, 222, 224, 226, 244
Wolfson, Susan 47–8, 101, 115, 117
Wollstonecraft, Mary 260
Woodmason, James 228
Wordsworth, William 8, 19, 35, 77–97, 118
    Evening Ode 82–6
    *Lyrical Ballads* 85–7, 93
    *Michael* 93–4
    "Mutability" 87–9
    *The Prelude* 84, 88–97
Wright, Joseph (of Derby) 224–5
Wroe, Ann 253

Yachnin, Paul 3
Yates, Mary Anne 39

CPSIA information can be obtained
at www.ICGtesting.com
Printed in the USA
BVHW040023080519
547643BV00006B/31/P